UNIX®
Shell Programming

THIRD EDITION

Lowell Jay Arthur
Ted Burns

John Wiley & Sons, Inc.
NEW YORK / CHICHESTER / BRISBANE / TORONTO / SINGAPORE

Publisher: Katherine Schowalter
Senior Acquisitions Editor: Diane Cerra
Associate Managing Editor: Jacqueline A. Martin
Editorial Production: G&H SOHO, Inc.

UNIX is a registered trademark of UNIX Systems Labs. Designations used by companies to distinguish their products are often claimed as trademarks. In all instances where John Wiley & Sons, Inc., is aware of a claim, the product names appear in capital letters. Readers, however, should contact the appropriate companies for more complete information regarding trademarks and registration.

Chapter and Part opening art is from the Dover Pictorial Archive series, copyright © 1978 by Dover Publications, Inc.
Figures 3.3, 3.5, and 11.6 are from *Application Prototyping* by Bernard Boar, copyright © 1984 by John Wiley & Sons, Inc.

This text is printed on acid-free paper.

This publication is designed to provide accurate and authoritative information in regard to the subject matter covered. It is sold with the understanding that the publisher is not engaged in rendering legal, accounting, or other professional service. If legal advice or other expert assistance is required, the services of a competent professional person should be sought.

Library of Congress Cataloging-in-Publication Data:
Arthur, Lowell Jay
   UNIX shell programming / Lowell Jay Arthur, Edward N. Burns. — 3rd ed.
     p. cm.
   Includes index.
   ISBN 0-471-59941-7 (paper)
    1. UNIX (Computer file) 2. UNIX Shells. I. Burns, Edward N. II. Title.
QA76.76.063A765   1994
005.4'3 — dc20   93-33453
                                  CIP

Printed in the United States of America
10 9 8 7 6 5 4 3

Upon a mountain height, far from the sea,
I found a shell,
And to my listening ear the lonely thing
Ever a song of ocean seemed to sing,
Ever a tale of ocean seemed to tell.

Eugene Field

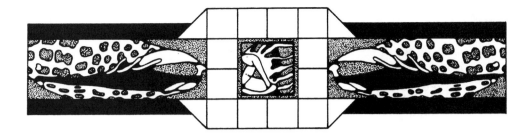

Contents

PART TWO
SHELL PROGRAMMING FOR RESULTS

About the Authors

Lowell Jay Arthur

Jay Arthur became a UNIX zealot at Bell Laboratories in Piscataway, New Jersey. Then, as a UNIX system administrator for Mountain Bell, he introduced one of the largest UNIX minicomputer systems ever implemented. He has worked on the creation of a fully integrated software cockpit for UNIX workstations. He is the author of six widely read books on software engineering including *Improving Software Quality, Rapid Evolutionary Development,* and *Software Evolution.* He is the author of forthcoming workbooks on Total Quality Management (TQM): *The Quality Improvement Coloring Book: Problem Solving Made Easy, The Quality Improvement Connect the Dots Book: Process Management Made Easy,* and *The Quality Improvement Book of Bows and Arrows: Hoshin Planning Made Easy.* Jay has over 21 years of work experience developing and maintaining software in IBM, UNIX, and PC environments. He has consulted with many firms nationally and internationally.

Jay is a quality-improvement instructor and facilitator with an extensive background in quality improvement, process design, and measurement. Since 1990, Jay has continuously been involved in implementing TQM in a large software organization. He has helped teams improve all aspects of the business: customer service, repair and installation, and information system development and maintenance.

Jay is also a certified master practitioner of Neuro-Linguistic Programming (NLP)—the programming language of the mind. He specializes in communication and performance enhancement to rapidly integrate improved quality techniques. He has a B.S. in systems engineering and an M.S. in operations research.

Edward N. Burns

Ted Burns has been building software systems for 13 years, the last 8 years as a member of the technical staff for U S West Communications. While pursuing his M.S. in computer science, he became a UNIX and AI (Artificial Intelligence) enthusiast. Since then he has exclusively developed UNIX-based application systems. Currently he is working on a UNIX-based expert system.

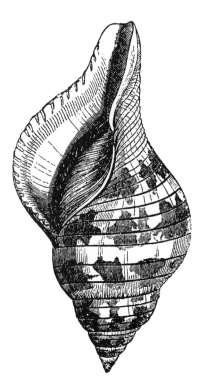

Preface

This book is like the shell of a chambered nautilus — sheltering you during your evolution from a novice to a power user of Shell programming. Along the way, you will learn the basics and travel the avenues to knowledge and wisdom. In Shell, as in life, there are three stages to growth: childhood, adolescence, adulthood; apprentice, journeyman, master; and so it is with this book — novice, user, and power user. We have added and expanded many chambers of knowledge and experience that will guide your growth through the book.

Shell unlocks the power of UNIX. It presumes that users can and will do remarkable things. Shell teaches us how to do things rapidly; one line of Shell can do the work of 100 lines of C language. Shell teaches programming through *composition* of existing programs, not through coding of complex, custom software. Shell teaches *reuse* in ways that support such advanced concepts as object-oriented programming.

To enable everyone to derive the maximum benefit from using the Shell, we have designed this book to carry you from beginning Shell usage all of the way through power user status. There are three major sections:

1. Shell for the Novice

2. Shell Programming for Results

3. Shell Programming for Mastery

Shell for the Novice leads you through files and processes and the power of Shell. It teaches you how to use Shell, from simple commands to more complicated programming.

Shell Programming for Results teaches you how to use these basic skills to create whole applications. People do things every day that could benefit from automation, but do not require a sophisticated database system. This section of the book will teach you how to master using Shell to automate your everyday needs. It also establishes the foundation for building more exotic applications as you evolve toward Shell mastery.

Shell Programming for Mastery steps into the world of software developers and systems administrators. This part of the book discusses rapid prototyping and other crucial software engineering activities in detail. There are new reference sections and extensions for power usage of Shell.

Throughout, the attention will be on UNIX and the varieties of Shell. There are two major flavors of UNIX: AT&T and Berkeley. From AT&T Bell Labs, we received the Bourne and Korn Shells; Berkeley gave us the C Shell. Bourne is the most common. C Shell is widely available in all Berkeley UNIX systems. Korn retains the power of the Bourne Shell while adding the power features of the C Shell. This book addresses all three shells, so regardless of your environment, it will support your growth and development. Unless otherwise noted, the Bourne and Korn Shell examples will appear on the left-hand side of the page, and the C Shell examples will be on the right-hand side of the page. In other instances, the C Shell examples will be prefaced by "csh:". Rather than retraining their customers, most vendors are providing all three shells with their UNIX systems. Now you can choose the shell that best suits your needs.

When I wrote the first edition of this book in 1984, UNIX was still a four-letter word and Shell was not far behind. You couldn't find a reference to either of them in any of the industry journals or magazines. The second edition, in 1990, found even wider acceptance because more people were using UNIX. Now references for UNIX shine from almost everywhere. Windowing systems on workstations have simplified the interface to UNIX. Once you have mastered the graphical user interface (GUI), you will want to step back behind the windows to explore the depth and power of Shell. Through the growth in popularity of UNIX, the use of Shell — the UNIX command language — has grown as well. We want to show you why.

Step by step, this edition will lead you into the depths of Shell and its usage. We hope that you will find the book as readable and enjoyable as we found the experience of writing it. We know that you will benefit greatly from the use of Shell to make your job more effective and efficient. We also know that, if you let it, the Shell will teach you elegant ways of thinking about application creation and evolution. It will teach you ways of doing things more quickly and efficiently than you ever thought possible. Have fun and enjoy your adventure in the world of UNIX Shell programming.

JAY ARTHUR
TED BURNS

Denver, Colorado
January 1994

UNIX®
Shell Programming

PART ONE

Shell for the Novice

The mind of the beginner is empty, free of the habits of the
expert, ready to accept, to doubt, and open to all the possibilities.

Shunryu Suzuki

Chapter One

The Power of Shell

The Shell is the key to improving productivity and quality in a UNIX environment. In the 1990s, unfortunately, the person who can make the best use of technology to get things done rapidly will be the one who retains his or her job. Whether you are a novice or a sophisticated user, the Shell can automate repetitive tasks, find where you left things, do things while you are at lunch or asleep, and a host of other time-saving activities. The use of the Shell can double, triple, or quadruple your productivity, making you more effective and more efficient. The Shell accomplishes this by letting you create tools to automate many tasks. To maximize productivity and quality, we have to learn how to automate mundane and complex tasks. The Shell enables you to rapidly construct prototypes of applications, programs, procedures, and tools. The speed with which you can build a working prototype, enhance it to provide exactly what you need, or just throw it away and begin again will allow you the flexibility to create exactly the right tool or application without a lot of coding, compiling, and testing. It will rarely be necessary to do things manually, because the Shell can grapple with almost any problem.

WHY SHELL?

Before we get into the meat of Shell, let's look at a few key reasons for using the UNIX Shell:

1. More and more data exists in a mechanized format all over the world. The networks to connect people to this information worldwide already exist and are being enhanced to provide an information "superhighway" that will offer information, communication, and entertainment to consumers. For people to

benefit from these rich sources of data, however, it must be transformed into information, knowledge, and wisdom (Figure 1.1). There are only a few ways that data can become these higher forms of understanding:

* *Selection* of data separates the wheat from the chaff. The amount of available information doubles every few years. Selection, like light, can help you illuminate the key pieces of information that you desire. Shell filter programs can help you select and display only the information you want to see, not the whole universe of information.

* *Combination* of data creates a collision course for two or more groups of data, and in this collision, information is created and knowledge is gained. Gregory Bateson (1979) suggested that we can only know something by comparing one thing to another. In other words, all understanding comes from the comparison of things. Additional Shell commands can help you compare and scrub data together to gain further insight about the opportunity or problem at hand.

* *Decisions and rules* help us further analyze the resulting information to gain knowledge. The Shell lets you ask IF-THEN-ELSE questions and repeatedly loop through reams of files and information in ways that will help you automate processes and evaluate information to create knowledge.

* *Serendipity* causes a person to mentally combine ideas, data, and information in a totally unexpected way. Shell commands offer so many ways to examine and evaluate existing information that serendipity is almost guaranteed.

2. UNIX was the first fully integrated CASE (computer-aided software engineering) toolkit. Integration of tools is the cornerstone of UNIX Shell.

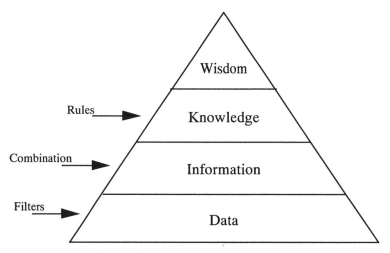

Figure 1.1   The Evolution of Data

UNIX will continue to be the platform of choice for IPSE (integrated project support environment). UNIX workstations are already leaving their early engineering applications and are being used as powerful front ends to assist business users in serving customers more effectively and efficiently. UNIX Shell can be a powerful tool for prototyping end-user applications and testing out new and improved ways of handling information for everything from customer contact applications to complex processing of databases.

3. Shell is a full programming language. It has:

   • Variables

   • Conditional and iterative constructs (IF-THEN-ELSE, CASE, DO WHILE, DO UNTIL)

   • Tailorable user environment

4. UNIX Shell is the original rapid prototyping tool, teaching such key concepts as modularity, reuse, and development through *composition* instead of coding. The Shell library of tools is the most widely reused library in the world other than perhaps a few FORTRAN math libraries. The UNIX philosophy is: Build on the work of others; stand on the shoulders of those who have gone before you. To be competitive in the 1990s, applications must be created quickly and be flexible enough to endure the nonstop changes brought on by the emerging global economy.

5. UNIX Shell is one of the original fourth-generation programming languages (4GL). Whole applications can be built quickly and effectively in Shell. Compare the power of Shell; what takes 1 line in Shell may take 10 or more lines in C++ or 100 lines in C (or COBOL). Some people complain that Shell has an awkward syntax, and it does, but no more so than most 4GLs.

6. Machines are cheaper than people. With Shell you can optimize your investment in people by creating look-alike environments for new users and developing an environment that can grow as the users grow. The key to productivity is to make user interfaces idiot-proof and easy to learn. Train the machine instead of retraining people.

WHAT'S IN IT FOR ME?

So what? you might ask. I've heard these claims before. Or you might be a user rather than a developer of systems. What's in it for me? How about the following?

1. Would you like to be more successful, more confident, more productive; receive more praise; and take more pride in your work? Shell is the key to

personal satisfaction and success. Shell allows you to compose whole applications in hours or days versus months or years in conventional environments. Completion of projects provides a major source of psychic income — self-esteem, recognition, and reward.

2. Would you like to be more effective and take advantage of opportunities? Shell gives you the ability to solve problems quickly and effectively. Shell can help you automate needed systems quickly to respond to market windows that close all too quickly. Programmers naturally tend to think that they must program in C or COBOL or some language. This is unnecessary. Composing systems from Shell programs will accomplish almost any task. Instead of waiting months or years for the "perfect solution," prototype applications built in Shell can be developed and refined and implemented. These can then be used as the requirements specification for the actual development of a "real" system, if needed. The ability to apply the full power of the UNIX Shell toolkit to immediate problems outweighs the efficiency penalties of using Shell. If you have time, you can go back later and tune up the performance of your application by coding the inefficient components in a programming language.

3. Do you need more time? Shell frees you from drudgery. Every job has its exciting parts and its dull parts. Dull tasks typically are repetitive and are easily automated with Shell.

4. Do you need more timely information? Shell can extract and massage huge quantities of information to meet your needs. Why look through a whole report when Shell can scan and retrieve important information for you effortlessly?

5. Do you need to integrate information from various existing systems? Using the communication facilities of UNIX and the power of Shell, this can be done at a fraction of the normal cost.

6. Are you having a hard time creating the applications that you or your clients really need? With UNIX Shell, you can rapidly prototype applications to make sure you have the requirements right before you build the production system. Even then, the Shell version may be completely satisfactory.

7. Would you like to be more creative? Are you having enough fun at work? Tinkering with Shell programming can be great fun for both the novice and the expert.

Beaten paths are for beaten men.

Shell, with its vast arsenal of tools that can easily be combined, lets you automate much of this repetitive activity. When I was at Bell Labs, I had the good fortune to work with John Burgess, a bearded, spectacled wizard, who was our resident UNIX toolsmith. All one needed to do was complain about something and by the next morning, John would automate it with Shell. The project I was on was successful in many ways because of his tool-building support. Since then, creating tools in Shell has become a way of life. Some tools are needed only once, and creating them ensures the accuracy of the resulting work. Some tools, like seeds, start small and grow into powerful aids for all of the work required.

8. Would you like to avoid retraining to use UNIX? Would you rather use familiar command names instead of UNIX commands? Shell lets you emulate any environment that you have used in the past. The Shell can easily imitate DOS (which I call "baby" UNIX) or an IBM MVS TSO environment. Using the smorgasbord of Shell tools, you can create commands that emulate the functionality of most systems. No need for retraining!

How can the UNIX Shell do all of these things? It must be complex! On the contrary, it is simplicity that allows this to happen, not complexity. Processing, interfaces, and data management are all dirt simple. This is what makes the Shell such a pleasure to use.

SHELL SIMPLICITY

How you use the Shell is perhaps one of its greatest simplicities. Unlike many programming languages, Shell commands do not need to be compiled (a translation process that is used to turn programming commands into something the computer understands) before execution. The Shell is an interpreted language, as opposed to compiled, meaning that when you type in a command its meaning is determined at that time. You can sit at your terminal and interact with the Shell directly. Immediate feedback about the task you are trying to perform makes it easy to prototype and test your ideas quickly.

Shell commands talk to one another through a simple and consistent interface called a *pipe*. The Shell uses the UNIX file system (which is a hierarchy, much like an organizational chart) which lets you organize files into cabinets and folders (directories). This hierarchy of directories and files yields a simple, clean view of all information in the system.

The UNIX system is another key to the Shell's ability. UNIX is portable; it runs on almost any computer hardware made today. So your investment in training, education, and development of Shell programs will be portable from system to system as you move around. UNIX also supports multiple users and multiple tasks. Again, your investment in Shell programming will support dozens of other users and allow for hundreds and even thousands of repetitive tasks to be done in the "background" while you work on something else.

The Shell is almost exactly what it sounds like: It is a friendly environment for users that protects each user from every other one. It allows users to do whatever they want without affecting anyone else. When a user logs into a UNIX system, the operating system automatically starts a unique copy of the Shell, under which the user can perform any function available. It is this protected yet powerful environment that gives each user the ability to be more productive.

THE UNIX SHELLS

There are several major flavors of UNIX utilized in the marketplace today. These are:

- Berkeley UNIX (BSD 4.3)
- AT&T System V Release 4
- SunOS
- XENIX

The AT&T System V Release 4 is an attempt to bring together the best of all the UNIX variations while adding some new commands and functionality to the UNIX operating system. With the recent sale of UNIX to Novell and with POSIX looming on the horizon as a standard, further unification and standardization will hopefully occur. Within these major UNIX environments, there are usually three Shells available: Bourne, Korn, and C (Table 1.1). All support processes—both foreground and background, pipes, filters, directories, and other similar standard features of UNIX. The original Shell was rewritten by S. R. Bourne around 1975, giving us one version of the Shell known as the "Bourne Shell," which runs on most UNIX systems. Bill Joy and students on the Berkeley campus of the University of California created another version of the Shell known as the "C Shell" that is useful for C language programmers. David Korn, at AT&T, created the "Korn Shell," which preserves the functionality of the Bourne Shell and incorporates many powerful extensions. These extensions include some nice features from the C Shell as well as many new commands. Which of these Shells will dominate the market is yet to be seen, but I expect the Korn Shell to dominate. This book describes all three Shells. Let's take a look at the three Shells and some of their key differences.

TABLE 1.1   The UNIX Shells

Shell	Originator	System Name	Prompt
Bourne	S. R. Bourne	`sh`	$
Korn	David Korn	`ksh`	$
C	Bill Joy	`csh`	%

Bourne Shell

The Bourne Shell is the most common of the three Shells (Table 1.2). Almost all UNIX implementations offer the Bourne Shell as part of their standard configuration. It is smaller than the other two Shells and therefore more efficient for most Shell processing. However, it lacks the interactive bells and whistles of either the C or Korn Shell.

Occasionally problems can arise from your programming or from the system itself. These exceptions can cause problems unless you have a way of dealing with them. The Bourne Shell allows exception handling using the **trap** command, which is discussed in detail in later chapters. The **trap** command is not available with the C Shell. Connecting one command to another or a file to a command is handled by a simple facility called *input/output redirection.* Bourne Shell input/output redirection is more versatile than C Shell. For example, unlike the C Shell, the Bourne Shell allows redirection of standard input and output into and out of whole control structures. The Bourne Shell can also take advantage of System V's *named pipes.*

To support structured programming, the Bourne Shell supports both local and global variables. Global variables must be *exported.* The Bourne Shell offers the IF-THEN-ELSE, CASE, FOR, WHILE, and UNTIL control structures. It relies, however, on the UNIX utilities **test** and **expr** to evaluate conditional expressions, unlike the C and Korn Shells, which evaluate expressions directly.

TABLE 1.2   Shell Functions

Function	Bourne	Korn	C
Availability	`most`	`least`	Berkeley UNIX; some System V
Variables	`local` `global (`**`export`**`)`	`local` `global (`**`export`**`)`	`local (`**`set`**`)` `global (`**`setenv`**`)`
Control commands	**`if-then-else-fi`** **`case-esac`** **`select`** **`for-do-done`** **`xargs`** **`while-do-done`** **`until-do-done`**	**`if-then-else-fi`** **`case-esac`** `for-do-done` `xargs` **`while-do-done`** **`until-do-done`**	**`if-then-else-endif`** **`switch-case-endsw`** **`foreach-end`** **`repeat`** **`while-end`**
Conditional evaluation	**`test, expr`**	`direct`	`direct`
Interactive		**`history`**	**`history`**
Aliasing	`functions`	`functions`	**`alias`**
Signals	**`trap`**	**`trap`**	
Efficiency	`fast`	`medium`	`medium`

C Shell

Developed at the University of California at Berkeley, the C Shell offers some advantages over the Bourne Shell: *history,* and direct evaluation and execution of conditions and "built-in" commands. Interactively, the C Shell keeps track of the commands as you enter them (history) and allows you to go back and execute them again without reentering the command. Or, if you want to, you can recall them, make modifications, and then execute the new command.

The C Shell offers *aliasing,* which allows the user to create alternatives for command names. The C Shell also offers greater control over background (behind the scenes) and foreground (at the terminal) tasks. In the Bourne Shell, if you start a command in background or foreground, it stays there until it ends. In the C Shell, you can move commands from foreground execution to background execution as required.

The C Shell offers two kinds of variables: regular (local) or environment (global). The C Shell uses **set** and **setenv** to establish these two kinds of variables.

The syntax of the C Shell is more like C language programming and offers all of the C conditional operators (==, >, etc.), which C programmers might find useful. The C Shell offers the IF-THEN-ELSE, SWITCH, FOREACH, REPEAT, and WHILE control constructs. The C Shell evaluates conditional expressions within these control structures directly.

Korn Shell

The Korn Shell retains the complete functionality of the Bourne Shell and combines many of the key features of the C Shell. It also includes many new commands. The Korn Shell is faster than the C Shell but slower than the Bourne for most processing.

The Korn Shell offers *command-line editing,* which allows you to modify entered commands using features found in several common UNIX editors. It also provides improved *history* management, which provides direct access to past commands. Further, it incorporates job control (background/foreground) and enhanced programming capabilities. The Korn Shell evaluates conditional expressions directly for efficiency and adds a **select** control construct (such as CASE) for menu-driven Shells.

Choosing a Shell

For the novice, I'd choose the Korn Shell. I find the Korn/Bourne Shell syntax simpler than and preferable to the C Shell. This simplicity, combined with the nice enhancements found in the Korn Shell, make it the Shell of choice. More experienced users, familiar with the C Shell, will benefit from staying with what they already know. Bourne Shell users, however, can benefit from the interactive power of the Korn Shell and will find the migration to the Korn Shell simple and straightforward.

Conventions

Throughout this book, Bourne and Korn examples are displayed on the left side of the page and C Shell examples on the right. Otherwise, C Shell examples will have a leading "`csh:`" to help users find them.

WHEN TO USE THE SHELL

Anytime you enter a UNIX command, you are using the Shell. To increase productivity, use the Shell whenever you are faced with:

1. Doing something to many files, or
2. Doing the same task repeatedly

It's as simple as that. By necessity, people perform repetitive tasks, such as:

- The dates or names in a group of documents must be changed.
- Reports must be produced every month.
- Status must be entered daily and reported monthly.

Each of these tasks can be automated with a Shell program.

You can also use the Shell interactively at your terminal to automate one-time tasks. There are many situations that could benefit from use of the powerful features of Shell, but they do not require the creation of a separate Shell program. These problems can be solved with interactive use of the Shell. We look at interactive Shell usage in more depth in Chapter 5, Shell Decisions and Repetitions.

> Choose your weapons to match the war.
>
> *Brad Cox*

You should not use the Shell when the task:

- Is too complex, such as writing an entire billing system,
- Requires high efficiency,
- Requires a different hardware environment, or
- Requires different software tools

Use the Shell to automate anything that requires data manipulation: selecting data, adding numbers, printing statistics, or whatever. Finding the right information in a mound of reports is simple for the Shell and cumbersome for people. Manipulating data and putting it into printable form is also tedious and unreliable. The Shell, as you will soon see, can do all of these things quickly and reliably.

PRODUCTIVITY AND THE SHELL

Studies (for example, Thadhani, 1984) have shown that an average programmer may spend 20 to 25 hours a week at the terminal. Ninety-five percent of that time involves "human-intensive" activities such as editing and data manipulation. As homes, offices, and businesses become increasingly automated, 20-25 hours may climb to 30-35. To make people more productive:

1. Response times must be kept to a minimum (under one second), or
2. People must be allowed to automate their human-intensive activities.

The Shell and its tools have been designed and optimized to automate many of these activities. It requires some insight into the Shell and its usage to derive these benefits, but it only takes a little ingenuity to become more effective and efficient. As you learn to use the Shell, you will gain invaluable insights into how to design robust, reusable, and flexible systems that can respond to continuously changing environments.

Since the Shell can automate most of the recursive tasks, which encompass 50 to 80 percent of the human-intensive activities, it is little wonder that the Shell can double or triple productivity. The simplicity of UNIX files and the file system design makes this possible. The simple IF-THEN-ELSE, CASE, and looping controls of Shell enable you to automate the decisions and actions that are the key ingredient in "artificial intelligence" applications.

Whether you are a beginner, apprentice, or master user of UNIX Shell, the following chapters will help you discover powerful ways to make use of the Shell. Part of the pleasure of Shell is the seemingly endless possibilities for exploring new and interesting ways to combine tools to create new tools and new ways of looking at information. Like Darwin on the HMS *Beagle,* enjoy your journey of discovery — a journey into the power of UNIX Shell.

Chapter Two

UNIX Basics

A good beginning makes a good ending.

English proverb

In the current rapidly evolving technological environment, UNIX must be one of the arrows in your quiver. In today's complex applications, more and more power needs to be placed at the fingertips of the user. UNIX workstations offer power and flexibility above and beyond personal computers, while offering the flexibility to run DOS applications as one of many windows in the system. There is no way to separate a discussion of the Shell from UNIX (although some single-tasking versions of Shell run under MS-DOS). Without the simplicity of the UNIX architecture, the Shell could not exist. The Shell derives much of its power from UNIX.

WHAT IS UNIX?

Is UNIX an operating system? a philosophy? or just a red-hot environment for personal productivity that runs on every hardware platform from a personal computer to the Cray Super computer? Answer: all of the above.

UNIX is one of the most flexible operating systems available. UNIX departed from most traditional approaches to operating systems in that it simplified much of the typical complexity, especially the reading and writing of files — input/output (I/O). UNIX simplified I/O by having all files and devices look the same to any command that used them. Files contain data as streams of characters — no records, no varying record sizes, and fewer problems. Because of this uniqueness, every utility program in UNIX has been designed to accept input from any other program. Each program can perform a single unique function or be connected to other programs, devices, or files via the Shell. This simple design gives UNIX and the Shell much of their power. UNIX offers one of the richest "libraries" of reusable software components and programs to be found in any system. As a result, you do less coding and more composing of applications from reusable parts, which translates into huge improvements in personal productivity and software quality.

Following the development of UNIX, many software developers contributed additional user-oriented tools. These tools were packaged as an extension to UNIX called the Programmer's Workbench (PWB). This has since been included in the standard package, UNIX.

THE UNIX KERNEL

Let's take a little closer look at how the UNIX operating system is structured. The system is layered like an onion. At the heart of the system is the "kernel." All programs that run on a UNIX system interact with the kernel to get their work done. Figure 2.1 shows a high-level depiction of the UNIX system.

The kernel sits above your computer's hardware, guiding all of the activity. All other programs, including the UNIX Shells, interact with your computer through the kernel. When developing applications for the UNIX system, we add new layers to the "onion" by employing software that exists in the lower layers. The figure shows another very important feature of the UNIX operating system: Since all programs are insulated from the computer hardware by the kernel, moving programs from one computer to another is much easier. This hardware independence is one reason that UNIX runs on so many different types of computer hardware.

While it is good to understand what the kernel is and how the various Shell

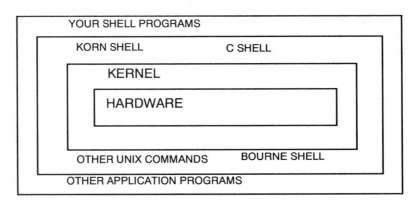

Figure 2.1   The UNIX System

programs fit into the overall UNIX system architecture, it is not something that you must be concerned with in day-to-day use of the UNIX system. In general, you interact with the kernel indirectly through the UNIX Shell and need not be concerned with any details about the kernel.

UNIX FILES

UNIX files are unique because they are basically free-form. Each file is just a sequence of characters (see Figure 2.2). Lines or records are delimited by the newline (\n) character. The end of a file is delimited by an end-of-file (EOF) or end-of-tape (EOT) character. Since every file can be read character by character and be output the same way, every Shell tool has been designed to handle this simple file architecture. Because of this design choice, the output from any program can be used as input to any other program. This design feature allowed the originators of UNIX to create simple, modular programs to perform single functions. Each function, although trivial when viewed as a single entity, becomes vastly more important when combined with other singular functions to do virtually any kind of activity.

UNIX files reside in a hierarchical file system or inverted tree (organization-chart style), like the one shown in Figure 2.3. To implement this structure, UNIX uses a special file known as a directory. You can think of a directory as a file cabinet, file drawer, or file folder, which is how you will see it displayed in a window. Each directory is a fork in the hierarchy, from which other branches may grow. This facility is useful for organizing files and information. In the example, my user identification (user ID), lja, resides under the file system /enduser. Under my ID are directories for source code (src), Shell commands (bin), and documents (doc). These names are short because so many people are terrible typists. Longer names such as *source code* or *documentation* can rarely be typed without error, and typing them is time consuming. Even my user ID, lja, is nothing but initials. Under src are directories for "C" language (c.d) and COBOL (cobol.d). The ".d" suffix makes them readily identifiable as directories. Under each of these directories are a variety of files that are represented by rectangles in the diagram. Just by use of directories and their names, I can usually find what I need in short order. Finding where you left something in a UNIX file system is often a challenge, especially if you

The UNIX Shell is the key to improving your productivity*n*
and quality in a typical UNIX environment*n*
The Shell can automate repetitive tasks,*n*
find where you left things,*n*
do things while you are at lunch,*n*
and perform a host of other time-saving activities.*n**0*

Figure 2.2   A UNIX File

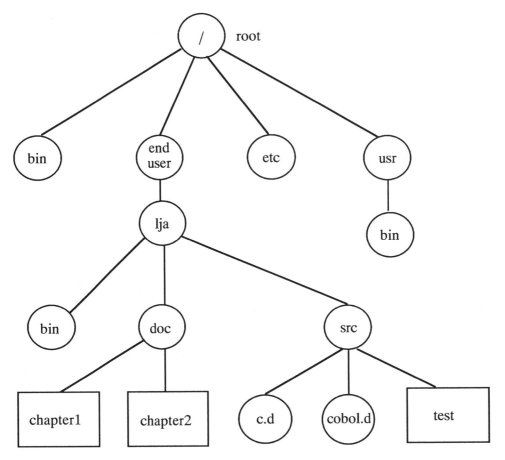

Figure 2.3   A UNIX File System

have 30-100 files in a directory. The **find** command, which is discussed later in this book, can often be used to locate files in the directory structure.

The UNIX file system is designed so that you can move around within the directory structure. Moving to a certain directory is much like opening the file folder or file drawer to reveal what is inside. UNIX provides several commands to allow you to move around the file system hierarchy and view what is contained in a directory. These commands are covered in detail in Chapter 4, Shell Commands.

Home Directory

A "home" directory is a standard UNIX directory that is assigned to you and usually is where you will create and edit files. The UNIX system associates a particular directory, in the overall directory structure of the system, as your home directory. After you log in to the system you will be located in your home directory. In the diagram of the UNIX file system, my home directory is lja. You are free to arrange your home directory however you wish. You can create and alter subdirectories (like bin, doc, and src in the diagram) to keep your files organized in any manner that makes sense to you. Normally the first time you log in your home directory will be empty. This may not be true if your system administrator sets up some standard files that are used by UNIX or perhaps others that are used by local utilities on your machine. Quite often a standard UNIX file named the .profile will have been created in your home directory. This file plays a large role in customizing your Shell environment at the time you log in. This is covered in more detail later in this chapter.

Path Names

UNIX provides a naming convention, called a path name, to uniquely identify a file or directory in the hierarchy shown in Figure 2.3. A path name starts with a / (slash) to indicate the root directory of the UNIX file system and is followed by a series of directory names, separated by / and ending with either a directory name (when referring to a directory) or a file name (when referring to a file). For example, my home directory has the full path name `/enduser/lja`. The full path name to my src directory would be `/enduser/lja/src`. The full path name to the test file located in the src directory would be `/enduser/lja/src/test`. A path name is used when we want to explicitly tell a UNIX or Shell command exactly which file or directory we want to work with. Shell and UNIX commands often use a file name or directory name as an argument. A common command form is:

```
"command filename"
"command directoryname"
```

When you are located in a particular directory, such as your home directory, it is referred to as your current working directory. Any files or subdirectories contained in that directory are in your current view; you do not need to specify a full path name in order to reference them. Your current working directory is your implied path name. For example, if my current working directory is my doc directory, the files chapter1 and chapter2 are within my view; they can be referenced directly without a full path name by using a format like "`command chapter1`". This is the same as saying "`command /enduser/lja/doc/chapter1`". Whenever you type a file name or directory name without a path, that file or directory is assumed to be located in your current working directory. This is sometime called a *relative path* because it is relative to your current working directory. If you need to specify a file or directory that is not located in your current working directory, then the full path name needs to be specified. UNIX needs to know exactly which directory or file you wish to access. It can know this only if you provide a full path name to the command. For example, if my current working directory is my /lja/doc directory and I want to reference the test file over in my src directory, then I would need to specify the full path to that file. This full path name is `/enduser/lja/src/test`.

UNIX does provide some shortcuts to help alleviate the typing chore. The symbol ".." (double period) represents the directory level one level above the current directory, or the parent directory. And the symbol "." (a single period) designates the current directory. These are discussed in Chapter 4 when we talk about specific file and directory commands.

Special Files

Directories and data files are not the only types UNIX offers. There are other, special "files" that are not really files at all, but devices such as terminal handlers, disk drives, tape drives, and so on. Using the simplicity of UNIX input and output, we can treat these devices like files — reading and writing information as if they were a simple file. These are discussed in detail in the advanced material later in this book. Any of these files can be processed using a Shell command to filter or enhance the data.

LOGGING IN

The first step you must accomplish before you can use UNIX or the Shell is to log in to your machine. This is usually a very straightforward process provided that you have a login ID and a password. If you don't have both your login user ID and your password, you won't be able to gain access to the system.

When you try to access your system, UNIX will display a prompt that looks something like this:

```
login: fuzzy
Password: was-he
```

After receiving the login prompt, you enter your login ID (*fuzzy* in the example), after which you receive the Password prompt. At this stage you must type in your password (*was-he* in the example). Your password does not display on the screen when you type it in. It is hidden for your protection. The password you use should be kept private. It is the method used by the UNIX system to prevent unauthorized entry into the system. The password should be changed frequently. On many systems, after a specified period of time, your password expires (ages) and the next time you log in the system requires you to change your password. In addition, you can change your password whenever you like on most systems by using a command to alter the password. We discuss how to change your password a little later in this chapter.

Your Initial Log In

The above procedure is the general method for logging in to a UNIX system; however, your first login session might be a little different. The main difference is that since you have not been on the system before, you may not have your own password. On many systems the system administrator will provide a default password that you use for your first login session. Once you provide the default password to the `Password:` prompt, the system will ask you to change your password to one that only you know. This will be the same process that you will follow when your password ages and expires on your system. Essentially your system administrator has provided a default password that is already expired. When the system determines that your password has expired, it forces you to provide a new one before you can gain access to the system. A typical first log in might look like the following:

```
login: fuzzy
Password: Welcome
Your password has expired.
Choose a new one.
Old password: Welcome
New password: was-he
Re-enter new password: was-he
```

Again, none of the passwords you type will actually display on the screen. Note that this same process is followed when your password expires in the future. When you reenter the password it must match what you typed before or you will be prompted for the new password again.

Choosing and Changing Your Password

An important part of the UNIX security system is centered on your password. It prevents intruders, more commonly called hackers, from entering the system. Hackers, however, are a determined bunch and they know that people often choose passwords that are easy to guess. There are actually lists of commonly used passwords that many hackers will try. When you choose a password you should try to avoid the common passwords that hackers often use. These passwords include things like your name, your spouse's name, the word *password,* the letter *X,* and other easily guessed passwords. If you use passwords like these, a hacker will have an easy time gaining access to your system and will be in a position to cause great damage to your files and directories. They will also be able to read most of the proprietary information that exists on the system. To prevent some of these password abuses, the UNIX system requires a password to have certain properties. Following are some of the rules that UNIX uses to check a password for validity:

- The password must have at least six characters.
- It must contain at least two alpha characters and at least one numeric or special character.
- It cannot be any permutation of your login ID.

To change your password you can use the **passwd** command. At the UNIX prompt you type the command "`passwd`" and the system prompts you for your old password, to make sure it is really you doing the changing, and then asks you to provide a new password. This process is the same as is used when your password expires through the password aging process.

Improper Login

Sometimes you may not type the login ID or password properly. When you do this, the system will respond with the following message:

```
login: fuzzy
Password: Welcom
Login incorrect
login:
```

Note that the system does not tell you which one is incorrect. Again, this is a security measure. Even if you type your login ID improperly, you will still get the password prompt. You usually get three to five attempts to get it right before your terminal is disconnected. Many times a message is displayed to the system administrator telling him or her that several unsuccessful attempts were made on your login ID. If you do not respond to the system prompt within a minute, your terminal is disconnected and your dial line is dropped or you are returned to your LAN prompt.

The Login Process

Back to the process of log in: Once you type in a user ID and a password, the system attempts to verify that you are indeed a valid user on the system and that your password is correct. This is done by searching a file called /etc/passwd. This file contains all the valid user IDs for the system along with their current passwords and some other very important UNIX information. You can look at this file for reference (passwords are shown in code), but you are not able to modify it. The information in the password file is critical to the UNIX system and should be changed with care by a system administrator. Let's take a look at some entries in the /etc/passwd file. (For this example we are looking at an older style of the UNIX passwd file because it is a little easier to see all the pieces with the old-style passwd file.)

```
fuzzy:Wpe5JdZ7XB3NI,2/..:108:100:the Fuzz:/staff/fuzzy1:/bin/sh
fred:WSwXMk5vpG37w,2/..:109:100:\
   Fred 303-111-4545:/prog/fred:/bin/sh
nancy:eL.dVgT3FM7Zs,2/..:314:100:\
   Nancy 454-222-1212:/staff/nancy:/bin/sh
```

```
elroy:yEspcrjOQ.P1U,2/..:110:150:\
  Elroy Jetson 303-999-8976:/support/elroy:/bin/ksh
stinkfot:jBsF82rrn2VYo,2/aG:201:400:\
  STINKFOOT 303-333-4444:/guest/stinkfot:/bin/ksh
```

The fields in the password file are separated by a colon ":". A few of the fields are of little concern at this stage, but others will lead to some insight into the UNIX login procedure. The first field is your login ID and is very important to the login procedure. The system uses this field to locate you as a valid user. If the user ID you type in is not found in the password file, you are not permitted to log in to the system. The second field is your encrypted (coded) password. UNIX stores your password in this encrypted form to permit other users to view the information in the password file without discovering what your password is. The new versions of UNIX do not have the encrypted password entry in this file. Instead you will see an asterisk (*) in this field; the encrypted passwords are stored in a separate file that no one can look at. This provides extra security since hackers could encrypt common passwords and compare the encrypted characters. But no matter which style is used, the results are the same: UNIX knows what your real password is by decoding this field. As you can see, UNIX goes to great lengths to protect the privacy of your password. The next field, an integer, is your UNIX user number. The UNIX system actually keeps track of who you are by using this number, which is associated with your user ID. This is used mainly by UNIX and is normally of no concern to users. Following the UNIX user number is the UNIX group number. UNIX uses this field to identify you as belonging in something called a user group. The group you belong to plays a role in what you are allowed to see and do on the system — in other words, what permissions you have. This is covered in greater detail in the section on UNIX permissions in Chapter 4. Next we have an informational field that can contain any information about the user, such as name and telephone number, as in the example.

The last two fields are very important to the login procedure once you have been identified as a valid user who knows the proper password. The second to last field in the password file tells UNIX what your home directory is. The importance of the home directory was discussed in the previous section on UNIX files. Once the login procedure is completed, you will be located in that directory.

The final field in the password file tells UNIX where to locate the Shell program to run for your login session. This is very important because this is where you indicate to UNIX which of the three Shells — Bourne, Korn, or C — you wish to use when you are logged in to the system. UNIX uses this password file field to locate the executable version of the Shell program and runs that program. The Shell provides you with a system prompt, often a "$" although this can be and usually is altered, indicating that it is ready to interact with you. Once the Shell is executing, everything else that you type at the terminal is interpreted by the Shell you choose to run. From that point forward all your interactions with UNIX are done through the Shell. The login procedure is complete and you are ready to enjoy the productivity gains provided by the Shell.

THE GRAPHICAL USER INTERFACE (GUI)

The previous sections discussed the basic UNIX login procedure. The end result of that login procedure was a user sitting at a terminal, Shell of choice installed, ready to take commands. In years past, this was how UNIX users started their login sessions. But with modern UNIX this may or may not be the end result of logging in. With the ever-increasing popularity and user-friendliness of graphical user interfaces (GUIs for short), the face of UNIX has changed. A GUI is another layer of software (around the kernel and the Shell) that changes the way a user interacts with the UNIX system. Instead of typing commands at a command-line interface, a method that requires lots of typing and memorization, the user is presented with a screen that usually contains a set of graphical objects to ease the burden of using the system. While the focus of this book is not on UNIX GUIs or windowing systems, these topics must be covered in a general way so that you can understand how the Shell and the GUI work in a synergistic manner. This should allow you to integrate the material learned in this book for use in your environment even if you are utilizing a GUI.

Some of the more frequently used objects in a GUI are windows, icons, pull-down menus, pushbuttons, and dialog boxes. Often the user interacts with these objects, by using either a mouse or some other device for selecting the objects, in conjunction with the keyboard. A window is a rectangular region on the screen that can usually be resized and moved and is at the heart of most GUIs. Often a particular software application runs inside a window. There can be multiple windows open on the screen at any one time. This ability allows the user of a GUI to run several applications on the screen at one time and to switch between them with ease. An icon is a small picture that appears on the screen and is usually associated with a command or application. To run that command or application, the user can simply point to the icon and double-click the mouse button. Pulldown menus are small windows that appear on the screen upon demand and provide the user with a list of allowable commands or options. These commands can be selected using the mouse to point to the option desired. A pushbutton is a small button often used to select some action. The user selects the action indicated on the button by again pointing to it with the mouse and double-clicking. These elements combine to make a GUI a user-friendly environment. They often relieve the burden of memorizing and typing lots of difficult commands and they show how functional a software application can be. In addition, and perhaps more importantly, a GUI provides a consistent way to interface with almost all applications developed to run under the GUI. By exploring the various components of the GUI, users can often discover many aspects of an application or system that they never knew existed.

There have been many popular GUIs in the marketplace in the latter part of the 1980s and certainly the early 1990s. Anyone who has had any exposure to computers since the late '80s has probably experienced a GUI. Perhaps the most successful GUI, as well as one of the first, belongs to the Apple Macintosh. Now the very popular Microsoft Windows provides a GUI for IBM-compatible personal computers. The UNIX GUI marketplace has begun to grow over the past several years. The development of a UNIX GUI first had to have a windowing system that met the needs of the users of UNIX systems as well as the philosophy of UNIX. These needs include the ability to run over a network, independence from any specific display terminal, and independence from hardware. The heart of almost all UNIX GUIs is the X Windows system.

The X Windows System

The X Windows system is a general-purpose window development and delivery system. It is a comprehensive package of software used to run and develop window-based graphical user interfaces. The X Windows system grew out of software projects that were done at MIT in the 1980s. It is based on a concept called the "client/server model," which permits the separation of software applications from the input/output terminal or device (a mouse, for instance). In this model there is a special application called the *server* that handles all input and output to the terminal, including the drawing of all types of graphical objects used to build a GUI, and any user interaction with those objects. The server interacts with another type of X program called the *client.* The client, or application program, tells the server what to draw on the screen based on information received from the server about what action a user took. Thus there is a two-way interaction between client and server. They send messages back and forth, with the server telling the client what the user did and the client telling the server what action to take based on this user action. The idea of sending messages is a powerful one. These messages can be sent locally, with the client and server running on the same machine; or over a network, with the client and server being located on different machines. An X client application program utilizes software provided with X (called the X library, or xlib) to tell the server what action to perform on the user's screen. Most of the basic X commands are very simple graphical commands, such as "draw a line from point A to point B".

While the xlib provides all that a user would need to build a full-blown GUI, it would be quite time consuming to do so. If everyone built a GUI or X client from the ground up using these primitive X library commands, each person would determine how windows and menus would look and feel. This would defeat one of the major advantages of a GUI. For this reason a number of X toolkits exist that help developers build GUI applications in a consistent and simplified manner. These toolkits provide a higher level of software support and more directly implement the objects found in a GUI. For example, in most X toolkits there is a command that is called to draw a window on the screen at a certain position and of a certain size. This window has all the properties that one would expect from a window, and every window has the same basic properties. You can see that this is a large step forward from the simple **xlib** command to draw a line from point A to point B. By providing this kind of support, the toolkits simplify the development task while at the same time helping to maintain a consistent method for interfacing with the GUI objects. Two of the more popular X toolkits are Motif and Open

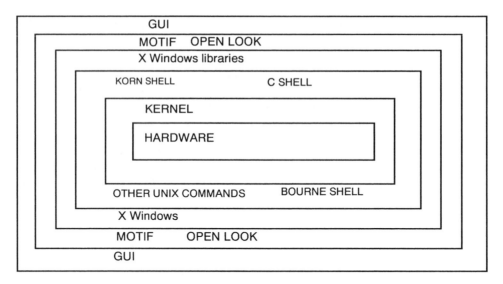

Figure 2.4   Graphical User Interface

Look. Both of these toolkits have a certain look and feel to the GUI objects that are utilized. But in the end they both do a good job of allowing the construction of attractive and consistent graphical user interfaces. Users who are familiar with Microsoft Windows on a PC will feel very comfortable with the Motif-style interface. The previous few sections have presented several new layers of software that are utilized to support a GUI in the UNIX environment. We might now view the software layers of our system in Figure 2.4.

While there are many X clients that run in a typical GUI environment, all of which perform some certain task, there is one client application that is particularly important to our discussion and is found in almost all X GUI environments. This client, perhaps the most widely used X client in existence today, is called *Xterm*.

Using Xterm

Xterm (or X terminal) is the key X client for several reasons. The first is that it provides a window in which a user runs a Shell session. When you start the Xterm client running in your GUI, a window appears, and in that window is the Shell prompt. From this point you can type Shell commands in that window and the Shell responds just as if no GUI existed. You are back to command-line interaction with the Shell. This direct connection to the Shell will be invaluable as you continue to learn Shell programming. Another very useful aspect of the Xterm Shell window is the ability to have more than a single Shell window running at a time. Using the ability of the X Window system, you can actually have two Shell sessions active at one time and switch between them whenever needed. If you have more than one Shell on your system (Bourne, Korn, or C), you can use these two windows to do different applications using different Shells, or you can just run two copies of the same Shell.

Another very important contribution of the Xterm client is that it provides a consistent terminal interface for all UNIX applications. If you are running X Window, it just does not matter what type of terminal you are utilizing. As soon as you start an Xterm window you successfully emulate a DEC VT102 terminal or a TETRONIX 4014 in that window. This means that developers can target any non-graphical character-based user interfaces for these types of terminals and know that anyone running in an X Window environment will be able to run the application properly. In the past this was not always the case. Users ran many different types of terminals, and developers had to anticipate and develop software with these many different terminal types in mind.

Starting an Xterm Window

The Xterm client can most often be started from the system or root menu of a GUI. In many GUIs the system menu can be found by holding down the left mouse button while pointing at the GUI background. (Background could be interpreted to mean not pointing at any GUI object.) When this is done a small menu will pop up. Often this window will have an Xterm option. While you continue to hold down the left mouse button, select the Xterm option and then release the mouse button. This action will often start an Xterm window. If this does not seem to work on your system, refer to the manuals that come with your machine to determine how an Xterm session is started.

Making the Most of Xterm

There are many nice features and options associated with Xterm clients. Many of these features can make using Xterm more user-friendly while others make it more productive. The next few sections point out some of the options available when utilizing Xterm. They do not go into great detail about how to accomplish these things. If you see something that would make your experience more rewarding or productive, please refer to the Xterm documentation for your system to determine how to utilize the feature outlined.

Emulation Options

As was just pointed out, the Xterm client is a VT102 emulation program. There are various options that can be controlled via Xterm to help provide an emulation that best fits your needs. These options can be set by using the VT102 emulation pop-up menu available from inside an executing Xterm window. To access this menu, strike the middle mouse button while holding down the Ctrl key on your keyboard. These menu options allow you to select or remove various emulation options, such as 80-column or 132-column mode. For a full description of all the emulation options, please refer to your system documentation.

General Xterm Options

The are several general Xterm options that can be set by running a pop-up menu inside the Xterm window. This general Xterm pop-up menu can be seen by holding down the left mouse button and the Ctrl key on the keyboard at the same time. The "logging" function in an Xterm session will record your actions in a log file. There are other useful functions available on this menu as well, including the ability to kill a program that is running in the window and the ability to redraw the window.

Multiple Windows

It is possible to have two Xterm clients active at the same time. You may be running a Shell program or application program in one Xterm window and have a need to run some other Shell command while in the process. Suppose, for example, that you are running a Shell program and at some point, after you have already answered numerous questions, the program asks you for a file name that it needs for processing. You cannot remember what that file name is, but you don't want to stop the program and look since you have already typed in a great deal of information. This problem is easily solved by starting another Xterm window and looking for the proper file name. Once you find the file name, you can return to the other window and type in the name without losing any of your work.

Cut and Paste

Another very useful feature when utilizing a GUI is the ability to "cut and paste" between windows. This powerful feature is generally applicable between any two windows, and it seems to be especially useful when working with Xterm clients. There is a fair amount of typing involved with command-line interfaces to Shell commands and application programs. Cut-and-paste operations can help reduce the amount of repetitive typing.

The idea behind a cut-and-paste operation is the utilization of a buffer or clipboard that is accessible to all windows. Text is cut or copied from one window to the buffer and is then pasted into another window as needed. The actual method for the cut/copy operation is done by highlighting or marking text for the cut operation. The marking operation can often be done most effectively with the mouse. Often text is marked by holding down the left mouse button and moving the mouse to highlight all text that is to be copied. When you move the mouse while holding down the left mouse button, the text is highlighted using reverse video. Releasing the mouse button automatically copies the text to the buffer. Now any other operations can be performed and the text will remain in the buffer. You can switch to another window, run a Shell program, or start your favorite application program, and the copied text will be available at any time for recall. To recall—or paste—the copied text, many systems utilize the middle mouse button.

To see how this might be useful, let's return to the example for using multiple windows. In this example the problem was a forgotten file name. Let's say that this time when we start our second window to determine the needed file name, instead of depending on our memory for typing the file name, we use the cut-and-paste operation. When we discover the file name in the second window, we cut the file name to the buffer, return to our first window, and use the paste operation to provide the file name to our Shell program. This avoids possibly forgetting the name again or typing it incorrectly.

The Look and Feel of the Xterm Window

The way the Xterm window looks on your screen, including colors, size, and fonts, can all be controlled. A default setting is provided with your system that controls how the window appears upon starting the Xterm client. Often these defaults are not to our liking. It is often nice to set the Xterm window color and fonts to our preference, for example. These in particular can make looking at the window for long periods of time much more pleasant. This is most often done by setting preferences in a file called .Xdefaults, but can also be done using Xterm menu options to set the preferences on the fly. For a list of all the available preference settings, see your local system Xterm documentation.

SUMMARY

UNIX is a powerful multiuser, multitasking operating system that provides a wealth of powerful user tools. At the heart of the UNIX operating system is the kernel. The kernel hides all other software from a particular hardware implementation. The software of a UNIX system is layered, with each layer using the functionality of the layer below in increasingly powerful ways. The simplicity of UNIX files and the file system structure gives the Shell much of its flexibility and power. The UNIX file system is arranged in an inverted tree structure, with directories representing branch points and files being stored under the directories. The directories traversed to reach a particular file or directory are called the path. All users on the UNIX system are provided with a special directory called their home directory where they perform much of their work. In order to log in to a UNIX system, you must provide a valid user ID and password that correspond with an entry in the /etc/passwd file. If you are utilizing a GUI, then the look and feel of the UNIX user interface is dramatically changed. Most popular UNIX-based GUIs utilize X Windows for creating the graphical objects used. In order to utilize the Shell at a command-line level when running an X Windows–based GUI, you must run the Xterm client. The Xterm client provides a terminal emulation window and allows character-based interaction with the Shell of your choice. The Shell and all of its facilities allow users to become more productive, automating the routine tasks and giving them time to pursue more creative and fulfilling work.

EXERCISES

1. When should the Shell be used:

   a. Interactively?

   b. For programming?

2. Describe UNIX file and file system structures.

3. How can you use the Xterm feature of X Windows to easily access the power of the Shell? What other ways can you use the power of the Shell via your GUI?

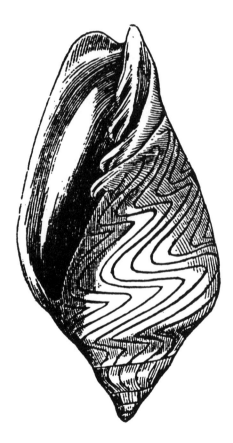

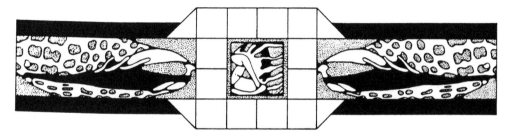

Chapter Three

Shell Fundamentals

There are certain fundamentals that hold true for almost all Shell commands. This chapter covers these fundamentals before covering the basic commands themselves. The principles learned in this chapter will be important building blocks for all Shell commands and Shell programs developed later. This chapter covers the basic command syntax of all Shell commands. In addition, we will look at special characters called "metacharacters" that help make using the Shell easier and more productive. We also introduce methods for controlling input to and output from commands using a technique called I/O (input/output) redirection. Finally, we will take a first look at using Shell commands together to achieve greater results than would be accomplished by using the commands individually. This method of command interaction is accomplished using a device called a "pipe." This will be our first step toward Shell programming.

COMMAND SYNTAX

The Basic Syntax

The syntax of English is *subject-verb-object.* Using Shell, the syntax is *verb-modifier-object:*

```
command -options argument(s)
```

The command can be any one of the hundreds of standard commands available to the Shell or a Shell command that you have developed. Shell commands operate on files, directories, and various devices — tapes, disks, printers, etc. You will need to choose your tool to match the task at hand. The wealth of Shell commands and their many uses will be explored further in subsequent chapters.

Options, like adverbs in English, modify the operation of the command; they change how the command operates. They cause the command to do one thing and not another, or they allow the command to effectively handle exceptions. Most options are single letters or numbers prefaced by a dash (-):

```
command -a -1 argument
```

Not all commands use options in the same way. Unfortunately, some options work differently in various versions of UNIX. If you get surprise results, check the system documentation for a description of how the command works in your environment.

Regardless of whether you use options or not, you will soon begin to discover one of the pleasures of Shell commands: They all tend to take an intelligent default action. By that I mean that if you use a command incorrectly, it might:

* give you a help message

```
rm
syntax: rm -[rf] file(s)
```

* exit gracefully with a return code
* do whatever will cause the least damage (e.g., leave a file unchanged)

Intelligent default actions prevent defects and can save you a lot of effort and rework. The *object* of a command is called an argument. This is described a little later in this chapter. Now let's look at the key file and directory commands.

While most newer Shell and UNIX commands follow the syntax just described, some of the older commands were developed before this syntax standard was set, and you may find some commands that do not follow this syntax. Today this syntax is well understood and used by developers. The details of how options and arguments should be defined is spelled out clearly in the documentation on the **getopts** command and is further discussed in this book when we look in detail at the command. As you progress and begin to develop your own Shell commands, you should keep this command syntax standard in mind. If you do, then UNIX Shell users will know how to execute commands that you develop.

What Is a Command?

All Shell commands start out with a command name. Just like most other things in UNIX, the command is a file that resides in the UNIX file system. UNIX knows, based on the syntax described previously, that the file name given as the command should be a file that contains executable commands. By "executable" we commonly mean that the file contains either instructions for the machine itself (machine code) or a further list of Shell commands for the Shell to examine. If this is indeed the case, then the Shell takes the proper action to execute the command. So when you specify a command name in the Shell syntax, you are really providing the name of an executable file.

Since commands are really files, we can specify command names in the same way that we specify file names: either as stand-alone file names or with a related path in front of the name. The Shell has a standard method of trying to locate the file name specified as the command name when no specific path name is provided. This method essentially consists of telling the Shell which directories within the file system should be searched, in addition to your current directory which is always in your view, in order to try and locate the command name. A *path* is often needed when you create a Shell command of your own. If your command file name is not located in any of these places specified to search for commands, then you must tell the Shell where it is by using a path. How to tell the Shell where to search for commands and how to build your own commands is covered in detail later.

More on Options

Options modify the normal behavior of the Shell command or provide some input for the command. Options are either a simple flag (-f) or a letter followed by a value (-f 47). This can be represented as "-x*value*" or "-x *value*", where **x** is the option and *value* is the value associated with that option. Some commands take values in both forms, others require that they be separated, and still others want no separation. How a command will behave in this respect often is hard to predict. Most new commands need the value separated by a space, so you should probably assume this to be true in most cases. The offenders usually are older commands. In cases where commands use multiple simple flags, the flags can be stacked into a single string, listed separately, or a combination of the two. The following command option lists are the same:

```
command -l -s -t
```

or

```
command -lst
```

or

```
command -ls -t
```

When you specify options, they usually come after the command, separated by a space, and before the argument — but they are never required.

More on Arguments

To be useful, commands have to do something — read, write, transform, or modify data in some useful way. The object of a command, an argument, can be a file, directory, device, or whatever. The argument usually follows the options, if any are specified, and always follows the command. It is differentiated from the option by the fact that it is not preceded by a "-". Many commands expect a file name as the argument. The file name can stand alone or be qualified with a path.

Command Interpretation

The Shells (sh, ksh, csh) are command interpreters; they read the Shell commands and figure out what to do. More formally, the Shell is an *interpreted* computer language. This means that every command entered is analyzed while you wait and is converted into a form the computer understands. This is different from some computer languages that convert the commands into a form the computer understands and stores them in the converted form to be run at any time in the future. These are *compiled* languages. A compiled language is often more efficient, since commands do not need to be converted while you are waiting, but interpreted languages are often easier to use, faster for more personal productivity, and more interactive. With an interpreted language you can get immediate feedback about the outcome of any commands you entered. Most interpreted languages, including the UNIX Shell, go through a standard looping procedure for reading and analyzing Shell commands. This is often called the *fetch-analyze-execute* cycle (Figure 3.1).

The Shell is always ready to read your next command. This is referred to as the *fetch* portion of the cycle. When you type in a Shell command at your terminal, the Shell fetches (or reads) that command. Next the Shell will *analyze* what it is that you entered on the line in order to make some sense of it. Finally, if the Shell determines that what was entered on the line forms some valid Shell command, it will attempt to *execute* that command.

When the Shell analyzes what you have entered on the command line, it uses

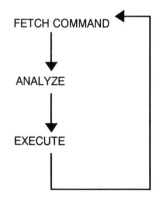

Figure 3.1   Shell Command Loop

the syntax that we described earlier in conjunction with special characters to determine what was entered. These special characters are called "whitespace" and consist mainly of a space, tab, or newline. The newline (a.k.a. the Return key) tells the Shell that you have completed entering the command. The Shell considers all characters up to the first whitespace character, disregarding any leading white space, to be the command. The remainder of the line, up to the newline character, is passed to the command as input. It is actually the executable command itself that looks at the options and arguments portion of the command line. All extra white space is ignored. For example, the following **ls** commands all behave the same since they vary only in the amount of white space contained on the line.

```
$ ls - l /usr/tburns
$      ls       -l      /usr/tburns
$ ls                            -l /usr/tburns
```

After analyzing the input entered in these examples, based on the rules given about white space, the Shell determines in all cases that the command to be executed is the **ls** command and that the options and arguments are -l /usr/tburns.

METACHARACTERS AND FILENAME GENERATION

The Shell assumes that anything on a command line that is not a command or an option is a file, directory, or special file. To simplify handling files and directories, there is another labor-saving Shell facility that:

- reduces the amount of typing necessary
- encourages good naming conventions
- simplifies Shell programming

The Shell provides the user with special characters (* ? [...]) to allow automatic substitution of characters in file and path names. These special characters, sometimes called *metacharacters,* are shown in Table 3.1.

When the Shell sees these characters on the command line, it interprets them as having special meaning. They are not the same as other letters, digits, and characters used to form file and directory names. Instead they are interpreted by the Shell with the meaning outlined in Table 3.1. For an example, let's say that we wanted to list all the files in our current directory that started with the letters "test". Let's also assume that we have three files that we want to list, each of which starts with "test": test1, test2, test3. This could be done by entering any of the following **ls** commands in conjunction with metacharacters:

```
$ ls test*
$ ls test?
$ ls test[123]
```

TABLE 3.1   Metacharacters

Metacharacter	Description
*	Matches any string of characters (including none).
?	Matches any single alphanumeric character.
[...]	Matches any single character or series of characters within the brackets.

KSH	
~	Your Home directory is substituted for this character.
~-	Your previous working directory is substituted for the characters.
~userid	The home directory of the user "userid" is substituted for the characters.
~+	Your current working directory is substituted for the characters.

Metacharacters can significantly reduce the keystrokes required to access a series of file names. There are a few drawbacks, however. In the previous example, I would have gotten different results if the following files existed in the directory:

```
test1  test2  test3  test4  test-5   testmess
```

The first command would have listed all six files. The second command would have listed the first four. The last command would be the only one that worked exactly as required. Metacharacters can reduce typing effort, but can give unexpected results depending on the files in a directory. When you are preparing to use a metacharacter in a file name to identify more than a single file to a Shell command, it is often a good idea to use the **ls** command to list the files that you would use when running the command. This prevents accidentally using incorrect files.

More on the * and ? Characters

The simple example just shown demonstrates the power of using metacharacters to match against multiple file names. Let's look a little more closely at using the * and ? characters to help generate lists of file names.

First it should be pointed out that any of the metacharacters can be used anywhere in a file or path name, not just at the end as in the example. Often we use the metacharacters at the end of file names because it is a natural way to find files that are named in a similar way. But the power of metacharacters can be used to look in multiple directories while looking for multiple files. For example, the following command will list all the files that end with "doc" and reside in any directories with names starting with the string "document_" residing in the directory /system/doc/.

```
ls /system/doc/document_*/*doc
```

The * metacharacter will match *zero or more* characters. In the example just given, any file that was named with some string of characters followed by "doc" would be matched as well as the file named doc if it existed.

Now of course, the metacharacters can be used in combination to generate file names as needed. For example, if we had documents named chapter1.doc through chapter20.doc in the document directories /system/doc/document_*/ and we wanted to use chapter1.doc through chapter9.doc, we could use the following command:

```
ls /system/doc/document_*/chapter?.doc
```

We can combine the metacharacters in any number of ways and make the expression more useful and, occasionally, more complicated. For example, let's say that our chapters listed in the example were further divided into files containing sections of the chapter using a naming convention such as chapter_chap#_section#. So, for example, "chapter_1_1.doc" would contain Chapter 1 Section 1. Let's say that we were interested in looking at all sections for Chapters 1 through 9. The following command would do the job:

```
ls /system/doc/document_*/chapter_?_*.doc
```

For another example, let's say that we were interested in seeing all the sections for Chapters 10 through 19. The following command works well:

```
ls /system/doc/document_*/chapter_1?_*.doc
```

As a further example, suppose we only wanted to see Section 1 of all the chapters. Again, using metacharacters makes it easy. The following command will list all the chapters in Section 1:

```
ls /system/doc/document_*/chapter_*_1.doc
```

As a final example, suppose that we only wanted to work with sections numbered > 9. The following command that combines more than a single ? would do the job since it would require that two characters occur for the section name. Sections 1 through 9 would not meet this criterion.

```
ls /system/doc/document_*/chapter_*_??.doc
```

Depending on how you organize your files and directories, and how you name your files, metacharacters can simplify all of your commands. It will require some exploration, but once you learn how to use metacharacters to simplify your work, you will wonder how you ever got along without them.

More on the [...] Metacharacter

The [...] "regular expression" metacharacter matches any one of the characters listed between the brackets. It also has a few other features that make it a powerful tool for Shell programming. First, you can specify ranges of characters by separating the characters with a "-" character (a-z). Second, you can use the negation symbol "!" as the first symbol after the [to match characters that are not found enclosed in the brackets(!a-z). Using the [...] in conjunction with "-" and "!" allows you to match on a wide range of character combinations. Let's look at a few examples that continue the use of /system/document/chapters.

If we only wanted to work with a few chapters—Chapters 1, 7, and 9, for example—the following command, which uses the [...] metacharacter, would do the trick:

```
ls /system/doc/document_*/chapter_[179]_*.doc
```

What if we wanted to work with Chapters 2 through 6? We could specify this as a range:

```
ls /system/doc/document_*/chapter_[2-6]_*.doc
```

How about all the chapters between 1 and 9 except Chapter 7? Easily done:

```
ls /system/doc/document_*/chapter_[1-689]_*.doc
```

Or if we wanted to eliminate Chapter 5, we could use two ranges as follows:

```
ls /system/doc/document_*/chapter_[1-46-9]_*.doc
```

Instead of wanting just Chapters 1 through 9 except Chapter 5, what if we wanted all chapters except Chapter 5? The negation symbol could be used to find everything but 5.

```
ls /system/doc/document_*/chapter_[!5]_*.doc
```

As you can see, the [...] is a powerful metacharacter. A few other important ranges are used frequently. The range [a-z] matches any lowercase character; [A-Z] matches any uppercase character. The range [0-9] matches any single digit as we saw in the preceding examples. The negation of these ranges is also powerful. The range [!a-z] matches any character that is not a lowercase character, and [!0-9] matches anything that is not a digit.

KSH

The ~ Character

The Korn Shell supports a special character that also helps reduce the amount of typing needed when specifying path names. This is the ~ (tilde character). When the Korn Shell sees this special character at the start of a path, your home directory name is substituted. Since you will often type your home directory at the start of a path name, it can really save typing effort. For example, we could list the contents of our home directory with the command:

```
ls ~
```

If our home directory was /usr/tom, then all the files in that directory would be listed with the **ls** ~ command. Let's say that we wanted to change to /usr/tom/bin. The following Korn Shell shorthand would do the trick:

```
cd ~/bin
```

The Korn Shell also offers a few other variations on the ~ substitution that can be very convenient at times. In a similar manner, they help reduce the typing needed to reference path names. The other forms were listed in Table 3.1.

The first of these forms is the ~- form, which is used to substitute your previous working directory. This can be very useful when you are working with files from two different directories. This situation occurs often. The Korn Shell makes referencing the files in the two different directories a snap. First **cd** to one of the directories, making it your current working directory. Then **cd** to the other directory, making it your new current working directory. The previous files in the first directory can be accessed with the ~- special character, while the files in the current working directory can be accessed using normal Shell conventions. This is especially useful when the path names are quite long. For example, let's say that we want to work with some files named doc-1, doc-2, doc-3 located in the directory /system/doc/userdoc. We need to reference these files often from our home directory /usr/tom. The following sequence of commands could be used to access the files:

```
cd /system/doc/userdoc  # Change to the doc directory
ls *                    # List what is in the directory
doc-1
doc-2
doc-3
cd ~    # Change to our home directory
ls ~-   # What, in the document dir again?
        # Notice no need to type path
```

```
doc-1
doc-2
doc-3
ls -l ~-/doc-1
```

Now if we need to reference one of the files in the document directory, there is no need to type the long path name /system/doc/userdoc over and over again, as would be required using other Shells. Simply place the ~- special character and the Korn Shell does the typing for you.

As if that were not enough to convince you that the Korn Shell is the easiest to use, there are still some other forms of tilde special characters. While these are probably not quite as useful as the ones already covered, they can be a convenient shortcut at times. The first has the form ~username, where *username* is the name of some user on your system. When the Korn Shell sees this series of special characters, it determines the home directory of the user specified in username and substitutes that home directory in the path. This is nice if you know a user's ID but not his or her home directory name. For example, the following command would change your directory to lja's home directory:

```
cd ~lja     # Switch to /usr/programmers/team1/lja
            # lja's home directory
```

The last form of tilde special character substitution is one used to reference your current working directory. While your current working directory is assumed to be the default path used by the Shell, the form often can be useful in Shell programs when the working directory might be changing and you want to reference the current directory in some way. As a simple example, consider:

```
echo The current directory is ~+
```

This command would echo to the user screen the current working directory name.

While we have clearly seen the power of metacharacters, care must be taken when using them. Complicated expressions using numerous metacharacters can be difficult to understand and may not always return the file or path names you expect. A good practice is to check the file names returned using the **ls** command with the expression to ensure that you are going to use the correct files. You can imagine the consequences of using the * metacharacter in conjunction with the UNIX command to remove files! Finally, you may have noticed that when files are named in a way that forms recognizable patterns, it makes using the metacharacters easier and more powerful. So when naming your files, use simple naming conventions. This can greatly increase your ability to access files using the Shell.

OTHER SPECIAL CHARACTERS

Other special Shell characters are shown in Table 3.2. These are characters that the Shell uses to determine special operations to be performed. These are different from the Shell metacharacters because they are not involved with forming file or directory names in a shorthand way. Instead they instruct the Shell to perform a special task. Some of these special characters are covered in the following sections of this chapter, while others are covered in later chapters when they are appropriate.

The Comment Character

As we progress through the book the examples become increasingly more detailed, and there are points where comments have been placed alongside Shell code to help clarify what the command or group of commands is doing. The Shell recognizes these lines as comment lines by the use of the # special character. Anytime the Shell sees this character it considers all following text, up to the end of the line, to be comments. The Shell ignores all comments. If the comment character occurs at the start of a line, then the entire line is a comment. If the comment occurs on

TABLE 3.2   Special Characters

Character	Purpose	Example
#	Shell comment character	`# execute command`
;	Sequential command separator	`cmd1; cmd2; cmd3`
\	Quote a character to remove special meaning (Also acts as command continuation indicator when used as the last character on a command line)	`\*`
&	Place the command in the background for execution	`cmd1&`
( )	Groups the *stdout* of commands	`(cmd1 | cmd2 ; cmd3)`
|	Create a pipe between commands	`cmd1 | cmd2`
<	Command input redirection	`cmd1 < file`
>	Command output redirection	`cmd1 > file`
${var}	Shell variable	`${variable}`
`cmd`	Substitute *stdout*	`var= `cmd2``
'string'	Quote all the characters in a string	`'1,000'`
"string"	Quote all characters but allow substitution	`"${var}$1"`
{cmd1; cmd2}	Execute commands in current Shell	`{ cmd1 | cmd2 }`

the same line as the command, it must be separated by a space or tab; otherwise it will be considered to be part of the command line. Following is an example of adding a comment line and a comment tag line that follows a command:

```
# This is a comment line and is ignored by the Shell.
ls /staff/tburns    # List tburns directory
```

When you begin to write Shell programs, you will want to use comments to describe what the program is doing. You may remember what the command does today, but you may not have a clue a month from now. Similarly, other people may borrow your programs. How can they learn and understand without your forethought about describing the program? Providing good comments in programs helps you and others understand what your program does. You will find that a few comments now can save lots of time in the future. They will jog your memory and provide insight into complicated Shell programs.

The Command Separator

Another very useful special character that can save time is the semicolon command separator character (;). This special character tells the Shell that you have completed one command and are about to begin another. This, of course, allows you to enter more than one command on a line. If you know that a series of commands will be needed to accomplish your desires, you may enter these commands on a single line separated by a semicolon. For example, if I wanted to change to my home directory and then list what files reside in the directory, I could issue the needed **cd** and **ls** commands on a single line:

```
cd /staff/tburns; ls *
```

The Quote Character

It should be pointed out that these special characters, or metacharacters, will sometimes need to be used as their normal character representation. When this happens the special meaning of the metacharacter can be ignored by using the quote special character (\, or backward slash) before the metacharacter. When the Shell sees the \ it will ignore the meaning of the next character. In essence, the \ character is a special character that tells the Shell not to consider the character following it to be special. The following command will remove a file with the name "*junk".

```
rm \*junk
```

REGULAR EXPRESSIONS

Throughout this book we use UNIX tools that utilize regular expressions. A regular expression could better be described as a pattern-matching expression. Regular expressions are formed by using letters and numbers in conjunction with special characters that act as operators. They can greatly aid in the ability to find and filter information in files. The most common UNIX tools that utilize regular expressions are ed, sed awk, the various forms of grep, and the emacs editor (an even richer set of regular expression operators). In addition, you will find other tools that utilize a more limited form of regular expressions. An example of this is filename generation in the Shell. While it does not support a full implementation of regular expressions, you will see that several of the regular expression operators are at work. (Unfortunately, the implementation is not completely consistent — note * and ? following.) Another example of a tool that supports regular expression is the **pg** command. In this section we cover each of the regular expression operators and learn how to build regular expressions using them. You will find this information to be applicable in many areas of UNIX.

Let's first take a grand tour of all the regular expression operators. Table 3.3 shows all of the regular expression character operators along with a brief description of how they operate. Any character that is *not* in this list and is used in a regular expression stands for itself and nothing else. These are often called ordinary characters. For example, all of the alphabetic and numeric characters stand for themselves when used in a regular expression.

Simple Regular Expressions

In this section we start to explore the building of regular expressions by examining simple regular expression patterns. The point of showing these somewhat trivial examples is to ensure that the difference between ordinary and special characters is understood. The following string is a regular expression that consists of the character *q* and would match just the character *q* and nothing else:

```
q
```

While this seems trivial, it shows that *q* is an ordinary character that can represent a regular expression. Simple regular expressions consist of no special operators and simply represent themselves. Further, the regular expression

```
quit
```

is a simple regular expression that would match the characters *q, u, i, t* in succession. Any character that is not listed as a special operator character in Table 3.2 can occur in a simple regular expression and will stand for itself and nothing else. For example,

```
column; row%
```

is a simple regular expression that in essence matches the string "column;row%". If for some reason we need to include a special character as part of a simple regular expression, then we can do so by preceding it with the escape character \. This

TABLE 3.3   Regular Expression Operators

Character	Description
.	Match any single character (like ? in filename generation).
[ ]	Match any character found between the brackets. This operator is used to form a class or set of characters to be matched. The - is used to describe a range of characters. For example, [0-9] matches all numeric characters and is the same as writing [0123456789]. Note that all characters (except ^ in the first position and - in a range) become ordinary when they appear between [ ].
[^]	Match any character not found between the brackets. The ^ acts as the complement operator for the set or character class. For example, [^0-9] would match all characters that are not numeric.
^	Match following regular expression only if it occurs at the start of a line.
$ '	Match preceding regular expression only if it occurs at the end of a line.
*	Match zero or more occurrences of preceding regular expression. (Note that this is different from filename generation, which matches any string.)
\{m,n\} \{$m,$\} \{m\}	This construct controls the number of times that the preceding regular expression matches, with m being the minimum and n being the maximum. If the regular expression occurs at least m times and at most n times, then it is assumed to match. There are variations on this as shown. If m occurs and n is missing (as in \{$m,$\}) then the regular expression must occur at least m times. If m occurs alone (as in \{m\}), then the regular expression must match exactly m times.
\	Used before any of the characters in this table to escape their special meaning. When a \ occurs in front of any special character, it stands for itself in that occurrence.
\\	The null regular expression that resolves to the last regular expression encountered.
\(reg_exp\)	Remember the reg_exp enclosed between ( ) for later reference. Each occurrence of ( ) is referenced based on its occurrence from the left side of the regular expression string.

character means that the next character should not be considered a special character but simply an ordinary character in the regular expression. The following example would match the string ABC*:

    ABC*

It should also be noted that a space participates in a regular expression as an ordinary character that must be matched by a space.

A simple regular expression can stand alone as shown here, but is often combined or concatenated with regular expression operators and other simple regular expressions to form complex regular expressions. This is of course the real power of regular expressions and deserves close inspection.

Matching Any Single Character Using .

A period is a special character in regular expressions that will match any single character. You use this in a regular expression anytime you want a single character to occur but it does not matter what that character is. For example, if we wanted to match all three-character strings that start with the letter *r* and end with the letter *n,* the following regular expression would do the trick:

```
r.n
```

This would of course match the strings run, ran, and ron, which form valid words, but would also match any of a long list of more nonsensical character strings — such as r1n, rxn, and r&n — as well as longer strings that contain r.n as a substring such as ronald or rink. The point here is not to overlook the fact that the period matches any character in the ASCII character set, not just numbers and letters.

As another example, let's say that we were filtering a file that contained five-character part codes. We want to match any part code that has the character *Z* as the third character. The regular expression that would accomplish this task could be written as

```
..Z..
```

This regular expression would of course match any character string five characters long that had a *Z* as the third character. In this example we will assume that our file only contained part numbers and no other strings. If that were not the case, this regular expression could get us into trouble if we did not use care to isolate just the part number.

Matching Sets of Characters Using [ ]

The left bracket starts the definition of a character set in a regular expression. Any characters that occur between the left and the right bracket are considered part of the set. The regular expression matches if any of the characters in the set occur in the string being examined. As an example, let's return to our three-character string that begins with *r* and ends with *n.* We saw previously that the period special character gave us many matches. If our intention was just to match three-character words that start with *r* and end with *n,* we might utilize the [ ] construct in our regular expression to help us narrow our matches. We might begin by assuming that we should narrow our search to just lowercase alphabetic characters. We can do this using a character class. Of course, we could list every lowercase character between the brackets, but luckily we can use a shorthand notation to represent this. The - is used to represent a range of characters. So the range [a-z] represents [abcdefghi...z] and thus forms our desired regular expression representing all lowercase alphabetic characters. Now getting back to our example, the full regular expression would be

```
r[a-z]n
```

This would eliminate any string that does not have a lowercase alphabetic character in the second position. But clearly this can still match lots of nonsense words (rbn, rcn, etc.). If we assume that a vowel needs to occur in the second position, we could further limit our regular expression by placing just the vowels in our character set. For example,

```
r[aeiou]n
```

would match more closely with our intentions of matching words that contain a substring that starts with *r* and ends with *n* (ran, run, ron, ronald, rink). Placing a space after the *n* in the regular expression would make it more closely match just three-character words that start with *r* and end with *n* followed by a space.

The [ ] construct is very powerful at limiting the scope of regular expression matching to particular characters or sets of characters. The range operator - can specify any sequence of characters as long as they are continuous in the ASCII sequence. For example, [A-C] represents just the uppercase characters ABC. Several commonly used ranges are listed as follows:

[A-Z]	all uppercase alphabetic characters
[a-z]	all lowercase alphabetic characters
[0-9]	all digital characters
[A-Za-z]	all alphabetic characters

In addition to the range operator, there is another operator that has special meaning within the brackets. If the first character after the left bracket is a ^, then the complement of the character set defined between the brackets is matched. This means that any character that is not in the set defined will be matched. For example, the regular expression

```
r[^A-Z]n
```

would match any three-character string that started with *r* and ended with *n* and did not contain an uppercase alphabetic character in the second position. This operator can be applied to the common ranges shown previously to form other very useful ranges. For example:

[^A-Za-z]	matches all nonalphabetic characters

One last point concerning the [ ] construct: All characters that occur inside the brackets are ordinary. The only characters that have special meaning within the [ ] are the range operator - and the ^ complement operator. These can of course stand for themselves if preceded by an \ escape character.

Matching the Start of a Line Using ^

If the ^ character occurs outside of the character class operator [ ] and at the start of a regular expression, then the expression that follows must match at the beginning of a line. For a very simple example, consider the following regular expression:

`^Windy`

This regular expression would only match the characters "Windy" if they occurred at the beginning of a line. All other occurrences of "Windy" would not match. Matching the beginning of a line can be a very useful tool when editing files and is a frequently used regular expression in sed and ed. The ^ character alone matches just the beginning of a line and can be used to insert information onto the front of a line using sed. For example, the regular expression

`^`

will match the start of every line in the file.

But the ^ character can really occur before any regular expression. Let's return to our previous example where we wanted to match a part number located in a file. If you recall, this was accomplished using the regular expression

`..Z..`

As we pointed out then, this regular expression could match only any character string in the file that contained a Z in the third position. We were safe as long as we just had part numbers in the file. Let's assume instead that the part number was at the beginning of each line in the file. Then the following regular expression, using the ^ special character, could limit the matching performed to just the start of the line:

`^..Z..`

You will find the ^ operator to be very useful in forming regular expressions since key information is often located at the start of a line of data. In addition, it is often easy to arrange it so that important information is located at the start of a line.

Matching the End of a Line Using $

Like the ^ special character at the start of a line, the $ character following a regular expression is used to cause a match to occur only if the preceding regular expression occurs at the end of a line. For example,

END$

would match only if the string "END" occurred at the end of a line. All other occurrences of the string would be ignored. The $ character can be used after any valid regular expression to force the match to occur only at the end of the line. Consider this example where we want to match the word *end*, but in any case mixture:

[E,e][N,n][D,d]$

This is often a good technique for matching user input where the input can be in any case and you want to look simply for the word regardless of case.

Consider the following example, which uses both the ^ and the $ regular expression characters:

^$

This regular expression will match all blank lines.

Matching Zero or More Characters Using *

The * character is used to match zero or more of the preceding character or regular expression. Note that this is different from the filename generation * symbol, which says to place any string in this position. (This is accomplished in regular expressions by the formation .*, which is any character repeated any number of times.) The * in regular expressions is simply a repeat symbol. The preceding character can repeat any number of times, including zero times, and still match. As an example, consider the following regular expression:

ZA*P

This regular expression would match the string ZP as well as the string ZAAAAAAAAAAAAAAAAAAAAAAAAAAAP. If we wanted to ensure that at least one occurrence of the *A* is to appear in the string, we could write the regular expression

ZAA*P

which would at a minimum match ZAP.

Of course, the * special character can be used after any regular expression to indicate that it is to repeat zero or more times. For example, here are several widely used regular expressions involving *:

[A-Za-z][A-Za-z]*	matches any string of characters (essentially matches all words)
[+\-][0-9][0-9]*	matches any integer with a preceding + or -

```
.*                          matches any string of characters
^ *$                        matches lines that have only spaces (blank lines)
```

Note that a .* alone will match the entire line since regular expressions match the longest possible string if any ambiguity exists. This is a good way to match all the lines in a file.

Matching a Specified Number of Characters Using \{m,n\}

The * character introduced in the previous section is very powerful but provides no control over how many occurrences of a character is considered valid as a match. It can range from 0 to some very large number of occurrences. Sometimes we would like to have a little more control when building regular expressions. The \{m,n\} construct provides three ways to control matching of repeating characters. These are:

1. Character must repeat within a range specified by m and n with m being the minimum number of times the character can repeat and n the maximum. This has the form \{m,n\}.

2. Character must repeat at least m number of times. This has the form \{m,\}.

3. Character must repeat exactly m number of times. This has the form \{m\}.

These forms often provide the control that we need when forming complex regular expressions. For example, consider the example from the previous section that described integers:

[+\-][0-9][0-9]*

Actually, this forces our integers to have a preceding + or - sign. This often is not the case when trying to match integers in general, which may or may not have a + or - sign in front. But without the \{m,n\} construct it would be very difficult to write a regular expression to match the general case integer. Using [+\-]* would simply not work for obvious reasons. But now that we can control the number of occurrences, the following regular expression should do the trick:

[+\-]\{0,1\}[0-9][0-9]*   matches any legal integer expression

Likewise, we could now form an expression that would match any real or integer number by using the following regular expression:

[+\-]\{0,1\}[0-9][0-9]*\.\{0,1\}[0-9][0-9]*   matches any real or integer
                                                  decimal expression

As another example, let's return to our part number and assume that the first two positions in the part number are alphabetic and the final two positions are numeric. Then our part number would look something like AAZ23. We may want to match a part number anywhere it is found and can assume that part numbers always have this form. Using the repeating control construct, we can form a regular expression that matches part numbers as follows:

```
[A-Z]\{2\}Z[0-9]\{2\}
```

The first part of the expression, [A-Z]\{2\}, says that we must have exactly two occurrences of uppercase alphabetic characters followed by a Z, which of course is followed by two numeric characters.

Save a Match and Compare Later Using \(...\) and \n

The \(...\) construct provides the ability to save a matched string in memory for comparison later in the regular expression. Any regular expression can be placed between the \(\) parentheses. Each time that a string is stored using this construct it is assigned a number 1 through 9 based on its position in the regular expression. These stored expressions can be referenced later in the same regular expression by using the \n construct in the place of a regular expression. For example, let's suppose that we had a file containing lines that were divided into fields based on the field delimiter ":". There are four fields on each line. We want to only select lines where the first field matches the third field and the second field matches the fourth. The following regular expression demonstrates how saved expressions are assigned numbers:

```
\(.*\):\(.*\):\1:\2:
```

The first field is matched and stored and \1 using \(.*\): which says to match any character string up to the first : (which is our field delimiter). The second field is stored as \2 by the second occurrence of \(.*\):. Finally, we recall the saved patterns by referencing \1 in the third field position and \2 in the fourth field position. If the third field matches the pattern saved for the first field and the fourth field matches the pattern saved for the second field, then the line matches.

Saving matched patterns is a very useful tool especially when using sed and ed, which allow the saved pattern to be used as a replacement value when editing a file. Note that this construct \(...\) is not available when using awk.

Creating More Complex Regular Expressions

In the previous sections several examples were used to demonstrate each of the regular expression special characters. As we progressed we developed increasingly complex expressions. As you can imagine, regular expressions are very powerful and can match or recognize a wide variety of strings. This is done by concatenating smaller regular expressions into longer strings. We saw this in

TABLE 3.4   Awk Extensions to Regular Expression Operators

Character	Description
+	Match the previous character one or more times. This is different from the * operator because zero occurrences do not match.
?	Match the previous character zero or one time only.
|	The OR operator, which means to match either regular expression pattern occurring on either side of the OR symbol: reg_exp1|reg_exp2
( )	A regular expression grouper that can be used to group entire regular expressions. Aids in removing ambiguities in complex regular expressions.

some of the latter examples in the previous sections. For example, the regular expression to match an integer or real decimal was given by

```
[+\-]\{0,1\}[0-9][0-9]*\.\{0,1\}[0-9][0-9]*
```

This is of course a concatenation of several smaller regular expressions. We can extend this concatenation into a wide array of complex regular expressions that will match all kinds of classes of strings. In fact, regular expressions are used in computer language compilers to help recognize valid syntactic components of the language.

Egrep and Awk Extensions to Regular Expressions

In addition to the regular expression characters just discussed, egrep and awk extend the capabilities of regular expressions by adding several other regular expression characters. These are outlined in Table 3.4. Note that these are only available in egrep and awk and cannot be used in other tools such as sed and ed. As was mentioned above, the \(...\) construct is not part of the egrep/awk regular expression special characters.

Matching One or More Characters Using +

The + operator is used much like the * operator described previously, except that the + operator does not consider zero occurrences to be a match. The preceding character must occur at least once. This is a very convenient operator since there are often situations where we want to ensure that the regular expression character occurs at least once. In the previous sections we saw examples of regular expressions that describe words and integers. In each of these regular expressions we had to take measures to ensure that a letter or digit occurred at least once, as is shown in the following:

```
[A-Za-z][A-Za-z]*
```

By using the + operator we can simplify the expression to be

```
[A-Za-z]+
```

This implies that at least a single alphabetic character must be found in order for a match to occur.

We could simulate the behavior of the + character using the \{1,\} construct which implies that the preceding character must occur at least one time.

Matching Zero or One Occurrence of a Character Using ?

Similar to the * and + operators, the ? matches zero or one occurrence of the previous character. This can be thought of as a special case of the \{m,n\} construct, where m is 0 and n is 1. The ? operator is provided because the need to specify zero or one occurrence arises frequently when developing regular expressions. In our previous example of a regular expression that matched integer or real number decimal representations, we looked for zero or one occurrence of a + and - sign and a decimal point. This regular expression was as follows:

```
[+\-]\{0,1\}[0-9][0-9]*\.\{0,1\}[0-9][0-9]*
```

Using the ? and the + operator, we can simplify this regular expression to the following:

```
[+\-]?[0-9]+\.?[0-9]+
```

Matching Either of Two Regular Expressions Using |

The | is an OR operator that can be used to specify two full regular expressions, either of which can match to cause a match of the regular expression. The syntax for using the OR operator is

```
reg_exp_1\reg_exp_2
```

which means either *reg_exp1* or *reg_exp2* can match to cause an overall match. For example, the simple regular expression

RED|TED

would match either the string RED or the string TED. This can be useful when we want to match several conditions in a single position in a regular expression.

FILTERS

As we discussed briefly in Chapter 1, a key way to turn raw data into useful information is to filter out the extraneous data. You should think of most Shell com-

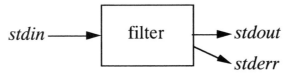

Figure 3.2   A Shell Filter

mands as filters, like the one shown in Figure 3.2. They have a single input, called standard input (abbreviated as *stdin,* see Table 3.5), that gives them a character at a time. Each command also has two outputs: standard output (*stdout*) and standard error (*stderr*). Each command filters data from the standard input or refines it in some fashion, and passes it to the standard output. Any errors that it encounters (if any) are passed to *stderr.* Errors rarely occur, however, because most UNIX commands are designed to take intelligent default actions in most situations. If, for example, you don't assign a file as *stdin,* then the Shell assumes that your terminal is *stdin.* If you don't assign a file as standard output, then the Shell again assumes that the terminal is standard output. One of the dumbest things you will ever do is type a command such as "**cat**" (concatenate and print) followed by a return and then wonder what happened:

```
cat
```

What is happening? See Figure 3.3. The Shell is waiting for you to type input from the screen, and it will display it back to you when you are done. To get out of this command, you have to hit the "break" or "delete" key, or type `Ctrl(d)` for end-of-file (EOF).

The **cat** command is the simplest of the Shell's filters. It does not change the data; it takes the standard input and reproduces it on the standard output. At first glance, this seems worthless, but if you want to view a file on your terminal, all you have to do is type the command:

```
cat file
```

The Shell will open the file and reproduce it on *stdout* (your terminal). Any errors detected, such as a missing file, will be passed to *stderr* (again, your terminal).

TABLE 3.5   File Descriptors

Name	I/O	File Descriptor
stdin	input	0
stdout	output	1
stderr	error output	2
user-defined	input/output	3-19

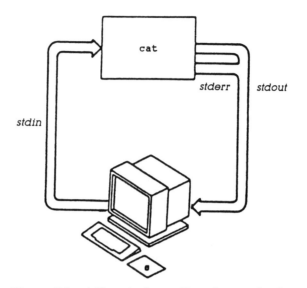

Figure 3.3 A Terminal as *stdin*, *stdout*, and *stderr*

Other filters extract only the data you want to see, while others add or change the data per your instructions. The **grep** command (Globally look for a Regular Expression and Print) will find every occurrence of a word or phrase in a UNIX file. For example, the following command will find all occurrences of my name in Chapter 1:

```
grep "Arthur" chapter1
Author: Lowell Jay Arthur
King Arthur and the Knights of the Round Table
```

Two occurrences were found. **Grep** filtered out all of the other lines in the file chapter1. Please notice that all Shell commands are *case sensitive.* Uppercase and lowercase letters are different. To illustrate how the Shell can use commands to modify and enhance data, imagine that I need to change all occurrences of "shell" to "Shell". The **sed** (stream editor) command is useful:

```
sed -e "s/shell/Shell/g" chapter1
```

Sed will open chapter1 as *stdin* and pass the file to *stdout* (the terminal) while changing all occurrences of "shell" to "Shell". Well, you might say, that is certainly useful, but I need the output in a new file. To create a new file with Shell, you need to use a facility called input/output redirection.

INPUT/OUTPUT REDIRECTION

Input and output redirection allows you to:

1. create files
2. append to files
3. use existing files as input to the Shell
4. merge two output streams
5. use part of the Shell command as input

You can use I/O redirection to change the direction of *stdin, stdout,* and *stderr,* or any other user-defined file descriptor (Table 3.5). A file descriptor is a numeric handle that UNIX uses to identify a file that is open for processing. Twenty files may be open at one time; their file descriptors are 0-19. The first three file descriptors are reserved for *stdin* (0), *stdout* (1), and *stderr* (2).

The syntax of the two most frequently used redirection activities is as follows:

```
file-descriptor-1 operator file-name      (e.g., 2> errorfile)
file-descriptor-1 operator file-descriptor-2 (e.g., 2> &1)
```

The first format opens a file as either input or output and assigns it to a specified file-descriptor. The second format duplicates or assigns one file descriptor to another. The Shell recognizes the operators shown in Table 3.6.

In the previous example, I could have used I/O redirection to save the output in a new file as follows:

```
sed -e "s/shell/Shell/g" chapter1 > newchapter1
```

TABLE 3.6   Redirection Operators

Operator	Action
<	Open the following file as *stdin.*
>	Open the following file as *stdout.*
>>	Append to the following file.
<<del	Take *stdin* from here, up to the delimiter `del`.
<&	Use file descriptor 2 as input wherever file descriptor 1 is used.
>&	Merge file descriptor 1 with file descriptor 2.
>>&	Append file descriptor 1 to file descriptor 2.
|	Pipe *stdout* into *stdin.*

The **sed** command knew to open the file, chapter1, as *stdin,* but I could have also written the command as:

```
sed -e "s/shell/Shell/g" < chapter1 > newchapter1
```

But what about *stderr*? Isn't it still directed to the terminal? Well, yes. Redirecting *stderr* into a file is occasionally useful to debug a Shell command. To do so, however, the Bourne and Korn Shells recognize the file descriptor for *stderr* (2) and the output symbol (>) to mean that *stderr* should be placed in a file:

```
sed -e "s/shell/Shell/" chapter1 > newchapter1 2> newerrors
```

Any errors will be put in the file newerrors. *Note:* This syntax will not work with the C Shell.

Sometimes, it is useful to combine *stdout* and *stderr* into one output stream and put it into a single file. To do so is simple:

```
     sed -e "s/shell/Shell/g" > newchapter1 chapter1 2>&1
csh: sed -e "s/shell/Shell/g" chapter1 >& newchapter1
```

The expression "2>&1" tells the Shell to assign *stderr* (2) to the same file descriptor as *stdin* (&1). Then, the Shell redirects both outputs into the file newchapter1.

The Shell has two other special features — appending to a file and using part of the Shell command as input — to handle special situations. The output redirection command, ">", creates a new file if the file name does not exist. If the file already exists, the Shell writes over it.

KSH

The overwriting of files is a mixed blessing. While it is convenient—you don't really need to think about the current status of an existing file—it can also be disastrous. If an already existing file has important information in it, the Bourne Shell does not indicate in any way that it is ready to overwrite the file. Your data is simply gone. You can help prevent this by ensuring that you redirect output to a certain directory or by restricting file permission on important files; but the Bourne Shell does nothing to warn you. The Korn Shell has added the noclobber option to help you prevent overwriting of important information. You set the noclobber option with the set command using the -o (option) option .

```
set -o noclobber    # Don't overwrite any existing files
```

Once this option is set, you will no longer be able to overwrite files using redirection of output. Instead, you will receive an error message that the file already exists. You can force the file to be overwritten by using the >| symbol for output redirection. This kind of overwrite protection is also available with the C Shell.

Sometimes, it is useful to write some text into a file and then add text to it as required. To do this, you use the symbol to append, ">>".

- If the file does not exist, then the Shell will create it.
- If it exists, the Shell will append text to the file.

A common example involves writing Shell procedures. Often, when using a Shell procedure, you want to create a file of errors and mail them to the person executing the command:

```
echo "First Error" > mailfile    # create a new error file
echo "Second Error" >> mailfile # append errors to the error file
echo "Third Error" >> mailfile  # append more errors
mail lja < mailfile             # mail the error file
```

The first error is detected and stored in a new mail file. The use of ">" creates a new file and avoids appending new errors to old errors in a similar file. All subsequent errors are appended to the mail file. Finally, the mail is sent to the person executing the command — one message is usually better than three separate ones.

The remaining redirection device, "<<", uses lines of data *within* the Shell command as input. Using this method of input to a Shell command is often referred to as a Here document. Using data within the Shell command is most often useful with the editor. Rather than having a separate file as input to the command, you can include it directly with the Shell command:

```
ed mailfile <<EOF!
g/Error/s//Terminal Error/
/First/d
w
q
EOF!
```

This command will edit the mail file using the subsequent lines, up to the first occurrence of delimiter line "EOF!", as input. The editor will replace all occurrences of "Error" with "Terminal Error", delete the next occurrence of "First", write the mailfile, and quit. This ability is useful when you need to edit more than one file and make the same changes to each.

By the way, you do not have to use "EOF!" — any word or character will do. For example, you could use "de" (*ed* spelled backwards).

```
ed mailfile <<de
s/Error/Terminal Error/
/First/d
w
q
de
```

Anything else will work equally as well.

To close an open file descriptor, use "&-":

```
exec 4>&-  # Close file descriptor 4
exec 1<&-  # Close stdin
```

The **exec** command causes any following Shell commands to be executed.

REDIRECTION USING C SHELL

The C Shell handles input/output redirection almost identically except for a couple of minor instances: combining standard output with standard error and overwriting existing files. To combine *stderr* with *stdout,* add an ampersand at the end of the redirection sign:

```
command arguments >& outfile
command arguments >>& outfile
```

The output file will contain all of the standard output and standard error data created by the Shell command. The C Shell also has a variable called noclobber that can be set to prevent accidental destruction of existing files:

```
setenv noclobber
```

When noclobber is set, it is an error for the output file name to exist. To override this protection, use the exclamation point:

```
command arguments >! outfile
command arguments >&! outfile
command arguments >>! outfile
command arguments >>&! outfile
```

Outfile will be rewritten or appended whether it exists or not. If the variable noclobber is not set, the exclamation points are ignored. It does so without concern for the format of the files, whether they exist or should be created. The Shell handles all of this for you. As you will see in the next chapter, input/output redirection gives you great flexibility to manipulate text.

Sometimes, however, it's unnecessary and somewhat inefficient to create a file for everything. Occasionally, you will want to pass the output of one Shell command directly to the input of another. Rather than create a file and have the second command read it, you can pass the data from one command to another using the Shell facility called *pipe.*

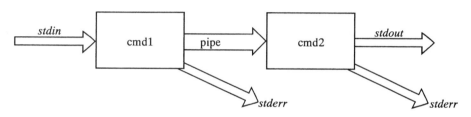

Figure 3.4   A Shell Pipe

PIPES

The "pipe" is exactly what it sounds like — a conduit to carry data from one command to another (see Figure 3.4). It connects the *stdout* of one command to the *stdin* of another — no messy temporary files to deal with, fewer errors, and greater productivity. Besides eliminating temporary files, the pipe allows the two commands to operate at the same time (asynchronously). As soon as the first command creates some output, the second command can begin execution. Figure 3.5 shows the difference in execution time between processes that execute synchronously and those that execute asynchronously. The pipe is not only useful but efficient as well.

In a previous example, I changed all occurrences of "shell" to "Shell" in Chap-

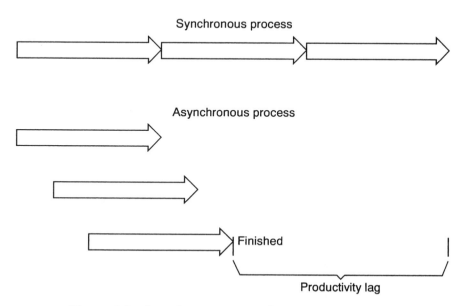

Figure 3.5   Asynchronous versus Synchronous Processes

ter 1. It might be useful to change all occurrences in all of the chapters and put them into a single file. The pipe would let me combine the **cat** and **sed** commands to do this simply:

```
cat chapter1 chapter2 chapter3 | sed -e "s/shell/Shell/" > book
```

Cat concatenates the chapter files and puts them on *stdout*. The pipe passes the data from the **cat** command to the stream editor command (**sed**), which then edits the data and writes it into the file named book.

It is also possible to redirect standard error into standard output and then pipe them both into another command as follows:

```
command arguments 2>&1 | nextcommand
                 csh: command arguments |& nextcommand
```

Aside from this minor difference, the Bourne, Korn, and C Shells all handle pipes in the same way.

Because it may be necessary to save the data passing through a pipe — to test that the command is passing correct data or just to retain the data for future use — there is a facility to save the information in a file. What better name for a pipe fitting than **tee**? **Tee** writes the standard input into a file and onto the standard output. **Tee** is as simple to use as a pipe:

```
cat chapter? | tee book | nroff -cm
```

In this example, **cat** pulls together all of the chapters, **tee** creates the compiled book, and **nroff** formats them.

Pipes are used to connect Shell commands to perform complex functions and improve efficiency. Rather than coding some new command to handle a needed function, Shell commands can be reused, coupled with each other, and shaped to handle even the most difficult information applications. Information passing through pipes can be saved in files with **tee.** Pipes are a key component of the Shell's flexibility and usability.

Named Pipes

Using Bourne or Korn Shell, you can create special devices called *named pipes*. Instead of accepting input from one program, they can accept input from any commands that write to them. Typically, only one *background* command will read the input, however. To see how this works, let's create a named pipe called LOG using the **mknod** (make node) command and run a background process **runlog** that will write log records to the logfile:

```
/etc/mknod LOG p
# log < LOG
```

```
while TRUE
do
 read line
 echo `date +'%H%M%S'` $line >> /usr/local/logfile
done < LOG
nohup nice log&
```

Now, all of the other commands we have running can write to the named pipe, **LOG,** and the **log** command will then read and create records with the output from these commands:

```
command1 > LOG
command2 > LOG
```

The handy thing about named pipes and their background commands is that they can be running all day while other commands come and go. This is a great way to reuse applications such as writing logs or error files.

SUMMARY

The basic Shell command uses the following syntax:

```
command -options argument(s)
```

The argument is often, but not always, a file or path name. The options are almost always specified with a preceding "-" character. Each section of the command—command name, option, and argument—is separated by at least a single whitespace character. Command options alter the actions a command performs.

Shell commands are really UNIX files that contain executable Shell code. Since commands are file names, they can be specified with a path if needed. The Shell has a default method for trying to locate command files in the file system. Commands are interpreted by the Shell using the fetch-analyze-execute cycle. Once a command is located and executed, options and arguments are passed to the command to be analyzed.

The Shell has certain characters that it reserves to have special meaning when seen on the command line. These characters, called metacharacters and special characters, perform a variety of tasks that make using the Shell easier and more powerful. The metacharacters are used to help match many file and path names that fit a certain pattern. The file names that match are generated for use with a particular command. This will alleviate the need to type a large number of similar file names when they all need to be accessed or processed in the same way. The Shell special characters tell the Shell to take some specified action. For example, the symbols < and > tell the Shell to redirect standard input and standard output.

Shell commands can be viewed as filters. They take input data from a file stream, called standard in (*stdin*), filter or transform the data in some way, and place the resulting data in the output file stream. The output file stream is called standard out (*stdout*). There is also a related output stream called *stderr* that is used by the Shell to output error information.

The redirection of I/O allows the input and output for a command to be redirected from the default file stream — your terminal — to a particular file name. Input redirection tells the Shell to read command input from the named file, while output redirection tells the Shell to place the results in the named file. Saving the results of a Shell command is very useful. It can then be used as information or as input to other Shell commands for further processing.

The idea of a pipe is to allow the connection of Shell commands to accomplish a transformation of input data. The pipe is a conduit between commands that attaches the standard input of one command with the standard output of another command. It is an efficient and easy way to accomplish the task of using a series of Shell commands. There is no need for intermediate files, and the Shell commands in the "pipeline" operate in an asynchronous mode.

EXERCISES

1. Describe the use of each of these Shell metacharacters:

    a. *

    b. ?

    c. [...]

    d. \

2. Given a directory containing the following files — Abel, Cain, George, Gorth, Greg, Sam, Ted, Trod — use the **ls** command to list only those files:

    a. consisting of three letters

    b. consisting of four letters

    c. that begin with a *G* followed by *e* or *o*

    d. that begin with *T* and end with *d*

3. Diagram and describe a typical Shell filter.

4. What are standard input (*stdin*), standard output (*stdout*), and standard error (*stderr*)?

5. What is input/output redirection?

6. Write a simple interactive Shell using I/O redirection to accept input from file1, put *stdout* in file2, and *stderr* in file3.

7. Write a simple Shell to redirect *stderr* into *stdout* and put the combined output in outerrfile.

8. Write a simple Shell to append to an existing file.

9. Write a simple Shell, using the pipe, to sort a file both before and after using **grep** to extract information from it. Which form is more efficient?

10. Use **pipe** and **tee** with the previous exercise to put the output of **grep** into a file before sorting the information selected.

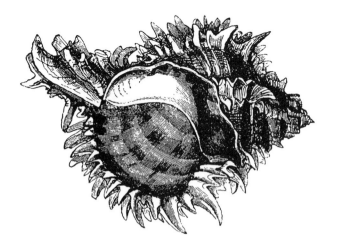

Chapter Four

Shell Commands

Almost any UNIX command is available for use with the Shell. This chapter explains how the Shell finds commands and files. It also introduces some of the most useful, but simplest, commands. From these simple tools, a Shell programmer can grow increasingly functional programs that will perform tasks that are hundreds of times more powerful than their basic Shell commands. These commands fall into several key categories:

File and directory

Selection

Combining and ordering

Transformers and translators

Editors

Printing

Security

Built-in

Before we get into these various kinds of commands, I need to explain that I'm not going to attempt to reiterate the UNIX manual pages for each command discussed. If you would like to know more — and believe me, there is much more to most commands than we have space to discuss in this book — then you will need to look up the commands either in your documentation or interactively on the UNIX system. To view the documentation for a command, use **man**:

```
man command_name
```

If you need to view it page by page, *pipe* the output into **more** or **pg**:

```
man command_name  |  more
```

Or, if you absolutely need a paper copy, you can *pipe* the output into either **lp** or **lpr**—the line printer commands—depending on which is appropriate for your system. I will encourage you to avoid paper output as much as possible. Printed reports seem to need to be copied multiple times and are ultimately thrown away. Electronic reports can be copied thousands of times and only consume a small quantity of disk space. Think ecologically. Only print things when you really need them:

```
man command_name  |  lpr
```

Now that we've handled the administrative details, we will begin our investigation into Shell commands. When reading about the Shell commands presented in the following sections, keep in mind the Shell basics covered in the previous chapter, including command syntax.

FILE AND DIRECTORY COMMANDS

Directories are like file cabinets and file folders; they allow you to organize your information effectively in various files. The standard maximum length of all file and directory names is 14 characters. File and directory names can include any of the following characters: '. _ a-z A-Z 0-9'.

The Shell file and directory commands are shown in Table 4.1. The most elementary directory commands are **pwd**, **ls**, **cd**, **mkdir**, and **rmdir**. Elementary file commands include **cat**, **cp**, **mv**, and **rm**.

TABLE 4.1   File and Directory Commands

Type	Command	Purpose
Directory	`cd`	change directory
	`ls`	list a directory's contents
	`pwd`	print working directory
	`mkdir`	make a new directory
	`rmdir`	remove an existing directory (if empty)
File	`cat`	concatenate file(s)
	`cp`	copy file(s)
	`csplit`	split a file based on arguments
	`ln`	link two names to one file
	`mv`	move file(s)
	`rm`	remove file(s)
	`split`	split a file into *n* line chunks

Directory Commands

Since it's easy to get lost in the file system, you will occasionally need to ask the question: Where am I? The **pwd** command does this for you:

```
pwd     # Please tell me what directory I'm in
/unix1/lja
```

KSH

The Korn Shell provides a method to allow your current working directory to always be displayed. It is a very nice feature and is covered in detail in the section on the Shell variable PS1. It helps prevent that lost feeling when moving around in the file system.

Another common question is: What's in this directory? The **ls** (list) command, without any options or arguments, gives a listing of all of the files and directories in the current directory:

```
Bourne/Korn      Csh
ls               ls
bin              bin doc src
doc
src
```

The **ls** command can be combined with numerous options, most commonly -l (for long) and -ld (for directory names only, not their contents), to give a more detailed listing of the current directory and its contents:

```
ls -l
drwxrwx---       3 lja    adm      992 Dec 1 05:39 bin
drwx------      28 lja    adm      496 Dec 4 12:28 doc
drwxrwxrwx      32 lja    adm     1008 Dec 3 18:22 src

ls -ld
drwxrwxrwx      32 lja    adm      437 Dec 3 18:22 .
```

It is possible, however, that there might be some hidden files in a directory. Hidden files have a period (.) as the first character of their name. Hidden files are normal UNIX files that are hidden from your normal view. In general they are files that you do not work with on a regular basis. You can change and create hidden files just like other files. To see all of the files in a directory, including those deliberately hidden, you should use the -a option:

Bourne/Korn	*Csh*
`ls -a`	`ls -a`
`.`	`. .cshrc .profile doc`
`..`	`.. .login bin src`
`.cshrc`	
`.login`	
`.profile`	
`bin`	
`doc`	
`src`	

There are many options to the **ls** command. We do not cover them all in this book, but there are a few others that are worth pointing out. There are several options that sort the file names in various orders based on date and times instead of the default sort order of names. These are the -t, -c, -r, and -u options. There are also several options that change the way the listing is displayed. These are the -x, -C, and -F options. One final option that is useful at times is the -q option that shows unprintable characters that may exist in your file name as "?". This can be a real help when your file name was mistakenly created with a character that does not display on your terminal. When this happens you cannot access the file because you don't know what the real file name is. You can't print it, edit it, or remove it. The -q option can help identify when this has happened.

Once you know where you are and have a list of the directories beneath the current one, you may want to move into another directory. The **cd** (change directory) command moves you from one directory to another:

```
cd directory_name
```

The **cd** command will change to any directory that is located under your current working directory. This command works just like other Shell commands when it comes to recognizing directory names. The directories under your current working directory are within view and do not need to be prefaced by a full path name. You should put related files in different directories (cabinets, drawers, or folders) to make them easier to find. Proper naming of directories and files will help you locate them.

Using the **cd** command without any arguments will transfer a user to the home directory:

```
pwd                          # Where am I?
/unix1/lja/src/application
cd                           # Take me home
pwd
/unix1/lja
```

To make a big leap and change to any other directory in the system, you would use the full path name to the other directory. For example:

```
cd /usr/bin
pwd
/usr/bin
```

KSH

Since changing directories is a frequent activity, the Korn Shell has a few shortcuts that can help out. Of course, the full set of ~ metacharacters are very helpful at reducing typing of path names—these were discussed in the previous chapter. The Korn Shell also provides an extension to the **cd** command itself, which is the cd - syntax. This command will return to your last working directory. For example:

```
cd /usr/bin      # Change to the /usr/bin directory
cd               # Home please
pwd
/usr/tburns
cd -             # Back to /usr/bin
pwd
/usr/bin
```

You will also need to create and delete directories. This is simple using **mkdir** (make directory) and **rmdir** (remove directory):

```
mkdir new_directory
rmdir old_directory
```

Rmdir, however, will not let you remove a directory if it still holds any files or subdirectories. To delete the directory, you first have to delete all of the files and directories within it. Only the entries . , .. can exist in the directory. More about deleting files in the next section.

```
ls -a    # List directory
         # Only . and .. occur—the only entries allowed for rmdir
         # to work
.
..
```

When you create a new directory with **mkdir**, the permissions that are placed on the directory may not allow others to access the directory you created. The permissions that are placed on your new directories and files are based on the setting of your umask value. You can of course change the permissions using the **chmod** command, but if you do not then the system default permission is assigned (usually rwxr-xr-x — umask 022). The **umask** command and what it does for file and directory permissions is covered later in this chapter. If the permissions are not set correctly for the directory, then others may not be able to read, write, or search it. This may indeed be what you want, but in general, there are probably others in your group that you like to have access your directories. If others will need to gain access to your directories and files, you can save yourself headaches by ensuring that your umask value is set properly.

Using the Shell interactively or with actual procedures often requires changing directories. Determining the current directory is also important. Both the **cd** and the **pwd** commands can be used anywhere at any time. You can then use **mkdir** and **rmdir** to create and delete directories as you require.

Pwd, ls, cd, mkdir, and **rmdir** handle most of the basic directory handling needs. They provide the ability to move within the file system, to see what is contained in the file system, and to alter the layout of the file system hierarchy. **Ls** and **pwd** are especially important; they produce their output on *stdout,* so they can be coupled with other commands via pipes to create more complex commands. Once you have set up directories, you will need to begin working with files of data and information.

File Commands

The most common file commands are **cat, cp, mv,** and **rm.** The **cat** command takes one or more file names as its arguments, opens the indicated files, and copies them to standard output. **Cat** allows you to display them on your terminal or redirect them into other files:

```
cat .profile    # Show me what's in my .profile
PATH=${PATH}:${HOME}/bin
export PATH

cat January february march > status_1Q_90
# Contents of files jan-march to status file
```

While **cat** is a very useful command, especially when the need to place the contents of a file to *stdout* exists, it can be awkward to view the contents of a file on your screen using **cat.** First, it does not scroll in any sensible fashion. The contents of a file are placed on your screen and continue to roll by until the entire contents of the file have been listed. (This can be somewhat controlled by using scroll control on your terminal, typically Ctrl-s to stop and Ctrl-q to continue.) Further, the **cat** command is not very good at handling files that contain nonprintable characters. It can just make a mess of the output listing to your screen and will sometimes lock your terminal. Often you can break out of this by sending **cat** a break (Delete key). The real power of **cat** is in handling multiple files and being able to stream their contents to the *stdout*. This allows easy redirection of their contents into a file or to some other command using a pipe.

But have no fear. UNIX provides a method for viewing files in a sensible manner. (See the section on screen-oriented print displays for a discussion of the **pg** command, which solves many of the **cat** command problems.)

The move (**mv**) and copy (**cp**) commands work similarly. You can move or copy one file to another:

```
mv file1 file2
# Move file named file1 to file2 - file1 no longer exists

cp file1 file2
# Copy file named file1 to file2 - file1 and file2 exist
```

Or you can move or copy many files into another directory:

```
mv file1 file2 file3 directory
cp file1 file2 file3 directory
```

Or you can copy all the files in a certain directory to another using metacharacters:

```
cp * /usr/fred    # Copy all the files in current directory to
                  # /usr/fred
```

At other times, you may want to remove (**rm**) one or more files:

```
rm file_name
rm file1 file2 file3
rm file*
rm file?
```

The **rm** command has a very nice feature that allows you to remove all files and subdirectories under the current directory. To do this you specify the -r option (recursive option) to the **rm** command. This is often used when you wish to remove a directory using **rmdir** and the directory contains files and subdirectories that also have files. The **rm** command with the -r option can be used to remove all these files and subdirectories in a single command. For example, suppose that we had the following directory with files and subdirectories:

```
cd /usr/fred/src    # Change to fred's source directory
ls -l *             # List all the directories and their contents
                    # and any files that exist
testprog:
total 154
```

```
-rwxrwxr-x     1 fred progmrs      28672 Apr 14 10:07 program1.
-rw-rw-r--     1 fred progmrs      10700 Apr 14 10:26 program2.c
-rw-rw-r--     1 fred progmrs       7936 Nov 10 12:02 program3.c
-rw-rw-r--     1 fred progmrs       3543 Feb 17 14:31 program4.c

prodprog:
total 38
-rw-rw-r--     1 fred progmrs       3130 Mar  3 1992 sight1.c
-r--r--r--     1 fred progmrs      19217 Feb 12 1992 sight2.c
-r--r--r--     1 fred progmrs      12072 Feb 12 1992 sight4.c
-rw-rw-r--     1 fred progmrs         91 Feb 25 1992 sight5.c

compile:
total 93
-rwxrwxrwx     1 fred progmrs          6 Aug 13 1991 msghandle.c
-rwxrwxrwx     1 tburns progmrs      1693 Oct 29 1991 market.c
-rwxrwxrwx     1 tburns progmrs       362 May 30 1991 constant.c
-rwxrwxrwx     1 tburns progmrs        95 Aug 13 1991 blue.c
```

So you can see based on the **ls** listing of /usr/fred/src that the directory contains three subdirectories—testprog, prodprog, and compile—all of which contain files. If we wanted to remove the /usr/fred/src directory, each of these three directories would need to be empty. We could **cd** to each directory and perform an **rm *** command and then **cd** back up to the /usr/fred/src directory and use the **rmdir** command to remove the directory (which is required to remove the src directory), or we could use the **rm -r** command and do all that with a single command.

```
cd /usr/fred/src
rm -r *     # rm all files and subdirectories
ls -la      # Show that all files gone except . and ..
.
..
```

Another nice option to the **rm** command is the -i option. This puts the **rm** command into interactive mode and it prompts you before it removes it.

```
rm -i junk1
junk1: ? y
ls junk1
junk1 not found
```

Sometimes when you use the **rm** command it will prompt you with a rather obtuse message that looks something like this:

```
rm junk2
junk2: 400 mode ? y
```

The remove command is prompting you to tell it whether file junk2 should be deleted. This occurs when the file you are attempting to remove does not have the correct permissions for you to be able to remove a file but the directory containing the file would allow you to delete files. The 400 mode is specifying what the permissions are on the file. If you answer **y** the file is removed; otherwise it is not removed.

Of course, when specifying file names to any of the commands talked about in this section, you can use any valid metacharacter(s) as needed to specify a file name. When using metacharacters with **rm**, please use care. Be sure that you are specifying the files that you think, and of course use the command **rm *** with caution as it will remove all files from your current working directory.

File Splitting Commands

Having put the files together using the **cat** command, you may need to split them apart. There are two key programs to support splitting files: **split** and **csplit**. **Split** chops files into smaller ones that contain a user-specified number of lines. To split the file book into 100 line files, I could use the following command:

```
split -100 book
ls
book
xaa
xab
xac
```

The files created by **split**—xaa, xab, xac—each contain 100 lines of the file book. Those file names are the default file names created by the **split** command. This might not give me exactly what I want, however. To split the book back into chapters, I could use **csplit**—a context split. **Csplit** splits files wherever it finds a match between its arguments and the content of the file. For example, to split the file by chapter, I could use the following:

```
csplit -f Chapter book "/Chapter 1/" "/Chapter 2/" "/Chapter 3/"
ls Chapter*
Chapter00
Chapter01
Chapter02
Chapter03
```

In this example, **csplit** created four files using the prefix (-f Chapter), dividing the chapters wherever it found the chapter headers. **Csplit** always begins numbering the created files from 00. The first file in this example would be a null file because "Chapter 1" is the first text the command encounters in the book file. Just remember that **split** works in *numbers of lines* and **csplit** searches for *strings of characters*.

Now that you know how to find and manipulate files and directories, it is important to learn how to extract information from either.

TABLE 4.2   Selection Commands

Type	Command	Purpose
Selection	**awk**	pattern scanning and processing language
	cut	select columns
	diff	compare and select differences in two files
	grep	select lines or rows
	head	. elecl header lines
	line	read the first line
	sed	edit streams of data
	tail	select trailing lines
	uniq	select unique lines or rows
	wc	count characters, words, or lines in a file

SELECTION COMMANDS

Every Shell user will need to select, extract, and organize information from existing files, thereby transforming data into usable information. Several Shell commands make it easy to select information (by row and column) and prepare it for
printing or processing. The commands to handle this important task are also
shown in Table 4.2.

To begin to understand why these commands are important and how they
work, we must again look at how to structure data files. All files are simple, "flat"
files, but through the addition of delimiters like the tab character, these flat files
become transformed. What was once a flat file can become a relational database
(Figure 4.1) or a spreadsheet (Figure 4.2). Why not use a true relational database
or a spreadsheet, you might ask? If you have access to one, do so. Most relational
database management systems (RDBMS) and spreadsheets, however, do not keep
their data in a form that is directly accessible by the Shell. You may have to
export data from the software packages to get them into a simple format usable by
the Shell. We discuss how to do this in later chapters, but for now you can keep
the same data in simple files that are easily accessible.

To get data from a spreadsheet or an RDBMS, you need to be able to select
information by row (horizontal) and column (vertical). **Grep, head, line, sed, tail,**
and **uniq** operate on rows. **Cut** operates on columns.

Social						
Security	<tab>	Last	<tab>	First	<tab>	Middle
Number	<tab>	Name	<tab>	Name	<tab>	Initial
527964942	<tab>	Arthur	<tab>	Lowell	<tab>	Jay
234567890	<tab>	Doe	<tab>	John	<tab>	D.

Figure 4.1   Relational Table

Month	\<tab>	Income	\<tab>	Expense
Jan	\<tab>	10000	\<tab>	9000
Feb	\<tab>	12000	\<tab>	10500
Mar	\<tab>	11500	\<tab>	9800

Figure 4.2   Spreadsheet

Line or Row Commands

There are some simple ways of getting information from files. The first is **line.**
Line can easily get the first line from a file. The first line is an excellent place to
put any heading information:

```
line < employee_file    # Print the first line of the file
SSN  Name  Street  City  State
```

Or we might want to look at only the first few lines of a file. Two commands
support previewing files: **head** and **sed.** If I wanted to view the first ten lines of a
file, the following two commands would be equivalent:

```
head file          # Print the first 10 lines of a file
sed -e '11,$d' file    # Also print the first 10 lines of a file
```

Similarly, I could use **tail** to view the last ten lines of a file:

```
tail file
tail < file
```

Although these commands are simple methods of extracting information from
a file, there are other, more exotic ways of selecting information. The **grep** command finds and selects information that is often hidden deep within files. It looks
for character strings in files and writes the requested information on *stdout.* I
might, for example, want to determine each of the chapters that has the word
PATH in it. To do so, I would enter the following command:

```
grep PATH chapter?
chapter2: PATH=${PATH}:${HOME}/bin
chapter2: export PATH
   .
   .
   .
chapter9: the PATH variable
```

Unfortunately, **grep** also provided all of the lines in each of these files that contains PATH. To get just the name, I would use the -l option:

```
grep -l PATH *
chapter2
chapter9
```

Or I might want to know which lines in the files contain PATH. I could use the **-n** option and enter the following command:

```
grep -n PATH chapter2
28:PATH=$PATH:$HOME/bin
29:export PATH
```

When using **grep** and looking for strings of more than one word, you must enclose the string in double quotes; otherwise **grep** thinks that the spaces or tabs between words separate the search string from the file names:

```
grep -l export PATH *
cannot open PATH
```

```
grep -l "export PATH" *
chapter2
```

The -i option on the **grep** command is also very useful. It tells **grep** to ignore differences in case when searching for matches on the string entered. Thus, if you were not sure what case the string was in, you could find it anyway. If you don't use the -i option, the case of the string searched for must match exactly with the case of the string in the file. For example,

```
grep -i PATH chapter2
```

would match not only the string PATH in the file but also Path, path, PatH, pATH, and so on. Without the -i option, only PATH would be matched.

One final option for **grep** that can come in handy at times is the -v option. This tells **grep** to return all the lines that *do not* contain the string or pattern specified. So if we switched the -n option on the following command with the -v option, we would get all the lines except 28 and 29:

```
grep -n PATH chapter2
28:PATH=$PATH:$HOME/bin
29:export PATH
grep -v PATH chapter2      # Returns lines 1-27 and 30 through the
                           # end of the file
```

There are two other forms of **grep**—**egrep** (extended **grep**) and **fgrep** (fast **grep**). **Egrep** looks for more than one string at a time, while **fgrep** looks for many strings that *exactly* match a line of the file. These two variations of the command provide efficiency when looking for multiple strings in the same files. For simplicity, however, I find it most useful to stick with **grep.**

Another useful command, word count (**wc**), can count the number of characters, words, and lines in a file. The counts of characters and words are useful for determining speed and productivity and for document content. The number of lines in a file, however, is often useful in Shell programs to determine the scope of a file. Sorts work more efficiently when they know the exact number of lines or records in the file. Also, if a command should create only 10 records instead of 10,000, you could use **wc** to check the outcome of the processing. To find out how many files contain the word *PATH*, for example, I could couple **grep** with **wc**:

```
grep -l PATH chapter? | wc -l    # How many files have string
                                 # PATH in them
2
who | wc -l                      # How many people are logged on
37
```

The -l option tells **wc** to return a count of the number of lines instead of the number of words. Likewise, the -c option tells **wc** to return the number of characters instead of the number of words.

Grep is the key tool for extracting information from fields of data. Another useful command is **uniq**. **Uniq**, in its simplest form, removes identical lines or rows from a file. Invariably, data is duplicated throughout files and databases. **Uniq** gets rid of the redundancy. For **uniq** to work, however, the file must be sorted. We'll see how to do this a little later in this chapter. Since the **uniq** command requires that data be in sorted order (for **uniq** to recognize two rows as identical they must occur next to each other in the file), we often use **sort** followed by **uniq**. For example:

```
sort parts_list | uniq    # Remove any duplicate part names from
                          # parts list
```

If **uniq** does not have an input file name, it reads standard in. If it does not have any output file name, then it places the unique file on *stdout*. The -d option is often useful. It reports the duplicate lines that exist in the file. So if, for example, the part "coupler" was repeated in the parts_list, the **uniq** -d option would list coupler. Now if the part "coupler" occurred 15 times in the file, the -d option would print it only once. To get a count of the number of times something is repeated in a file, use the -c option. It prints each line in the file and the number of times it is repeated.

Column Commands

Cut does exactly what its name suggests — cuts files into pieces that can be pasted back together in some other usable fashion. **Cut** can operate on a character-by-character or field-by-field basis or some combination of both. These columns can be put back together later using a command called **paste**. **Paste,** unlike **cut,** works line by line to put new files together.

One of the most simple examples of using **cut** involves finding a person's name in the /etc/passwd file using just his or her logname. If you entered the following commands you would get the lines shown:

```
who
root   console Jan 2 6:00
lja    ttyp0 Jan 2 8:30
```

```
grep lja /etc/passwd
lja:password:user#:group#:Jay Arthur x9999:/unix1/lja:/bin/sh
```

This is more information than needed. **Cut,** however, can extract the required fields. Fields in /etc/passwd are delimited by a colon (:). Field 1 is the login name; number 2, the password; and so on. All you really need are fields 1 and 5. **Grep** and **cut** can retrieve this information:

```
grep lja /etc/passwd | cut -f1,5 -d:
lja:Jay Arthur x9999
```

In the preceding example, the -f option indicated the fields that were to be cut. In this case, field 1 and field 5. Fields can also be specified as ranges using a dash. For example, an option of -f1-5 would have returned the first five fields of the passwd entry. The -d option is followed by the delimiter character. The **cut** command uses the character to define fields. In this case the (:) is used to indicate fields.

When creating files using Shell, use delimiters to take advantage of **cut** and **paste.** Most files currently created or maintained in the UNIX system have delimiters to facilitate their use.

Even without delimiters in a file, **cut** can be used in character mode. When this is done the **cut** command looks forward the number of characters specified and begins the cut at that position. If the character count is a range, for example 2-7, then the characters starting at position 2 through position 7 are used as a column. There is no need for a field delimiter in this form. This can be useful in files that have fixed-length columns, but will give very inconsistent results using files that have variable-length columns such as the passwd file. As an example, some of the outputs from Shell commands are not delimited. The output of the **ls -l** command has no delimiters. **Cut** can be used, on a character-by-character basis, to extract only the data required:

```
ls -l | cut -c1-15,55-    # Cut out file permissions and file
                          # name from ls output

drwxrwx---    3 bin
drwx------   28 doc
drwxrwxrwx   32 src
```

As another example, let's say that we have the following file containing employee information:

```
1234567890123456789012345678901234567890
John       engineer  173760978
Paul       marketing 152908976
George     software  130547689
Henry      personnel 152769078
Skip       engineer  168890965
```

All the rows are 30 characters long and each column is 10 characters wide in this file. With a file like this, we can use the **cut** command successfully by utilizing the character mode of the command. The following **cut** command would list the employee name and the social security number:

```
cut -c1-10, 20-30 emp_file    # List the employee name and social
                              # security number
John       173760978
Paul       152908976
George     130547689
Henry      152769078
Skip       168890965
```

Like **grep**, **cut** is an incredibly powerful command for operating on tables of data, removing the fat from the meat of the information you require. Having looked at ways of selecting information, let's look at ways of combining and ordering the selected data to create even more useful information.

COMBINING AND ORDERING COMMANDS

Having selected the data you need, the next logical step is to further refine it using the commands shown in Table 4.3. Using selection commands, you can extract information from a file in any form required. Once the data is cut into several slices, however, you will want to recombine the file's contents in a different order to present the information in a more usable form.

Paste

Paste can put files together in useful ways. **Paste** works on single files, multiple files, or the standard input. The syntax of the **paste** command takes several forms:

```
paste file(s)               # Paste two or more files together
paste -d"list" file(s)      # Paste files using specified delimiters
paste -s -d"list" files     # Paste subsequent lines of files
paste - -                   # Paste two subsequent lines from stdin
```

TABLE 4.3   File Processing Commands

Type	Command	Purpose
Joining	**cat**	concatenate files
	join	join two files, matching row by row
	paste	paste multiple files, column by column
Ordering	**sort**	sort and merge multiple files together
Transform	**sed**	edit streams of data
	tr	transform character by character
Printing	**awk**	pattern scanning and processing language
	cat	concatenate and print
	pr	format and print
	lp	print on system printer
Security	**chmod**	change security mode on a file or directory
	umask	set default security mode

Using the **ls** command, for example, you can easily create a multiple-column listing of a directory's contents:

```
ls -a | paste - - - -
.                ..        .cshrc     .login
.profile    bin      doc          src
```

The dashes tell **paste** to use one line from standard input in each of those positions. The same result could have been obtained with the following commands:

```
ls -a > dirlist
paste -s -d"\t\t\t\n" dirlist
.                ..        .cshrc     .login
.profile    bin      doc          src
```

The -s parameter tells **paste** to merge subsequent lines from the same file. The -d parameter tells **paste** to use the characters between the double quotes as delimiters between subsequent lines. In this case, the first three delimiters are tabs (\t); the last delimiter is the newline character (\n). The following command would produce an output with two items per line:

```
paste -s -d"\t\n" dirlist
.cshrc     .login
.profile    bin
doc          src
```

Paste can also put two files together once they have been separated. Using the passwd file, let's extract two of the fields and put them back together in a different order:

```
cut -f1 -d: /etc/passwd > temp1
cut -f5 -d: /etc/passwd > temp2
paste temp2 temp1 > loginlist
pr -e20 loginlist
```

```
Jay Arthur x9999      lja
Paula Martin x9999    pgm
```

This could also be accomplished using **awk:**

```
awk -F: '{print $5 $1}' /etc/passwd
Jay Arthur x9999      lja
Paula Martin x9999    pgm
```

The secret to making people more productive is to select the right data and present it in a usable format. **Grep, cut,** and **paste** provide a tremendous facility to extract only the data needed, recombine the fields, create a new file, or print the information with another command. **Grep** and **cut** select the data required; **paste** combines selected data into a usable format.

These commands provide the basic tools of a relational database: select and join. It takes a while to gain an understanding of the use and relationships among these commands, but once this occurs, you will wonder how you ever got along without them.

Sort

In many cases, sorting the data makes the resulting output even easier to use. In other cases, it may be necessary to merge two files that have already been sorted on a common key. The **sort** command performs both of these functions. Sorted output often contains duplicate lines of data; **uniq** will remove them or display only the repeated lines. **Uniq** facilitates the removal or selection of duplicate data — a common requirement in Shell programming.

When we sort rows of data in a file, we want the rows to be arranged in some order based upon some fields contained in each row of the file. We call these fields *sort keys*. The sort keys defined to the **sort** command can be defined as fields, which are groups of characters delimited by white space (a tab or space), or as a group of characters that you define based on the position these characters have in the file. The **sort** command will then take the sort keys and order the rows in the file based on the sort key value. The order can be either the ascending (the default) or descending order of the keys. Once again, **sort** is designed to work easily with **grep, cut,** and **paste.** For efficiency, **sort** should be used after the data has been selected with **grep** and **cut.** Why sort a whole file when you can sort a small subset of the total data? For example, I could sort the passwd file by user ID and then extract all of the users under the file system /unix1:

```
sort -t: +0 -1 /etc/passwd | grep unix1 | cut -f1 -d:
lja
pgm
```

This example forces the Shell to sort the entire passwd file and then extract the pertinent information. It would have been more efficient to extract the data and then sort it:

```
grep unix1 /etc/passwd | cut -f1 -d: | sort
lja
pgm
```

Looking at the previous two examples, you might wonder why the first one had the options: +0 -1. These options told **sort** to use field 0 as the sort key. Since there was only one field in the second example, no options were necessary. Why does **sort** count from field 0 and character 0? I don't know. It has confused more people than it has helped. I presume that because C language counts from 0, **sort** was designed to take advantage of humans instead of the opposite. Figure 4.3 shows a variety of **sort** commands and the sort keys that will be used.

To specify that the fields are delimited by other than a common tab character, you must specify the character using the -t option. In the passwd file example, the delimiter was a colon (:). In some files, it may be a blank: -t" ". If there are no consistent field delimiters in the file, use 0. (character position) to identify the start and end positions. To sort a long listing of a directory by the number of characters in each file, in descending (reverse) sequence, use the following command:

```
ls -al | sort +4nr
-rwxr-xr-x    1    lja    adm    12839   Jun 23 05:12   .profile
-rwxr-xr-x    1    lja    adm     4839   Jun 23 05:12   .cshrc
-rwxr-xr-x    1    lja    adm     4139   Jun 23 05:12   .login
drwxrwxrwx   32    lja    adm     1008   Dec  3 18:22   src
drwxrwx---    3    lja    adm      992   Dec  1 05:39   bin
drwx------   28    lja    adm      496   Dec  4 12:28   doc
```

`sort -nr file`	sort in reverse numerical order
`sort -t: +0 -2 file`	sort on fields 1 and 2 delimited by a ":"
`sort +0.20 -0.25 file`	sort on characters 20–25
`sort -rt" " +3 -4 file`	sort on field 4 delimited by blanks
`sort -m file1 file2`	merge file1 and file2

Figure 4.3   Various `sort` Commands

Merge

Sort can organize any UNIX file by fields or characters. Occasionally, the need arises to combine two or more files that are already sorted. In these cases, it is more efficient to merge the files. The output of the **ls** command, for example, is already sorted. To get a sorted listing of the commands available to a user under the /bin and /usr/bin directories (this is where many Shell commands reside), the following commands would provide equivalent outputs:

```
ls /bin > binlist
ls /usr/bin > usrbinlist
sort binlist usrbinlist > cmdlist

ls /bin > binlist
ls /usr/bin | sort -m binlist - > cmdlist
```

Since merging is more efficient than sorting, the second set of commands is preferable. The second command uses the dash (-) to tell **sort** to look for one of its inputs on *stdin* (the output of "ls /usr/bin"). This eliminates one temporary file, another efficiency consideration. The file, cmdlist, can now be printed or included in a memo or user guide.

As previously mentioned, problems can occur when there are duplicate command names in /bin, /usr/bin, and user bins. To identify these potential problems, you could manually compare the three listings of /bin, /usr/bin, and $HOME/bin. This is nothing but drudgery and is prone to error. It can be automated using **join,** which reads two files as input and puts out a single file containing a "join" of only those lines from both files that match on a specified field (normally the first, and in this case the command names):

```
ls /bin > binlist
ls $HOME/bin > homebinlist
join binlist homebinlist
cat
sort
```

Sort and **uniq** can automate this analysis when more than two files are involved:

```
ls /bin > binlist
ls /usr/bin > usrbinlist
ls $HOME/bin > homebinlist
sort -m binlist usrbinlist homebinlist | uniq -d
cat
sort
```

There are two commands, **cat** and **sort,** that are duplicated in two of the three directories. These could be located easily:

```
egrep cat\|sort *binlist
binlist:cat
binlist:sort
homebinlist:cat
homebinlist:sort
```

Similarly, **uniq** could have been used to create a merged listing of the three directories, excluding all duplicate command names:

```
sort -m binlist usrbinlist homebinlist | uniq > cmdlist
```

In other instances, use **uniq** to show only those lines that are not repeated. When comparing two directories that should have identical contents, the only concern is the files unique to each directory. To list them, use the following command:

```
ls dir1 > dir1list
ls dir2 | sort -m dir1list - | uniq -u > differences
```

Sort, merge, join, and **uniq** are powerful tools for manipulating information to prepare it for human consumption. Combined with selection commands, they provide a marvelous facility to automate the common functions of data selection, combination, and ordering. The remaining needs of a Shell programmer are to transform or translate the information into another form, and to print the results.

TRANSFORMERS AND TRANSLATORS

There are two main facilities for transforming or translating data (see Table 4.3) — **sed** (the stream editor) and **tr** (translator). **Sed** transforms incoming data by executing editor commands on the standard input. **Tr** translates incoming data, character by character, based on conversion tables specified by the user. In Chapter 13 we look at ways to build custom filters that go beyond these two, but for now, let's look at ways to use these standard transformers.

Sed is used in pipes in place of the standard line editor (**ed**). The syntax for the **sed** command is:

```
sed edit_command file
```

where *edit_command* is an **ed** like editor command and file is the name of the file to be acted on by the editor commands. If no file name is specified, then standard input is assumed. The original file is never altered. In order to get the transformed version of the file, you must redirect the output from the **sed** command.

For simple substitutions, the editor commands can be put on the command line:

```
sed -e "s/shell/Shell/" Chapter1 > newchapter1
```

In this example, the editor command "s/shell/Shell/" is applied to each row of data in file Chapter1. The resulting row of data, after the edit command has been applied, is placed in the file newchapter1. The edit command in this case is telling **sed** to substitute the first occurrence of the text "shell" with the text "Shell". To replace all occurrences of the text "shell" you would need to use the global option on the substitute line, as shown:

```
sed -e "s/shell/Shell/g" Chapter1 > newchapter1
```

For more complex transformations involving many substitutions, you can put the editor commands in a file and specify them as input to **sed**:

```
sed -f sedfile Chapter1 > newchapter1
```

where *sedfile* contains the following edit commands:

```
s/shell/Shell/
s/c language/C Language/
```

The **sed** command is a full-function editor. It has the ability to perform many different types of translations on a file. The edit_command portion of the **sed** command can control what rows should have the edit commands applied as well as what the edit function itself should be. In the example just presented the substitute command was applied to the entire file. We could have limited this to just certain rows by using a row range in the beginning of the *edit_command*. The following command would have limited the substitution to only the first five rows of file:

```
sed -e "1,5 s/shell/Shell/" Chapter1 > newchapter1
```

The row range is presented at the start of the edit command in the form *start_row,end_row*. If only a single number is used, then just that row is affected. We can also limit the rows affected by the edit command by specifying a match action. This means that only rows that contain a specified string will have the edit command applied. The string to match on is specified between slash characters. For example, the following command would apply the substitute action to only the rows in the file that contain the string "Unix".

```
sed -e "/Unix/ s/shell/Shell/" Chapter1 > newchapter1
```

TABLE 4.4 Common *sed* Edit Commands

Edit Command	Description	Example
s	Substitute the first string for the second	"s/gold/silver"
d	Delete lines from the file	"1,5d"
i	Insert text in the output file	"i/This is an inserted line/"
a	Append text in the output file	"a/This is an extra line/"
c	Change lines	"c/This is changed text/"
p	Print certain lines from the file (can be used to select rows from a file)	"1,5p"
w wfile	Write changed rows to a file	"w output"

Now that we have seen how to better control the application of edit commands in the file, let's look at some other common edit commands that are available with **sed** to aid in the transforming of data. Some of the more common commands are outlined in Table 4.4.

This is really not all the **sed** commands. Once you start putting **sed** commands into edit script files using the -f option, **sed** really turns into an edit command language that allows you to manipulate the text in a variety of ways. See your manual pages on **sed** for further details.

The print option can be used to select certain ranges of rows from the file. If you use it with the -n option, **sed** can be viewed as a selection command. The -n option tells **sed** to print just the lines that were selected with the p option. Usually **sed** prints all lines to the standard output. For example, to print the first ten lines of a file, use the following command:

```
sed -n "1,10p" file1 > output    # Print the first 10 lines of file
                                 # 1 to output. No changes made
```

Sed is an efficient method of transforming a file into some other usable format. For example, the output of the word count command (**wc**) looks like this:

```
wc -l file
   35 file
```

File has 35 lines in it. Using **sed,** the numbers can be extracted by removing blanks, tabs, and the characters *a* to *z* as follows:

```
wc -l file | sed -e "s/[ \ta-z][ \ta-z]*//g"
# Sed using regular expressions
35
wc -l < file
      35
```

The translate command, **tr,** works similarly to the **sed** command, but it changes the standard input character by character rather than string by string. **Sed** operates on rows and strings, but is hard to use on a character-by-character basis. The **tr** command has the following syntax:

```
tr from_string_list to_string_list
```

where the *from_string_list* and *to_string_list* must have one-to-one correspondence. The **tr** command will substitute using this one-to-one correspondence between *from_string_list* and *to_string_list*. Use the following command to translate a file from uppercase into lowercase:

```
tr "[A-Z]" "[a-z]" < uppercase > lowercase
```

The expression "[A-Z]" signifies the uppercase letters from *A* to *Z*. The second expression "[a-z]" tells **tr** to substitute the lowercase letters, on a one-for-one basis, with the uppercase letters. Doing this with **sed** would take a file with 26 editor commands; **tr** is much simpler.

Tr can also be used in other situations that require transformations. If I wanted to change Chapter 1 into a file of just words and obtain a sorted listing of the words and the number of times they were used, I could issue the following command:

```
tr "[ ]" "[\012]" < chapter1 | sort | uniq -c
```

In this example, **tr** translates blanks into newline (\012 is the ASCII code for newline; any ASCII code can follow a \) characters (one word per line). These are then sorted in alphabetical order and counted by **uniq**. This output would show all of the words in the document and the number of times they occur. It can be used to identify overused words that should be varied to improve the quality of the prose.

Similarly, to convert a file delimited by colons (:) to a file delimited by tab characters, you could use either of the following commands:

```
sed -e "s/:/\t/g" < colonfile > tabfile      # The \t represents a
                                              # tab
tr "[:]" "[\t]" < colonfile > tabfile
```

The **tr** command has some useful options as well. The -d option tells **tr** to delete the characters in the *from_string_list*. For example, the following **tr** command would strip all the tab characters from chapter1:

```
tr -d "[\t]" < chapter1    # Get rid of all the tab characters in
                           # chapter1
```

Another useful option is the -s option, which tells **tr** to squeeze out all extra occurrences of the substituted character. If after substitution the character occurs more than once in the text, the extra repeated characters are squeezed from the text. This is often used to remove repeated characters in text by specifying the from_string_list and to_string_list to be the same. A very useful **tr** squeeze command is to squeeze all the multiple spaces from a document:

```
tr -s "[ ]" "[ ]" < chapter1    # Remove any extra spaces in
                                # chapter1
```

The following command will remove all multiple tabs from a file:

```
tr -s "[\t]" "[\t]" < chapter1
```

Both **sed** and **tr** are useful for translating and transforming a file or input stream. **Sed** is stronger for use with strings, words, or lines. **Tr** is stronger when operating on characters. Each plays an integral part in the use of the Shell.

EDITORS

UNIX editors (see Figure 4.4) are also commands available to the Shell. The specifics of using each editor have been left out of this section because editor usage varies from installation to installation.

Sometimes it is not possible to **grep, cut, paste, sed,** or **tr** a file into a required format. A few lines may need to be added to a file or human analysis will be needed. In these cases, you can use the editor of your choice from within a Shell command. Editors are an important tool to manipulate text. When used repetitively within a Shell procedure, they become more beneficial.

ed	line editor
emacs	a screen editor
se	another screen editor
vi	the most common screen editor

Figure 4.4   UNIX Editors

Ed

As previously described, the standard UNIX line editor, **ed,** can use commands typed in-line as follows:

```
ed file <<eof!
/First/
a
These are the times that try men's souls
And mine too for that matter.
.
w
q
eof!
```

This would find the line with the first occurrence of the word "First" and append the next two lines after that line. This facility is occasionally useful in Shell commands.

Vi, Se, Emacs, and Other Editors

From the terminal, **vi** or any of the other editors can be invoked interactively. They can also be used in Shell commands to present a file to a user for editing:

```
vi chapter?
```

The UNIX line and screen editors are an easy way to create or modify a file. They have many uses in Shell programming.

PRINTING

The previous sections have discussed various ways of selecting information from files, translating the information into other forms, and sorting the information into a meaningful order. These are the essential steps in preparing information for use. The final step displays the information on the user's screen or printer.

All of the Shell commands have *stdout* and *stderr* files that can be displayed on the screen or a printer. The output of these can be redirected into files or devices. But these outputs are rarely formatted for easy human consumption. The facilities for formatting output are **cat, more, pg, pr, nroff,** and **awk.** Some are screen-oriented; others are more paper-oriented.

Screen-Oriented Displays

Cat, as we have seen, reads a file and "prints" it exactly as found. **Cat** is effective for simple viewing of a file. For more relaxed viewing, **pg** (page) or **more** (the ucb version of page) will display the file one page at a time.

The command to display a C language file on a screen and pause between pages would be:

```
pg file.c
```

or

```
more file.c
```

When a full screen of information is displayed, the **pg** command will stop and prompt for input. The default **pg** prompt is a colon (:). When you receive the prompt on the bottom left side of the screen you have several options. You can continue scrolling a screen at a time or you can jump around in the file moving backward and forward a certain number of pages. To move forward, enter a +n at the prompt where *n* is the number of pages to move forward. To move backward in the file, enter −n. It is also possible to search the file for patterns. At the prompt, enter the command /**text** where the text is the test that you want to search for in the file. Several other features exist and can be found in your manual pages on **pg.** You will find **pg** to be a much easier way to view the contents of a file on your screen. The other method of viewing files is to use a screen editor such as vi or Emacs, as was discussed earlier.

Paper-Oriented Displays

Regardless of how much people talk about "paperless" offices, there seems to be no end to the amount of reports that need to be printed and distributed. Shell provides you with many ways of formatting reports.

Pr

Pr prints files with simple headings and page breaks. Where **cat** lists a file exactly as it exists, **pr** provides the file name and date of last modification in the title and provides facilities to break the output every so many lines for clarity. The command line to print a C language file would be:

```
pr file.c
```

The same command to display the file on a 25-line terminal screen and pause between pages would be:

```
pr -l24 -p -t -w79 file.c
pg file.c
more file.c
```

To print a file, delimited by colons (:), with a special heading and 20-character-width fields:

```
pr -e:20 -h "Special Report" file
```

To obtain a more attractive listing, use the print command (**pr**):

```
ls -a > dirlist
paste -s -d"\t\n" dirlist | pr -e20
.              ..
.cshrc         .login
.profile       bin
doc            src
```

Or more simply:

```
ls -a | pr -2 -e20
.              ..
.cshrc         .login
.profile       bin
doc            src
```

Nroff and Tbl

Nroff formats documents using nroff and mm macros, but it can be used with files whose fields are delimited by unique characters, like the password file. **Tbl,** the table preprocessor, creates the input to nroff.

Tbl requires a text file like the following:

```
.TS          ⎫
tab(:) ;     ⎬ tablestart
l l n n l l l. ⎭
text file
.TE          ⎬ tableend
```

The password file can be formatted with **tbl** and **nroff** as follows:

```
tbl tablestart /etc/passwd tableend | nroff
```

Awk

For those users with even more rigorous reporting requirements, **awk** (a pattern scanning and processing language named after its developers — Aho, Weinberger, and Kernighan) provides many of the capabilities of C language. It allows variable definition and control flow, but is interpretive and therefore more responsive to the user's needs than compiling and testing C language programs.

One of the previous examples formatted the /etc/passwd file using **awk** to print the third and fifth items in the file:

```
awk -F: '{print $5 $3}' /etc/passwd
```

This example could be expanded to print the other fields of the /etc/passwd file as follows:

```
passwdprnt
BEGIN { FS = : }
{ printf "%-3s %.4d %.4d %-35s %s\n", $1, $2, $3, $4, $5 }
```

"$1" represents the first field in the passwd file; "$2", the second; and so on. The format shown following the **printf** statement uses the same conventions of the C language **printf** statement. The command to print the file would be:

```
awk -f passwdprnt /etc/passwd
```

Awk uses the passwdprnt file as the program to process the file /etc/passwd. The resulting output would be:

```
lja     1     1     Jay Arthur x9999 /unix1/lja
pgm     2     2     Paula Martin x9999 /unix1/pgm
```

Awk, pr, and **nroff** give the user a variety of ways of printing information already selected and sorted by the commands already described in this chapter. These formatted reports simplify human interaction with UNIX and are desirable. Human effectiveness is only as good as the information presented and its format.

Modern Word Processing

There are several modern word processors now available for the UNIX environment. These programs provide the robust features of PC-based word-processing programs and allow for powerful control over printing, fonts, spelling, and general text manipulation. In many cases these programs are UNIX implementations of PC-based products. Of course, these programs are not free. You must purchase them from the software vendor or from someone who sells the program. All of the text manipulation and printing tools talked about till now have been standard Shell commands available on almost all UNIX systems. If you are doing a great deal of document development and maintenance, an investment in one of these word-processing programs could be worthwhile. Here is a sample of some of the word processors available on many of the popular UNIX platforms:

Word Perfect for UNIX	a full-function word processor that is equivalent to the PC-based version
Microsoft Word	a full-function word processor that is equivalent to the PC-based version
FrameMaker	a full-featured desktop publishing package

SECURITY

Security is an important feature of UNIX and the Shell. You can create files and, by setting the permissions, allow people to read, write, or execute your file. The permissions are established in binary as shown in Figure 4.5. Two commands affect the accessibility of a file: **umask** and **chmod.** The long form of the list command (**ls -l**) will display the accessibility of any file or directory that the user can read.

There are three levels of security: what the owner of the file can do, what his or her related group can do, and what the world can do. The different levels or modes are also shown in Figure 4.5. Within each of these levels a file can be set to be (or not be by the absence of the flag) readable (r) by that level, writable (w) by that level, or executable (x) by that level. Let's look at a few examples to help clarify. Here is a sample **ls -l** listing showing file permissions for files in a directory:

```
ls -l *
-rw-r--r-- 1 fred1 progmrs 271353 May  4 17:55  mail
-rwxrwxrwx 1 fred1 progmrs 0      Oct 13 1992   calendar
-r--r----- 1 fred1 progmrs 131    Jan 19 14:44 cost.data
drwxrwxrwx 1 fred1 progmrs 15     Apr 21 15:38 junk
```

The first file listed by the **ls -l** command, mail, has the permissions rw- (read and write) for owner, r-- (read only) for the group of users in group progmrs, and r-- (read only) for all users. No one has execute permissions on this file. The next file is wide open. It has the permissions rwx (read, write, and execute) for the owner,

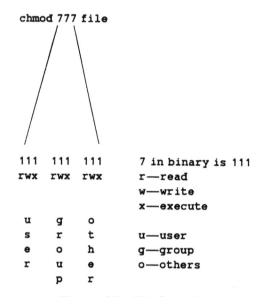

Figure 4.5   File Security

group, and the world. The next file, cost data, is read only for the owner and the group. The final file, junk, is a directory as indicated by the *d* in the first position. The directory is wide open to owner, group, and the world. As you can see, if the permission is not present on the file, then a dash (-) character appears in place of the *r*, *w*, or *x*.

The file permissions used by the Shell on files is often very confusing to new Shell users. The commands that follow allow two different methods for indicating the file permission flags. First there is the numeric method, which represents each flag as a number total based on position. Then there is a method that uses the alpha characters just like the **ls** command shows. Let's look at each in detail.

The numeric method uses a digit number in the range of 1 through 7 to represent the flags for each of the levels—owner, group, and the world. For example, the number 777 says that the owner, group, and all users have read, write and execute permissions (rwx) (see Figure 4.5). How did we get this number? Each flag position holds a value that is added together to get the number used for the level. The read flag has a numeric value of 4, the write flag a numeric value of 2, and the execute flag a numeric value of 1. So if all three flags are present, the sum of each of the flags is used to come up with the numeric indicator. Thus an rwx permission is equal to a 7 (4+2+1). A read-only permission totals 4; a read and execute permission totals 5. Only eight values are possible, as listed in Table 4.5.

The numeric method uses a number for each level, as was indicated previously. The number represents the various levels—owner, group, and others from left to right. The character method uses the characters *r*, *w*, and *x* to represent the permission flags, and they are used in conjunction with + and - symbols to represent addition of the permission and removal of the permission respectively. Used in conjunction with this are the flags that represent the levels. The flag u is for the owner of the file, the flag g is for group, and o is for all others. The combination of these flags sets the permissions. For example, ug+x adds the execute (x) permission for the owner and the group to the existing permissions (add 1 is another way to look at it). The permission flag setting of o-rwx would remove all the permissions for the others on the system. Finally, u+rwx adds all permissions for the owner.

TABLE 4.5   Permissions

Numeric	Permission Description	Character Representation
0	no permissions	---
1	execute permission only	--x
2	write permission only	-w-
3	write (2) + execute (1) permissions	-wx
4	read only permission	r--
5	read (4) + execute (1)	r-x
6	read (4) + write (2)	rw-
7	read (4) + write (2) + execute (1)	rwx

If all that seems a bit confusing, that's because it is. The character method of specifying permission flags was added after many people complained of how confusing the numeric method is. While it is true that it is confusing at first, it is also more abbreviated. That is why you will still see many UNIX power users using that method of specifying file permissions. Use what is comfortable for you. Soon enough, both methods will make sense.

The **umask** command sets up the default security for any file or directory created. The default security for a file is 666 (read and write permission for everyone). The default security for a directory is 777 (read, write, and execute). Without the execute bit, directories cannot be searched. The **umask** command tells the operating system which permissions to exclude when creating a new file or directory. **Umask** is executed at login time by either /etc/profile, $HOME/.profile, $HOME/.cshrc, or $HOME/.login. The most common **umask** command is:

```
umask 022
```

which says to omit write permission for the user's group and the world. Everyone can read your files or directories, but no one can write in or over them. If you wanted to keep the world out of your files, put the following command in your .profile:

```
umask 027
```

which lets your group read your files or directories, but prohibits any other users from accessing your files in any way.

Once the file or directory has been created with default security, you will occasionally need to change the permissions. The change mode command (**chmod**) allows you to do so:

```
chmod 755 shellcommand
chmod +x shellcommand
```

When you write a Shell command with one of the editors, the file is normally created with read and write permissions, but not execute. To make the file executable, you must change the permissions as shown above. To let just your group and yourself execute the command, you would enter:

```
chmod 750 shellcommand
chmod ug+x,o-rwx shellcommand
```

Sometimes, you will create an important file that you do not want to delete. The remove command, **rm,** will remove anything for which you have write permission. To get **rm** to ask you before it removes the important file, you can change the file's mode:

```
chmod 444 importantfile
chmod -w importantfile

rm *
rm: importantfile mode 444 ?
```

The **umask** and **chmod** commands allow control of file and directory access. Changing permissions is necessary and continuous in a UNIX environment. Knowing how to make files accessible and executable is an important part of creating Shell commands, but now we need to understand how the Shell finds commands.

BUILT-IN COMMANDS

The Shell, for efficiency, includes several built-in commands. The Bourne Shell has the fewest, relying on existing commands to do the work. For this reason, it is the smallest and fastest of the three Shells. The Korn and C Shells have the most built-in commands, so they are noticeably larger but not noticeably slower. The Shell built-in commands are shown in Table 4.6. They are discussed in more detail in future sections.

TABLE 4.6   Shell Built-in Commands

Bourne/Korn Shell	C Shell	Purpose
:	:	null command
	alias	create a command name alias
	bg	run current command in background
break	break	exit enclosing FOR or WHILE loop
	breaksw	break out of a switch
cd		change directory
continue		continue next iteration of FOR or WHILE loop
	default	default case in **switch**
	dirs	print directory stack
	echo	write arguments on *stdout*
eval		evaluate and execute arguments
exec		execute the arguments
exit	exit	exit Shell program
export		create a global variable
	fg	bring a command into foreground
for	foreach	execute FOREACH loop
	glob	perform filename expansion

Continues

TABLE 4.6   *(Continued)*

Bourne/Korn Shell	C Shell	Purpose
	goto	go to label within Shell program
	history	display history list
if	if	IF-THEN-ELSE decision
	jobs	list active jobs
	kill	kill a job
	limit	limit a job's resource usage
	login	terminate login Shell and invoke login
	logout	terminate a login Shell
newgrp		change to a new user group
	nice	change priority of a command
	nohup	ignore hangups
	notify	notify user when job status changes
	onintr	control Shell processing on interrupt
	popd	pop the directory stack
	pushd	push a directory onto the stack
read		read a line from *stdin*
readonly		change a variable to read only
	repeat	repeat a command *n* times
set		set Shell environment variables
	set	set a local C Shell variable
	setenv	set a global C Shell variable
shift	shift	shift the Shell parameters $* or $argv
	source	read and execute a file
	stop	stop a background process
	suspend	stop the Shell
	switch	CASE decision
test		evaluate conditional expressions
times	time	display execution times
trap		manage execution signals
ulimit		limit file sizes written by child processes
umask		set default security for files and directories
	unalias	discard aliases
	unlimit	remove limitations on resources
	unset	unset a local variable
	unsetenv	unset a global variable
until		UNTIL loop
wait		wait for a background process to complete
while	while	WHILE loop
	% job	bring a background job to foreground
expr	@	display or set Shell variables

How the Shell Finds Commands

Most Shell commands reside in directories called "bins": /bin and /usr/bin. Others, important only to the system administrator, reside in /etc, /usr/rje, and /usr/adm. Users can create their own bin directories. For the majority of users, the commands available in /bin and /usr/bin will be of most importance. The /usr/ucb bin contains the Berkeley 4.2 BSD commands. On Berkeley systems, System V commands can be found in /usr/5bin.

When a user logs in, the Shell sets up a standard environment using several variables (see Table 4.7). The Shell uses the PATH (sh, ksh) or path (csh) variable to find each **bin** that a user can access. The PATH variable is initialized at login time. To find out the default paths available, try the following command:

```
echo $PATH          csh: echo $path
:/bin:/usr/bin:        . /bin /usr/bin
```

The response means that you have all of the standard Shell commands available for execution. The Shell uses the PATH variable to determine where to search for commands and in what order you want to search the bins. The current value of PATH indicates that the Shell will first search the current directory, then /bin, and finally /usr/bin. The current directory is represented by a null name, followed by a colon. You can change the order of the search by redefining the value of PATH as follows:

```
PATH=/usr/bin:/bin::      set path=( . /usr/bin /bin )
```

TABLE 4.7   Shell Variables

Bourne/Korn Shell	C Shell	Purpose
CDPATH	**cdpath**	search path for **cd**
	cwd	full path name of current directory
HOME	**home**	path name of the user's login directory
MAIL	**mail**	name of user's mail file
PATH	**path**	the Shell's search path for commands
PS1	**prompt**	the primary prompt string
		"$" for Bourne/Korn Shell systems
		"**hostname**%" for C Shell systems
		"#" for superuser
PS2		the secondary prompt string: ">"
IFS		internal field separators (space, tab, newline)
	history	number of commands remembered by history
	ignoreeof	ignore end of file
	noclobber	don't overwrite existing files
	noglob	inhibit filename expansion

which reverses the order of the search. If you had a user bin under your home directory, you might add it to the search path using another Shell variable, HOME:

```
PATH=${PATH}:${HOME}/bin        set path=( ${path} ${HOME}/bin )
```

Using my log in as an example, this would change the value of PATH to:

```
/usr/bin:/bin::/unix1/lja/bin
```

Whenever I execute a command, the Shell will first look in /usr/bin, then /bin (the current directory), and finally my user bin. This means that I can type a command name and the Shell will find it; I do not have to type in the full path name to use a command I have created. This is an important feature of the Shell that helps improve productivity; bins full of user commands can be placed anywhere in the system and be accessed directly via the PATH variable.

The system administrator can redefine PATH to include common user bins by inserting the following two lines into /etc/profile:

```
PATH=:/bin:/usr/bin:/local/bin
                        set path=( . /bin /usr/bin /local/bin )
export PATH
```

The **export** command makes the PATH variable available to all subsequent processes initiated by the user.

Because users would rather not change the PATH variable during every session, the user may further modify the PATH variable automatically at login time. The PATH variable can be modified using either /etc/profile or the .profile in the user's home directory. In a C Shell system, the PATH variable can be modified in the user's .login or .cshrc files which reside in the user's home directory. You can create the .profile (csh: .login/.cshrc) file in your HOME directory and add the following two lines to include your own command bin:

```
PATH=${PATH}:${HOME}/bin
export PATH
```

These two lines will add your bin to the Shell's search path. The Shell can now automatically look in all command bins to find any command you request. Problems can occur, however, if there are two commands with the same name in different bin directories; the Shell will execute the first one it finds. This is especially important in systems that have all three Shells: Bourne, Korn, and C. Not all System V commands behave like Berkeley commands. To obtain System V commands, put them first in the PATH variable. On Berkeley UNIX systems, reverse the positions of /usr/5bin and /usr/ucb:

```
PATH=:/bin:/usr/bin:/usr/5bin:/usr/ucb
                    set path=(. /bin /usr/bin /usr/ucb /usr/5bin)
```

That's about all you need to know about the PATH variable. If you execute a command but it doesn't behave like the documentation, you might suspect the PATH variable is pointing to libraries in the wrong order.

The Bourne and Korn Shells also use an environment variable, CDPATH, with the **cd** command to reduce typing. The user can set up CDPATH in their .profile to include any of their major directories. Then, no matter where they are in the directory structure, all they have to do is **cd** to the directory name and the Shell remembers where those directories are and changes to them without extensive typing. For example, if there was an entry in the .profile as follows:

```
CDPATH=$HOME/doc
export CDPATH
```

and you are already in the /usr/bin directory, you could change into the doc directory by typing:

```
cd doc
```

The directories can also be listed like the PATH variable to give immediate access to any of the major directories:

```
CDPATH=$HOME/bin:$HOME/doc:$HOME/src
export CDPATH
```

Using the **cd** command, the user can change from one directory to another without typing long path names. The Shell will print the path name of the directory it has changed into:

```
cd doc
/unix1/lja/doc
```

SUMMARY

Shell commands are usually found in directories called bin. The most frequently used directories are /bin and /usr/bin. As a user or toolsmith develops new Shell tools, they can be placed in local bins that can be directly addressed via the PATH variable.

The most commonly used file and directory commands are **ls, cd, cat,** and **grep.** The output of these commands has been structured to maximize their utility when combined with other commands — such as **cut, paste, uniq,** and **pr** — that select portions of their output and report the information required.

Ordering the output in a meaningful way is the job of **sort,** which handles both sorting and merging information. The **join** command also can be used to integrate information from two different files.

Once output files have been created, the information they contain can be translated by **sed** or **tr. Sed** operates on strings of information; **tr** operates on characters. More complex transformations that require operator intervention can be handled by using the UNIX editors. These can be invoked directly from the Shell or Shell procedures.

The output of these commands can be formatted for ease of use with the **awk, pr,** and **nroff** commands. Each of these commands can work on files of lines and the fields within those lines. **Awk** and **pr,** in particular, are good for prototyping report programs. **Awk** allows the user to create detailed reports that are not easily possible with the other two commands.

These basic commands are the roots of more advanced usage of the Shell. Understanding how they interact with each other via the pipe or by input/output redirection is essential to advanced Shell usage.

EXERCISES

1. Describe the importance of PATH and CDPATH.

2. Describe the **ls, pwd,** and **cat** commands.

3. Describe the **grep, cut,** and **paste** commands.

4. Describe the use of **sort, merge, join,** and **uniq.**

5. Name the different Shell translation commands and the type of data (strings, characters, delimiters) they are best designed to handle.

6. Write a Shell to extract, sort, and print all users in the global file system. (Use the /etc/passwd file as input.)

7. Using the Shell from exercise 6, extract only those users with multiple entries in the /etc/passwd file.

8. Write a Shell to translate the /etc/passwd file into uppercase and translate the ":" delimiters into tab characters.

9. Describe the usage of **umask** and **chmod.** How do they offer security in a UNIX file system?

10. Write the **umask** command to prohibit all other users (except for the owner) from accessing files created by the user. Write the **chmod** commands to make Shell programs executable by:

    a. the owner

    b. the owner and his or her group

    c. the world

11. Write the **pr** command to print the /etc/group file on the user's screen and printer.

12. Write a simple **awk** command to print the same information from the /etc/group file as in exercise 11.

Chapter Five

Shell Decisions and Repetitions

Who can control his fate?

Shakespeare

The chapters to this point have provided information about using simple Shell commands. To make full use of the Shell, however, requires the use of a special set of Shell commands that control what happens and when. These commands allow the user to decide among:

- two different actions (IF-THEN-ELSE)
- many actions (CASE)
- looping through an action many times (FOR, REPEAT, WHILE, and UNTIL)

All third-generation programming languages have these basic control structures: IF-THEN-ELSE, CASE, DO WHILE, and DO UNTIL. Using these control structures in conjunction with the Shell commands that we learned in Chapter 4 makes the Shell a full-blown programming language capable of many powerful information-processing tasks. Using these capabilities of the Shell we will be able to build powerful programs to solve many problems. This chapter discusses the use of these control structures. The next chapter talks about how to construct a Shell program.

The Bourne, Korn, and C Shells all provide these control structures, although the C Shell differs in many respects (see Table 5.1). The Bourne and Korn Shells rely on the **test** command to handle the evaluation of all conditions. In the C

TABLE 5.1   Shell Control Structures

Structure	Bourne Shell	Korn Shell	C Shell
IF	`if [...]`	`if [...]`	`if (...)`
THEN	`then`	`then`	`then`
ELSE-IF	`elif`	`elif`	`else if`
ELSE	`else`	`else`	`else`
ENDIF	`fi`	`fi`	`endif`
CASE	`case`	`case`	`switch`
	`value)`	`value)`	`case: value`
	`;;`	`;;`	`breaksw`
	`*)`	`*)`	`default:`
	`esac`	`esac`	`endsw`
FOR	`for`	`for`	`foreach`
	`do`	`do`	
	`done`	`done`	`end`
REPEAT	`xargs -1`	`xargs -1`	`repeat`
UNTIL	`until`	`until`	`-`
	`do`	`do`	
	`done`	`done`	
WHILE	`while`	`while`	`while`
	`do`	`do`	
	`done`	`done`	`end`

Shell, evaluations of conditions are performed directly by the Shell. The Korn Shell has made some enhancements to the **test** command; these are covered in detail in this chapter. The Shell also provides mechanisms for executing repetitive commands interactively: **xargs** (csh: **repeat**) and **find**. Each of these control structures permits loops and decisions to be made by Shell procedures. The ability to test conditions and take actions is the most important feature of the Shell command language.

SHELL VARIABLES

The Shell lets you establish variables to hold values while you process them. It provides several standard variables (see Table 4.7 and Table 5.2) that are always accessible with the Shell providing values for these variables. Variable names can be of any reasonable length and must begin with an alphabetic character or "_" followed by any of the characters "a-z, A-Z, or 0-9".

Variables hold values that are manipulated by a Shell program while processing. A variable may be set to a value once or many times in the course of a Shell

TABLE 5.2   Shell Variables

Bourne and Korn Shells	C Shell	Purpose
`$#`	`$#`	number of positional arguments
`$0`	`$0`	command name
`$1, $2 ...`	`$1, $2 ...`	positional arguments
	`$argv[n]`	positional arguments $1 ...
`$*`	`$*, $argv[*]`	$1 $2 ...
`$@`		$1 $2 ...
`$-`		Shell options from **set** command
`$?`		return code from last command
`$$`	`$$`	process number of current command
`$!`		process number of last background command

program. It may also be referenced, to extract the value that it contains, as many times as needed. A variable either is set to some single value or it is said to be unset (has never existed as a variable). It is possible to unset a variable once it has been set by using the **unset** command. A variable may also be set but may contain the null value or empty string. This is not the same as being unset. If a variable contains the null value, it is set. This difference between a variable's being set or null is important because often in the course of writing Shell programs we need to determine if a value is set or null. Also, the Shell variable operators, discussed in the next section, make a distinction between a variable's being set and null. Shell variables are an integral part of Shell programming. They provide the ability to store and manipulate information within a Shell program. The variables you use are completely under your control. You can create and destroy any number of variables as needed to solve the problem at hand.

You establish your own variables by simply assigning values to variable names:

```
temp_name=/usr/tmp    csh: set temp_name=/usr/tmp
month=01                   set month=01
```

Note that when assigning variables values using the = assignment operator, there are no spaces between the = and the variable name and variable value. If you leave a space the Shell will try to interpret your variable value as a command to be executed. When the Shell finds the assignment operator, it will create the value on the left side of the =, if it does not already exist, and assign it the value provided on the right side of the =. If the variable already exists it will receive the new value, replacing the old value that the variable contains.

To access the values stored in the variables, you insert the variable name (preceded by a dollar sign) wherever you need it:

```
cp file $temp_name
echo "Current month is $month"        # Show the user the value of
                                      # the month
Current month is 01
```

Whenever the Shell sees a $*var_name* it substitutes the value that is stored for that variable into the command line at that location. To be perfectly accurate and prevent errors, you should enclose the name in braces:

```
cp file ${temp_name}
echo "Current month is ${month}"
```

Otherwise, establishing other variable names can lead to problems when the Shell tries to interpret your commands:

```
temp=/tmp/                   set temp=/tmp/
echo $temp_name              echo $temp_name
/usr/tmp                     /usr/tmp
echo ${temp}_name            echo ${temp}_name
/tmp/_name                   /tmp/_name
echo ${temp_name}            echo ${temp_name}
/usr/tmp                     /usr/tmp
```

You can see that when the Shell attempts to substitute the variable value in the command line, it has no way to distinguish between the variables named $*temp* and $*temp_name*. The Shell scans forward from the $ character looking for the end of the variable name string. It considers the end to be any character that cannot be used to form a variable name. In this case it is the space character. When a variable name is formed, its value is substituted. Thus, in the preceding example, the variable $*temp_name* is substituted when no brackets are used instead of the variable $*temp* followed by the string "*_name*". The { } characters prevent this type of ambiguity by defining exactly what the variable name is. When we use $*{temp}_name* the Shell knows that we want to use the variable $*temp*, not $*temp_name*.

You can assign values to variables directly or from the output of various Shell programs. For example, to create a variable called *current_month* and assign the system's value for month, we could use the date command:

```
current_month=`date +'%m'`        set current_month=`date +'%m'`
```

The characters surrounding the date command (`) are called accent graves. They tell the Shell to execute the command in a subshell and to put the resulting value in place of the command. So, the date command returns only the month (%m), a value between 01 and 12. This powerful capability will be explored in more detail as the book progresses.

Because variables can be changed throughout the execution of a Shell program, looping and testing can be done without repeating the logic many times. The examples in the following sections expand and clarify the benefits and usage of Shell variables.

CONTROLLING VARIABLE ASSIGNMENTS

The Shell also provides variable operators used for assigning values to variables under varying conditions. In general, the operators take action based on whether the variable named is set or not, or whether the variable is null or not null (Table 5.3).

As is pointed out by the Action column, these variable operators provide a method for taking some action based on whether the variable is set or not. These operators are more convenient than testing for the condition using the IF Shell command. The operators exist because these are actions that are frequently performed when utilizing Shell variables.

The operators shown in Table 5.3 also have a related set of operators (see Table 5.4) that provide a method of checking for whether the variable is null in addition to whether it is set. The difference between whether a variable is set or whether it

TABLE 5.3   Shell Variables

Variable Operator	Action	Description
`${varname}`	Nonambiguous variable substitution.	Simple variable substitution occurs with the value of *varname* being substituted.
`${varname=value}`	Assign a default value for the variable if a value does not exist.	If *varname* does not have a value, then *varname* is set to *value*. *Varname* is then substituted in the statement.
`${varname+value}`	Utilize value if *varname* is set.	If the variable, *varname*, contains a value, then the alternate value, *value*, is substituted instead of the value of *varname*. If *varname* is not defined, then null is substituted.
`${varname-value}`	Assign a temporary default value for a variable if one does not exist.	If the variable, *varname*, contains a value, then it is substituted; otherwise the value, *value*, is substituted but is not assigned to *varname*. (different from = operator)
`${varname?value}`	Issue an error message if the value of the variable is not set to any value.	If the variable, *varname*, contains a value, then it is substituted; otherwise an error message containing the value, *value*, is printed and the Shell exits.

TABLE 5.4 Variable Default Actions

Variable Operator	Description
`${varname:=value}`	If *varname* is not set or the value is null, then *varname* is set to *value*. *Varname* is then substituted in the statement.
`${varname:+value}`	If the variable, *varname,* is set and is not null, then the alternate value, *value,* is substituted instead of the value of *varname*. If *varname* is not defined, then null is substituted.
`${varname:-value}`	If the variable, *varname,* is set and is not null, then it is substituted; otherwise the value, *value,* is substituted but is not assigned to *varname*. (different from = operator)
`${varname:?value}`	If the variable, *varname,* is set and is not null, then it is substituted; otherwise an error message containing the value, *value,* is printed and the Shell exits.

is null was discussed previously. The related set of operators utilize the ":" symbol to also include the not null condition in the variable operator check. Let's look at a few examples of using these assignment operators. These examples should help make it clear how the variable operators help simplify variable assignment.

Perhaps the most widely used of the operators is the default assignment operator "=". The operator will assign a value to a variable if no value exists. Very convenient.

```
${file_type:="doc"}    # If file type is not set or it is null
                       # then make the value "doc"
```

This situation can occur whenever the Shell program is expecting a value to be set by a user. If the variable file_type was to be entered or set by the user, then we have no way of ensuring that this was done properly. The user may have forgotten to set the value of the variable or may have entered a null value. These conditions may make your Shell program work improperly. So we need to ensure that file_type has some value assigned by checking that value. If the user does not provide the value, then we will assume a default value. The {file_type:="doc"} conveniently provides that default value. Consider the following check that uses an "if test" to ensure that the variable is set:

```
if [ !file_type]    # Is the variable file_type null?
then
  file_type=doc    # If it is, then set it to doc
fi
```

The "if test" logic is covered in detail in the section on the Shell test and IF command constructs. As you can see, this test is quite a bit more work and is prone to typing and logic errors. The variable operator "=" accomplishes the same task and is less prone to errors.

KSH

Array Variables

The Korn Shell provides several extensions to the standard variables available with the Bourne Shell. One of these is the ability to have array variables. An array is a set of similar items that are referenced with a common (set) name. Items in the set can be assigned values using the assign operator and they can be referenced just like any other variable. Arrays are a very convenient way to store lists of information that you may need to use in your Shell program. They are a very powerful programming tool and are used universally in all major programming languages. As you begin programming you will discover endless applications for array variables.

There are 512 elements that can be contained in an array variable using the Korn Shell. The method of indexing an array variable to either assign or reference the variable is to use the [ ] characters following the variable name. The index numbers start with 0 and go through 511 on most versions of the Korn Shell. For example, to make an array containing a list of cities, the following Shell assignments would work:

```
cities[0]=DENVER
cities[1]=SEATTLE
cities[2]=DALLAS
cities[3]=HOUSTON
cities[500]=PHILADELPHIA
```

Each position of the array can be viewed as a variable that can be set or unset, null or not null. Note that the assignment can be random. We assigned the slot cities [500] without assigning any values between 4 and 499. You can think of the array as a variable that contains slots, with each slot holding a value that is indexed by a unique number.

```
                        Cities Array

                        Slot/Index    Value
                        0             DENVER
                        1             SEATTLE
Cities[2]  =======>     2             DALLAS
                        3             HOUSTON
                        .
                        .
                        .
                        500           PHILADELPHIA
```

To reference an element of the array, simply utilize the [ ] syntax following the variable name referenced by the $ operator. There is a minor problem with referencing array variables directly in what would seem to be the most obvious manner, namely $cities[3]. This syntax is valid Bourne Shell syntax and is interpreted as such by the Korn Shell. What you get is the following:

```
echo $cities[3]
DENVER[3]
```

The Korn Shell sees $cities as the name of a variable and substitutes the [0] element of the array for cities (the default action if no index is provided for the array variable) and then appends the string "[3]". To remove this ambiguity you must enclose the array variable reference in braces { }. For example, to utilize the third element of the array, enter the following:

```
echo ${cities[3]}
HOUSTON
```

Any element of the array can be referenced individually and be used anywhere that a normal variable would be used. The Korn Shell also allows the index reference enclosed in the brackets "[ ]" to be an arithmetic expression. So, for example, the reference to an index element could be based upon an expression using integer variables:

```
typeset –i x=2 y=1
echo ${cities[x+1]}
HOUSTON
echo ${cities[x+y]}
HOUSTON
```

The **typeset** command is used to assign an integer type to the variables x and y. This is also a Korn Shell extension and is discussed in the next section.

The Korn Shell also provides some special operators to help in the processing of array variables. The first is the [*] array reference operator. When [*] is used as the index to an array variable, the entire array contents are expanded and substituted. Each element of the array is separated by a space. Any unset or null elements are not expanded. For example, the cities array would expand as follows:

```
echo cities[*]
DENVER SEATTLE DALLAS HOUSTON PHILADELPHIA
```

A related operator [@] performs the same task but treats the elements of the array as quoted strings.

To determine the number of elements in an array, the Korn Shell provides an # operator. This is a very useful operator since it allows you to perform a loop to access the elements of an array no matter how many elements might be contained in the array. The # operator is placed before the variable name and is used in conjunction with the [*] operator. For example,

```
echo ${#cities[*]}
501
```

Note that in this case it considered the array to have 501 elements even though many of the elements were not set. This is because we placed Philadelphia at the five hundredth array position. Moving the PHILADELPHIA array assignment to position 4 would give the expected array count:

```
cities[0]=DENVER
cities[1]=SEATTLE
cities[2]=DALLAS
cities[3]=HOUSTON
cities[4]=PHILADELPHIA
echo ${#cities[*]}
5
```

Assigning Variable Types and Properties

The Korn Shell provides a method for assigning types and properties to variables. Of particular interest is the ability to assign a variable a type of integer. This gives the Korn Shell the ability to use the variable directly in situations where it is expecting a numeric argument. An example of this was shown in the previous section when we used the variables x and y directly in array subscripts as well as directly in an arithmetic expression that was then used as an array subscript. In order to define a variable as an integer type, we use the **typeset** command:

```
typeset -i counter=1
```

Note that we can define the variable type and provide an initial value (1 in this case) using the **typeset** command.

In general, the syntax of the **typeset** command is as follows:

```
typeset [-+options] [var_name=value]
```

where the most frequently used options are shown in the **typeset** entry of the built-in command reference at the end of the book and *var_name* is the variable name that is having the properties set. Note that options are turned on by using the "-" and turned off by using the "+".

Assigning a variable to be of type integer is not the only thing that can be done with the **typeset** command. It also provides the ability to assign properties to string variables. For example, a string can be made to be a fixed length with either left or right justification. It is also possible to force a variable to contain only uppercase or lowercase letters. Variables can be made read-only and can be defined as immediately exported. Refer to the list of options shown in the reference section on Built-in commands (Appendix E).

As an example, let's make a variable read-only and then try to assign a value to it:

```
typeset -r mode=update    # Set the variable mode to read-only
                          # and assign value update
echo $mode
update
mode=add    # Try to change the value of mode to add
ksh: mode: is read only
```

ENVIRONMENT VARIABLES

Environment variables are used by the Shell for processing and can also be accessed and set by you. This provides control over your login environment. An example of an environment variable is *PATH,* which was discussed previously. This variable is used by the Shell to determine where it should search for commands. Some environment variables are assigned a value when you log in, others are set by the Shell, and still others are your responsibility to set. They are called environment variables because the Shell utilizes these variables to control the way your environment behaves. Really these variables are no different from any other variables other than the fact that they have special meaning to the Shell and the fact that the Shell provides a value for many of them. They can be referenced and changed just like any other variable. Some of the more important environment variables are shown in Table 5.5. These are not all the environment variables and you should refer to your manual pages (**man ksh, man sh**) for a complete list.

All the variables described contain values that help control how your environment will look and behave. All the values can be changed during your login session by simply assigning a new value. For example, if we wanted to change the time between mail checks to 30 seconds, we could simply assign a value of 30 to the variable MAILCHECK:

```
MAILCHECK=30
```

KSH

The Korn Shell provides a very nice extension to the PS1 variable. The Korn Shell will reevaluate the contents of the PS1 variable and make substitutions for any variables found in the string. This is not done in the Bourne Shell. For example, if we set our PS1 variable as shown following, then the current working directory will be displayed as part of our Shell prompt. Setting your

PS1 variable in this manner allows you to determine your current working directory at a glance.

```
PS1='${PWD}: '
```

With our PS1 environment variable set as shown, the following prompt will be displayed if the current working directory is /usr/tburns:

```
/usr/tburns:
```

Several of the variables shown are unique to the Korn Shell. In particular, the HISTSIZE and HISTFILE are used to control the Korn Shell's command history, which allows you to recall recent commands for reexecution.

TABLE 5.5   Key Environment Variables

Bourne	Korn	C	Description
CDPATH	CDPATH	cdpath	Search path for **cd** command.
HOME	HOME	home	Path name of the user's home directory set at login time.
MAIL	MAIL	mail	Name of the user's mail file.
PATH	PATH	path	The Shell's search path for commands.
PS1	PS1	prompt	The primary prompt string displayed at log in: "$" for Bourne/Korn "hostname %" for C Shell "#" for the superuser
PS2	PS2		Secondary prompt string used when you start a subshell: ">" by default
	HISTFILE		File name used to save command history.
	HISTSIZE	history	The number of commands remembered by history.
IFS	IFS		Internal field separator (space, tab, newline) used to separate command words.
	LOGNAME		Your login ID is contained in this variable, which is set by the Shell at log in.
PWD	PWD		Current working directory path name set by the Shell.
	EDITOR		Command editor used for editing commands on the Shell input line; can be emacs, gmacs, or vi.
MAILCHECK	MAILCHECK		The time, in seconds, that passes before the Shell checks your mail file to see if you have received any new mail.

SPECIAL VARIABLES

In addition to the environment variables just described, the Shell also maintains some special variables. These variables, shown in Table 5.2, are always set by the Shell. These variables are still just like any other variables from the aspect of referencing the variables; they are always available using $ to reference them. But many of the variables are maintained by the Shell and cannot be changed through assignment. These special variables are most often used when you write a Shell program. The variables $0 to $9 are assigned the parameters passed to the Shell program. This makes arguments accessible to your Shell program without your needing to do anything special. These play a more prevalent role when we begin building Shell programs in the next chapter and are covered in detail there.

QUOTING

Now that we have learned about variables and the way the Shell performs substitution in command-line expressions, we will look at the various ways the Shell has to control the evaluation of the variable name. This method of controlling both variable name substitution and filename substitution (covered in Chapter 3) is referred to as quoting. Quoting protects white space that occurs in a string as well. This protection of white space causes quoted strings to be interpreted as a single word by the Shell. This is needed when we want a string to contain spaces but be evaluated as a single argument to a command. The Shell respects four different "flavors" of quoting, outlined in Table 5.6.

Quoting can seem confusing at first, but it is needed to protect strings from the default action of the Shell—evaluate and substitute. While this feature of the Shell provides much of the Shell's power, it is not always what we want. Previous examples have demonstrated this feature, but now that we have explored variables in detail, we can take a more in-depth look at quoting.

As was mentioned in the previous paragraph, the Shell's default action is to evaluate and substitute. The command line is scanned, and whitespace characters divide the command line into words and any special characters are evaluated and substituted. The evaluated words are parsed in a manner consistent with Shell command syntax:

```
command -options arguments
```

But the standard command-line evaluation is not suitable in all cases. An often cited example (because it occurs often) is using a space-delimited string in conjunction with the **grep** command. The **grep** syntax is:

```
grep expression file_name_list
```

The Shell passes each word (strings separated by white space) following the **grep**

TABLE 5.6   Quote Characters

Quote Character(s)	Substitution?	Filename Substitution?	Variable Name Recognized?	Whitespace Description
No quotes	yes	yes	yes	With no quoting, each word that is separated by white space is interpreted by the Shell with full file name and variable substitution.
Single quote `'string'`	no	no	no	Everything within the quotes is protected. No evaluation occurs. The string is viewed as a single argument to a command.
Double quotes `"string"`	no	yes	no	The string is evaluated but only certain characters are recognized as significant. These characters are $, \ (backslash), and `` (backquote). The corresponding action is taken when these characters are found. All other characters are protected.
Backslash `\c`	n/a	n/a	n/a	The character following the backslash is protected from evaluation by the Shell.
Backquotes `` `cmd_string` ``	yes*	yes*	yes*	The cmd_string is evaluated by a subshell and the results of running the command are substituted in place of the cmd_string. The subshell evaluates the command string in the normal way, including embedded quoting.

*This is true as long as no other quoting is embedded within the backquotes. Any quoting done within the backquotes will be interpreted in the standard way by the subshell executing the command.

command as arguments. The first is taken to be the expression to search for in the files that follow. But consider the following **grep** command:

```
grep Error file number error.log
grep: can't open file
grep: can't open number
```

The intention was to search for the string "Error file number" in error.log, but with the white space separating the expression string, the word "Error" was considered the expression to search for and the words "file" and "number" were considered part of the filename list. Of course, these files don't exist and therefore the error message from **grep**. (It is even more confusing when one of those file names happens to exist.) So the solution to this problem and many other, related problems is the judicious use of quote characters.

The Single Quote

The single quote is the most restrictive of the quote characters used. It tells the Shell to ignore evaluation of the string between the single quotes. White space is ignored as well as any special characters ($, *, ?, etc.). The string is treated as a string literal and is passed as a single argument to commands. So to solve the **grep** problem just cited, we could enclose the expression in single quotes followed by the file name:

```
grep 'Error file number' error.log
```

Grep now sees the expression as "Error file number" and the file list as error.log. Literally anything can occur between the single quotes. For example, let's say that we wanted to show the message "Enter $amount or * to see all entries in the list or ? for help menu" to the user. If we utilize the **echo** command in the normal manner, you can imagine the results.

```
echo Enter $amount or * to see all entries in the list or\
  HELP? for help menu
Enter or ETransfer HELPX HELPY RMAIL awk bin calendar cat
shellpgms to see all entries in the list or HELPX HELPY for help
menu
```

Well, this is not exactly the string we wanted to display to our user! Of course, substitution by the Shell is the culprit here. Let us look more closely at what happened. First the Shell tried to interpret $amount as a variable name. Since there was no variable defined, it returned null. The * had file substitution performed and was replaced with the list of all the files in the current directory. Finally HELP? was interpreted as a filename substitution as well and was replaced with two file names HELPX and HELPY. The single quote can be used to eliminate this problem. If we surround the string with single quotes, no evaluation will occur.

```
echo 'Enter $amount or * to see all entries in the list or\
  HELP? for help menu'
Enter $amount or * to see all entries in the list or HELP? for
help menu
```

The single quote took care of all our substitution problems. This is very useful in many cases but also very restrictive. Let's say that really we wanted the user to be prompted with a particular amount to be entered that is stored in the variable

$amount. The single quotes surely won't do the trick. We need a quote mechanism that allows partial substitution to occur. This leads us to a discussion of the double-quoted string.

The Double Quote

The double quoting of strings tells the Shell to evaluate the string but to recognize only certain characters as special when the evaluation is done. The three special characters recognized are the $ variable indicator, the backquote characters (` `), and the backslash character (\). Notice that this list does not include file substitution wildcard characters (*, ?, etc.). This means that while variable substitution does occur with double quotes, filename substitution does not. This is very nice. It can get rid of the sometimes pesky (but powerful) filename substitution while keeping the ability to substitute variables. Notice also that a single quote is not recognized. Thus single quotes contained within double quotes hide the single quote from the Shell evaluation.

The substitution that is performed on a variable contained in double quotes is slightly different from the normal command-line substitution of a variable due to the protection provided by the double quotes. This can be seen in the following example:

```
MYSTRING="HELLO     CRUEL     CRAZY     WORLD"
echo $MYSTRING
HELLO CRUEL CRAZY WORLD
echo "$MYSTRING"
HELLO     CRUEL     CRAZY     WORLD
```

You can see that placing the variable in double quotes protected the spaces that were embedded in the string MYSTRING. The double quotes, while allowing variable substitution, differ from the normal substitution in the Shell. The Shell will normally take a variable and strip any extra white space and recognize each element as separate. In this simple case, each word was stripped of leading spaces and was passed to the **echo** command. The **echo** command receives each word as an individual argument and prints the arguments with a single space between each. In the case where the string is quoted, then the spaces are protected and the **echo** command receives the string as a single argument — the string containing spaces — and prints it.

Let's return to the example that we used in the previous section to explore substituting within double quotes in a little more detail. Suppose that in the example given with the user input string (following) that we really wanted to show the user a particular amount for the variable *$amount* but wanted the remainder of the string to print just as it is without filename substitution.

```
amount=99.99
echo "Enter $amount or * to see all entries in the list or \
  HELP? for help menu"
Enter 99.99 or * to see all entries in the list or HELP? for help
menu
```

As you can see, the double quotes did the trick, providing the ability to substitute the *amount* variable with a value of 99.99 while not performing any file substitution on the file substitution metacharacters (* and ?).

The Backslash

The backslash quote character is a little different from the other quote characters, all of which occur in pairs while the backslash stands alone. It is a unary operator. The backslash quote simply protects the character following from being evaluated by the Shell. In essence, it is a way to protect any character at any time. The only place where a backslash character is not recognized is within the single quote characters. It is often used within a double-quoted string to protect a double quote character that occurs with the string. Look at the following **grep** command for an example:

```
grep "Error \"TIME=$SECS\"" error.log
```

The **grep** expression that we wish to search for is "Error "TIME=$SECS"" where **SECS** is a variable that is to be substituted. This of course requires the double quotes around the string. But in order to protect the double quotes around the TIME string from being evaluated, we must use the backslash.

As another example, let's consider the user prompt string that we have looked at previously. We could have used the backslash quote mechanism to protect the string from filename substitution or variable substitution by using the backslash character to protect the special characters that indicate to the Shell that it is to take special action. The following examples show the use of the backslash character to protect the string as needed. The first shows how to protect the string from variable name and filename substitution; the second allows for variable name substitution to take place. Note that using this technique does not protect the string from whitespace evaluation.

```
echo Enter \$amount or \* to see all entries in the list or \
  HELP\? for help menu
Enter $amount or * to see all entries in the list HELP? for help
menu

echo Enter $amount or \* to see all entries in the list or \
  HELP? for help menu
Enter 99.99 or * to see all entries in the list or HELP? for help
menu
```

We also could have protected the spaces by using double quotes and then also protected the variable evaluation by using the following command which encloses the string within double quotes. Remember that the backslash character is recognized within double quotes.

```
echo "Enter \$amount or * to see all entries in the list or \
  HELP? for help menu"
Enter $amount or * to see all entries in the list HELP? for help
menu
```

The backslash quote character is a powerful tool that really helps control Shell evaluation, but it also serves another function for the Shell. When the backslash character occurs as the last character on the line, the Shell considers it as a continuation and prompts you for more input using the secondary prompt string. The secondary prompt string is assigned using the PS2 environment variable. It is good to know what your secondary prompt string is so that you can determine when the Shell is asking for more input. This sometimes occurs when you make an error, and seeing the secondary prompt string can be confusing unless you are aware of what it is set to. The secondary prompt allows you to enter the remainder of the line and then executes the command as a single line.

```
PS2=more:
echo "This is a long input line that I would like to continue \
more: on the next line but have the Shell consider it single line"
This is a long input line that I would like to continue on the
next line but have the Shell consider it single line
```

When typing long command lines, this can be a handy feature.

The Backquote

The backquote is a very powerful tool, especially when programming because it causes the Shell to treat whatever is between the backquote characters as a command and substitute the output in place. This is often called command substitution. You will find it endlessly useful when programming, particularly when assigning values to a variable. For instance, let's look at a simple example where we want to assign the variable *TODAY* with today's date using the UNIX **date** command. Seems simple enough, but not unless we have the backquote command substitution at our disposal.

```
TODAY=date        # Assign TODAY the value of date?
echo $TODAY
date

TODAY=`date`      # Assign using command substitution
echo $TODAY
Sun Jan 2 13:27:28 MDT 1994
```

As you see, the string date was first assigned to the variable *TODAY*. The Shell regards any characters to the right of the equal-sign to be part of the literal that you wish to assign. No evaluation is performed. The backquote characters cause the evaluation to take place with the output of the date command in its place. This assigns the *TODAY* variable the date string as expected.

Any valid command can occur with the quotes, even more than a single command by using the command separator, with the command entered being evaluated just as if it had been entered on the command line. This is because the command is actually executed in its own subshell. This of course means that events that occur within the subshell will not be retained upon return to the calling Shell. You will find the command substitution to be a powerful and necessary tool as we explore Shell programming.

TEST

At the heart of each control structure is a conditional test. The **test** command can determine if a given name is a file or a directory; whether it is readable, writable, or executable; and whether two strings or integers are greater than, less than, or equal to each other. Features of **test** also allow AND, OR, and NOT logic.

Test, like any other Shell command, always returns a true (0) or false (1) value in the Shell variable $?. All Shell commands should return a zero (0) when successful and a nonzero value (usually 1 or -1) when they fail.

If a file exists and it is readable, the result is True (0):

```
test -r filename        test -r filename
echo $?                 echo $status
0                       0
```

Similarly, if two strings are not equal, **test** returns a false (nonzero):

```
test "myname" = "lja"        test "myname" = "lja"
echo $?                      echo $status
1                            1
```

When comparing two strings or a variable to a string, it is best to put both strings in double quotes. That way, if one is null, the **test** command will still know how to evaluate the comparison. If the following $*variable* evaluated to null, then the **test** command would only receive two arguments (=, and "lja") and would issue an error message. The double quotes prevent this from occurring. This is a common Shell programming error, so use care and avoid passing test null variables. You can use the -n test to determine if a variable is null or not.

```
test "$variable" = "lja"
```

Under the Bourne Shell, **test** can be written by enclosing the conditions in brackets. The C Shell uses parentheses:

```
if [ -r file_name ]          if ( -r file_name ) then
```

Either of these two versions is preferable because they make the control structures easier to read. The readability becomes apparent when looking at any of the control structures: IF-THEN-ELSE, CASE, DO WHILE, or DO UNTIL. More on using these with **test** in the following sections.

Most tests will be performed on variable names created in the Shell. So use of the control structures will also depend on the use of variables.

KSH

The Korn Shell provides some extensions in the area of the **test** command. First there are several new tests provided. These are in addition to the tests that are already provided with the Bourne Shell. These new test conditions are outlined in Table 5.7.

In addition to the test conditions listed previously, there are a few other extensions that relate to the **test** command itself. First, it is possible for the numerical comparison tests to have numeric expressions instead of just integers. This is very convenient for calculating and comparing at the same time. This often occurs in programming for a wide range of tasks—perhaps a counter for a loop or an index for an array variable. Following is a simple example:

```
if [ "q -z" -ne "w + 2" ]     # Numeric expressions in test
                              # conditions - only Korn
```

In addition to these extensions to the regular **test** command, the Korn Shell provides a more flexible test condition of its own. This test condition uses the syntax

```
[[ test_cond ]]
```

where *test_cond* is any of the test conditions that are outlined in Table 5.7. This alternate form of the **test** command also allows the AND and OR operators (-a and -o), used to form compound test conditions, to be expressed as && for an AND condition and || for an OR condition. Many people, especially C programmers, will find this a familiar form of expressing compound Boolean expressions. Many people find the double brackets to be quite a bit more readable.

TABLE 5.7   Korn Shell Test Conditions

`-S file1`	True if *file1* is a UNIX socket
`-G file1`	True if the group ID of *file1* matches the effective group user running the test
`-O file1`	True if the file's owner is the effective user ID of the user running the test
`-L file1`	True if *file1* is a UNIX symbolic link
`file1 -nt file2`	True if the file named *file1* is newer than the file named *file2*
`file1 -ot file2`	True if *file1* is older than *file2*
`file1 -ef file2`	True if *file1* has the same UNIX device and UNIX file system i-node number as *file2*

EXPR

Like **test, expr** evaluates arguments and returns true (0) or false (1) for comparisons. Otherwise, **expr** returns a numerical value from an arithmetic evaluation. **Expr** uses essentially the same numerical evaluators as the C Shell:

```
if expr $a = $b        if ($a == $b) then
```

Expr will also work for string comparisons:

```
if expr "$my_name" = "Jay Arthur"
                               if ("$my_name" == "Jay Arthur")
```

Expr can also perform numerical evaluations, which are more straightforward in C Shell:

```
a=`expr $a + 1`        @ a += 1
```

Note that when we use the **expr** command, we must use the backquote characters to perform command substitution when we wish the output to be assigned to a variable (most often the case). This is because the **expr** command is a UNIX command and the output from the command must be substituted in the Shell. The **expr** command is the only method to perform integer calculations in the Bourne Shell. You will often use **expr** to calculate counters of all types as well as for conditional checks on integer values in all of the conditional expressions. These are covered in the following sections of this chapter. The **expr** command expects each operator and operand in the arithmetic statement to be separate arguments. Of course, this means that you should not single-quote or double-quote the arithmetic statements. Table 5.8 contains the commonly used arithmetic operators that work with the **expr** command. Note that all the operators work with integers only.

TABLE 5.8   Expr Operators (in precedence order)

Operator	Description	Returned Value
*	integer multiplication (*Note:* the * special character must be protected from Shell substitution or syntax error occurs.)	integer
/	integer division	integer
%	remainder function returns remainder after integer division	integer
+	integer addition	integer
-	integer subtraction	integer
=	equality	true/false
!=	not equal	true/false
>	greater than	true/false
>=	greater than or equal to	true/false
<	less than	true/false
<=	less than or equal to	true/false

As indicated in Table 5.8, the multiplication symbol (*) must be protected from the Shell either by enclosing it in single quotes or by using the backslash quote character:

```
i = `$i \* 15`    # Protect the multiplication from substitution
```

KSH

The Korn Shell, on the other hand, has some nice enhancements in this area. A full discussion of the arithmetic abilities of the Korn Shell is found in Chapter 7, but a brief discussion seems in order here. By using the integer variable types provided in the Korn Shell, it is possible to do straightforward arithmetic expressions where and how you might expect. No need for the **expr** command. The following shows a few examples of using the integer variables in situations where the **expr** command would be used in the Bourne Shell.

```
integer x=1    # Declare x as integer and set to 1
x=x+1          # Add 1 to the counter x—no expr command needed
echo x         # What's the value of x
```

Notice that when we form arithmetic expressions using the Korn Shell, the variables on the right of the "=" do *not* have a $ preceding them. The Korn Shell attempts to interpret anything on the right side of the "=" as arithmetic expressions or integer constants. (We cover this in detail when we talk about Korn Shell arithmetic.) The following example shows the use of an arithmetic expression as an array subscript:

```
integer x = 2
integer y =3
echo ${cities[x+y]}
HOUSTON
```

Finally, let's see an example where an arithmetic expression is used as in conjunction with a control structure. We look at control structures for the remainder of this chapter.

```
integer loop_count=1
while [ loop_count -le 25 ]
do
  echo ${CITIES[loop_count]}
  loop_count=loop_count+1
done
```

This example shows the use of arithmetic expressions while using control structures and should be helpful when working with many of the commands discussed next. The **while** command shown in the example is talked about later in this chapter. (These are not all the details related to Korn Shell arithmetic, but more of a quick tour to help you out with arithmetic that will be needed when we discuss the control commands in the following sections. More detail about Korn Shell arithmetic will be covered later.)

SEQUENTIAL CONTROL STRUCTURES

Several devices control execution of sequential commands. They are the following:

;	command delimiter
( )	command grouping with execution in subshell
{ }	command grouping with execution in current Shell
``	command substitution
&&	**test** for true return code and execute
||	**test** for false return code and execute

The command delimiter, ;, allows for more than one sequential command on one line:

```
cmd1; cmd2; cmd3
```

The grouping parentheses, ( ), and braces, { }, combine the *stdout* and *stderr* of multiple commands into one stream for ease of processing:

```
(cmd1; cmd2 | grep) | wc      # Execute group in the current Shell
{ cmd1; cmd2 | grep } | wc    # Execute group in a subshell
```

When using the grouping braces, note that they must occur separated by a space. If they are not isolated in this way, they are considered to be just another character.

Note that this cannot be accomplished in the C Shell. The output of each command must be placed in a temporary file and then processed by later commands:

```
cmd1 > /tmp/tmp$$; cmd2 | grep >> /tmp/tmp$$
wc /tmp/tmp$$
```

The command substitution allows for the nesting of commands and their application to variables:

```
var=`grep "line" chapter? | line`
```

The two **test** operators, && and ||, test the previous command's return code to decide whether to execute the next command or not:

```
command1 && command2    # Execute command2 if command1 returns
                        # true
command1 || command2    # Execute command2 if command1 returns
                        # false
```

The && and || commands are very convenient when writing Shell commands that are dependent on each other. They allow you to check the status of the previous commands without writing an IF statement (covered in the next section), as shown below:

```
command1                # Execute command1
if [ $? -eq 0 ]         # Check for good return code from command1
then
  command2
  command3
fi
```

By using the || and && commands in conjunction with the grouping statements, we can control the execution of groups of commands:

```
command1 || { command2; command3}
```

This would not have been possible without the grouping statements. For example, the following command would not have the same effect:

```
command1 || command2; command3
```

This series of commands will always execute command3.

These commands control simple sequential execution of commands. To gain further control and the ability to turn information into knowledge, we need decisions.

IF-THEN-ELSE

You will often want to **test** whether a file exists before attempting to modify it. The simplest way to make a true/false test is with the IF-THEN-ELSE (Figure 5.1). Bourne and C Shell versions of the IF-THEN ELSE are almost identical. There are two forms of the IF-THEN-ELSE:

```
if [ test conditions ]          if ( test conditions ) then
then
  command_list                     command_list
else                            else
  command_list                     command_list
fi                              endif
```

It should be noted that the ELSE portion of the if syntax is optional. It is possible to check for a condition and if it is not true, then perform no action. This form of the **if** command would have the following syntax:

```
if [ test conditions ]          if ( test conditions ) then
then
  command_list                     command_list
fi                              fi
```

In the preceding examples of the **if** command syntax, it should be noted that the command_list can be a single command or a group of commands. In most cases, you will want to take one of two actions. If a file exists, for example, you might want to print it on the screen. If not, you might want to create it. A simple test to do so would look like this:

```
if [ -r filename ]                        if ( -r filename ) then
then                                      ...
  cat filename
else
  echo "Enter the data for filename"
  cat > filename
fi                                        endif
```

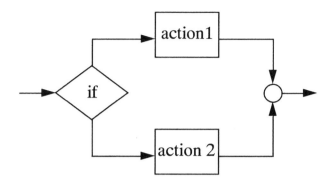

Figure 5.1   IF-THEN-ELSE

Some Shell commands will run in the background, without user interaction. They may also be run interactively. To test whether to send messages to the terminal or to mail them to the user (rather than interrupting what the user is currently doing), you could include the following logic in your Shell:

```
if [ -t 0 ]    # (If the standard input is a terminal)
then
  echo "Error Message"
else    # (The command is running in background)
  echo "Error Message" | mail ${LOGNAME}
fi
```

You may also test if a parameter has a value and take an action:

```
if [ "$PATH" ]                      if ( "$?path" ) then
then                                ...
  echo $PATH
else
  echo "No path is specified"
fi                                  endif
```

Test automatically assumes that if there are no parameters, it should return a false exit status. This test is particularly useful when applied to user-created variables and parameters.

The Bourne Shell offers a feature that the C Shell does not — an operator to nest IF-THEN-ELSE constructs, **elif,** which is useful for implementing CASE control structures.

```
if [ -d ${variable} ]
then
```

```
   process-the-directory ${variable}
elif [ -f ${variable} ]
then
   process file ${variable}
else
   error
fi
```

The IF-THEN-ELSE is useful for two-path decisions and nested tests of the form shown, but to test a single variable for more than one value, use the CASE construct.

CASE AND SWITCH

Many times, a Shell command will create variables or receive parameters that can have many different values. Although the IF-THEN-ELSE can be used to test each of these values and take action, the CASE control structure (Figure 5.2) is more convenient. The following form is a very simple and common example of the **case** command where the value contained in $variable is matched against value1, value2, value3, and value4. If a match is found, then the corresponding actions are performed.

```
case $variable in       switch ( $variable )
value1)                    case value1:
  action1                    action1
  ;;                         breaksw
value2)                    case value2:
  action2                    action2
  ;;                         breaksw
value3|value4)             case value3:
                           case value4:
  action3                    action3
  ;;                         breaksw
*)                         default:
  default action             default action
  ;;                         breaksw
esac                       endsw
```

The last test, "*)", is a default action; if no other value matches, then the default action is taken. Often, you will need to issue an error message and exit from the Shell without doing anything when none of the values are matched.

The more general syntax of the **case** command is the following:

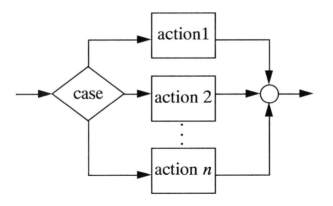

Figure 5.2   CASE

```
case match_string_expression in
   [match_pattern | match_pattern ] ..)
     action_command_list ;;
.
.
.
   esac
```

In the general-purpose CASE statement, the match_string_expression can be any string expression or command list that evaluates to a string expression. For example, it is possible to use a command substitution as the value of the match_string_expression:

```
# Count control files and run report if proper number found
case `ls control*` in
  control1)
    run_report1 ;;
  control2)
    run_report2 ;;
  control3)
    run_report3 ;;
  *)
    echo "Don\'t know what to do with control files"
esac
```

Really any expression that evaluates to a string can be used for the match_string_expression. A further enhancement that is provided with the CASE statement, something that cannot be done with the **test** command used with an IF-THEN statement, is the ability for the match_pattern to contain a file-matching pattern. This is done using any of the characters provided in filename substitution (for example, *, ?, etc.). This is really where the default case is generated from: An asterisk matches any string. But general patterns can be formed using the file-generation characters. Use caution when specifying general patterns. The match patterns are executed in the order written. Place more specific patterns first so that they will match before more general patterns. If you don't do this, they will never execute. The following example demonstrates:

```
case `ls control*` in
  control?)
    run_report1 ;;
  control[2..5])
    run_report2 ;;
  control[6..9])
    run_report3 ;;
  *)
    echo "Don\'t know what to do with control files"
esac
```

In this example, the more general case (control?) will match before any of the more specific cases. Since the match patterns are executed in order, the more specific cases (control[2..5], and control[6..9]) will never be executed because any condition that they match will be matched by the more general condition that is first in the list of match patterns. To fix this we just need to rearrange so the more general case (control?) is after the more specific cases.

CASE structures are particularly useful for processing parameters to the procedure. For example, the Shell variable, $#, contains a count of the number of parameters passed to a Shell command. When working interactively, $# is zero (0). When using a Shell command, the value can run from zero to several hundred. Most Shell commands require some parameters (at least a file to operate on) as information to begin processing. $# should be greater than zero. To test for the number of parameters, use the CASE construct and $#:

```
case $# in                              switch ($#argv)
  0)                                      case 0:
    echo "Enter file name:"               ...
    read argument1                        ...
    ;;                                    breaksw;
  1)                                      case 1:
    argument1=$1
    ;;
  *)                                      default:
    echo "Invalid number of arguments"    ...
    echo "Syntax: command filename"
```

```
      exit 1
      ;;
esac                                                    endsw
# Main processing begins here
```

Assume for a moment that you use Shell to create a monthly report and that the processing differs from month to month. To test and properly execute the command, you could use the **date** command and test for each of the months:

```
current_month=`date +'%m'`
case ${current_month} in
  01)
    January
    ;;
  02)
    February
    ;;
  .
  .
  .
  12)
    December
    ;;
  *)
    echo "Problems with the date command"
    ;;
esac
```

The Shell executes the command line:

```
case 01 in
```

January, February, and so on are the actual names of commands that have to be executed.

The CASE control structure can also be used for character strings. Multiple character strings can be specified to default to the same action:

```
case $current_date in              switch ( $current_date )
  01|Jan|January)                    case "01":
    January                          case "Jan":
    ;;                               case "January":
  02|Feb|February)                     January
    February                           breaksw
    ;;                                 ...
  ...
esac                               endsw
```

The CASE and SWITCH constructs are a powerful way of handling many comparisons and many different actions. Sometimes, however, an action needs to be repeated using different files or different information.

LOOPING COMMANDS

The commands to handle repetitive operations are **for, while,** and **until** (csh: **foreach, repeat,** and **while**).

For and Foreach

The **for** (Bourne Shell) and **foreach** (C Shell) control structures (Figure 5.3) permit looping through a series of actions while changing a variable name specified on the command line. Both interactively and in a background mode, the use of Shell will require processing many different files the same way. The common form of these control structures is:

```
for variable in value1 value2 ...        foreach variable ( value1 \
do                                           value2 ... )
  action on $variable                      action on $variable
done                                     end
```

The **for** structure will repeat the action commands a specified number of times — once for each value listed in the list of strings "value1 value2 ...". The optional list of strings can be any expression that evaluates to a list of strings (file names, command substitution, etc.). If you omit the list of strings, then the Shell defaults to use the special variable $* which represents all the arguments passed to the Shell. When the **for** loop executes, the variable takes on each value in the list of values. Each iteration of the loop assigns the next value in the value list to the variable.

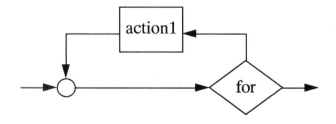

Figure 5.3   FOR

For example, to edit all of the files for this book, replacing "shell" with "Shell", I could use the following commands:

```
for file in chapter*        foreach file ( chapter* )
do
ed - $file <<eof!
g/shell/s//Shell/g
w
q
eof!
done                        end
```

This could also be done for files with many different names:

```
for file in file1 filename xyz etc
```

FOR control structures, as well as any of the Shell control structures, can be nested inside of one another. For example, to process all of the files in the directories bin, doc, and src, I could use the following nested control structure:

```
for dir in bin doc src      foreach dir ( bin doc src )
do
  cd $dir                   cd $dir
  for file in *               foreach file ( * )
  do
    if [ -f $file ]             if ( -f $file )
    then                       then
      process $file               process $file
    fi                         endif
  done                       end
  cd ..                      cd ..
done                        end
```

For each of the directories, the Shell would change into that directory. Then, for each file it would test to ensure that the variable $*file* is really a file and not a directory, and then the Shell would execute the command "process" on each file name. When the Shell finished with all of the files under bin, it would change up to the parent directory and then start working on the doc directory. Nesting control structures is a convenient way to handle complex operations that would otherwise require extensive typing to accomplish the same ends.

The **for** construct is not the only way to handle looping through repetitive operations. The **while** and **until** constructs provide another alternative.

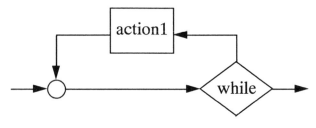

Figure 5.4 WHILE

While and Until

The **while** construct (Figure 5.4) takes a form similar to the **for** construct:

```
while command list        while ( expression )
do                            actions
  actions                   end
done
```

In the following example, let's use a variable, *month,* and the **while** loop to process every month's activity:

```
month=1                        set month=1
while [ ${month} -le 12 ]      while (${month} < 12)
do
  process ${month}               process ${month}
  month=`expr $month + 1`        @ month += 1
done                           end
```

Using the Bourne or Korn Shell, you can do something you can't do in the C Shell — direct *stdout* into a conditional statement using the pipe:

```
for file in Chapter?
do
  cat $file | \
  while read line  # read a line
  do
    process $line
  done
done
```

This is a great way to process a file one line at a time. Or you may need to process the *stdout* from the command using a pipe:

```
for file in file1 file2          foreach file (file1 file2)
do
  line < $file                     line < $file >> /tmp/tmp$$
done | wc > header_count         end
                                 wc < /tmp/tmp$$ > header_count
```

You may need, at some time, to start an infinite loop. The **test** command recognizes the existence of any value as true:

```
while [ 1 ]              while ( 1 )
do
  process something        process something
done                     end
```

To prevent looping forever or forcing the user to break out of the loop by using one of the Break or Delete keys, you will need to break out of the loop. The **break** command, as shown in the following example, is the way to jump out of a loop without causing logic problems.

```
while [ 1 ]
do
  if [ end condition ]
  then
    break
  else
    process something
  fi
done
```

Sometimes the processing will need to continue without processing anything. The **continue** command handles these requirements:

```
while [ 1 ]
do
  echo "Enter file name"
  read filename
  if [ -r $filename ]
  then
    process $filename
  else
    continue
  fi
    echo "Processed file ${filename}"
done
```

The **while** construct can also use **test** on variable names and files, processing them accordingly:

```
while [ "$variable" = something ]
do
  process $variable
done

ls |\
while [ -r $file ]
do
  process $file
done
```

The **until** form of the loop (Figure 5.5), available with the Bourne Shell only, is used less often. It executes the processing at least once and then tests the conditions.

```
until [ end conditions ]
do
  processing
done
```

The difference between the **while** loop and the **until** loop is the point at which the test is performed. The **while** loop first examines the test condition to ensure that the loop should be executed. If the result of the test or command is **true**, then the loop is executed. With the **until** loop, the condition is checked at the end of the processing loop. Thus the processing specified with the **until** loop will always be executed at least once. You should take this into account when writing **until** loops.

Below is an example of an **until**:

```
until [ "`who | grep lja`" ]
do
  sleep 60
done
```

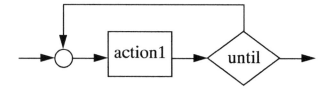

Figure 5.5   UNTIL

The **until** example shown previously is useful when watching for known hackers to enter the system under a specific ID. A generalized hacker check could watch for the user ID to appear on the system and then send mail and call the system administrator:

```
# Hacker Check
until [ "`who | grep $1`" ]
do
  sleep 60
done
echo `date` there's a hacker in the machine | mail lja
# Call my office phone (or home phone)
cu 5551234
```

The C Shell also includes the **repeat** form of loop, which executes a command a specified number of times:

```
repeat 10 command
```

Aside from **for, foreach, while, until,** and **repeat,** there are a few other ways of handling loops and the processing of many files: **xargs** and **find**.

KSH

Select Statement

The **select** statement is unique to the Korn Shell. It is provided to allow for the easy creation of menu-driven user input. The **select** statement acts like a combination of a **while** and a **case** statement. The syntax of the **select** statement is shown as:

```
select variable in [ words ... ]
  do
    command list
  done
```

The words, determined by whitespace separation, are printed on the standard error (usually your terminal) with a number associated to each word printed. The Korn Shell uses two standard variables to facilitate the **select** command—the PS3 prompt string and the variable named REPLY. After printing the menu based on the words listed, the user is prompted with the PS3 prompt string. The user input is then read into the variable REPLY. If the first character in the REPLY variable is a valid number that was associated with a word menu option, then the variable is set to the corresponding word.

If this is not the case, then the variable is set to null but REPLY still contains what the user entered.

Whenever the user enters something on the prompt line, the variable is set (possibly to null), REPLY is set, and the command list is executed. Usually this command loop checks for a valid menu option and then takes some action based on the option that the user entered. After executing the commands listed in the command list, the user is again prompted for input. If the user does not enter any input the menu is redisplayed. The executed **do** loop is an endless loop. You, or the user, must break the loop execution. As a Shell programmer you will almost always want to provide your users with a menu option that allows them to gracefully exit the loop. To exit the loop in the Shell, the **break** or **exit** command can be used. The user can usually break out of the loop by exiting the Shell in a forced manner (i.e., with a **break** command—Del key on the keyboard). This might sound confusing, so an example will help clear the fog index.

```
PS3="Hello master! What function would you like today oh wise\
    one?: "
select option in "Create Gold Bullion" "Alter the weather" \
    "Create happiness" "Create despair" \
    "Create a new World" "End it all" "Exit"
do
  echo "You chose to $option"
  case $REPLY in
    1) echo "Programmers wish computers could do this" ;;
    2) echo "Dream on" ;;
    3) echo "Sometimes computers do this" ;;
    4) echo "Most often computers actually do this" ;;
    5) echo "Don't know the ingredients for a new world." ;;
    6) echo " Sorry you can't stop it now" ;;
    7) echo "To serve you has been a pleasure"
      exit;;
  esac
done
```

The results of running this example are shown below:

```
1) Create Gold Bullion
2) Alter the weather
3) Create happiness
4) Create despair
5) Create a new World
6) End it all
7) Exit
Hello master! What function would you like today oh wise one?: 4
You chose to Create despair
```

```
Most often computers actually do this
Hello master! What function would you like today oh wise one?:
1) Create Gold Bullion
2) Alter the weather
3) Create happiness
4) Create despair
5) Create a new World
6) End it all
7) Exit
Hello master! What function would you like today oh wise one?: 6
You chose to End it all
Sorry you can't stop it now
Hello master! What function would you like today oh wise one?: 7
You chose to Exit
To serve you has been a pleasure
```

Note that when the user simply entered nothing, the variable option was set to null and the menu was redisplayed without executing the contents of the **do** loop. If the user enters an invalid option, the variable option is also set to null and REPLY is set to what the user actually entered. You can of course take some default action in this case. Most often you will want to issue an error message of some sort. You can see that the **select** statement is a very easy way to create menu-driven user interfaces.

Xargs, Repeat, and Find

The Shell provides two other facilities for handling repetitive operations: **xargs** (csh: **repeat**) and **find**. **Xargs** simplifies the implementation of loops when you need to execute only one command with a list of files. The problem is more complicated when every file under a user's ID must be examined or when entire file systems must be changed. The **find** command has the ability to look through entire directory trees for specific files or directories and then execute commands on those file or directory names.

Xargs takes lines of input and executes commands, substituting the input lines wherever specified. You could view **xargs** as a command constructor and executor. **Repeat,** in the C Shell, executes a command a specified number of times. (**Xargs** performs this function for Bourne and Korn Shells.) **Find** searches downward from a specified directory and can execute commands, substituting file or directory names into the command. **Xargs** is useful when interactively executing the same command on many files in a directory. **Find** is more useful for examining entire directory structures and executing commands.

Some Shell commands, such as remove (**rm**), only work on a maximum number of files (100). Since the command

rm *

results in an error message when there are more than 100 files, **xargs** can be used to execute the **rm** command with the first 100 and then the remaining files:

```
ls | xargs -n100 rm -f        ls | repeat 100 rm -f
```

When executed, this **xargs** command will generate **rm -f** commands followed by a list of 100 file names. The file names are generated by the **ls** command and piped to the **xargs** command. If the -n option was removed, then **xargs** tries to construct as many arguments as it possibly can. **Xargs** uses an internal buffer to store the command, and once that is full the command is executed. The -n option provides control over how many arguments should be allowed.

Similarly, a series of existing files can be copied to other names:

```
ls chapter* | xargs -i cp {} old{}
```

The -i option of the **xargs** command places **xargs** in insert mode. The command is constructed by replacing the string { } (this is the default; string could be any string) with the word read in from standard input. In this case the word is a chapter name. This command creates a duplicate set of the chapters from a book named oldchapter1, etc. Instead of creating duplicate copies, however, it would be better to store each of the chapters in the source code control system (SCCS):

```
ls chapter* | xargs -i admin -n -i{} $HOME/doc/sccs/book/s.{}
```

This command stores the chapters in the directory $HOME/doc/sccs/book for later retrieval and update.

There are other options under the **xargs** command that should be explored. For instance, it is impossible to execute the command for each line read from standard input, to print the command generated before executing it, and to print the command and then prompt for authorization to execute the command. See your manual pages for details on these options.

It is common for users to change from one work group to another. To allow other members of their group to access a file, they could either change each file and directory one at a time, or they could use **find**:

```
cd $HOME
find . -exec chgrp newgrp {} \;
```

which says "Find all of the files and directories under my log in and change the group ownership of each one to the new group." Note that the **find** command recursively searches each subdirectory of the directory named as the starting path. In this case the starting path is ".", the current directory $HOME, but it could have been any path name. The braces indicate where the **find** command should substitute the name of each file and directory found during its search. The same ability can be used to change the mode on all of the files or to copy the files from one place to another:

```
cd $HOME/bin
find . -exec chmod 775 {} \;
find . -print | cpio -pd new_place
```

Find can also test each name and take action. To change mode on all of the directories under the login directory, you could use:

```
cd $HOME
find . -type d -exec chmod 770 {} \;
```

The **find** command has many different tests that can be performed on files to control which files are listed. It is possible to check for files owned by a particular user ID, a particular name (often used to locate lost files), a particular size, or last access time, just to name a few. See your manual pages for full details.

The **find** command used to print the location of file names would have the following format:

```
find $HOME -name chapter1 -print
```

This command would print the location of files named chapter1 found anywhere under my login directory or any of its subdirectories.

Find can even ask you if it is okay to execute the command:

```
find . -type d -ok chmod 770 {} \;
```

The option -ok works just like -exec except that **find** will prompt you before executing the command.

Rules of Thumb

- Use **xargs** or **repeat** when working on a list of files.
- Use **find** to operate on all of the directories and files under a specific directory.

They both work well when using the Shell interactively.

SUMMARY

In order to store information that you want to use in Shell procedures, you must utilize a Shell variable. A Shell variable is a storage area that has a handle, which is the name you used when assigning a value to the Shell variable. To retrieve the contents of a variable you must precede the name of the variable with the $ character. The Shell provides a number of operators that can be used in conjunction with a variable to provide default assignment values. The Korn Shell offers some nice extensions to Shell variables by providing array variables, as well as typed variables. By providing an integer variable type, the Korn Shell provides enhanced arithmetic capabilities.

The Shell provides many facilities for controlling actions. The use of repetitive control structures such as **for, foreach, repeat, until, while, xargs,** and **find** will improve your productivity. The **test, if-then-else,** and **case** commands each help improve the reliability and usability of your commands.

The Shell control structures are the foundation of good Shell programming. Use them wisely and productively. They can be used productively in two ways: interactively at the terminal or as the basis for interactive and batch commands that automate much of a UNIX user's work. These subjects are explored more fully in the next two chapters.

EXERCISES

1. Name the control structures in the Bourne and C Shells and describe their use.

2. What Shell facility handles all conditional tests for the Shell control structures? Which Shell variable contains the return code from a conditional test?

3. What other Shell commands can be used to handle repetitive processes?

4. What Shell facility handles errors and interrupts?

5. Write the IF-THEN-ELSE statement to test whether a variable name is a directory. Write the same test for file names.

6. Write a CASE statement to test a variable name for the values "data", "source", "comments", or anything else.

7. Write a **for** loop to process all of the files in a directory.

8. Write an infinite loop to prompt the terminal user for file names to be removed and remove them. Use **trap** to exit gracefully when finished.

9. Write an infinite loop to check a directory for files, print them using **pr** if any are found, remove them after printing, and then sleep for 15 minutes (900 seconds).

10. Use **xargs** to process all of the files in a directory.

11. Use **find** to locate all of the files in a user's ID named *.c (C language source code) and print them with **pr**.

12. Write the **trap** statements to handle:

    a. ignoring hangup signals

    b. removing temporary files when QUIT or INTERRUPT is received

    c. removing temporary files when the command ends normally

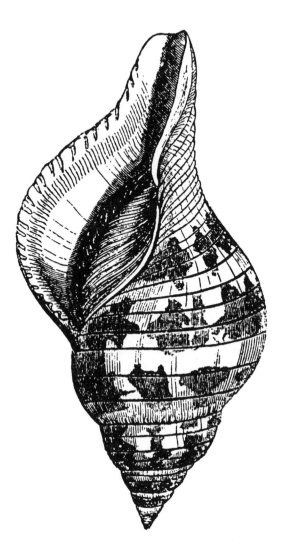

PART TWO

SHELL PROGRAMMING
FOR RESULTS

Great is the art of beginning, but greater is the art of ending.

Longfellow

Chapter Six

Shell Programming

Shell programming is little more than combining the commands and control structures you have learned up to this point. You can program interactively or by combining Shell commands in an executable program (a UNIX file that holds the commands) that you and others can execute. Shell procedures are simple ways to automate complex processes as well as simple everyday ones.

INTERACTIVE SHELL USAGE

One of the most productive ways to use the Shell is interactively at the terminal. People familiar with the Macintosh or any other WIMP (windows, icon, mouse, and pointer) interface will ask: Why bother? As an avid Macintosh user, I agree, for some applications. If you want to start up a single application program and do just one thing to one file, icons and mice are a great way to go. If, however, you want to start up many commands and do many things to many files, you'll need the Shell. The commands to do this are shown in Table 6.1.

TABLE 6.1 Looping Commands

Command	Operations	Files	Variables
for	many	many	one
repeat	many		
xargs	one	many	one
while	many		many
until	many		many

When creating a Shell program (as described in the next chapter), you will often use the Shell interactively to *prototype* or test out how the command will ultimately work. It is also useful when you are having some problem in your Shell program and you want to test portions independently to ensure that they are working properly. A quick way to do this is by typing the Shell commands interactively. So interactive use of the Shell will also serve the development of Shell programs.

SHELL SETUP

As a user logs into and out of UNIX, several files come into play to set up the environment for the user and the Shell (Table 6.2). We briefly touched on these files when discussing the login procedure in Chapter 2. One of the final stages of the login procedure is the execution of your .profile. The Shell does this automatically for you. You can put any Shell commands (except .exrc) in these files that you would use elsewhere, but each file has a specific use.

In the Bourne and Korn Shells, /etc/profile is defined by the system administrator to set up the common Shell environment for all users. To override or enhance these system defaults, you can place any commands you want in ${HOME}/.profile. As you log in, UNIX executes /etc/profile and then ${HOME}/.profile before creating a Shell for you. ${HOME}/.profile is an excellent place to create specific global variables such as *PATH* or to send yourself a good morning message or to change the default system prompts:

```
PATH=${PATH}:${HOME}/bin      # Add bin to PATH
PS1="#@%\\! "
PS2="More Input!> "
export PATH PS1 PS2
echo "G'day mate!"
```

${HOME}/.profile is also an excellent place to place *Shell functions*, which will be discussed in the advanced material. The Korn Shell also permits alias commands to be placed in your .profile. For a simple example, however, let's take the **dir** command of MS-DOS:

TABLE 6.2 Setup Files

Bourne and Korn Shells	C Shell	Purpose
`/etc/profile`		System-wide setup procedure
`.profile`		User-specific setup for **sh** or **ksh**
	`.cshrc`	User-specific setup for **csh**
	`.login`	Commands executed at *login*
	`.logout`	Command executed at *logout*

```
dir()
{
  ls -l
}
```

Some of the more important environment-specific variables that often are set in your .profile are shown in Table 6.3. As was discussed in Chapter 5, the setting of many of the environment variables is up to you, while others are provided automatically by the Shell. You may override or change any of the environment variables to customize your work environment.

The commands and variables shown in Table 6.3 are really the very basics that you will want to have in your .profile. As you become a more powerful user, your .profile will grow and become increasingly sophisticated — all in an effort to utilize the full power of the Shell with a customized environment.

In the C Shell, ${HOME}/.cshrc performs similar functions. It is the perfect place to set key Shell variables:

```
set noclobber       # Don't clobber files during execution
set history=20      # Keep track of 20 previous commands
set prompt="#@%! "
set path=${path}:${HOME}/bin
echo "G'day Mate!"
```

${HOME}/.cshrc is also an excellent place to put aliases for commands:

```
alias dir 'ls -l'
```

The ${HOME}/.login file executes after .cshrc. It is an excellent place to set terminal characteristics with stty and to set environment variables with setenv:

```
stty erase '^H'          # Set erase to a backspace
setenv PRINTER MYroom    # Set PRINTER default to MYroom
```

TABLE 6.3   Variables/Commands Commonly Set in .profile

PATH=PATH:/your directories here	Append your important directories to the default Shell search path.
MAIL=/usr/mail/mylogin	Tell me about my incoming mail.
umask 022	Set your default file creation mask.
PS1="NEXT:"	Set your primary prompt.
TERM=vt100	Tell the system what type of terminal you are running with.

In a Sun workstation or any X Windows–based environment, you can also use .login to execute the window manager:

```
sunview
```

If you are using the C shell, the ${HOME}/.logout file runs after a user logs out of UNIX, so it's best to have only background processing in this file. It can say good-bye and then clean up junk files or whatever:

```
clear     # Clear screen
echo "G'bye Mate!"
nohup nice find -name 'junk*' -exec \rm '{}' \; &
```

The final setup file, ${HOME}/.exrc, sets up the environment for the vi editor and allows you to define macros for use in that editor. For example, to maintain the same indentation as the previous line, a user could set autoindent. Then the program would automatically follow the current indentation:

```
set autoindent
```

Or, for documentation, you can set wrapmargin to automatically insert a *line-feed* whenever you get close to the right-hand margin:

```
set wrapmargin=10
```

USING THE SHELL INTERACTIVELY

Any time you execute any command — **ls, cat,** or **who,** for example — you are using the Shell interactively: *Stdin, stdout,* and *stderr* are all directed to the terminal. Combining commands via the pipe or executing existing Shell programs contributes to productive interactive use of the Shell.

You should use the Shell interactively whenever you need:

- immediate results (list a directory with **ls**)
- to interact with the command (it asks you questions)
- to perform a repetitive operation on a one-shot basis (look for and operate on specific files in a directory)

Using simple commands, like the editors, is an effective use of the Shell, but less productive than joining Shell commands together to perform complex operations for you. Learning to use **grep, cut, paste,** and numerous other tools effectively is the essence of productivity improvement. The Shell provides a consistent environment of reusable tools that can be joined together to manipulate virtually any text into some required form. The hard part is developing the mental focus to understand this flexibility and use it in everyday activities. The Shell can quickly extract and format information, or it can handle more complex, recursive procedures.

In-Line Procedures

Selecting and reporting information is an excellent way to improve productivity with the Shell. Files containing fields and delimiters, such as /etc/passwd, can be inspected and printed:

```
cut -f1,5 -d: /etc/passwd | pr
lja  Jay Arthur
pgm  Paula Martin
```

Or you can print a document and mail it to many users:

```
nroff document_file | mail user_id user_id user_id
```

Using data selection commands such as **grep, cut,** and **uniq** can quickly eliminate extraneous information. Reporting commands such as **awk, cat, pr,** and **nroff** can then format the remaining information. For further information on these commands, refer to Chapter 3. Another good way to use the Shell interactively is with looping procedures.

Looping Procedures

In everyday usage, you will need to perform many operations on many files. The main Shell facilities to help you are **for, find,** and **xargs. While** and **until** are also useful occasionally. **Find** is invaluable when you have left a file somewhere under your log in but have no idea where. To find the file from your HOME directory, type:

```
find . -name lostfile -print
./doc/unix/lostfile
```

Once you have identified that **find** is locating the proper file names, you can execute commands on those files. I would not, however, recommend executing commands that remove or change files before you have determined that **find** is obtaining only the file names you require. Otherwise, you could lose or corrupt a large number of files and never know it was done. If you are in doubt, use the -ok feature of **find** to check each file name before executing the command:

```
find . -name s\* -ok rm -f {} \;
./doc/unix/book/s.chapter1? n
./doc/unix/book/s.chapter2? n
```

```
./src? n
./src/slop? y
./src/sludge? y
```

Without these checks, **find** would have removed the SCCS files containing Chapters 1 and 2. Re-creating them would not be fun unless the system administrator could restore them from backup. A simple command to remove all junk files, however, would be:

```
find . -name junk\* -exec rm -f {} \;
```

Find is useful for any task that requires looking down through directory structures, finding files, and executing commands to modify or delete the files. It does not work well, however, when you want to work on just the files in the current directory. For these looping processes, you need **for** and **xargs**.

For lets you perform multiple operations on specified files. **Xargs,** on the other hand, can execute only one command per file. One of the most frequent uses of the **for** loop involves editing files in the current directory to change an old word to a new one:

```
for file in chapter?
do
ed $file <<!
g/shell/s//Shell/g
w
q
!
done
```

The **for** command substitutes chapter0 through chapter9 for the variable *file* and executes the editor commands that follow.

Similarly, **for** could calculate the average length of each word in each chapter:

```
for file in chapter?
do
    totalchar=`wc -c ${file} | cut -c1-7`
    totalwords=`wc -w ${file} | cut -c1-7`
    average=`expr ${totalchar}/${totalwords}`
    echo ${file} ${average}
done
```

These are fairly simple examples, but they show the basic interactive uses of **for**.

Xargs works well on files in a directory when you want to execute only one command:

```
ls junk* | xargs -i rm -f {}
```

Adding, getting, or creating deltas of files in SCCS is another application of **xargs**. In the following example, all of the chapters can be added to SCCS with one command line:

```
ls chapter? | xargs -i admin -i{} -y"First draft" s.{}
```

Xargs is a handy way to process many files at one time. For more complex loops, the Shell user will need **while** and **until**.

The **while** loop can be used interactively when you want to set a variable to a value and loop until it reaches some other value. The following simple example calculates the sine of all angles between 1° and 90°:

```
angle=1
while [ ${angle} -le 90 ]
do
  sine=`echo "scale=2;s(${angle})" | bc -l`
  echo "Sine of ${angle} = ${sine}"
  angle=`expr ${angle} + 1`
done
```

All of the values would print out on the terminal. These values could also be directed into a file or printed with **pr**.

Note that the **while** loop simplifies interactive commands that change variables other than file names. **For** and **xargs** are more effective with files.

All of these commands—**find, for, until, while,** and **xargs**—allow the user to execute repetitive actions on files and directories. When the user needs to interact with these commands, the process should be run in foreground. Whenever possible, however, these commands should be run in background so that the user can continue working.

Command History and Editing

Once startup processing completes, the Shell begins reading commands from the terminal. Both the C Shell and Korn Shell have the ability to keep track of commands as you enter them from the terminal. The Shell stores these commands in memory and allows them to be recalled, modified, and executed.

History substitution, in the C Shell, begins by typing the character "!" There are lots of exotic ways to modify or execute previous commands in csh. The simplest way is to directly execute a previous command:

!!	execute last command
!*n*	execute previous command line *n*
!-*n*	execute current command line minus *n*
!*str*	execute the previous command line beginning with *str*
!?*str?*	execute the previous command line containing *str*

You can also select specific words from a previous command using these as a prefix:

!!:1 !!:3   select words 1 & 3 from the last command
!!:2-4   select words 2-4 from the last command

You can also substitute words:

!?gerp?:gs/gerp/grep/ replace 'gerp' with 'grep' and execute

There are more exotic substitutions than this, and if you use the C Shell, I suggest you explore them. They can speed your effort at the terminal.

KSH

The Korn Shell handles history somewhat differently (see Table 6.4 on page 155). The ability to recall commands and perform editing on those commands is a very powerful feature of the Korn Shell and one that should be fully explored by anyone who is using the Korn Shell on a regular basis.

The Korn Shell provides command history—the ability to recall previously executed commands—by saving all commands entered in a UNIX file. By searching the file looking for a previous command to execute, you can save a great deal of typing. The name of the file used to store the commands in is assigned via an environment variable, *HISTFILE*. This is most often set in your .profile. If you do not provide a name, then the Shell will default to $HOME/.sh_history. The number of commands that the Shell keeps in the file is controlled by *HISTSIZE*, which again is most often set in your .profile. The default for this value is 128. You may want to set this higher if disk space on your system is not a problem and you perform a great deal of interactive Shell work.

The Korn Shell provides two methods for interacting with the commands stored in the history file. The first (and older) method is through the use of the **fc** command. This command allows you to see what is in the command history file and to edit and reexecute the commands. The second method of interacting with the command history is through the command editing mode. This is an enhancement to the Korn Shell that allows your command line to behave like your favorite editor (as long as your favorite editor is vi or emacs, that is). By using commands that are taken from the editors, you can manipulate the command text much like you manipulate a line of text in the editor itself. The beauty is that this is built right into the Shell. It is always available without invoking an editor. By using editor-like commands, you can scroll back through the history file, select commands, edit them, and reexecute directly on the command line!

We will look at the older **fc** command first. The **fc** command provides a way to view and manipulate the command history file. You can view the contents of the file, edit the contents through a specified editor, and execute commands in the history file all through the **fc** command. The first form of the command is used for viewing and reexecuting the contents of the file and has the syntax:

```
fc [-e editorname ] [-nlr] [first_line] [last_line]
  -n no number in listing
  -l list the contents of command file; don't edit and execute
  -r reverse the listing order
```

The syntax of this command is really a bit confusing and is one reason that many people prefer using command editing to access previous commands. But if you use the **fc** command and only wish to list the commands to see what is in the file, you *must* specify the -l (for list) option. If you do not specify -l, then the **fc** command assumes that you want to edit and reexecute a command in the file.

There are several ways to list the commands stored in the history file. First, you can use the **fc -l** command with no other options. This will list the last 16 commands that you entered on your screen. This default command is also provided in a built-in alias called **history**. Typing the **fc -l** command or the **history** command will yield the listing shown:

```
fc -l

6414  fc -l -30
6415  fc -l
6416  man .profile
6417  jobs
6418  history
6419  fg
6420  fc -e emacs -l
6421  fg
6422  exit
6423  emacs
6424  fc -l
6425  fg
6426  envp
6427  aqcb_stat
6428  fg
6429  fc -l
```

As you can see, each command that is listed is preceded by a number. That number is assigned when the command is placed in the file and can be used with the **fc** command to specify a particular command that you wish to work with. The **fc** command will always let you specify a particular command from the list or a range of commands. For example, let's say we wanted to see the last four commands in the commands list. We could type the command

```
fc -l 6426 6429
```

```
6426  envp
6427  aqcb_stat
6428  fg
6429  fc -l
```

There is another numbering scheme that can be used with the **fc** command. The commands are determined relative to the last command entered. For example, the last command entered is -1, the second-to-last command entered is -2, and so forth. Thus, we could have listed the previous four commands by using the following command:

```
fc -l -4
```

```
6426  envp
6427  aqcb_stat
6428  fg
6429  fc -l
```

It is also possible to use a string value for the values of first_line and last_line. This will search back through the command stack for the first command that starts with the string listed. If you do not provide an end line, then the command history is listed to your screen starting with the command that contains the string given through the last command entered. You can even use a string for both starting and ending lines or a combination of string and number references.

Now that we know how to see what is in the command file, how do we reexecute the commands? There are two methods of reexecution supported through the **fc** command. First is the edit/reexecute method, or there is the direct reexecution with no editing. The first method of edit and execute uses the **fc** command as we saw previously, only without the -l option. When this is done, the **fc** command allows you to edit, through an editor that you specify, the command(s) from the command history file. If you use the -e *editor_name* option that editor is executed and loaded with the commands specified from the command list. The commands can be listed in the same method as was done with the -l option above. Any of those techniques is valid. Once you have edited the commands and exited your editor, the command(s) are executed by the Shell. In order to provide a default action, the Shell will use the editor listed in the FCEDIT environment variable if no editor name is given. If you are using the **fc** command, you will want to set the FCEDIT variable in your .profile. This will prevent the need to specify an editor when you wish to edit commands. The following command would edit and reexecute the previous command from command history using the default editor listed in FCEDIT (in this case the emacs editor).

```
FCEDIT= /usr/local/bin/emacs
fc -5
```

The next method for simple reexecution of the commands from command history, without editing them first, is to use the following form of the **fc** command:

```
fc -e - [old=new] [line]
```

In this form of the **fc** command the -e - option tells the **fc** command that you do not wish to invoke an editor but simple to reexecute a command directly. The *line* is a particular line from the command history file that you want to reexecute. The line that you wish to reexecute can be specified in any of the ways that were discussed before. You can specify a particular line number, a relative line number, or the string representation of the command. If you specify old=new, then a substitution of the old string with the new string is performed on the command that you reexecute. This is a quick edit on a previous command.

It should be pointed out that the command with only the -e - option will reexecute the last command that you entered. This is so common that the Korn Shell provides a standard alias for this function. The alias is the r alias. Entering r on the command line will reexecute the previous command in the command history file. The alias is simple to set to the **fc** command shown:

```
r=fc -e -
```

Let's perform a simple command reexecution:

```
ls *    # List the contents of the directory
master_usr.doc
ums_mail.doc
ums_memo.doc
ums_notes.txt
ums_team.txt
ums_todo.txt
fc -l -1    # Show me the last command on the command stack
6612  ls *
6613  fc -l -1
r    # Rerun the ls command
master_usr.doc
ums_mail.doc
ums_memo.doc
ums_notes.txt
ums_team.txt
ums_todo.txt
```

```
fc -e - *=*.doc -1     # Change the ls command to show only doc
                       # files
master_usr.doc
ums_mail.doc
ums_memo.doc
```

Command Edit Mode

As was mentioned before, the Korn Shell also provides a more advanced way of editing and reexecuting commands from command history, through a feature called command editing. Essentially this provides vi, emacs, and gmacs editing capabilities to each command line previously entered. Any command line entered can be edited in very powerful ways with commands that you are already familiar with (given that you use vi or emacs). Even if you do not use the vi or emacs editor, it is probably worth learning a few commands that can be great time-savers when typing many interactive Shell commands.

The first step in using command-line editing is to tell the Korn Shell that you wish to do so. This can be accomplished in several ways. One is to invoke the Korn Shell with the -o option set to the command-line editing option you wish to use. The second is to use the **set** command to do the same. And finally, the easiest and most flexible method is to set the *VISUAL* or *EDITOR* global variable. The Korn Shell searches for these variables to determine if command-line editing should be invoked. If the string assigned to either of these variables ends with a valid editing mode indication (emacs, gmacs, vi), the Korn Shell will install that style of command-line editing. Often the *EDITOR* variable is set in your .profile. The following example would invoke emacs style command editing as well as point to the location of the emacs editor for any other commands or Shell programs that may need to invoke an editor:

```
EDITOR=/usr/local/bin/emacs
```

Once you have set your Korn Shell session to one of the editor options, your command line becomes a single-line editor window onto the command history file. It is much like editing the command history file with emacs or vi but only viewing a single line of the file at a time. The single line that you are viewing is the current Shell command line. This editor window contains many of the commands that you would use if you were editing the line in vi or emacs itself. It also provides the ability to move around in the command history file by using editor commands to see the previous or next line. It is also possible to search for particular commands in the command history file and reexecute them at will. In general, most of the common editing commands that you use when editing a file with your editor of choice are available to you at the command line.

There are many command-line edit options available, based on your editor choice; the major ones used for each of the editor options are indicated in Tables 6.5 and 6.6. To get a full list of all the commands that are available, see the manual pages on the Korn Shell (man ksh). If you are not familiar with vi or emacs and are a heavy Shell user, it would be worth the effort to gain at least a basic understanding of one of these editors. The command-line edit options will make much more sense and will give you greater productivity in the Shell.

Foreground and Background Procedures

Any time that you need immediate answers, execute Shell commands in foreground at the terminal. When you can afford to wait—the command takes a long time and will tie up the terminal, which you could use for other productive work—you can submit the command in background. The Shell facility to handle this is simple and easy to remember: &. The ampersand at the end of a command line tells the Shell to run the command in background. Initiating background processes can be very productive and is something everyone should learn how to use. Recall a previous example:

```
ls chapter? | xargs -i junkproc {} &
2304
```

The Shell started up a background process and printed out the process number (2304). This number is used to reference the process. The Shell variable $! contains the number of the last background process initiated.

You can also ask a command to **sleep** for a number of seconds and then execute:

```
(sleep 900 ; ls chapter? | xargs -i junkproc {})&
2717
```

TABLE 6.4 History Commands

Korn Shell	C Shell	Purpose
r	!!	execute last command
r n	!n	execute previous command line n
r -n	!-n	execute current command line minus n
r cmd	!cmd	execute the previous command line beginning with cmd
	!?str?	execute the previous command line containing str
r str=str2 cmd	!cmd:s/str1/str2/	substitute and execute last cmd

TABLE 6.5 Common Vi Command Editing*

Command	Mode	Description
`<Enter>`	I	Execute the command on the command line.
`<Esc>`	I	Enter command mode. When using the vi editor you have two different modes—an input mode where typed characters are actually entered on the line, and command mode where the editor takes the next character to be a special command that will act on the input text in some way.
`<Erase>`	I	Delete previous character.
`^w`	I	Delete previous word.
`^d`	I	Exit the current Shell. If this is your login Shell, then you will be logged off the system.
`a`	C	Add text following the current cursor position after returning to input mode.
`dd`	C	Delete the entire line.
`cc`	C	Delete entire line and return to input mode.
`i`	C	Insert text before the cursor position, return to input mode.
`[n] G`	C	Make line *n* the current line in the command history. If *n* is not provided, then look at the last entered command.
`u`	C	The previous command is undone and the command line is returned to its original state.
`?command_string`	C	Search for the command string in the command history file. The search is done in a forward direction. The first command in command history that contains the *command_string* is made the current line in the edit window.
`/command_string`	C	Search for the command string in the command history file. The search is done in a backward direction. The first command in command history that contains the *command_string* is made the current line in the edit window.

*Note that the mode is either I for input or C for command mode. The command shown is only effective when you are in that mode.

Processes may also be submitted to background so that you can hang up (log off the machine) and let the process continue. (All processes are killed otherwise.) The facility that allows this is called **nohup**:

```
nohup nightlyprocess&
15342
```

TABLE 6.6   Common Emacs Command Editing*

Command	Description
`^f`	Move the cursor forward one character.
`^b`	Move the cursor backward one character.
`M-f`	Move the cursor forward one word. (The escape version of the command usually acts on a word instead of a character.)
`M-b`	Move the cursor backward one word.
`^d`	Delete the current character.
`^k`	Kill from the current cursor position to the end of the line.
`^a`	Move cursor to the start of the line.
`^e`	Move cursor to the end of the line.
`^p`	Move to the previous command in the command history file. Repeated ^p commands continue to move backwards through the command history stack.
`^n`	Move to the next command in the command history file. Repeated ^n commands will continue to move forward in the command history file.
`^rcommand_string`	Search backward through the command history file for the first line that contains *command_string*. Note that you must hit Return after typing in the command string.

*The common emacs notation is used here where ^ is Ctrl and M- is escape.

Nohup stands for no hangup. It prevents the process from terminating when a user logs off. Any output generated by the command on either *stdout* or *stderr* is placed into a file called nohup.out, which can be examined later to determine the success or failure of the processing.

To be kind to your fellow UNIX users, the priority of any background processes should be lowered to speed up terminal response time. The Shell facility to lower priorities is called **nice**. It should be used as follows:

```
nice command arg1 arg2 arg3 ... &
nohup nice command arg1 ... &
```

Note that both **find** and **xargs** lend themselves to background execution. **For, while,** and **until** are more easily initiated in foreground. But they can be executed in background by use of parentheses, which cause the **for** command to be initiated in a separate subshell that is placed in the background:

```
( for file in *
do
  cp $file newdir
done
)&
2413
```

While and **until** loops can be initiated in background in the same fashion.

Some systems have a command that allows execution of commands at a specified time. The **at** command allows a UNIX user to execute commands at night, on weekends, or on holidays, without ever logging in to UNIX. It takes the following forms:

```
at 6pm nightlyprocess
at 6pm
nightlyprocess1
nightlyprocess2
cntl(d)
```

Nightlyprocess[12] will be executed at 6 P.M. with all of the user's characteristics. The **at** command is an excellent way to offload CPU- and I/O-intensive activities to the evenings or weekends. When you begin to experience degraded response time on a UNIX system, consider using **at** to reduce prime time system load.

Bourne Shell Job Control: The Bourne Shell uses **kill** and **wait** to control background jobs. There are times when you will need to kill a process:

```
kill $!    # Kill the last job placed in the background
2717 killed
```

Or you will need to wait on it to complete:

```
wait 2304
```

C Shell Job Control: The C Shell offers some additional job control features that can suspend background processes (**stop**) or switch them in and out of foreground: **bg** and **fg**. To stop a foreground process, either type stop or press Ctrl-z. To stop a background job, type:

```
stop %job
```

To pull a job back into foreground in csh, list the jobs using **jobs** and then select the job using % or **fg**:

```
jobs
1 find...
3 nohup...
%1
fg %1
```

Then you can send the job back with **%** or **bg**:

```
%1
bg %1
```

KSH

As you may have guessed, the Korn Shell also provides some nice job control extensions. It behaves a great deal like C Shell job control, but with some ease-of-use enhancements. The **jobs** command is used to display the stopped and background jobs that are currently active for your session. The list produced is used to manage the jobs using the other Korn Shell job management commands (**bg, fg, kill**). By using this list, you can tell the Shell which job to work with when using the other commands. After entering the command **jobs** at your terminal, you might see a display that looked something like the following:

```
jobs
[1]+ Stopped  emacs tester.c
[2]- Stopped  zap
[3] Running  counter
[4] Done  magic
```

The number in the brackets represents the job number associated with executing this UNIX process. You can use this job number to manage the jobs that you are executing. This is done by referring to %num wherever a job is called for in any of the Korn Shell job management commands. Suppose that we wanted to begin executing our emacs editing session again. This could be done by bringing the emacs edit session back to the foreground by entering the command

```
fg %1
```

In this case, the "%" symbol is a way to refer to a job number. Table 6.7 on page 161 outlines other ways to reference particular jobs when using the job control commands. In Table 6.7, the current job and previous job are indicated by the + and - designation shown in the preceding jobs printout. The + is the current job (the most recently stopped) and the - is the previously stopped job. The job control commands work with the current job when no job is indicated.

Fg Command

The **fg** (foreground) command is used to move a job that currently is stopped or is in the background to the foreground. This will make the job the currently active job associated with your log in. The foreground command has the following syntax:

```
fg [job_name]
```

where the *job_name* is any of the valid job names listed in Table 6.7. If no job_name is provided, then the current job name is used. For example, we could have started the emacs edit session listed in the preceding jobs list by entering just **fg** with no job number. Since the emacs job is the current job (as indicated by the +), it would be the job selected by the **fg** command. We could have specified any of the other jobs by providing a job identifier and that job would have become the current job. To move a job from the foreground to the background, issue the Ctrl-z command. This will place the currently active job in a stopped status.

Bg Command

The **bg** (background) command is used to move a job that is in a stopped status (using Ctrl-z) into the background for execution. The **bg** command has the following syntax:

```
bg [job_name]
```

where *job_name* can be a job number from the jobs list or a process number. If no *job_name* is provided, then the current job is moved into the background. The **fg** command can be used to return the command into the foreground.

Kill Command

When using the Korn Shell, the **kill** command is used to send a specified signal to a job. It has the following syntax:

```
kill [ -signal] job_name
```

The signal can be the name of any of the signal commands used in UNIX, or it can be the corresponding number that is related to the signal. The available signals and their related numbers are listed in Appendix E. The job can be identified using any of the methods outlined in Table 6.7. It can be a job number or a process number. If no signal is specified, then the TERM (software termination) signal is sent to the job, which will usually cause the job to terminate. There are many UNIX signals, and the way that any particular command responds can vary. However, most Shell commands respond and terminate when they receive the default TERM signal. Signal processing is covered in greater detail later in this chapter.

TABLE 6.7   Korn Shell Job Identifiers

Job Identifier	What It Represents
number	the UNIX process ID
% number	job control number printed by **jobs** command
%+	current job
%-	previous job

INTERACTIVE SHELL SUMMARY

Interactive Shell usage can be highly productive. It can extract and report useful information. It can repetitively perform complex processes on files, directories, or whatever. Use of repetitive procedures and background processing promotes productivity. Processing can even be delayed into non–prime time with commands such as **at**.

Interactive Shell helps test prototypes of new Shells. It can also be used to prototype C language programs to eliminate bugs before coding the commands in a more efficient form.

Once you begin using the Shell interactively and discover that many interactive processes require too much typing, it is time to learn about Shell programming — putting those interactive commands into an executable file that you can reuse to further improve your productivity.

Complex commands should be created as Shell procedures. Trying to perform complex activities interactively is usually frustrating because syntax errors can easily negate all of your typing. If you try an interactive command a couple of times without success, consider putting the whole thing into a Shell procedure that can be edited (using your favorite editor) and corrected as errors are uncovered.

WHEN TO CREATE SHELL PROGRAMS

You gain the most power from the Shell when you create a Shell program, commonly called Shell procedures, Shell programs, or just plain "Shells" for brevity. Create Shell programs (Figure 6.1) anytime you need to perform:

- a complex procedure using many command lines
- a procedure from which all users can benefit
- the same simple command over and over again

The advantage of Shell is that it has access to many small functional commands. These reusable commands can be combined to automate increasingly complex functions that you normally would do manually.

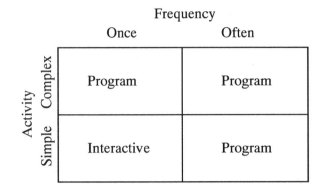

Figure 6.1   Interactive and Shell Programming

CREATING SHELL PROGRAMS

To create a Shell program, Shell commands are combined in various ways to accomplish the user's needs. This is the fun part. Users create procedures by entering Shell commands into a UNIX file via any of the available editors. To make the Shell file executable, all you have to do is change its mode:

```
chmod 755 shellproc
```

Rules of Thumb

1. Try each command line interactively, to make sure it works correctly.

2. Build the program using one of the editors interactively, one line at time, testing as you go.

Try each command line interactively, making sure that it works as expected. The following simple example extracts a user's name from the password file by login name and reports it:

```
grep lja /etc/passwd | cut -f5 -d:
Jay Arthur
```

If the field displacement or delimiter of the **cut** command had been wrong, I would have known it immediately. I can now include this command in a Shell procedure with faith that it works like I want it to.

You can execute commands directly from the vi editor as you create programs by typing:

```
:! shell_command
```

Then as you write your Shell program, you can test it right from vi by using the following:

```
:w
:!your_shell_program -options argument(s)
```

To make commands reusable, however, you will need to know about argument lists.

If you are using the emacs editor you can accomplish the same type of testing by opening a Shell window buffer in emacs, and when you receive a command line prompt you can enter the name of the command that you are building and testing. Emacs also supports a direct execution, much like vi, by using the **M-!** command (ESC-!).

Option and Argument Lists

Most Shell programs will need to have options and arguments on the command line, just like a typical Shell command:

```
command -options argument1 argument2 . . .
```

When creating a Shell procedure, you will probably want to pass it the name of one or more files or you will need to give it some special information to affect its processing. This can be done easily with options and arguments:

```
shell_program -a file1 file3 file5
shell_program -k "Jay Arthur" "lja"
```

The Shell recognizes each of these arguments and assigns them special variable names that can be accessed within the program—$1, $2, $3:

```
shell_program -a file1 file3 file5
  $0  $1  $2  $3  $4
```

These special variables were covered briefly in Chapter 5 (see Table 5.2) but deserve some more attention here. As you can see from the preceding example, each portion of the Shell command is assigned a default special variable name $0–$9. These variables can then be accessed in your Shell procedure to refer to the arguments passed. The $0 argument is always the name of the Shell program. The remainder of the variables ($1–$9) are the actual arguments the user of your Shell supplied. The number of arguments passed is stored in a special variable set by the Shell. The $# stores the count of the number of arguments passed. In the preceding example it would contain the value 4. This is useful in looping commands that access the arguments.

To edit each of these options and arguments, we can use much of what we have already learned about looping in the Shell:

```
edit_status=TRUE
for arg in $* # Loop through arguments
do
  case $arg # Process options
    -a)
      process option -a
      ;;
    -k)
      process option -k
      ;;
    *)
      if [ `echo $arg | cut -c1` = '-' ]
    then
        echo "Option: $1, invalid"
        edit_status=FALSE
      elif [ -f $arg ]
    then
        process $arg
    else
        echo "Invalid File Name $arg"
        edit_status=FALSE
    fi
    ;;
  esac
done
exit ${edit_status}
```

In this example, I edited all of the arguments to the command (rather than edit until I found one problem and then exit). Then, at the end, I checked for a valid status to decide whether to exit or continue processing the program.

The Shell variables ($1, $2, $3, etc.) can be changed as they are used by use of the **shift** command. **Shift** moves each argument ($1 through $#) to the left, changing the previous argument list as follows:

```
shell_program file3 file5
  $0   $1   $2
```

Shift is used with WHILE loops to process arguments:

```
while [ "$1" ]    csh: while ( "$1" != "" )
do                        ...
  process $1
  shift
done                      end
```

This example processes each argument and then shifts the remaining arguments. When there are no more arguments, **test** will return a false value to the **while** loop and the command will exit successfully. **Shift** makes looping through arguments simple and straightforward. **Shift** is also useful when processing two or more arguments at a time:

```
while [ "$1" -a "$2" ]        while ( "$1" != "" && "$2" !="" )
do
  process $1 $2
  shift;shift
done                          end
```

It should be noted that the Bourne Shell only allows for the arguments $0-$9. If you have more than nine arguments, then you must use **shift** to access the arguments beyond the $9. The Shell will not recognize $10 as an argument reference. It will interpret this as the $1 followed by the 0 character.

KSH

The Korn Shell does permit the direct reference to variables beyond $9 by using the numbers $10-$99. The only restriction here is that the variables beyond $9 must be enclosed in braces to retain consistency with the Bourne Shell. So to access variable $10 in your Shell program it must be written as ${10}.

There are two other Shell variables that reference the arguments $1 through $#—$* and $@. These are used when one Shell procedure invokes another with the argument list. The two are almost identical except in how they pass the arguments when they are quoted—$* passes all of the arguments to the receiving command as a single argument:

```
shell_program file?
# shell_program
rm "$*"
```

is the same as

```
rm "file1 file3 file5"
```

$@ passes the arguments as they were originally specified so that the command can work properly:

```
rm "$@"
```

is the same as

```
rm "file1" "file3" "file5"
```

If the executed command had been another Shell procedure instead of a **remove** command, that procedure's arguments would have varied as follows:

```
subshell "$*"
(subshell "file1 file3 file5")
$1 = "file1 file3 file5"
```

The following substitution would have occurred using $@:

```
subshell "$@"
(subshell "file1" "file3" "file5")
$1 = file1 $2 = file3 $3 = file5
```

The $* form is useful with **echo** to display all of the arguments:

```
echo "$*"
file1 file3 file5
```

Without the double quotes, **$*** and **$@** are equivalent, but these two can cause confusion and problems, so be careful.

Arguments to a Shell program should be edited using either the IF-THEN-ELSE construct for single arguments or the CASE construct for programs with more than one argument. Editing arguments helps improve a program's reliability.

A Shell program that expects a single argument, perhaps a file name, should test for too many arguments and for a valid file name:

```
if [ $# -eq 1 ]                       if ( $#argv = 1 ) then
then
  if [ -f $1 ]                          if ( -f $1 ) then
  then
    process $1                            process $1
  else                                  else
    echo "$1 invalid file name"           ...
  fi                                    endif
else                                  else
    echo "$0 syntax: $0 filename"         ...
fi                                    endif
```

Most Shell programs, however, will have many options and files. One special command, **getopt,** can parse **$*** and separate flags when they have been clumped together by a user (e.g., -abct is actually -a -b -c -t). Some utility programs work

this way, so it can be useful to design commands to handle users this way. To use
getopt, you simply reset the Shell's positional parameters (**$***) by supplying a
string of options:

```
set `getopt abct $*`
```

Once the positional parameters have been reset using **getopt,** a program with
more than one argument can use the CASE construct to handle the argument edits:

```
case $# in                              switch ($#argv)
  0) # oops no arguments                    case 0:
    echo enter argument1                        ...
    read arg1
    echo enter argument2
    read arg2
    ;;                                      breaksw
  2)                                          case 2:
    arg1=$1                                      ...
    arg2=$2
    ;;                                      breaksw
  *)                                          default:
    echo "$0 syntax: $0 arg1 arg2"
    ;;                                      breaksw
esac                                    endsw
```

Or a program may expect a series of options as well as file names or whatever.
Options should be separated from the remaining arguments:

```
while [ `echo $1 | cut -c1` = "-" ]
do
  case $1 in
    -a|-b|-c)
      options="${options} $1"
    ;;
    *)
      echo "$1 is not a valid option"
    ;;
  esac
  shift
done
```

Then, the tests for the remaining arguments can be performed using the CASE
construct or IF-THEN-ELSE. Editing arguments is an important part of building
reliable Shell programs.

When creating a Shell procedure, you will probably want to pass it the name of one or more files, or you will need to give it some special information to affect its processing. This can be done easily with options and arguments.

KSH

In addition to this manual method, which in the Bourne Shell is the best method, the Korn Shell also provides a more automated way of accessing and processing the arguments passed. This is done through the **getopts** command. This is the Korn Shell version of the UNIX **getopt** command and should be used in place of the UNIX command wherever possible. This new Korn Shell version is more powerful and also functions as a built-in command instead of a UNIX call.

The **getopts** command is used to parse argument lists passed to a Shell in a standard manner. The syntax of the **getopts** command is:

```
getopts options_str opt_variable [args .. ]
```

The **getopts** function was designed to handle all of the various forms of command-line options used when executing Shell and UNIX commands. For example, a typical UNIX or Shell command that accepts command-line arguments can take those arguments in various forms as shown:

```
grep -bi group file.test
```

or

```
grep -b -i group file.test
```

The **getopts** command parses the argument list and allows the Shell program to examine its arguments in an organized and consistent way no matter which order a user inputs options. The Shell program need only utilize the **getopts** command, and the flexibility of specifying options on the command line is automatically provided. **Getopts** provides this functionality by utilizing a few standard variables and information passed to the command in your Shell program.

In order to utilize the **getopts** command, you must specify which command-line options are valid. This is done by providing a string of legal options for the command in the options_str. For example, if we were to use the string "abcf: " for options_str in the **getopts** command, we are telling **getopts** to accept the options -a, -b, -c, and -f followed by any argument (such as a filename). The colon (:) following an option specifies, as was illustrated by the previous example, that a variable has arguments or groups of arguments. If the options_str begins with a colon, then the **getopts** command allows your Shell program to handle illegal options (options entered by the user but not in the options_str). This is described in the next paragraph. If you don't specify a colon at the start of the options_str, then **getopts** provides a standard error message when an illegal option is entered.

Each time that **getopts** is called (you are responsible for calling it until all command line arguments are parsed), it parses the options and provides the next option to you in the variable named in opt_variable in the **getopts** command. Let's take a look at another example:

```
getopts :xyzf: $BULL_ARG
```

Now each time we call **getopts** it will return the options passed to the Shell program, provided they are valid options listed in options_str, into the variable $BULL_ARG. If the variable $BULL_ARG does not exist, then **getopts** creates it. If the option is preceded by a minus sign (–), then only the option letter appears in $BULL_ARG. But if the option was preceded by a plus sign (+), sign then $BULL_ARG contains the + followed by the option letter. If your options_str indicates error checking, as the string does in the example by preceding all options by a colon (:), then an illegal option assigns a value of ? to $BULL_ARG.

In conjunction with passing your program the option that was just parsed, the **getopts** command also sets two global variables—$OPTIND and $OPTARG. OPTIND tells you which option indicator will be processed next, and OPTARG holds the arguments for the option parsed. For example, if a user had called the Shell containing the **getopts** command listed previously using the command

```
foo -f "stuff"
```

then the variable $OPTARG would contain "stuff" when $BULL_ARG contained "f".

The optional args that can be passed to **getopts** indicate that you would like **getopts** to parse the parameters found in the string. If you do not provide an argument (the usual case), then the standard positional parameters are parsed ($1, $2, etc.). Often if an argument is provided, then it is the special Shell variables "$*" or "$@".

The main function of **getopts** is to read options and arguments passed to your Shell program by a user. This is usually done by putting the **getopts** command into a **while** loop in conjunction with a CASE statement. This is demonstrated by the following Shell program called showopts:

```
USAGE="showopts [-q] quit mode [-v] verbose mode(default) [-h] \
   help -f filename"
  while getopts :qvf: h WHICH_OPTION
    do
      case $WHICH_OPTION in
        q ) echo "You selected the option $WHICH_OPTION indicating\
          Shell is in quit mode"
```

```
        echo "No messages will be displayed during Shell execution"
        Q_MODE=1;;
        v) echo "You selected the option $WHICH_OPTION indicating \
           Shell is in verbose mode"
        echo "All informational and error messages will be \
           displayed"
        V_MODE=1;;
          f) echo " You selected to work with file named \
             $OPTARG";;
          h) echo "You selected the help option. The format of \
             this command is $USAGE"
        exit(-1);;
            ?) echo "$USAGE"
               exit(-1);;
    esac
  done
  if (( [ Q_MODE -eq 1] && [V_MODE -eq 1])
  then
    echo "Quit mode and verbose mode are exclusive of each other; \
       pick one or the other"
    exit(-1)
  fi
```

Now if we enter the following command, let's see what happens:

```
showopts -q -f FRED

You selected the option q indicating Shell is in quit mode
No messages will be displayed during Shell execution
You selected to work with file named FRED
```

Variables in Shell Programs

Assigning values to variables is an important feature of creating Shell procedures. Previous chapters showed how variables work with control structures (IF-THEN-ELSE, CASE, FOR, UNTIL, and WHILE). The Bourne and Korn Shells assign variables differently than the C Shell does. The C Shell requires the user to **set** variables, while the Bourne and Korn Shell allows simple assignment:

```
variable=value        set variable=value
```

Shell users can also create variables to improve maintainability and reusability of the procedure. A simple example involves keeping all of the boilerplate for documents — letters, memos, forms, whatever — in a unique directory. To allow for future changes in the directory name on various systems, you might create a variable that points to the boilerplate directory:

```
docdir="/unixfs/boilerplate"
```

Then, create a Shell called getdoc that selectively retrieves boilerplate from the directory:

```
# getdoc
docdir="/unixfs/boilerplate"
if [ -r ${docdir}/$1 ]
then
  cp ${docdir}/$1 $2
  echo "$1 boilerplate created as $2"
else
  echo "$1 boilerplate not found in ${docdir}"
  echo "Valid templates are:"
  ls ${docdir}
fi
```

Setting and using the variable *docdir* ensures that the command can later be changed to point to other directories on other machines by changing only the variable assignment, not the entire procedure. Using variables for path names is definitely desirable: They are easily maintained and more reliable.

A common problem with new Shells is that variables are referenced before they are assigned a value. To counter the effects of this problem, the Shell can be told to treat unset variables as fatal errors:

```
set -u
```

Or, you can specify a default value for a variable:

```
if [ -d ${docdir:=/unixfs/boilerplate} ]
```

The Shell checks to see if docdir has a value; if so it uses it, otherwise, it uses /unixfs/boilerplate. Having meaningful defaults for variables means never having to say you're sorry. They prevent improper operation of the Shell. For example, suppose that you had a command that did the following:

```
cd $temp
rm -rf *
```

If *$temp* has no value, the Shell will change to $HOME and remove all of your files. This could have been avoided by using a default value of /tmp:

```
cd ${temp:=/tmp}
rm -rf *
```

which would only remove those files in /tmp that belong to your user ID.

Variables can also be set to the output of Shell commands by use of the accent grave characters (backwards apostrophe). For example:

```
cmdpath=/usr/bin/nroff           set cmdpath=/usr/bin/nroff
dirname=`basename ${cmdpath}`    set dirname=`basename \
                                   ${cmdpath}`
echo $dirname                     echo $dirname
/usr/bin                          /usr/bin
```

The **set** command can also be used to set the command variables ($1, $2, $3, etc.). To set these variables to all of the file names in the current directory, use the following command:

```
set - *
```

To set $1 to a new value, **set** can also be used as follows:

```
set - "new value for $1" "new value for $2" . . .
```

Another ability of the Shell involves setting variables *before* execution using the command line:

```
var1=value var2=value command -options argument1 argument2 . . .
```

Although this may not sound very exciting at first, we could use it to act like a mail merge — adding names and addresses to a letter before printing:

```
name="Jay Arthur" address="Radio Free Denver CO" l_print \
  query_letter
# l_print
sed -e "s/name/${name}/g" -e "s/address/${address}/g" $1 | nroff
```

In this example, I set the variables *name* and *address* before executing the command **l_print.** Within **l_print,** I had access to these two variables, used them with **sed** to change query_letter, and then formatted and printed the letter with **nroff.** This is one of many ways that presetting variables can be used in the Shell.

Variables are an important part of writing good Shell procedures. They can be assigned both string and numeric values from any source, including the output of other Shell commands. Put them all together with arguments, commands, and control structures, and you have the ability to manipulate files into any required format.

Built-in Commands in Shell Programs

The Shell uses certain commands that are built in. The Bourne, Korn, and C Shell built-in commands were shown in Table 4.6. The commands **break, cd, exit, export, set, shift,** and **test** have been demonstrated in prior examples. Of equal importance are the **eval, exec, read,** and **wait** commands.

The **eval** command lets the user build command strings and then use them as if they were part of the Shell program. For example, a complicated Shell command might have to determine the proper input and output filters for a given command. Rather than execute the command many different ways, the Shell could create a variable containing the correct input filters and one containing the proper output filters. The complete command could be evaluated and executed as follows:

```
inputfilter="cmd1 | cmd2"
outputfilter="cmd3 | cmd4"
eval "$inputfilter | command | $outputfilter"
```

which would be the equivalent of executing the commands:

```
cmd1 | cmd2 | command | cmd3 | cmd4
```

Using **eval** can increase the flexibility of many Shell programs by allowing you to dynamically create Shell commands based on user input. The overall net effect of the **eval** command is that the line passed to **eval** is scanned by the Shell two times. First substitution is performed and then the line is evaluated again to determine the Shell line that is to be executed. For example, let's say that we had built the following line of Shell code in the variable OUTPUT, based on some information provided by the user, and then try to use this portion of code in conjunction with the **cat** command:

```
OUTPUT=" maxfact > maxfactout"
cat $OUTPUT
```

Here are the results of the maximum factor calculation:

```
cat: cannot open >
cat: cannot open maxfactout
```

As you can see, the Shell performed the substitution of $OUTPUT, but then the redirection symbol was not properly evaluated. You can use **eval** to perform the evaluation of the redirection operator:

```
OUTPUT=" maxfact > maxfactout"
eval cat $OUTPUT
```

This time the output is redirected to the file maxfactout because of the double evaluation caused by **eval**.

The **exec** command will execute a command in place of the current command without creating a new process. The Shell that currently is running is replaced and the new command runs in its place without any subshell being created. This is occasionally useful if control need never return to the parent Shell and can reduce the number of processes running on your machine. A more useful form reads a Shell program as input and executes the commands as if they were part of the current Shell program:

```
. shell_module        source shell_module
```

This facility encourages modularity (a key quality design goal of all software) and helps to encourage reuse of Shell programs. The Shell code in shell_module is reusable by any Shell program that needs it. Reusability, in turn, can reduce maintenance costs — rather than fixing ten versions of the same code, only one module need be changed.

The **read** command gets a line from standard input. In most cases, *stdin* will be a terminal. The **read** command is the main input mechanism you will use in your Shell programs. The syntax of the **read** command is:

```
read [var_name ... ]
```

Each word read from the standard input is assigned to the variables listed as var_name. If there is more input than variable names, then the last variable named in the list var_name receives the remainder of the input. The **read** command returns an exit code of zero unless it detects an end-of-file condition. If the user is entering input from the terminal, then the Ctrl-d sequence indicates the end-of-file condition.

In most Shell programs, if the user does not enter the correct number of arguments, it is better to ask for them than to exit and demand that they be entered on the command line. A combination of **echo** and **read** handles the job nicely:

```
if [ $# -eq 0 ]
then
  echo "Enter filename"
  read filename
else
  filename=$1
fi
```

Read can also get a line of input from a file or pipe used as standard input:

```
shellcommand < file
```

or

```
command | shellcommand
# shellcommand
while read inputline
do
  process inputline
done
```

This could also be handled by the **line** command, although **read,** because it is built in, is faster:

```
while inputline=`line`
etc.
```

The **read** command is a handy function to get information from the standard input and assign the result to a variable that can then be handled like any other.

KSH

The Korn Shell provides some extensions to the **read** command that increase its flexibility. The major enhancement provided is the ability to read from files other than the standard input. The syntax of the **read** command is:

```
read [ -prsu[n] ] [name ? prompt] [var_name ...]
```

where the -p and -u options have the following meaning:

-p   Read from the input pipe of a process spawned using |&. If an end of file is read, then the spawned process is cleaned up so that another can be spawned.

-u [n]   Read from the file associated with file descriptor n. If n is not supplied, then 0 is used.

As with the Bourne Shell version, the Korn Shell reads from standard input unless the -p or the -u option is used. The -p and -u options provide the ability for a single Shell procedure to read input from more than a single file. If no variable names are provided to place the read input into, then the Korn Shell uses a default variable REPLY to store what was read. Another enhancement provided is the prompt string option. If the first variable named in the var_name list is followed by a ?, then the **read** command will use the prompt string to prompt the user for input.

The **wait** command, as its name implies, waits for a background process to complete before continuing. A Shell program might start a background process, do some other processing, and then have to wait for the background process (or processes) to complete before continuing. **Wait** is a patient command:

```
command&    # Put the command in background
```

other Shell commands

```
wait $-     # Wait for the last background command to finish
wait        # Wait for all background commands to finish
```

continue processing.

Wait, like the rest of these built-in commands, meets special needs of the Shell programmer. They help make it simple to build useful Shell procedures.

HOW THE SHELL FINDS COMMANDS

Most Shell commands reside in directories called "bins" — /bin and /usr/bin. Others, important only to the system administrator, reside in /etc, /usr/rje, and /usr/adm. Of course, you can create your own bin directories to store all your Shell procedures. In fact, the directory can really be any valid UNIX directory name, but it is customary to place Shell programs in directories called bin. The only stipulation is that the Shell procedure stored in the directory must have its mode changed to executable. For the majority of users, the commands available in /bin and /usr/bin will be of most importance. The /usr/ucb bin contains the Berkeley 4.2 BSD commands. On Berkeley systems, System V commands can be found in /usr/5bin.

When a user logs in, the Shell sets up a standard environment using several variables (refer to Table 5.5). As was discussed in previous chapters, the Shell uses the PATH (sh, ksh) or path (csh) variable to find each directory path that should be searched to find commands. The PATH variable is initialized at login time. To find out the default paths available, try the following command:

```
echo $PATH          echo $path
:/bin:/usr/bin:     . /bin /usr/bin
```

The response means that you have all of the standard Shell commands available for execution. The Shell uses the PATH variable to determine where to search for commands and in what order you want to search the bins. The current value of PATH indicates that the Shell will search first the current directory, then /bin, and finally /usr/bin. The current directory is represented by a null name, followed by a colon. You can change the order of the search by redefining the value of PATH as follows:

```
PATH=/usr/bin:/bin::        set path=( . /usr/bin /bin )
```

which reverses the order of the search.

If you had a user bin under your home directory, you might add it to the search path using another Shell variable, HOME:

```
PATH=${PATH}:${HOME}/bin        set path=( ${path} ${HOME}/bin )
```

Using my log in as an example, this would change the value of PATH to:

```
/usr/bin:/bin::/unix1/lja/bin
```

Whenever I execute a command, the Shell will look first in /usr/bin, then /bin (the current directory), and finally my user bin. This means that I can type a command name and the Shell will find it; I do not have to type in the full path name to use a command I have created. This is an important feature of the Shell that helps improve productivity; bins full of user commands can be placed anywhere in the system and be accessed directly via the PATH variable.

The system administrator can redefine PATH to include common user bins by inserting the following two lines into /etc/profile:

```
PATH=:/bin:/usr/bin:/local/bin
                        set path=( . /bin /usr/bin /local/bin )
export PATH
```

The **export** command makes the PATH variable available to all subsequent processes initiated by the user.

Because users would rather not change the PATH variable during every session, the user may further modify the PATH variable automatically at login time. PATH can be modified using either /etc/profile (usually done by the system administrator) or the .profile in the user's home directory. In a C Shell system, PATH can be modified in the user's .login or .cshrc files, which reside in the user's home directory. You can create the .profile (csh: .login/.cshrc) file in your HOME directory and add the following two lines to include your own command bin:

```
PATH=${PATH}:${HOME}/bin
export PATH
```

These two lines will add your bin to the Shell's search path. The Shell can now automatically look in all command bins to find any command you request. Problems can occur, however, if there are two commands with the same name in different bin directories; the Shell will execute the first one it finds. This is especially important in systems that have all three Shells. Not all System V commands behave like Berkeley commands. To obtain System V commands, put them first in the PATH variable. On Berkeley UNIX systems, reverse the positions of /usr/5bin and /usr/ucb:

```
PATH=:/bin:/usr/bin:/usr/5bin:/usr/ucb
                    set path=(. /bin /usr/bin /usr/ucb /usr/5bin )
```

There is a command in the Bourne Shell, the **type** command, that will allow you to see which version of a command is being executed by the Shell. It will echo back the full path name used to locate the command as well as what type of command was entered as an argument. It is convenient when the command does not appear to be doing what you think it should be doing and you want to see where it is being executed from. For example, if we had a Shell procedure proj_status and we wanted to see where the Shell was executing this command from, we would enter the **type** command:

```
type proj_status
proj_stat is /usr/tburns/shellpgms/proj_stat
```

As you can see, the full path the Shell used to locate the command is printed. This eliminates confusion over exactly which command is being executed. The **type** command will also tell you if the command is a built-in command or if it is a hashed command.

```
type test
test is a shell builtin
```

KSH

The Korn Shell provides the **whence** command to find the path name used to locate commands. **Whence** is similar to the **type** command but offers an option that is not supported by the Bourne Shell. The -v option provides information about the command much like the **type** command does. But the **whence** command used alone will provide just the full path name used to locate the command and can be used as input to another command. This cannot be done using the **type** command. The following command would allow the emacs editor to be loaded on the script proj_status:

```
whence proj_status
/usr/tburns/shellpgms/proj_stat
emacs `whence proj_status`
```

As was mentioned, the -v option provides verbose output about what type of command was passed as an argument:

```
whence -v proj_status
proj_stat is a tracked alias for /usr/tburns/shellpgms/proj_stat
```

The **whence** command provides information about what type of command was passed even when the -v option is not provided. It will report whether the command is a regular command, a function, or an alias, or is unknown to the Shell. The response provided depends on the type of command. A normal command causes **whence** to respond with the full path name of the command. If the command passed is an alias, then the alias is echoed to the screen. A function passed as an argument causes **whence** to respond with just the name of the function. Finally, if the command is not known, then no response is provided. For example, the alias *r* gets the following response from the **whence** command:

```
whence r
fc -e -
```

That's about all you need to know about the PATH variable. If you execute a command but it doesn't behave like the documentation, you might suspect that PATH is pointing to libraries in the wrong order. Or if you type a command name and the Shell issues an error message saying that the command cannot be found, check your PATH variable to ensure that is pointing where you believe the commands exist.

The Bourne and Korn Shells also use an environment variable, CDPATH, with the **cd** command to reduce typing. The user can set up CDPATH in his or her .profile to include any of his or her major directories. Then, no matter where the directory is, all the user has to do is **cd** to the directory name and the Shell remembers where those directories are and changes to them without extensive typing. For example, if there was an entry in the .profile as follows:

```
CDPATH=$HOME/doc
export CDPATH
```

and you are already in the /usr/bin directory, you could change into the doc directory by typing:

```
cd doc
```

The directories can also be listed like the PATH variable to give immediate access to any of the major directories:

```
CDPATH=$HOME/bin:$HOME/doc:$HOME/src
export CDPATH
```

Using the **cd** command, the user can change from one directory to another without typing long path names. The Shell will print the path name of the directory it has changed into:

```
cd doc
/unix1/lja/doc
```

SHELL PROGRAMMING

To illustrate the prior facilities and concepts, let's develop a few Shells, ranging from simple to complex.

The **who** command tells who is logged on to the system at any time, but it only tells the person's login ID, not his or her name. This information is in the password file, but not in a form that can easily be used. Let's develop a command, called **whois,** to extract the user's name from the password file and print only the relevant information.

First, we need to extract the user ID from the /etc/passwd file and then extract only the person's name. **Whois** will have the following form:

```
# whois userid
if [ $# -eq 0 ]                                    if( $# == 0)
then
# No user ids supplied
  echo "Enter userid"
  read userid
else
  userid=$1
fi
grep $userid /etc/passwd | cut -f5 -d:
whois lja
Jay Arthur
```

To make this command work on more than one user ID, it could be modified as follows:

```
# whois userid(s)
if [ $# -eq 0 ]
then
# No user ids supplied
  echo "Enter userid"
  read userid
  grep $userid /etc/passwd | cut -f5 -d:
else
  while [ "$1" ]
  do
    grep $1 /etc/passwd | cut -f5 -d:
  done
fi
```

The command could be made more efficient by using **egrep** and pasting all of the arguments together as follows:

```
# whois userid(s)
if [ $# -eq 0 ]
then
# No user ids supplied
  echo "Enter userid"
  read userid
else
  userid=`echo $* | sed -e "s/ /\|/g"`
fi
egrep $userid /etc/passwd | cut -f5 -d:
```

Another simple Shell procedure might need to look through all directories
under the current one and execute commands entered by the user. This command
should also trap interrupts (discussed in more detail later in the chapter) and allow
processing to continue:

```
# dirsearch [ directory name ]
# Search the specified directory for other directories
# In each one, prompt the user for commands to be executed.
if [ -d "$1" ]
then
  cd $1                        # Change directory to $1
else
  dir=`pwd`                    # dir=current directory
  for file in *                # All files in directory
  do
    if [ -d $file ]            # Directory ?
  then
      cd ${dir}/${file}
      while echo "${file} ?"
      trap "exit 0" 1 2 3
      read cmd                 # Read command
    do
      trap "" 1 2 3
        eval $cmd $file        # Execute command
      done
      cd ..
    fi
  done
fi
```

Another simple but useful command displays information on the screen a
page at a time. Using **cat** to display a file often causes the important information

to disappear before the user can hit the no scroll key. Simple commands to display pages on 25-line terminals are **more** and **pg**. The same can be accomplished with **pr**:

```
pr -p -t -123 filename    # Pause every 23 lines
more filename
pg filename
```

But on other occasions, it would be nice to page through the output of another command:

```
nroff -cm document | more
```

These can be combined into a single Shell that handles whatever it's given:

```
# Page [files]
case $# in
  0)
# If the terminal is standard input and
# There are no arguments
# Prompt for a file name
  if [ -t 0 ] # Standard input is a terminal
  then
    echo "What file? "
    read filename
      more ${filename:=/dev/null}
  else    # Read from standard input
      more <&0
  fi
    ;;
  *)
    while [ "$1" ]
    do
      clear
      more $1
      shift
    done
    ;;
esac
```

Another example involves a directory that contains files or commands spooled by another command. If the first line of each file contains a header line with the user's ID and other information, the user can check the status of those jobs as follows:

```
# Status
spooldir=/usr/spool/whatever
cd ${spooldir}
( for files in *         # All files in spool directory
  do
    line < ${files}      # Read first line
  done
) | grep ${LOGNAME}      # grep userid from first lines
```

In this example, **line** will extract the first line of each file in /usr/spool/whatever. Because the FOR loop is enclosed in parentheses, all of the output from each of the **line** commands is placed on *stdout*. Instead of many separate streams of information, the Shell combines the output of each of the **line** commands into a single stream that can be piped into **grep**. **Grep** then looks through the stream for header lines that match the user's login name, ${LOGNAME}.

Another simple need of a Shell user would be to execute a series of commands, but execute them at intervals so that the system's other users would notice little degradation. The program, **today,** to read a command from an input file and execute it at 15-minute intervals, would look like this:

```
# nohup today commandfile&
exec 0< $1              # Open commandfile as stdin
while
  read cmd              # Get line from commandfile
  test -n "${cmd}"
do
  eval ${cmd}           # Execute command
  sleep 900             # Sleep 15 minutes
done
```

The possibilities for creating useful commands seems endless. It requires some ingenuity to pick the best combination of commands, pipes, redirection, and Shell constructs to build a new Shell, but with a little experience it is easy. One of the best ways to get new ideas is to study the Shells that come with UNIX—those in /bin, /usr/bin, and /usr/ucb/bin.

Handling Error Conditions

There are two major types of error conditions that you should check for in your Shell script if it is to be well behaved and of high quality. First, there are internal errors in your script itself. This is generally caused by some command's failing to perform as expected or the user's not providing the necessary information to the Shell program. The second type of error is an external error that the Shell procedure must respond to properly. These types of errors are sent to your Shell procedure in the form of a signal sent by the system telling you that some system-level event has occurred that will have an effect on your Shell procedure. An example of this would be if the user of your Shell procedure hangs up while in the middle of processing. Quality Shell procedures handle these events in a reasonable way (when possible) and take action based on the event that occurred. In the sections that follow we will look at each type of error condition and what you should do to handle them.

Internal Errors

User-Error Conditions

User-error conditions are unique and need to be tested for on a case-by-case basis. In general, you need to ensure that the user is not allowed to provide invalid input that will cause the Shell to behave incorrectly. A quality Shell program will always tell the user some meaningful error message when an incorrect action is performed. It should also provide a means to allow the user to correct the action if at all possible. Well-designed user interface is the key to developing useful Shell procedures. An integral part of a well-designed user interface is the quality of error messages provided as well as the degree to which the Shell procedure protects the user from erroneous input that will cause problems in the procedure. A good first step, as is demonstrated by several of the preceding Shell program examples, is to always check the options and arguments passed to the Shell to ensure that there are no invalid arguments or options. This can best be done by using the **getopt** command if you are a Bourne user or the **getopts** command if you are a Korn Shell user. The **getopts** command provides a foundation for defining how the user will input options and arguments and provides a foundation for parsing those options and arguments in your Shell procedure.

Command Failures

Another error that can occur in your Shell procedure is some unexpected command failure. For example, perhaps your Shell procedure needs to copy a UNIX file to obtain some information that will be used in processing. If this file no longer exists, then you will not be able to continue processing properly. You will need to check to ensure that you copy the file properly; otherwise, the results of later processing by the Shell command may be unpredictable. Each time a Shell command is executed, the special variable $? is set to the return status of the command. This provides you with the ability to check and ensure that the command worked properly. By convention, a command returns zero when it was properly executed and a non-zero value when it has not. Any time you execute a critical command in your Shell procedure you should check to be sure that it returned a zero return code. If it did not, then you should take some reasonable error action. As a side note, your Shell procedures should try to follow the same convention. If your Shell finished properly, then you should return a zero. Providing this type of standardization makes your Shell more reusable by both you and others. As an example of checking the return code, let's look at the following copy statement Shell fragment. The **cp** command returns 0 when the copy was completed successfully and a non-zero return code otherwise.

```
cp /shellpgms/var_skel .    # Copy the skeleton file to the
                            # current directory
if [ $? != 0 ]
  then
    echo "Sorry the Shell program was unable to copy file \
      /shellpgms/var_skel \n"
    echo " to your current directory - \
      The Shell program cannot continue\n"
    exit 1    # Exit the Shell and return an invalid return code
fi
```

Now if the copy command did not work properly, the user will get an error message indicating that the Shell procedure cannot continue. It would also be possible to check for error conditions using the **test** command to ensure that the files and directories to be copied from and to exist. This can be done before the copy command itself. The real point to be made is that you should check the status of every critical command in your Shell procedure to be sure that it worked as you expected it to work.

External Errors

Signals and the Trap Command

The second type of error is an error that occurs externally to your Shell process. Certain kinds of actions by the user and the system can cause errors that will interrupt your Shell program. These errors are captured by the UNIX system and are passed to your process as a "signal." The system is signaling your Shell procedure (a UNIX process) that there is a problem and some action may need to be taken. This action can be any valid Shell action, or it may be no action at all. You control how your Shell procedure will respond in each case.

The **trap** command lets you handle signals: phone lines hanging up, breaks, deletes, kill commands, and many others. Each of these is a *signal* described in Section 2 of the UNIX User's Manual under signal(2). Some of the more common interrupt signals are listed in Table 6.8. Note that this is not a complete list of signals. For a list of all signals, please see Appendix E under the **kill** command.

The Shell **trap** command allows you to decide which signals you want to handle and the action that should be performed when a particular signal is "caught" by your Shell program. The syntax of the **trap** command is shown as:

```
trap [ command_list] [signal_list]
```

TABLE 6.8   Common Interrupt Signals

Signal Name	Signal Number	Description
EXIT	0	exit from the Shell procedure
SIGHUP	01	hangup (user disconnects in some way)
SIGINT	02	interrupt (user hits Del key on keyboard)
SIGQUIT	03	quit (user hits Ctrl - \ on most keyboards)
SIGKILL	09	kill (cannot be caught or ignored)
SIGALRM	14	alarm clock
SIGTERM	15	software termination signal (default sent by **kill** command)

where the command_list is a Shell command(s) to be performed when the Shell receives any of the signals found in signal_list. In the case of the Bourne Shell, the signal must be a numeric value. Using the Korn Shell, it is possible to refer to all signals by the string name arguments shown in the above table. The **trap** command with no arguments will provide a list of all existing traps that have been set. Please note that it is not possible to trap a signal 11 (memory fault) or a signal 9 (sure kill). A signal 9 is designed to be a critical signal that ensures some method for killing a UNIX process that otherwise won't complete properly. The default action for all signals, if you do not specifically take some other action using the **trap** command, is to terminate the Shell program and exit. So if you choose not to trap some particular signal, your Shell procedure will terminate with no action taken. While not the most graceful way to leave your Shell procedure, the default action may be appropriate in some cases. In most cases, though, you will want to catch a signal and take some sort of reasonable action, such as cleaning up files and exiting properly.

Most often, when the Shell receives a signal, you will want to remove all temporary files and exit gracefully with a return code. This is accomplished by executing the following command:

```
trap (rm tmp*;exit 0) 1 2 3 14 15
```

When the Shell receives a hangup (1), interrupt (2), quit (3), alarm (14), or software termination (15) signal, it will remove the temporary files (**rm tmp***) and exit with a false value (**exit 0**). In other cases, the command may be working on many files and you would like to know where to restart the command:

```
trap (echo ${filename} > stopfile; exit 0) 1 2 3 14 15
```

Stopfile will contain the name of the last file used by the command.

In addition to taking some particular action, it is also possible to ignore a signal by taking no action at all. If you specify a null string for the commands to be executed, then the Shell will trap the signals specified and take no action at all. Your Shell will continue to execute as if it had not received any signal. This can be useful when you do not want a Shell procedure to be interrupted at some critical stage of processing. You could decide to ignore the interrupt signal by using the following statement:

```
trap "" 1 2 3
```

Actually, this statement ignores signals 1, 2, and 3. These are the most common methods a user uses to stop a Shell that is processing. In general, you will want to allow the user a way to stop the Shell from processing, but in certain cases you will want to ensure that the Shell is not stopped unless it absolutely must. In these cases, the ignore trap is a very useful tool.

It is also possible, as you may already have determined, to change how a trap behaves at particular points in your program. As was discussed, we might want to ignore some signals for certain portions of our Shell program but then reset them back to some other action after the critical code has completed.

```
trap "" 1 2 3                  # Ignore user interruptions
  do some critical processing
trap 1                         # Reset trap for signal 1 back to
                               # default action, leave temp files
trap (rm tmp*;exit 0) 2 3      # Remove temp files if user exits
```

Note that the **trap** command without any command resets the trap to the default action, which is to terminate and exit with a return code of 0. This is not the same as the null command, which causes the Shell to ignore a signal.

By setting a trap for a signal 0, you can specify some action that is always to be performed when the Shell procedure exits with a 0 return code. This can be useful for cleanup routines or just to issue a message of some kind.

```
trap "echo The Shell procedure has completed properly \
  with no errors" 0
```

One other note about the **trap** command: If a Shell ignores a signal, then all subshells also ignore that signal. If, however, a Shell takes some action based on a signal, then all subshells take the default action on that signal. In other words, trap actions are not inherited by subshells.

These are simple examples, but every Shell command should clean up after itself and take some meaningful action when interrupted. **Trap** encourages the active rather than passive handling of signals.

Trap is not available in the C Shell, but a similar command, **onintr**, handles trapping signals and takes remedial action.

KSH

The Korn Shell adds a few nice features to the **trap** command. First, the signals can be listed by name as well as by number. In place of omitting the command to reset the trap action to its default, it is permissible to use "-" with the Korn Shell to indicate a desire to reset signal action.

The Korn Shell also defines some special signals that cause commands to be executed at particular times. These are very handy for debugging Shell programs. In particular, if a signal is ERR, then the commands listed are performed any time a command returns a non-zero return code. The EXIT signal (or 0) performs the commands after a function if the trap was done inside a function, or after exiting the Shell if not inside a function.

TESTING AND DEBUGGING SHELL PROGRAMS

Before subjecting the rest of the user community to your new Shell program, it is a good idea to test the Shell thoroughly. The Shell provides a couple of interactive debugging facilities in the form of Shell parameters (-vx).

You can execute a procedure and the Shell will display every command line as it was written in the Shell procedure:

```
sh -v shell_program
```

Similarly, the Shell will display each command executed and the values substituted for variables:

```
sh -x shell_program
```

Let's look at an example of the output from the debugging options. We will use the whois Shell developed earlier in the chapter as an example. For illustration, though, let's assume that we made a simple syntax error in the Shell. The **read** command was misspelled as *reaf* instead of *read*. The **whois** command is shown:

```
# whois userid
if [ $# -eq 0 ]
then
# No user ids supplied
  echo "Enter userid"
  reaf userid
else
  userid=$1
fi
grep $userid /etc/passwd | cut -f5 -d:
```

Now let's try to run this command and see what happens:

```
whois
Enter userid
whois: reaf: not found
```

Not only do we get an error message indicating that the Shell could not find a command called **reaf**, but the Shell also hangs up and causes us to exit with an interruption. If we wanted to see what had happened, we could run the Shell with the -x option to observe what exactly had occurred. The results of doing this are:

```
sh -x whois
+ [ 0 -eq 0 ]
+ echo Enter userid
Enter userid
+ reaf userid
whois: reaf: not found
+ cut -f5 -d:
+ grep /etc/passwd
```

Each line that is preceded by a + is a line that the Shell has evaluated and has performed variable substitution on. Lines without a + are the normal output supplied by the Shell. Now that it is possible to see the trace of all commands as they are executed, it is very easy to spot errors. We can pinpoint that the **read** command was misspelled, and we can see exactly where the error occurred. While in this simple example it is fairly obvious, in larger Shell programs it can be difficult to determine where error messages are generated from. The reason the Shell appears to "hang up" and not finish properly is also clear. The **grep** command is now incomplete since no user ID was provided. The **grep** command is simply missing an argument.

While the -x option is most useful in solving most bugs, the -v option can be used to trace the flow of a Shell program. The -v option simply prints the Shell lines, just as they are in the Shell program, to your terminal.

```
sh -v whois tburns
# whois userid
if [ $# -eq 0 ]
then
# No user ids supplied
  echo "Enter userid"
  reaf userid
else
  userid=$1
fi
grep $userid /etc/passwd | cut -f5 -d:
Ted Burns 303-965-8949
```

Sometimes it may be difficult, using the -x option, to determine what line has executed after all the variable substitution has occurred. You can use the -v and -x options together to see a before and after image of the Shell lines as they execute. While this may be useful at times, I usually find it to be more confusing overall and only use it when I just can determine what line has been executed.

There are several other options that can aid in debugging a new procedure (refer to Table 6.8). Any of these commands can be set within the procedure by use of the **set** command:

```
set -x
```

Any of the currently set options are contained in the Shell variable $-.

```
echo $-
x
```

Another useful technique in Shell debugging uses a global variable in conjunction with the **set -x** command to turn debugging on and off in your Shell procedure. If we tie the turning of the -x option in all Shells to some global variable, then we can turn debugging on and off in a snap just by setting a global variable to some particular value. For example, let's call our global variable DEBUG. Then at the top of the Shell we check to see if the variable is set to "on". If so, then we turn debugging on in the Shell. To turn debugging off, we simply set the DEBUG variable to "off". Don't forget that you must export the DEBUG variable. Here is what the whois Shell would look like with the DEBUG code installed:

```
# whois userid
if [ "${DEBUG}" = "ON" ]
then
  set -x
fi
if [ $# -eq 0 ]
then
# No user ids supplied
  echo "Enter userid"
  read userid
else
  userid=$1
fi
```

Now if we wanted to turn the -x option on, we would simply do the following:

```
DEBUG=ON
export DEBUG
```

When the **whois** command executes, the -x option is turned on and the debug lines are displayed to your screen. To turn debugging off, you simply do something like the following:

```
DEBUG=off
export DEBUG
```

The setting of the DEBUG variable can be made an alias to simplify the process: alias debug='DEBUG=ON; export $DEBUG'.

While at first glance this approach may not seem to have much of an advantage, it actually provides several valuable things. First, if you are consistent and always place this code at the top of every Shell program that you write, then you have a very consistent and easy method for turning debugging on and off in all your Shell procedures. Where this really becomes advantageous is when you are working with Shell programs that call other Shell programs to perform some work. If you try to debug this series of Shell programs using the standard "sh -x" invocation, you will find that it does not work as expected. The called Shell programs do not have the -x option set since they are invoked as a subshell. As an example, let's say that we modified the whois Shell program to call a general-purpose password grep procedure. This procedure is passed the user ID and the column to cut from the password file. A simplified version of this general-purpose grep and cut follows. Note that for simplicity much of the error checking that should be done is not.

```
# A general purpose password file grep and cut
if [ "${DEBUG}" = "ON" ]
then
  set -x    # Turn debugging output on
fi
if [ $# -eq 0 ]
then
  echo "No arguments supplied for passgrep - \
    Arguments are userid and field number
to cut"
fi
grep $1 /etc/passwd | cut -f$2 -d:
```

Now if we call this routine from inside the **whois** command instead of doing the grep directly, we have problems when we try to use the "sh -xv" to debug. This is what we get when we try to debug the Shell program:

```
sh -x whois tburns
+ [ = ON ]
+ [ 1 -eq 0 ]
```

```
userid=tburns
+ passgrep tburns 5
Ted Burns 303-965-2349
```

As you can see, there is no debug information provided for the passgrep Shell. This problem can be overcome using the global environmental variable as shown:

```
debug     # Turn on debugging
whois tburns
+ [ 1 -eq 0 ]
userid=tburns
+ passgrep tburns 5
+ [ 2 -eq 0 ]
+ cut -f5 -d:
+ grep tburns /etc/passwd
Ted Burns 303-965-8949
```

Both Shell procedures have debugging turned on. When Shell procedures start to become large and call many other Shell procedures, this debugging technique can save hours of headaches trying to locate a problem. Another useful tip is to place other information in the debug code that sets debugging on. For example, you could echo the name of the Shell that is being invoked as well as the arguments passed to the Shell. These can be very useful when trying to track down problems. But any information that might be useful can be placed inside the debug check. Here is an example:

```
if [ "${DEBUG}" = "ON" ]
then
  echo "Entering whois command and turning debugging on"
  echo "The arguments passed to the whois shell are $*"
  set -x
fi
```

Using this technique, you can also set various debugging levels in your Shell program. By setting DEBUG to particular values, you can provide various levels of debugging output, or maybe debug only particular Shell programs or functions. For example, maybe we want to have a detail and a trace debug output with detail providing debug information for every statement and trace just showing which procedures are being called. This could be done by setting DEBUG=DETAIL or DEBUG=TRACE and checking for these values and turning debug on and off as needed. There are lots of ways this technique can be used to provide flexible and complete debugging information.

To increase your speed, you can use **vi** and test the command interactively as you develop it. Once you're in **vi** and you've created the first few lines of the Shell program, write the file (**:w**). Then you can execute it without leaving **vi**:

```
:w                    :w
:!sh -vx %            :!csh -vx %
```

:   gets you to the **vi** command line
!   tells **vi** to execute the following Shell command
%   **vi** fills in with the current file name (the Shell program)

If you use the vi editor (or other full screen editors with an escape (!) facility), you won't believe how fast you can develop and test Shell programs. The emacs editor provides the same capability by using a Shell window or by exiting to a Shell prompt using the Ctrl-Z command to place emacs into the background.

SUMMARY

Shell procedures are simple to create — put a group of commands into a UNIX file and make the file executable. Shells should be created anytime it requires too much typing to enter the commands interactively or when the series of commands can be reused by many users.

Arguments, variables, pipes, input/output redirection, Shell control constructs, and all of the existing commands are available for command construction. Because of the simplicity of command interfaces, one Shell program can interface with another Shell or a native command. Increasingly complex processes can be automated with groups of Shell programs. Whole systems can be built with Shell. Once the system has been shaken out and the user's requests for changes decrease, Shell programs can be rewritten in C language for efficiency. But writing in C language before all of the requirements are known often is a burden. Use Shell to design a working model of what is needed. If it becomes too complex or slow, it can be rewritten in C. Otherwise, Shell is more maintainable and the Shell program should be used.

Subsequent chapters give further examples of Shell programs. Examples are the best way to learn Shell concepts. Then, trying your own Shells will help cement an understanding of how Shell programming can automate much of the routine, daily work of a user, programmer, analyst, or manager.

EXERCISES

1. Describe the two types of interactive Shell procedures.

2. Describe the difference between foreground and background processes. What is the Shell character that puts commands into background?

3. What command allows the Shell user to run commands in background and hang up?

4. In what other ways can interactive Shell usage serve the development of Shell programs?

5. Write an interactive command to search through your directories, removing junk files. Make sure the command runs after 10 P.M. to reduce system load.

6. Write a background command to edit all of the files in the current directory, replacing the word *while* with *until*.

7. How are Shell programs created? How are they made executable?

8. What Shell options allow for "verbose" testing of Shell programs?

9. Which Shell variables contain the arguments to a Shell?

10. What Shell command changes the values of these variables?

11. Describe the difference between $* and $@.

12. What are the Shell built-in commands?

13. Write a Shell program to test for arguments: arg1, arg2, and arg3. If they are not present, prompt the user for them.

14. Write a Shell program to test for arguments of the form -c, -d, -e, and so forth. Set arguments by the same names (c, d, e) to TRUE (1) or FALSE (0) depending on whether the argument exists on the command line.

15. Write a Shell program to loop through the arguments on the command line and process them if they are files.

16. Combine exercises 14 and 15 into one program to loop through the dashed arguments such as -c, shifting the Shell variables, and then loop through the remaining arguments processing them if they are files.

17. Expand exercise 16 to prompt the user for file names if none are specified. Multiple file names are possible, so loop through the prompt sequence until the user enters a return without any file name.

18. Describe and write a program to use accent grave characters to assign values to variables in a Shell program.

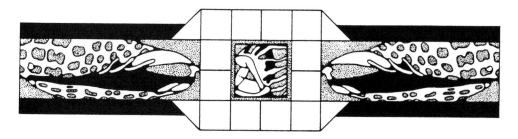

Chapter Seven

User Shell Programming

To this point, we have looked at Shell and all of its facilities to gain a foundation of understanding. To have benefit in the real world, however, we need to know how to compose application systems using the Shell and its supporting tools. This chapter will help most users experience ways to build an entire system using Shell. These systems will ultimately result in enhanced effectiveness and efficiency.

In Shell, we compose systems from various programs written in Shell. In the world of software, there are five basic program designs (Figure 7.1) that make up virtually all systems:

1. *Data input* — Users enter data and information.

2. *Information queries* — Users request specific information and it is displayed.

3. *Information output* — Screens and reports condense the data into useful views of the information contained in the database.

4. *Database update* — Data input by users and passed from other systems changes the base of information in the database. The three key actions against the database are *add, change,* and *delete.*

5. *System interfaces* — Input from and output to other systems, since all systems interrelate in some fashion or other.

As we discovered in Chapter 4, virtually all Shell utilities will support one of these categories. Shell programs may consist of one or more of these designs.

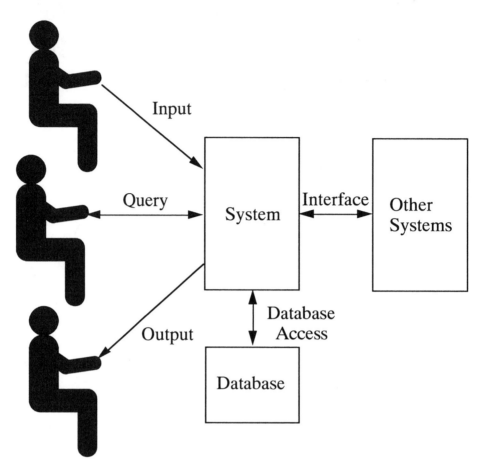

Figure 7.1   Program Types

The *input* process creates information. The input process may consist of:

- displaying a menu
- getting the user's selection
- displaying the input fields
- reading and validating the input

Once valid up-to-date data is in the database, the user may want to *query* the database to extract information. Queries are both an input and an output process. *Outputs* may be either screen displays or reports. To create an output, you will want to:

- *select* information
- *organize* it
- *format* it
- and finally *display* or *report* the desired information

Getting the data into the database is a trick in itself. The *update* process adds, changes, or deletes data from the database. Finally, all systems interact with each other, sharing data. *System interfaces* link application with application and machine with machine.

The following sections delve into each of these five basic program designs and ways to implement each in Shell. In this chapter we will be developing portions of an employee payroll application. The layout of this system is shown in Figure 7.2. Before looking at each section of the system, we must explore the relational database that will be used in many of the examples developed for our application system. Following this, we will look at building the data input portion of the system.

THE SHELL RELATIONAL DATABASE

Grasp, if you will, that one of the keys to Shell power is the ability to use UNIX files and Shell commands to form an elementary relational database management

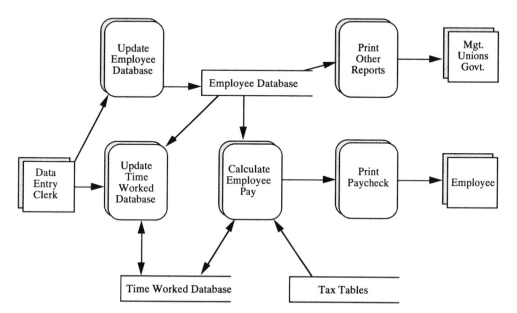

Figure 7.2   Payroll System Design

system (RDBMS). Databases are the primary problem-solving tools of industry; where else can you find everything there is to know about your business in an automated form that can easily be analyzed? The *relational table* — a table much like a spreadsheet — stores data and information in the simplest usable form: rows and columns. A *relational model* of a user's system consists of a collection of interrelated tables.

Traditional relational databases use lots of resources, require complicated setup and lots of training, and use proprietary data storage formats. Using the Shell and relational files, on the other hand, gives you the power to use all of the existing Shell tools to massage your data into any shape or form. The simplicity of implementing an RDBMS in Shell, added to the straightforward files it uses, gives you a powerful tool for data processing and information gathering. To harness this power, let's begin by looking at the design and use of the relational database.

Relational Database Design

All applications require some kind of database. The relational database is the current industry workhorse. Before we begin examining how to implement this data model in Shell, I'd like to give you the key to successful software system development:

Design the data first.

If you don't absorb anything else stated in this book, remember that well-designed data will minimize the amount of effort you spend to build and maintain a software system. It maximizes the flexibility of the resulting system, reduces duplication of data, and builds a safe foundation for the future. Relational databases accent this power and flexibility.

Relational databases store data in tables. Within the table are *rows* and *columns*. In Shell, we use plain files with fields separated by delimiters to implement these tables. The most common delimiter character is the *tab* (\t). The format of these tables is:

	COLUMN 1		COLUMN 2		COLUMN 3
row 1	*index/key*	*delimiter*	data_item	*delimiter*	data_item...

The first field is the index or key to what's in the rest of the record. The key should *uniquely* identify all subsequent data items. To begin to illustrate the nature of database design and the relational model, let's use the simple model of a payroll system shown in Figure 7.2. There are three database tables:

- Employee
- Time Worked
- Tax Tables

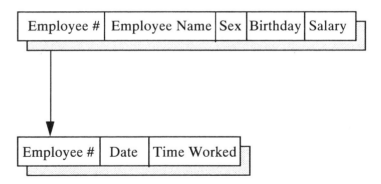

Figure 7.3   Partial Payroll Database Design

The employee number (Figure 7.3) — the employee's social security number (SSN), for example — could be the key to an *employee* record:

SSN	LAST	FIRST	MIDDLE	SEX	BIRTHDAY	SALARY
527964942 \t	Arthur \t	Lowell \t	Jay \t	M \t	1951/12/18 \t	35000 ...

In this example, I used my SSN, last name, first name, middle name, birthday, and salary to define a row in a table. I used a tab character (\t) as the delimiter between fields. *SSN* is the primary key; *last name* could be a secondary key. This will simplify sorting, organizing, and retrieving the information later. *Birthday* contains three other subfields: year, month, and day. You can create subfields by using a different delimiter character — in this case the slash (/). You could also use the colon (:), semicolon (;), blank ( ), or any other character as a delimiter between fields and subfields. A word of caution, however: Do not use a delimiter character that might commonly appear within the row, record, or field. Errors will result when the Shell attempts to separate fields based on such a character.

Notice also that I put the data items in the order that we most often like to organize information: alphabetical by last name and chronologically by year/month/day. The *query* and *reporting* tools can handle putting the data back into user-friendly order.

In a well-designed relational table, there are rarely more than seven data items. If your table needs to be larger, there should be more than one table. There are *many-to-one* relationships that require additional tables. For example, I might represent days and time worked in another table:

SSN	DAY	TIME WORKED
527964942 \t	1990/01/02 \t	9.5
527964942 \t	1990/01/03 \t	7.0
527964942 \t	1990/01/04 \t	8.5

These separate tables can then be processed independently, merged or joined based on their primary keys. Joining tables together often creates the greatest insights and knowledge about your system, your customers, and your company.

Finally, we might have to show relationships between tables. We might define the company's department table as follows:

DEPARTMENT NUMBER		DEPARTMENT NAME
1	\t	Corporate Headquarters
47	\t	Information Systems

We could then define the relationship between employees and departments (*many-to-one*) in another table, as follows:

DEPARTMENT NUMBER	(HAS AN)	EMPLOYEE SSN
47	\t	527964942
47	\t	513234567

There are also *many-to-many* relationships. In today's modern-day corporate culture, with matrix management, an employee could work for multiple departments:

DEPARTMENT NUMBER	(HAS AN)	EMPLOYEE SSN
47	\t	527964942
12	\t	527964942

One command that combines existing tables by matching on specific fields is **join**. **Join** does not merge lines. When it finds matching records in the two input files, it creates a single output record containing any or all of the fields in both records. Imagine two files with the following lines in each file:

```
   FILE1                 FILE2
Arthur:555-1234    Arthur:123 Main:Denver:CO:80202
Martin:555-2345    Martin:245 Juniper:Denver:CO:80202
Smith:555-3456
```

The command **join -t: file1 file2** will produce:

```
Arthur:555-1234:123 Main:Denver:CO:80202
Martin:555-2345:245 Juniper:Denver:CO:80202
```

Only the matched lines are joined to create an output line. The -t option tells **join** to use the colon as the field separator character. The output produced is the matched field, which in this case is the first field by default, followed by fields from file1 followed by the fields from file2. To generate an output line for all lines in file1, the command could be changed to:

```
join -a1 -t: file1 file2
Arthur:555-1234:123 Main:Denver:CO:80202
Martin:555-2345:245 Juniper:Denver:CO:80202
Smith:555-3456
```

To get just the name, phone number, and zip code from these files, **join** would be invoked as:

```
join -a1 -o 1.1 1.2 2.5 -t: file1 file2
Arthur:555-1234:80202
Martin:555-2345:80202
Smith:555-3456
```

The -o option specifies that only fields one and two (1.1 and 1.2) in file1 and the fifth field of file2 (2.5) should be output.

As shown in these examples, **join** updates files by adding fields or creating whole new files with subsets of the fields in the original files. It is another tool in the arsenal for updating files.

Paste works similarly to **join** by putting two files together regardless of their order:

```
paste -d: file1 file2
Arthur:555-1234:Arthur:123 Main:Denver:CO:80202
Martin:555-2345:Martin:245 Juniper:Denver:CO:80202
Smith:555-3456
```

In this form, **paste** gives the user another way to create tables. It is more primitive than **join,** but it often serves a useful purpose in Shell programming.

That's a brief overview of the various kinds of relational table designs using UNIX files. To summarize, here are a few key rules for tables:

1. Use a single unique delimiter (\t) between columns.

2. Use a different unique delimiter (/:;) between subfields.

3. Organize the data for machine efficiency: primary keys first, secondary keys next, then data items.

4. Restrict the number of fields per table to fewer than ten data items or redesign the table.

5. Create additional tables for multiple occurrences of data items' (one-to-many, many-to-one, or many-to-many) relationships.

6. Small tables — under 50 rows/records — are more efficient than larger tables. They are faster to sort and faster to access sequentially.

Now let's take a look at how to use this foundation to construct the inputs, queries, outputs, updates, and interfaces to an application system.

DATA INPUT

User Interfaces

The user interface software is the portion of the system that allows an end user to utilize the functionality of a system. It is the window that exposes the user to the capabilities of the software you have developed. It is perhaps the most important part of a software system because it determines how a user will interact with your software. Clearly this emphasis can be seen in today's modern software market with its increasing use of graphical user interfaces (GUIs). A user-friendly interface will permit a user to utilize all the functionality with ease. You can have some of the best software imaginable, but if it is difficult to use and understand (a poorly designed user interface), then it will never be utilized as it should be. Even if your software does everything that the user ever wanted it to do, if he or she cannot figure out how to make it work, it is worthless as a productivity tool. As a matter of fact, a poorly designed user interface can make software counterproductive. People spend more time trying to figure out how to make the system work properly than the time they save using the system. A good portion of all system design and development time should be spent ensuring that the system will be easy to use and understand. Clearly, a good user interface is a key goal in the development of any system, but what makes a good user interface?

A full discussion of user interface design and development is clearly beyond the scope of this book, but there are a few key qualities that any good user interface should possess. These are discussed further in the following paragraphs:

- The user interface should be easy to use.
- It should expose the functionality of the system.
- It should provide help to the user when it is needed.
- It should provide understandable, helpful, and clear error messages.

The first property, and perhaps the most evasive quality, is ease of use. What does it mean for a user interface to be easy to use? While what is easy for one person to use may not be the same for the next, there are some things that will always make a user interface easier to use. These properties should be built into any user interface whether it is a state-of-the-art graphical user interface or a menu-driven system such as the one we will be developing in this chapter. Some of these properties follow.

1. *Consistency, Consistency, Consistency.* Perhaps the number one rule of a good user interface is to make it consistent. Nothing is more annoying (or counterproductive) to a user than an inconsistent user interface. For example, let's say you have a menu-driven system that consists of a number of screens that are arranged in a hierarchy. If the user leaves one screen and returns to the next screen up in the hierarchy by selecting a particular option from the screen, then make this option the same on all screens. Don't make the "Exit" option one thing on one screen and something else on the next. This forces the user to be familiar

with each screen and increases the chances that the user will select the wrong thing. As another example, suppose you make a user enter the same data in a different manner in various places on your screen. Let's say you force a date to be entered as "mm/dd/yy" in one date field and as "yyyy-mm-dd" in another. I can assure you you will not have a very happy user. Consistency is perhaps the "golden rule" of user interface design.

2. *Make it clear what the user is to do and how to do it.* When a user is presented with a screen, it should be clear what he or she is supposed to do on the screen and how to go about doing it. This can be done in a wide variety of ways, from field highlighting to increased verbiage on the screen. For a simple example, let's say that the user was presented with the following very poorly designed screen:

```
    Employee System
Add
Change
Delete
Exit

   _____
```

It should be clear that this screen leaves much to be desired. What is the user to do here? Is one of these options to be selected? What is going to be added, changed, or deleted? How will the user tell the system to take that action? Does he or she enter the number that corresponds to the option or the name of the option? Does "exit" mean return to the previous screen, or does it mean that the program will end? As you can see, this is the kind of ambiguity that a user cannot tolerate if the system is to be usable by many. Here is an improved version that mainly relies on increased verbiage on the screen.

```
    Employee System
    Employee Update Screen
Select one of the following actions you wish to perform:
    Add a new employee to the system
    Change an existing employee
    Delete an existing employee
    Return to the main system screen
Select the option and enter the corresponding number ==>  _____
```

While this is a simple example, it points out the need to communicate clearly with the user.

3. *Provide lots of feedback to the user.* Users like to know what is about to happen, what's happening right now, and what went wrong. For example, when a user takes some invalid action, don't just provide a beep with no feedback. Give the user a clear indication of what is wrong and how it can be corrected. If the system is doing some work that takes a fair amount of time, let the user know that the system is working on it. Perhaps provide a message that shows the progress

being made. Don't just leave the user sitting there wondering whether the system is doing the right thing (or anything, for that matter).

4. *Understand your users and how they work.* If you know the way that a user works, you can design a user interface that better fits his or her needs. For example, if you know that users perform some particular function 90 percent of the time, don't make that option difficult to find or use. Be sure that it is the central focus of the user interface.

The second major goal of a user interface is to expose the functionality of the system. If users cannot determine what the system can do for them, they will not utilize it as they should. This means that all of the available options in the system should be accessible in a straightforward manner. For example, if you are making a menu-driven system, try to expose as much of the functionality on a single screen as possible. Don't make the user dig six levels deep to find applicable functionality. Deep-screen nesting hides functionality.

In addition to these user interface goals, a user should always have the ability to ask for help. If the current screen seems confusing to a user, he or she should be able to pull up a more complete description of how the screen works. The user should never have to guess what action to take. There are many ways to provide help for users. They may be able to swap to a help screen, for example, by always entering a particular value, or maybe they can find more specific help information by entering a "?" in the field. But one thing that should be made clear is that your help should be useful. If you are not going to provide complete and thorough help, then your users will be calling you every time they use the system.

Finally, the user interface should provide clear and helpful error messages. If the user does something wrong, it should be clear what the problem is and how it might be fixed. Anyone who has used software systems in the past knows the frustration of receiving an error message such as "Beep - Invalid Entry". Well, what was wrong with it? What entry are you talking about? What are the valid entries? Don't leave the user guessing what went wrong. Remember that users like good and verbose feedback.

Now that we have discussed some of the salient features of a well-designed user interface, let's write some Shell programs that will provide the user interface portion of our system.

Creating Menus/Screen Input

Through the use of terminal description files, /etc/termcap and /etc/terminfo, the Shell supports a huge array of terminal types — everything from the old vt100 to Sun workstations. To use these files to simplify screen handling:

1. The TERM variable must be set to the appropriate terminal type.
2. The System V **tput** command must be available on your system (see Table 7.1). If it is not, then you can use the **clear** and **echo** commands to create the menus outlined next. While not as flexible as the Shell that follows, they can generate and control menu screens and user input screens.

TABLE 7.1   Tput Capabilities

Option	Action
bel	echo the terminal's "bell" character
blink	blinking display
bold	bold display
clear	clear the screen
cols	echo number of columns on the screen
cup *r c*	move cursor to row *r* and column *c*
dim	dim the display
ed	clear to end of the display
el	clear to end of the line
lines	echo number of lines on the screen
smso	start stand out mode
rmso	end stand out mode
smul	start mode <u>underline</u>
rmul	end underline mode
rev	reverse video (black on white) display

KSH

As was discussed in Chapter 5, the Korn Shell provides the **select** statement to aid in the construction of menu screens. Please refer to Chapter 5 for a full discussion on how to use the **select** command.

Since most of the capabilities of **tput** are simple character sequences, you can store most of them in variables and then use the variables to improve efficiency:

```
term_bel=`tput bel`
term_blink=`tput blink`
term_bold=`tput bold`
term_clear=`tput clear`
max_cols=`tput cols`
term_dim=`tput dim`
term_ed=`tput ed`
term_el=`tput el`
max_lines=`tput lines`
last_line=`expr $term_lines - 1`
term_so=`tput smso`
term_eso=`tput rmso`
term_su=`tput smul`
term_eul=`tput rmul`
term_rev=`tput rev`
```

Once these are set, you can proceed to set up the screen any way you please using variables and **tput** cursor movements. For example, let's create a Shell to center one or more text lines beginning on a given row:

```
# Center_text row_number input_text_file
max_cols=`tput cols`
max_lines=`tput lines`
row_number=$1
shift
cat $* | \    # Read from stdin
while read input_text
do
    line_length=`echo $input_text | wc -c`
    tput cup $row_number `expr \( $term_cols - $line_length \) \
    / 2`
    echo $input_text
    row_number=`expr $row_number + 1`
    if [ $row_number -ge $max_lines ]
  then
      echo "Too many lines for the screen"
      break
  fi
done
```

We could also center rows on the screen, beginning at a certain column:

```
# Center_lines col_number input_lines
max_lines=`tput lines`
col_number=$1
shift
cat $* > /tmp/tmp$$     # Create temporary file
number_of_lines=`wc -l < /tmp/tmp$$`
row_number=`expr \($max_lines - $number_of_lines \) / 2`
cat /tmp/tmp$$ | \
while read input_line
do
    tput cup $row_number $col_number
    echo $input_line
    row_number=`expr $row_number + 1`
    if [ $row_number -ge $max_lines ]
  then
      echo "Too many lines for the screen"
      break
  fi
done
```

Using these two tools, we can now create a menu screen for the Time Reporting System using **tput.** We can create a header file (trs_header) and a menu file (trs_menu) containing the menu of choices:

TRS_HEADER	TRS_MENU
Time Reporting System	1. Add Time Worked
Time Worked Data Input	2. Change Time Worked
	3. Delete Time Worked
	x. Exit

The first thing we'll do is print the header on the screen and then center and indent the menu choices. Finally, we'll print and ask the user to input a choice:

```
term_clear=`tput clear`
max_lines=`tput lines`
last_line=`expr $max_lines - 3`
echo $term_clear
trs_prompt="Please enter your choice> "
trs_indent=15
center_text 0 trs_header
center_lines $trs_indent trs_menu
tput cup $trs_indent $last_line
echo $trs_prompt
read reply
case $reply
1)
    add_time
    ;;
2)
    change_time
    ;;
3)
    delete_time
    ;;
  `x'|`X')
    exit TRUE
    ;;
*)
     echo "Invalid choice You must enter 1, 2 or 3 or X to exit "
    ;;
esac
```

Once the user selects an action, we can have a series of screens to add, change, or delete the data. Since the basic screen mask will be used by all of these Shell programs, we can create the command, **time_screen,** as follows:

```
# time_screen
center_text 0 trs_header
tput cup 4 0; echo "SSN:"
tput cup 6 0; echo "Date:"
tput cup 8 0; echo "Time Worked:"
```

We could then add time reporting data by first displaying the field names and their default values, and then getting the data for each field. As you read through the example, notice how to edit each field, especially the SSN, and how to add the record to the database:

```
term_clear=`tput clear`
max_lines=`tput lines`
last_line=`expr $max_lines - 3`

echo $term_clear
text_indent=15

time_screen                # Display time worked screen mask

Date=`date %y/%m/%d`    # Set date
tput cup 6 $text_indent; echo $Date
tput cup 8 $text_indent; echo "8.0"

while [ TRUE ]
do
  tput cup 4 $text_indent; read SSN
  if [ -z "`grep $SSN employee.db`" ]      # Check for SSN
  then
    tput cup $last_line 0; echo "$SSN not in Employee Database"
  else
    break
  fi
done

tput cup 6 $text_indent; read tmp_date
  if [ ! -z "$tmp_date" ]    # Not default date
  then
    Date=$tmp_date
  fi

tput cup 8 $text_indent; read time_worked
  if [ -z "$time_worked" ]    # Default time worked 8hrs
  then
```

```
    time_worked=8.0
fi
```

```
echo "${SSN}\t${Date}\t${time_worked} >> time_worked.db
```

Getting valid file or directory names, correct string and numeric variables, and so on, is essential to having a Shell program execute correctly and reliably. To ensure that all variables, files, and special files are valid, you must edit the data and names. Is the file name correct and is the file readable? writable? executable? Is the name a directory, block special, or character special file? Is a variable equal to a specified value or other variable? Each of these questions is answered by editing the data within the Shell procedure (see Figure 7.4). The primary commands for editing data are **test** and **awk**.

Test combined with IF-THEN-ELSE handles most edits on arguments or data in a Shell program. The CASE statement handles the rest of the edits normally required.

Expr can be used to edit the content of fields. **Expr** will compare a variable to a regular expression and return a count of characters matched. So, for example, we can evaluate alphabetic and numeric variables as follows:

```
expr $var : '[a-zA-Z]*'        # Count alphabetic characters
expr $var : '[-+]*[0-9.]*'     # Count numeric characters
```

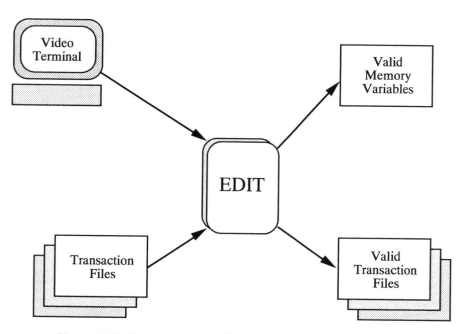

Figure 7.4   Interactive and Sequential Edit Program Design

To ensure that we got only what we expected, we could compare the returned length to the total length of $var:

```
if [ `expr $var : `[-+]*[0-9.]*'` -eq `expr $var : `.*'` ]
then    # It's numeric all the way through
else    # It's not
fi
```

Another useful and very powerful editing program is **awk**. **Awk** can edit fields using the matching operator (~). (Please see the section later on in this chapter on awk syntax for details.) In the following examples, we can test each field of the time_worked table for validity and numeric input:

```
$0 ~ /[0-9]+/
$1 ~ /[0-9][0-9]\/[0-9][0-9]\/[0-9][0-9]/
$2 ~ /[0-9]+/
```

Similarly, we could edit the last_name field from the employee record as follows:

```
$2 ~ /[A-Z][a-z-]+/
```

Input data, including Shell command-line arguments, is normally entered by humans and, as such, is most prone to error. It should always be edited for validity before using it in processing. If the user does not enter a valid value, then an appropriate error message should be displayed.

Screen Output

Using the existing input command, we can modify it to display information from the database one record at a time. To do this, let's create two commands — one to display the screen mask, called **trs_view,** and another to display the data, called **time_data**:

```
# time_data input_record text_indent
  SSN=`echo $1 | cut -f1`
  Date=`echo $1 | cut -f2`
  time_worked=`echo $1 | cut -f3'

  tput cup 4 $2; echo $SSN
  tput cup 6 $2; echo $Date
  tput cup 8 $2; echo $time_worked

# trs_view time_worked.db    or trs_view 3< file
term_clear=`tput clear`
max_lines=`tput lines`
last_line=`expr $max_lines - 1`
```

```
echo $term_clear
text_indent=15

if [ "$1" ]     # File specified
then
  exec 3< $1    # Open fd 3
    # Else the command must be executed with 3< file
fi


time_screen     # Display time worked screen mask

while
  input_record=`line <&3`    # Read record from stdin
  test ! -\ "$input_record"
do
    # Display time worked data
  time_data "$input_record" $text_indent
  if [ -t 0 ]    # Terminal is stdin?
  then
    tput cup $last_line 0; echo "Press Return for Next Record"
    read next
  fi
done
```

We could display the whole database one record at a time using the following command:

```
trs_view time_worked.db
```

Or we could sort it first:

```
sort time_worked.db > /tmp/tmp$$
trs_view /tmp/tmp$$
rm /tmp/tmp$$
```

This command will be useful for updating existing records as well as displaying the results of queries.

Screen Query

We can use essentially the same chunk of code to query the database by painting the screen, getting the user's selection criteria, and then searching the database and displaying the results:

```
# trs_query
term_clear=`tput clear`
max_lines=`tput lines`
last_line=`expr $max_lines - 1`
echo $term_clear
text_indent=15

if [ "$1" ]     # File specified
then
  exec 3< $1    # Open fd 3
  # Else the command must be executed with 3< file
fi


trs_screen    # Display time worked screen mask

while [ TRUE ]
do
  tput cup 4 $text_indent; read SSN
  if [ -z "$SSN" ]    # Not selecting by SSN
  then
      break
    elif [ -z "`grep $SSN employee.db`" ]       # Check for SSN
  then
      tput cup $last_line 0; echo "SSN not in Employee Database"
  else
      break    # Valid SSN
  fi
done
tput cup 6 $text_indent; read Date
tput cup 8 $text_indent; read time_worked
if [ "$SSN" -a "$Date" -a "$time_worked" ]
then
  grepstr="$SSN\t$Date\t$time_worked"
elif [ "$SSN" -a "$Date" ]
then
  grepstr="$SSN\t$Date"
elif [ "$Date" -a "$time_worked" ]
then
  grepstr="$Date\t$time_worked"
elif [ "$SSN" ]
then
  grepstr="${SSN}"
elif [ "$Date" ]
then
  grepstr="${Date}"
```

```
elif [ "${time_worked}" ]
then
  grepstr=$time_worked
else
  exit FALSE
fi
grep "$grepstr" time_worked.db > /tmp/tmp$$
trs_view /tmp/tmp$$
rm /tmp/tmp$$
```

This would show one record per page (Figure 7.5). If, instead, we would like to see multiple records per page (Figure 7.6), we could substitute the following for the display portion of the previous program:

```
echo " SSN    Date    Time Worked"
grep "$grepstr" time_worked.db
```

This Shell program is a simple example of how we could query the time_worked database for information by SSN, date worked, or time worked. More exotic queries can be handled using **awk**.

The output from the previous example was fairly crunched together. Instead of using **more,** we could use the advanced formatting features of **awk** to beautify the output (Figure 7.7):

```
                  Time Reporting System
                    Time Worked Data

        SSN:  527964942
        Date:  1990/01/02
        Time Worked:  8.0
```

Figure 7.5   Time Worked Output Screen

```
                  Time Reporting System
                    Time Worked Data

        SSN:           Date:        Time Worked:
        527964942      1990/01/02        8.0
        527964942      1990/01/03        9.5
        527964942      1990/01/04       10.0
```

Figure 7.6   Multiple Record Output Screen

```
                    Time Reporting System
                    Time Worked Data

      SSN:             Date:      Time Worked:
      527-96-4942    01/02/1990       8.0
      527-96-4942    01/03/1990       9.5
      527-96-4942    01/04/1990      10.0
```

Figure 7.7   Formatted Output Screen Using awk

```
echo " SSN    Date    Time Worked"
awk 'BEGIN { FS=OFS=~\t" } \
  { split($2, Date, "/") \
    printf(" %3d-%2d-%4d %2d/%2d/%4d %4.1f\n", \
    substr($1,1,3), substr($1,4,2), substr($1,6,4), \
    Date[2], Date[3], Date[1], \
    $3) }'
```

These are just a few of the ways that you can gather input from a screen, query a database, and output to the screen. Later in this chapter we look at more exotic ways to use **awk** to select and format information for reports. Next, however, let's look at what it takes to update a database.

DATABASE UPDATE

Updating a file or database means adding, changing, or deleting data from it. Earlier in this chapter we learned some ways to take input data from a screen and *add* a record to the database by appending the record to the table. Now let's consider ways to *change* and *delete* records from the database.

The design of a simple sequential update program is shown in Figure 7.8. There are one or more possible transaction files or screens that affect the original or master file. The master (or old) file is used as input and a new file is created as output. Any errors are directed onto *stderr*. In the following paragraphs we explore methods of performing the update function using Shell tools and commands.

The Shell commands that handle most of the common updates to UNIX files are **awk, cat, echo, join, merge, paste, sed,** and **tr**. The UNIX editors also update files, but they do so manually rather than mechanically. This section deals with the automated forms of file update. First let's explore methods for creating the new master file itself.

The simplest update program is **cat,** which can create new files, concatenate several files into one new file, or append one file to an existing file. Each of these forms of update is shown in the following examples:

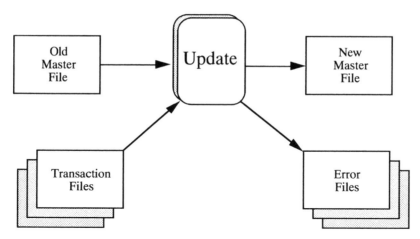

Figure 7.8   Update Program Design

```
cat > file               # Enter data from the terminal
cat file1 file2 > file3  # Create a new file from two
cat file3 > file4        # Append file3 to file4
```

In each of these examples, **cat** adds data to a new or existing file. Similarly, **echo** can combine fields and add a single record to a database:

```
echo "$field1 $field2 $field3" >> table.db
```

Cat and **echo** work well for creating or adding lines to a file as long as there is no concern about the order of that information. When the information should be in a particular order, however, either **sort** or **merge** (sort -m) serves as a better update program. **Sort** can put one or more files into a specified order. This form of update is best used on unsorted files:

```
sort file1 file2 > file3
```

When the transaction and master files are already in order, however, it is more efficient to simply merge them:

```
sort -m table.db trans1 trans2 > newtable.db
```

A simple example involves listing two directories and merging the files found:

```
ls /bin > binlist
ls /usr/bin > usrbinlist
sort -m binlist usrbinlist > combinedlist
```

When updating files in this way, duplicate entries may cause problems. There should not be two identical records in the resulting new master file. To eliminate duplicates, the output can be passed through uniq:

```
sort -m table.db trans1 | uniq > newtable.db
```

or

```
sort -mu table.db trans1 > newtable.db
```

Each of these examples using **sort** assumed that the first field in each file was the sort key. Other keys can be specified with positional parameters passed to the sort utility.

To update tables safely using these tools, we will need to create a temporary copy of the revised file, rename the old one as backup (bak), and rename the temporary file to the database name:

```
update employee.db > tmp$$
mv employee.db employee.bak
mv tmp$$ employee.db
```

Now that we have looked at methods to create the new master file from the transaction files and old master file, let's look at how we might apply changes to the actual data within the master file. The commands that actually change information within a file or table are **tr** and **sed. Tr** translates characters within a file. **Sed** can also be used to add, delete, or update records from the table. To change the lowercase text in the file to uppercase would require the following command:

```
tr "[a-z]" "[A-Z]" < file2
ARTHUR:123 MAIN:DENVER:CO:80202
MARTIN:245 JUNIPER:DENVER:CO:80202
```

Sed lets the user update fields within the file. For example, assume that everyone moved to San Francisco, California. **Sed** could handle all updates as follows:

```
sed -e "s/Denver:CO/San Francisco:CA/" file2
Arthur:123 Main:San Francisco:CA:80202
Martin:245 Juniper:San Francisco:CA:80202
```

Or the edit commands, including the zip code change, could have been placed in a file called city_state:

```
s/Denver/San Francisco/
s/CO/CA/
s/80202/74539/
```

Then **sed** could be invoked as follows:

```
sed -f city_state file2
```

To delete information from files, **sed** can selectively delete lines or parts of fields from files. To delete all of the records for people on Juniper Street and the word "Denver" from file2, the following command would be required:

```
sed -e "/Juniper/d" -e "s/Denver//g" file2
Arthur:123 Main::CO:80202
```

"**/Juniper/d**" is a line editor command to delete lines containing the word "Juniper." "**s/Denver//g**" is the line editor command to substitute nothing (//) for each occurrence of the word "Denver." Using these editor commands, **sed** acts like a program that updates fields or deletes lines. We could encapsulate the *update* capability into the following command which will update the time worked database with a new time worked amount provided by the user:

```
trs_screen     # Paint the screen
tput cup 4 $text_indent; read SSN
tput cup 6 $text_indent; read Date
if [ "$SSN" -a "$DATE"]
then
  search_string="${SSN}\t${Date}"
elif [ "$SSN" ]
then
  search_string="$SSN"
elif [ "$Date" ]
then
  search_string="$Date"
else
  echo "You must supply either the SSN or the Date"
  search_string="999999999"
fi

cp time_worked.db time_worked.bak     # Create backup of database
grep "$search_string" time_worked.db | \
while
  read record
do
  echo $record | trs_view                     # Display the
                                              # record
  sed_string=`echo $record | cut -f1,2 -d' '`  # Create the Sed
                                              # edit string
  tput cup 8 $text_indent; read time_worked   # Get new time
                                              # worked
```

```
#***********************************************************
# The following sed statement will update the time worked db
# with new info
#***********************************************************
  sed -e "/${sed_string}/s/[0-9.]*\$/$time_worked/" \
    time_worked.db > tmp$$
  mv tmp$$ time_worked.db       # Create new database from update
fi
```

It would then be simple to apply this same technique to display a given record and ask for confirmation before deleting the record.

Each of the commands presented in this section serves a specific purpose when updating UNIX files. Once the files have been updated and put in correct order, the data will need to be retrieved and printed. The commands to do so are described in the next sections on data selection and reporting.

DATA SELECTION

Both queries and reports will need to select data (Figure 7.9). Selecting information from files can be handled in a number of ways with the Shell. Information can be selected row-by-row, field-by-field, or both. The primary commands that perform data selection are **awk, cut, grep,** and **uniq**.

Uniq is perhaps the simplest. It works on a line-by-line basis, eliminating duplicate lines or every line except for the duplicate lines. **Uniq** assumes that its input is sorted. Given the following sorted file, called names, note how **uniq** selects the various lines in the file:

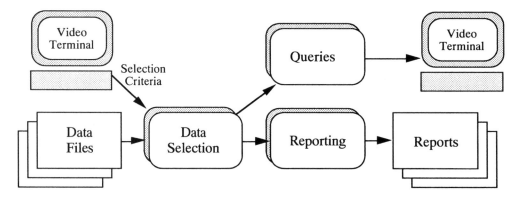

Figure 7.9   Data Selection and Report Program Design

Original FILE	UNIQ NAMES	UNIQ -U NAMES	UNIQ -D NAMES
Arthur	Arthur	Arthur	Martin
Martin	Martin	Smith	
Martin	Smith		
Smith			

The first example removes the duplicate name, "Martin." The second eliminates "Martin" entirely. The final example eliminates all names except "Martin." **Uniq** also has other options available. For example, it is possible to return a count of the number of duplicated lines and to skip portions of the file. **Uniq** provides an efficient tool for selecting information from files that contain duplicate lines.

Grep also operates on a line-by-line, row-by-row basis. It looks through a file for lines that contain the specified regular expression. Any matching records are selected. The extended grep (**egrep**) and fast grep (**fgrep**) commands provide for selecting on more than one regular expression at a time or by matching entire lines.

Given the following file, **grep** and its cousins can extract information and place it on *stdout*:

```
Arthur Denver CO
Martin Denver CO
Smith Colorado Springs CO

grep "Denver" file

Arthur Denver CO
Martin Denver CO

egrep "Martin\|Smith" file

Martin Denver CO
Smith Colorado Springs CO

fgrep "Martin Denver CO" file

Martin Denver CO
```

Grep provides other options that increase its flexibility. For example, if you use the -i option, **grep** will ignore case distinctions when it compares the file with the match string. The -c option prints a count of the number of matches that were found in each file. And the ever-useful -v option tells **grep** to return everything in the file that does not match the regular expression.

We can see the results of using the -v option in conjunction with **grep** in the following example:

```
grep -v "Arthur" file
Martin Denver CO
Smith Colorado Springs CO
```

There are still other options for **grep** that can be found in your manual pages.

To select information on a field-by-field basis requires the use of **cut** or **awk**. **Cut** can select fields from a file based on the character positions or based on the delimiters that separate the fields. An example of selecting fields uses the time_worked database. The fields selected are the SSN (f1) and time worked (f3):

```
cut -f1,3 time_worked.db    awk -F"\t" 'print $1, $3' time_worked.db
527964942 8.0
527964942 9.5
527964942 10.0
```

Fields can also be selected by their character position within a file. Consider a long listing of a directory:

```
ls -l
drwxrwx---    3 lja      adm        992   Dec 1 05:39   bin
drwx------   28 lja      adm        496   Dec 4 12:28   doc
drwxr-x---    2 lja      adm        192   Sep 5 17:55   jcl
drwx------    2 lja      adm        816   Sep 5 16:15   job
drwxrwxrwx    2 lja      adm       3760   Dec 3 09:37   rje
drwxrwxrwx   32 lja      adm       1008   Dec 3 18:22   src
              1           2          3      4     5        6
12345678901234567890123456789012345678901234567890123456789 0
```

Fields can be selected by column:

```
cut -c16-24,55-

lja     bin
lja     doc
lja     jcl
lja     job
lja     rje
lja     src
```

In this example, **cut** selected only the information contained in columns 16-24 and 55 through the end of each line; it shows its ability to select specific information for future reporting. In this particular example, the output was suitable for human consumption.

Grep and **cut** can be combined to extract information line-by-line and field-by-field. The output of **grep** can be piped into **cut.** In the following example, the

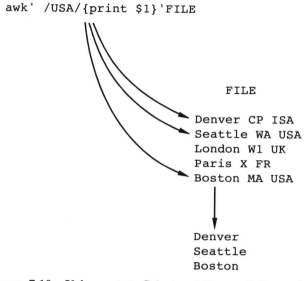

```
awk' /USA/{print $1}'FILE
```

FILE

Denver CP ISA
Seattle WA USA
London W1 UK
Paris X FR
Boston MA USA

Denver
Seattle
Boston

Figure 7.10   Using awk to Select and Report Information

commands extract all of the users in the "unix1" file system from the /etc/passwd file and then extract the user's name from the file:

```
grep "527964942" time_worked.db | cut -f3
8.0
9.5
10.0
```

Grep and **cut** are good for quick work, but do not handle formatting of the information. **Awk,** however, handles both row-by-row and field-by-field data selection (see Figure 7.10) as well as formatting data for reports or screens. Why not use it all of the time instead of **grep** and **cut**? Well, **awk** has to interpret a data selection and reporting program and then process the file. For less sophisticated processing, **grep** and **cut** are optimized to do their job more efficiently. When more exotic data selection criteria are applied to a file, however, **awk** gives the user more flexibility.

Awk Syntax

```
awk     'program' files—interactive use
awk -f program_file files—programming
```

The previous example could have been written in **awk** and summed as follows:

```
BEGIN { FS=OFS="\t" } # Field separator is a colon
/527964942/ { print $3; sum += $3 }
END { print sum }
```

The preceding program sets the field separator (FS) to a tab (\t) and then in the processing section looks for all records that match the string "527964942" and prints the third field in the records matched. Assuming that this **awk** program was stored in a file called Arthur_time, the command could be executed as follows:

```
awk -f Arthur_time time_worked.db
9.5
7.0
8.5
8.0
33
```

As data selection criteria become more complex, **awk** can greatly enhance the user's ability to get at the information stored in files. In another example using the previous long listing of a directory, **awk** can extract the lines containing files last updated in September and can print just the owner, group, and file name as follows:

```
ls -l | awk '/Sep/ { print $3, $4, $8 }'
```

Without a specified field separator (FS), **awk** assumes that a blank delimits fields. The following lines show how **awk** would pick up the fields from each record:

```
$1          $2  $3    $4    $5  $6   $7      $8
drwxr-x---   2  lja   adm   192 Sep 5 17:55   jcl
```

The resulting output would be:

```
lja adm jcl
lja adm job
```

Awk can also select information from fields within each line. In the following **awk** program, the hours and minutes are selected from a long directory listing:

```
split ( $8, hourmin, ":")
print hourmin[0];    # Print the hours first
print hourmin[1];    # Print the minutes next
```

This particular example splits the hours and minutes field ($8) by use of the delimiter (":") and places the two resulting numbers into the two-dimensional array hourmin. The following two statements print the hours (hourmin[0]) on one line and the minutes (hourmin[1]) on the next. This would produce two lines for each line from the long listing. The same processing using **grep** and **cut** would have been more complex. **Awk** handles the processing more clearly.

As shown in these examples, **awk** can handle the functions of **grep, cut, paste,** and **pr**. **Awk** is a powerful programming tool that also has the basic control structures IF-THEN-ELSE, FOR, and WHILE and much more. In addition to selecting data, **awk** also provides the ability to format the data in a flexible manner. Almost any data selection or reporting need can be programmed in **awk**.

Once the information has been extracted from a file using **grep, cut, sed,** or **awk,** it needs to be reported in ways that humans can best use. There are many Shell commands that support clear concise reports. The following section describes them in detail.

REPORTING

The design of a typical report program is shown in Figure 7.11. Notice that it is very similar to the design of a typical command, using *stdin* and *stdout*. Each of the standard Shell commands produces report-like output that is fairly legible. The **cat** command will reproduce files on either the terminal screen or a printer. Commands such as **ls** and **who** generate readable listings. But when data selection commands such as **grep, cut,** and **awk** have been used on files, a more specific reporting mechanism often is required to make the output readable.

There are two major facilities for reporting information: **pr** and **awk. Pr** produces paginated reports that fit the printed page or a terminal screen. **Awk** can handle more exacting report specifications with "C"-like precision. **Lp,** the print manager, handles the simple spooling and printing of output to a wide variety of printers.

Printing files or selected information on a printer is more useful when the output is offset by eight characters to allow room for a three-hole punch on the left-hand side:

```
pr -o file | lp    csh: pr file | lpr -i8
```

Files with field delimiters such as the tab (\t) can be printed more legibly with **pr:**

```
cut -f1,3 time_worked | pr -e20
527964942  8.0
527964942  8.5
527964942  10.0
```

Figure 7.11   Report Generation Program Design

Printing these two fields in reverse order would have been much more difficult. You should try using **cut, paste,** and **pr** to print the fields in the reverse order. It is easier to use **awk** when manipulating fields. The **awk** program to reverse these fields and print them would be:

```
awk -F'\t' '{ print $3, $1 }' time_worked.db

8.0  527964942
8.5  527964942
10.0  527964942
```

To obtain a more readable version of this report, the program could have used **printf,** an **awk** function that is exactly like the C language function by the same name:

```
BEGIN { FS="\t" }
{ printf "\t%-10.1f %-10s\n", $3, $1 }

  8.0  527964942
  8.5  527964942
  10.0  527964942
```

The **printf** statement uses a *format* statement (enclosed in double quotes) to describe how the output should look. In this example, there is a tab character, a right-aligned floating point (use a *d* instead of an *f* for integers), number of length 10 (%-10.1f), another (right-aligned) string (%-10s), and a newline character (\n). The first and third fields of the time_worked database are formatted in reverse order using this format specification. Increasingly more complex formatting operations can be handled with **awk** and **printf.**

Awk is the best Shell tool for formatting detailed reports. For more information, see the awk references in the bibliography (e.g., Aho et al., 1988). Now, having all of the four key programs available for application use, let's look at ways to plug our system into the others around it.

SYSTEM INTERFACES

Other systems often provide input to or accept output from our system via disk, tape, or electronic transmission (Figure 7.12). The commands that interface with other systems are shown in Table 7.2.

Ar typically manages libraries of C object modules. If a file is on disk, there is usually little problem getting the file into or out of the system. To copy files from one disk to another, **cpio** is a useful mechanism. **Cpio** can be used with either disk or tape. **Tar,** like **cpio,** packages and compresses information for storage on tape:

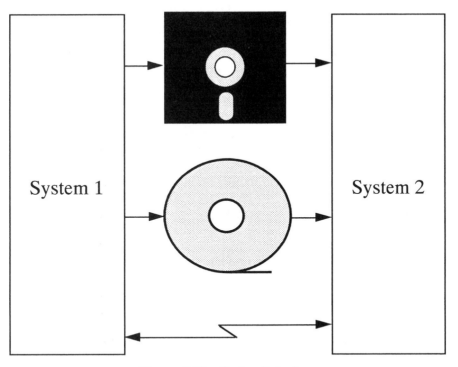

Figure 7.12   System Interfaces

INPUT INTERFACE	OUTPUT INTERFACE
`ar x archive.a`	`ar q archive.a file1 file2 ...`
`cpio -i < /dev/mt0`	`ls file*	cpio -o > /dev/mt0`
`ls olddir/file*	cpio -pdl .`	`ls file*	cpio -pdl new_dir`
`tar xf -	application`	`tar u file*`

Both disk and tape interfaces have their place, but they often are cumbersome. (Trust the postal system with my tape? Never!) Nothing beats the immediacy of electronic transmission. Using a modem, we can call another UNIX system using **cu:**

`cu 95551234`

On a local area network, we can use **rlogin** or the more powerful **telnet** to access another UNIX system, log in, and accomplish file transfers. Over wider networks, we can use **ftp** (ARPANET file transfer protocol) to move files around the nation and the world. **Mail** allows for direct contact with users on virtually any system. **Uucp** handles file transfers with a greater degree of security. **Send** lets a little old UNIX system flog a big IBM mainframe with job requests, retrieve

TABLE 7.2 System Interfaces

Interface	Command	Description
Disk	`ar`	archive and library maintenance
	`cpio`	copy input/output
Tape	`tar`	tape archive
	`cpio`	copy input/output
Transmission	`cu`	call another UNIX system
	`ftp`	file transfer program (network)
	`mail`	electronic mail
	`rjestat`	remote job entry (RJE) status
	`send`	RJE job submission
	`rlogin`	remote login to a system on the network
	`uucp`	UNIX-to-UNIX communication program
	`uustat`	status of uucp
	`uuto`	uucp file copy
	`uupick`	uucp file pickup
	`uux`	UNIX-to-UNIX command execution

information, and hack it up for more exhaustive processing in Shell. And a host of other communication programs, such as Kermit, wait in the public domain. Some examples of these commands follow:

```
rlogin network_system
ftp remote_hostname
mail system!system!username
uucp system!filenames destination_system!dir
uuto filenames system!user
uupick
```

For most application developers, intimate knowledge of these commands will be unnecessary. The UNIX wizard, however, will find them to be a vital tool in the worldwide quest for knowledge.

WORKING WITH NUMBERS

Every Shell programmer encounters the need to work with numbers: a sine here, a sum there, and an occasional graph. A significant part of UNIX is text, but the other part is numbers. Manipulating them and integrating them with the Shell is simple. There are only a few commands in the Bourne Shell that affect numbers: **bc, dc,** and **expr.**

Aside from handling various string comparisons and evaluations, **expr** also handles basic integer math: addition, subtraction, multiplication, and division. This facility is useful for simple mathematical processing and for controlling loops. Interactively, **expr** can handle simple calculations:

```
expr 327 + 431
758
expr 431 / 327
1
```

In loops, it can handle repetitious calculations. For example, the following command would sum all of the numbers from 1 to 100:

```
while [ ${i:=1} -le 100 ]
do
    total=`expr ${total:=0} + ${i}`
    i=`expr ${i} + 1`
done
echo $total
```

Expr can also control the number of times a loop executes. Since the Bourne Shell has no **repeat** control construct, **expr** and **while** handle the repetition of processing.

```
while [ ${i:=1} -le 10 ] # Repeat 10 times
do
    process something
    i=`expr ${i} + 1`
done
```

The C Shell can handle simple integer arithmetic using standard C language operators: +, -, *, /, and %. When assigning values to parameters, the C Shell can use the integer operators of C: +=, -=, *=, /=, ++, and —. The following example demonstrates the use of integer arithmetic:

```
if ( $variable + 1 > $maximum) then
    @ var1 += 5
    @ var2--
endif
```

KSH

The Korn Shell provides some nice extensions to enhance the arithmetic capabilities of the Bourne Shell while at the same time remaining compatible. We have already explored some of the integer arithmetic capabilities of Korn Shell and will now cover them in greater detail. First we must review how to make a variable an integer type.

The Korn Shell, as discussed in Chapter 5, allows you to assign a variable to be of type integer. As you will recall, this is done using the **typeset** command. The following example will declare counter to be of type integer:

```
type -i counter
```

Once a variable is declared as integer, the Korn Shell recognizes it as such and permits arithmetic operations to be performed directly using standard mathematical notation. The assignment operator "=" can be used in a straightforward manner—no need for the Bourne Shell **expr** command. For example, the loop shown that adds the numbers 1 through 100 using Bourne Shell could be written in Korn Shell as follows:

```
typeset -i i=1    # Set the variable i = 1 and tell Korn Shell it
                  # is an integer type
typeset -i total=0
while [ $i -le 100 ]
do
  total=total+i
  i=i+1
done
echo $total
5050
```

Notice that there is no need for the **expr** command here. Once the variable is declared integer, the assignment is done directly. It should be pointed out that when the integer variables are used, there is no preceding $ in front of the variable. When evaluating an arithmetic statement, the Korn Shell does not require the $, although the statement still works properly if the $ is present. Please note that if you do not declare the variable as an integer, the Korn Shell will treat it as a string just as the Bourne Shell does. This is to maintain compatibility with the Bourne Shell. This can give you unexpected results, as you can imagine, as shown using the preceding example but not defining the variable total to be of type integer:

```
typeset -i i=1    # Set the variable i = 1 and tell Korn Shell it
                  # is an integer type
while [ $i -le 100 ]
do
```

```
    total=total+i
      i=i+1
done
echo $total
total+i
```

In this case, total was assigned the string value "total+i"—not at all what we had in mind. The other thing to keep in mind is that you cannot place a space between the operator (in this case +) and the operands unless you quote the string. While this is to be expected, it is not obvious at first. So the expression total=total + 1 would not be evaluated properly due to spaces; the expression total="total + 1" is just fine.

The Korn Shell provides more arithmetic operators than the Bourne Shell, as is shown in Table 7.3 on page 231. These arithmetic operators can be combined to form expressions. An integer expression consists of integer variables, integer constants, and the operators shown in the table. Forming arithmetic expressions using these components ensures that the Korn Shell will understand how to evaluate it properly. But if you use a noninteger variable in an expression (a variable that is not defined as an integer variable using **typeset**), then the Korn Shell will attempt to evaluate it as an expression instead of an integer. If the variable does not evaluate properly, an error will occur. Let's look at an example of how this works:

```
integer i                        # Set the variables to integer
                                 # using the Korn Shell alias
                                 # integer j

integer first_total=0
integer second_total=0
total_expr="10 * (j / i) + 5"    # Set the total integer expression
j=20
i=5
first_total="$total_expr + j"
second_total="$total_expr + i"

echo $first_total
echo $second_total
65
50
```

As you can see, the total_expr was evaluated as an integer expression. In this case it did indeed contain a valid integer expression and the results were calculated properly. A few other things should be pointed out in this example. First, we utilized the integer alias that is a standard alias in the Korn Shell. This is simply an alias for the **typeset -i** command. The *total_expr* variable is also an example of developing a more complex arithmetic expression containing several variables and operators. Note that the parentheses can be used to control precedence evaluation, as you would expect.

As you may have determined by now, the variable on the left side of the assignment statement is what allows the Korn Shell to determine whether it should perform arithmetic evaluation on the right side of the assignment or not. If the variable is defined as an integer, the Korn Shell performs arithmetic evaluation on the right side of the expression; otherwise the right side is treated as a string. But what if you want the left side of the assignment statement to be a string variable but still perform arithmetic evaluation on the right side? The Korn Shell provides this ability through the use of the **let** command.

The Korn Shell **let** command allows you to specify when arithmetic evaluation is to take place. It forces the Korn Shell to look at the statement on the right side of the assignment operator as an expression instead of a string. If the variable on the left side of an assignment operator is a string variable, then the assignment is made anyway. The syntax of the **let** command is

```
let "expression ..." or (( expression))
```

where the *expression* is any valid arithmetic expression as described previously. (No need for $ in front of variables.) The **let** command returns an exit code of zero if the last expression in the expression list returns a nonzero value and 1 otherwise. Note that the expression should be enclosed in quotes if the **let** command is used. This helps remove ambiguity in the expression. You can place white space in your expression and it will be evaluated properly. It also helps remove the ambiguity between the Shell operators and the arithmetic operators (i.e., < less than and Shell redirection). The (( )) form of the **let** command is provided for convenience and does not require the quotes; quotes are assumed. It should be pointed out that the **let** command allows multiple expressions to be entered for evaluation, while the double parentheses form of **let** allows only one. All the characters between the ((and the)) are treated as **let** "characters." Let's look at an example of how the **let** command can be used. Let's restructure our previous example that totals the integers 1 through 100 to use the **let** command.

```
let "i=1" "total=0"
while (( i <= 100))
do
  ((total = total + i))
  ((i=i+1))
done
echo $total
5050
```

There are several things that are different in this Shell procedure. First, notice that we do not use the **typeset** command to define the variables used as integer. Instead, we have used the **let** command to force assignment to string variables. The next thing to notice is that we used the **let** command to control the WHILE loop. This is taking advantage of the fact that the **let** command returns an exit code. In this case we have tested to see whether the variable *i* is less than or equal to 100. If this is true, then the loop continues because of the exit value returned by **let**. This notation is often clearer than the standard test condition used before. It provides for the use of standard mathematical notation to describe test conditions. Most people understand the meaning of <= but are often left guessing at the meaning of the test operators (-le, -eq, etc.). The modified version of the Shell also uses the **let** command to calculate the total and loop control variable *i*. Notice that even though we are assigning to noninteger Shell variables, the $ construct need not precede the variable names.

The combination of the **let** command and the use of integer variables allows for a more intuitive approach to working with integer expressions in your Shell procedures that utilize the Korn Shell.

Handling more complex mathematics and floating-point numbers requires the use of **bc** or **dc**. The desk calculator, **dc**, works just like a desk calculator, but is not as flexible as the basic calculator, **bc,** for use with Shell programs. Using a syntax not unlike C or the C Shell, **bc** provides for unlimited precision arithmetic. It can also work in bases other than base 10. (This is also a capability that the Korn Shell has. Please see your manual pages on the Korn Shell). **Bc** has at its

TABLE 7.3   Korn Shell Arithmetic Operators

Operator	Action Performed
-	unary negation (make a number negative)
!	logical negation
~	bitwise NOT
*	multiplication
/	integer division
%	remainder after integer division
+	addition
-	subtraction
<<, >>	left shift, right shift
<, <=	less than, less than or equal to
>, >=	greater than, greater than or equal to
==, !=	equal to, not equal to
&	bitwise *and*
^	bitwise exclusive *or*
|	bitwise *or*
&&	logical *and*
||	logical *or*
=	assignment

command the IF, FOR, and WHILE control structures. It also has access to various functions — sqrt, length, scale, sine, cosine, exponential, log, arctangent, and Bessel functions. Users may define functions using **bc** that can be included to handle complex math operations.

When executed, **bc** first reads any files that were specified as arguments. User-defined functions can be stored in these files. Then, **bc** begins to read the standard input, which can be a file, a device, or a terminal. Two of the previous examples could be accomplished with **bc**:

```
echo "327 + 431" | bc      # Add 327 and 431
758
echo "scale=2;431 / 327" | bc     # Divide 431 by 327
1.32
```

In the first example, the **echo** command creates an input string for **bc**. The first example adds 327 and 431. The second example first sets the decimal accuracy (scale) to two. Then, the division of 431 by 327 is echoed into **bc**. Unless set to another value, the *scale* of every **bc** command defaults to zero decimal places.

For simple integer arithmetic, **expr** or Korn Shell arithmetic is the best choice. But when higher precision is required, **bc** handles the job nicely.

The **bc** command can also use the math library functions to calculate various limited equations. To calculate the sine of all angles from 1 to 90°, the basic calculator can be invoked in a WHILE loop:

```
while [ ${angle:=1} -le 90 ]    # For angles < 90
do
  # Calculate the sine to four decimal places
  sin=`echo "scale 4;s(${angle})" | bc -l`
  echo "Angle=${angle} Sine=${sin}"    # Print the result
  i=`expr ${angle} + 1`                 # Increment the angle
done
```

Functions stored in files can be handled by **bc** to process more complex equations. The following functions handle converting Fahrenheit to Celsius:

```
scale=2
define f(c){    /* convert Celsius to Fahrenheit */
   auto f    /* Fahrenheit variable */
   f = ( c * 1.8 ) + 32    /* convert */
   return(f)    /* return value */
}
define c(f) {    /* convert Fahrenheit to Celsius */
   auto c    /* Celsius variable */
   c = ( f - 32 ) / 1.8    /* convert */
   return(c)    /* return value */
}
```

Assuming that these functions were contained in a file called temp, conversions could be handled by invoking **bc:**

```
bc temp      # Invoke bc with fahrenheit/celsius conversions
f(100)       # Convert 100 degrees celsius to fahrenheit
212.00
c(32)        # Convert 32 degrees fahrenheit to celsius
0.00
quit
```

Or the results could be stored in a variable:

```
fahrenheit=`echo "f(100)" | bc temp`
celsius=`echo "c(0)" | bc temp`
```

Although these are simple examples, **bc** can use functions to process significantly more complex arithmetic equations as the need arises. It can also handle other functions required by programmers, such as conversion of numbers from one base into another.

Computers use base 2 for their calculations, but most of them display their information in octal (base 8) or hexadecimal (base 16). These conversions can easily be handled by **bc** by assigning an input base and or an output base. An octal calculator would set both input base (*ibase*) and output base (*obase*) to 8:

```
bc
ibase=8    /* set input base to octal */
obase=8    /* set output base to octal */
11 + 7     /* octal 11 + 7 = 20 octal */
20
quit
```

The same facility is available for the hexadecimal environment. Or hexadecimal or octal can be converted directly to decimal:

```
bc
ibase=8      /* input base is octal, output base is decimal /*
10           /* octal 10 is 8 decimal */
8
ibase=16     /* input base is hexadecimal, output base is decimal
             */
10           /* hexadecimal 10 is 16 decimal */
16
quit
```

In the previous example, an octal 10 is equal to a decimal 8 and a hexadecimal 10 is equal to a decimal 16. When reading octal or hexadecimal dumps of data or programs, these calculators can improve any programmer's productivity.

SUMMARY

As you have seen, you can construct complete application systems using the Shell as a fourth-generation language. You can create Shell systems anytime that a simple system will serve many users. As this system grows and evolves, it may eventually need to be rewritten using an actual database—Oracle, Ingress, Informix, Unity, Unify, or some other RDBMS. This leads us to one of the fundamental laws of software engineering:

Any system that works has always evolved from a simple system that works.

In any situation, a Shell prototype will serve as an excellent model for the development of a needed system. The prototype system can then serve the needs of customers and clients until the final product is available. This prototype system is composed of the five common types of software programs—input, output, query, database update, and interface. This chapter has demonstrated the key commands and Shell programs that support each of these types of program designs. Any Shell user who wants to maximize his or her effectiveness and efficiency should become familiar with the system-building capabilities described in this chapter.

EXERCISES

1. When should you use the Shell to create application systems?

2. Describe the format of a relational table.

3. What are the five basic program designs most often created in Shell?

4. Which Shell commands are used in each of the basic program designs?

5. Build the input, output, query, and database update programs for:
    - the employee database
    - the tax tables

6. Write the paycheck program for the payroll system.

7. Why are data modeling and design so important?

Chapter 8

Structuring Shell Programs

Now that we have looked at how to write Shell programs in Chapter 6 as well as the components that make up a Shell system in Chapter 7, we are ready to spend a little more time exploring Shell program structure. In this chapter we look at what makes up a well-structured program and how to use Shell functions to aid in developing that program.

As your Shell programs increase in complexity, good structure will be essential. Without good structure, larger Shell programs can become difficult to follow and understand and even more difficult to maintain and modify. Applying structured techniques while developing your programs will greatly aid you, and maybe more importantly others, to understand, maintain, and modify your programs with greatly improved productivity. Structured programming techniques have long been recognized as a key to quality software systems and are used extensively by professional programmers and system developers throughout the world. By applying these techniques to your Shell programs, you can achieve the same benefits.

You may feel that giving time to your program structure will slow you down and make you less productive. The voice of experience tells us that this is not true in the long run. By giving some thought to the structure of your Shell program, especially one that is not used as a prototype, you will save yourself hours of time and frustration. Even Shell systems that are being used for a prototype are better off being developed in some structured manner. When the time comes to replace the prototype with C language code, you will want to be able to understand what functions the Shell performs.

At the heart of structured programming is the function. The function provides you — the Shell programmer and developer — the ability to divide your program into small packages that perform particular tasks. Most robust software development languages, including the UNIX Shell, provide some method for building functions. Shell functions are most often used in the following situations:

1. To store often-used sequences of commands in the login Shell environment.

2. To provide structure to Shell programs by dividing up long command sequences into logical units.

3. To increase the reuse of code in the Shell procedures. This prevents redundant coding of the same process in numerous spots in the Shell program.

With this in mind, let's explore Shell functions.

SHELL FUNCTIONS

A function is a group of commands that are assigned a name that acts like a handle to that group of commands. In order to execute this group of commands defined in the function, you simply call the function by the name you provided. The syntax for defining a function in either the Bourne or Korn Shell is:

```
Bourne:  function_name ( ) { command_list; }
Korn:  function function_name ( ) { command_list; }
```

where the *function_name* is the name by which you want to refer to the function and the *command_list* is a list of one or more valid Shell commands. The function name can be any valid Shell variable name. Please note that a space must occur after the left brace ({) and the first command as well as before the right brace (}), which follows the semicolon of the last command in *command_list*. This is so that the Shell will recognize the braces as special keyword characters. The parentheses following the *function_name* alert the Shell to the fact that you are attempting to define a function. The function is read into memory and is executed any time that you invoke the function name. Invoking a function after it has been defined is done in the same manner as any other command. Simply type the name at the Shell command prompt or place the name in your Shell procedure.

Declaring Functions

As an example, let's declare a simple function and see how it behaves:

```
dir( ) {
ls -la | pg
}
```

This function, called dir, simulates the MS-DOS directory command. It invokes the **ls** command with the -la option and pipes the output to the **pg** command for browsing. Now if we type `dir` at the command line, the results are a listing of our current directory, much like an MS-DOS listing, piped to pg. Functions can be defined by placing the function in a file and making the file executable, as with any other Shell program, or they can be entered interactively at the command line. With the interactive approach the Shell will prompt you, using the secondary prompt string, for input until it sees the right brace:

```
dir( ) {
More: ls -la | pg
More: }
```

In this example, our secondary prompt, $PS2, was set to "More:" and we were prompted for input until the right brace is seen by the Shell, indicating that the function definition is complete. While the interactive approach is useful for temporary functions, it is prone to error and you must retype the functions each time you log in. This is not very efficient, and the entire point of functions is to increase efficiency.

If you attempt to define a function using a name that already exists, one of two things will happen. If the name is a function you will redefine that function. If the name is an alias you will not redefine the alias but will instead run the alias.

KSH

Korn Shell Autoload

The Korn Shell allows you to declare a function as undefined and then load that function when it is first invoked. To declare a function as undefined, you use the **typeset** command with the -fu options flags. For example:

```
typeset -fu function_name
```

would declare *function_name* as undefined.

When the Korn Shell attempts to execute this function for the first time, it recognizes that the function is not defined and searches the path names defined in the variable *FPATH* for a file with the same name as the function. When it finds this file it executes the commands that contain the function definition for *function_name*. If the *FPATH* variable is not defined, then the current directory is searched. The *FPATH* variable is defined, in the same manner as your *PATH* variable. Once the function is loaded, all subsequent calls run the function directly.

FUNCTIONS AND YOUR ENVIRONMENT

Functions can perform a wide variety of keystroke-saving work. By defining small functions such as the dir function cited previously, you can save lots of typing and frustration. As an added benefit you can place functions in your .profile so that they are defined when you log in. In this respect functions are much like forming aliases in the Korn Shell but are much more powerful since they allow for any number of commands to be included in the definition. Functions can be very powerful tools in helping customize your environment and saving lots of typing effort. Once you get the hang of building them to accomplish repetitive typing chores, you'll have dozens in your .profile. A good way of organizing them is to place them in another file called .myfuncs and then execute .myfuncs from your .profile. This can help keep your .profile orderly. You can even use this approach to define groups of functions that you may use for particular tasks—for example, store the related functions in a file and then execute that file in your current Shell:

```
. testfunctions    # Read in and define test functions in my Shell
                   # environment
```

What if we always wanted the standard **ls** command to behave in the same manner as the dir function? In order to do this we could have named the function **ls**.

```
ls( ) {
/usr/bin/ls -la | pg
}
```

If we do this, then we have in effect redefined the meaning of **ls** for our Shell session. Now when we type `ls` at the command line, it would execute the ls function and not the standard **ls** command. It is important to understand this naming priority that functions have. It can be a powerful tool in customizing your environment. Note that it is actually necessary to access the original **ls** command by using its full path name. Once you define the ls function, any reference to that calls the ls function. So if we were to define the **ls** command as shown next, we would cause problems:

```
ls( ) {
ls -la | pg
}
```

While your intention may have been to invoke the UNIX **ls** command, what was accomplished was a recursive call to the ls function (the ls function calls the ls function calls the ls function. . .), which in this case causes an endless loop and never returns. Actually, recursive calls can be a very powerful programming technique. (We cover recursive calls later in this chapter.) Just use care when redefining UNIX commands.

Listing Function Definitions

Now that we have seen how to define functions, let's look at ways to list the functions that are active in our session. If you are using the Bourne Shell, the functions are listed along with variables by using the **set** command. Since variables and function names are stored together, their names must be unique when using the Bourne Shell. Note that if you define a function when using Bourne Shell and then assign a variable the same name, your function definition will be lost.

KSH

When you are using the Korn Shell, listing of function definitions is done using the **typeset** command with the -f option. The **typeset -f** command is also stored as a standard alias in the Korn Shell called functions. The **typeset** command or functions alias will list all your function definitions. They are not listed with the **set** command as in the Bourne Shell. This brings out a distinction between the Korn and Bourne Shells' handling of functions. In the Korn Shell functions are not stored with the variables. Thus they are not listed with the **set** command and the variable name and function name conflict that exists with the Bourne Shell does not exist. It is possible, when using the Korn Shell, to have variables with the same names as functions. This removes the potential for defining functions and having them overlaid with variable names by a simple naming mistake.

Removing Function Definitions

In order to remove function definitions using the Bourne Shell, you use the **unset** command as shown:

```
unset function_name
```

where *function_name* is the name you provided for the function when you defined it. This is the same method used to unset variable names. This seems logical since the Bourne Shell stores functions as variable names. Once the **unset** command is executed, the function is no longer available.

KSH

The Korn Shell also uses the **unset** command in conjunction with the -f option flag to remove function definitions. This is needed because the Korn Shell stores function names separately from the variable names and also permits overlap between the function and variable names. The syntax of the **unset** command is:

```
unset -f function_name    # Remove a function name
unset var_name            # Remove a variable name
```

FUNCTION EXECUTION

After declaring your function, it is a simple matter to execute the function; simply type the name of the function just as you would any other command. The Shell locates the function and executes the associated commands. While this is very similar to using other Shell commands or Shell programs that you have written, there are differences.

Once the function is declared it is stored in your environment and is executed directly. This differs from the typical command where the Shell must read the file and then interpret the commands contained in the file. This latter method is much more demanding and thus much slower than a function call.

Commands stored in a function are not executed in a subshell; they are executed in your current Shell. This is very similar to invoking a Shell program with the dot (.) command:

```
. shell_pgm
```

where the *shell_pgm* is some Shell procedure that you (or someone else) have created. If you recall, this command tells the Shell to execute the command in your current Shell environment. This is different from invoking the Shell directly, which causes the commands to run in a subshell. Since functions are executed in your current Shell, any changes to the environment performed in the function are permanently made to the current Shell. Upon return from the function execution, the changes made to the environment remain intact. Most importantly, the following changes remain in effect after return from the function call:

1. All changes to variables are basically permanent. This means setting of variables, unsetting, and exporting.

2. Any changes to the current directory remain in effect.

3. Any files used are also shared.

So use care when you execute a function call. It does behave differently from a normal Shell program call.

The commands in the function are executed until either the end of the function is reached, or an exit or return statement is encountered. If an exit statement is coded in your function, then both the function and the invoking Shell are exited. (We have seen examples of the **exit** command previously.) The return statement is a way to exit just the function with the option of returning some particular value. The syntax of the return statement is `return  n,` where *n* is an integer value that you would like returned as an exit status to the calling Shell. This value can be tested for using the $? variable to check to see what action the function performed. Did it complete properly or does some other action need to be taken? The return statement provides the ability to leave a function whenever you choose. For example, if some error condition occurs, you can return from the function and inform the calling Shell program that some problem has occurred. If you do not supply a return statement and the end of the function is reached, then an implied return is performed with the exit status equal to the exit status of the last command performed in the function. After completion of the function you are returned to the spot where the function was called from. If this was the command line, then you are returned to the command line; if the function was executed from within a Shell program, then a return starts execution at the line following the function call in the program.

If your function has an error when processing under the Bourne Shell, the function and its calling Shell are exited.

KSH

The Korn Shell, on the other hand, does not abort the entire Shell program when an error occurs in a function. Only the function is aborted. Control is returned to the calling Shell program.

Passing Arguments to Functions

Arguments are passed to functions in the same manner as any other Shell procedure. Simply type the arguments following the command name, in the normal fashion, and the function will be able to access these arguments in the variables $1...$9 in the case of the Bourne Shell. Of course, the Korn Shell can access variables beyond $9, as was discussed previously.

There is one small anomaly that you should take note of. When you call a function with arguments from inside a Shell program, the function arguments replace the arguments originally passed to the Shell program. Of course, the solution to this problem is to store the arguments in a variable before you make the call to the function and then, upon return, replace the arguments if there is a need to do so. This can be done using the **set** command.

Another related approach is to parse all the arguments prior to any function calls and store any arguments in your own variables. The nice thing about this approach is that you can assign arguments to variable names that have more meaning than $1, $2, and so forth. When your programs start to get large and filled with numerous function calls and calls to other Shell programs, it is easy to lose track of what is being stored in the special variables $1 through $9. Good variable names are a key to easy understanding and maintenance of any program. Even though this approach is preferable, however, it may not always be possible. In those cases, the first approach of storing the arguments and then restoring them can always be used.

FUNCTION SCOPE

Function declarations have rules about where the functions themselves are applicable and what variables are accessible to the functions while they are executing. These rules are referred to as *scoping rules*.

When using the Bourne Shell, function declarations are local to the Shell in which they are defined. This means that any Shell program that runs in a subshell will not have access to the functions that were defined in the parent calling Shell process. In other words, it is not possible in the Bourne Shell to export functions to make them available to called Shell procedures.

KSH

The Korn Shell does allow for functions to be exported. This permits Shell programs that are executing in a subshell to access functions that were defined in the parent Shell program. This is done in the same manner as exporting variables. The syntax for the export is:

```
export func_name
```

where *func_name* is the name of your function you want exported. With some older versions of the Korn Shell, the **typeset** command must be used to export functions.

Once a function begins executing, there is the issue of which variables are available to the function. Since functions run in the current Shell, all variables defined in the current Shell procedure are available to all the functions declared in that Shell process. Also, any arguments passed to the function are available to the function in the special variables $1...$n as was mentioned before. Also, any variables defined in the function itself become available to the calling Shell procedure as well as to all other functions that may be called. Variables that participate in this kind of global sharing are called *global variables*. They are shared globally between all functions and procedures. By exporting a variable, you make it global not only to functions but also to any Shell programs that run in a subshell.

KSH

The Korn Shell does provide for local variables in functions. This means that the variable is visible only in the function where it is declared and is not shared by the calling Shell or any other functions. Once the function is finished executing and a return to the calling procedure is performed, the variable and its value are no longer available. A variable declared as local in a function becomes global to any functions it calls. In order to define the variables as local variables, you must use the Korn Shell **typeset** command.

When using the Bourne Shell, all traps are shared between the calling Shell program and the function. Thus, if a trap is reset in a function, it is reset for the calling Shell as well. The exit trap (signal 0) is not activated in the Bourne Shell when a function returns. This is not entirely true for the Korn Shell.

KSH

In the Korn Shell, all traps are shared except for the exit and the err traps. If an exit trap (signal 0) is activated in a Korn Shell function, it is executed upon return from the function. This can be a very nice debugging tool. The err trap is available in the Korn Shell only and is performed every time a command returns an unsuccessful return code. With Korn Shell functions, the err trap can be defined in the function and will be executed any time an error exit status is returned in the function. This is also a very powerful debugging tool.

PLACING FUNCTIONS IN YOUR SHELL PROGRAM

Now that we have looked at the basic mechanisms used to declare and use functions, let's look more closely at how to use functions to improve our Shell program structure. In order to use Shell functions, they must first be defined. This is true in both your login Shell environment and your Shell programs. This means that your Shell programs will have all function definitions at the top of your file. This allows all functions that are to be called to be defined before they are used. The layout would look something like the outline shown here:

```
# Typical Shell layout Skeleton
# Section 1 - Function Definitions
function1 ( ) { command_list
               return 0; }
function2 ( ) { command_list
               return 0; }
.
.
.
functionN ( ) { command_list
               return 0; }
# Section 2 - Main Shell Program Body
commands
.
.
function1
function2
.
.
more commands and function calls as needed
exit
```

In this skeletal layout, the functions used in a Shell program are defined before the main code begins to execute. This allows the functions to be called from the main procedure whenever you need to perform the task accomplished by the function.

The layout just shown has one slight disadvantage. The functions that are defined in the Shell program as shown are available to this Shell program only; they cannot be used by other Shell programs that you might construct. If you are developing numerous Shell programs, the sharing of Shell functions can be very beneficial. It can save you hours of time by reducing the need to code and test Shell procedures. We can overcome this problem by placing the functions in a file(s) and then executing the file to declare the functions. This way, numerous Shell programs can share the same common and reusable functions. The skeletal outline for this is shown next. In a Shell program file, funcfile, we provide the function declarations:

```
# File funcfile contains common function definitions
function1 ( ) { command_list
               return 0; }
function2 ( ) { command_list
               return 0; }
.
.
.
functionN ( ) { command_list
               return 0; }
```

Then, in our Shell program, we include the function declarations:

```
# Typical Shell layout Skeleton
# Section 1 - Function Definitions
. funcfile    # Declare function definition in the current Shell
# Section 2 - Main Shell Program Body
commands
   .
   .
function1
function2
   .
   .
more commands and function calls as needed
exit
```

As you can see, when using the Bourne Shell you must execute the common function file using the "." command to ensure that the functions are declared in the current Shell. Also note that when using the Bourne Shell the functions declared in this Shell program are available to this Shell process only. If you call another Shell program that executes in a subshell, the functions will not be available.

KSH

By using the ability of the Korn Shell to export functions, this limitation can be overcome. If we were to export the functions after they are declared, they would be available to all other Shell procedures that execute as subshells.

GOOD PROGRAM STRUCTURE

Now that we have seen how to define functions in our Shell program, we should spend a little time discussing what good program structure is. When you are designing programs in any programming language, a well-structured program will greatly facilitate understanding of the program. To provide a well-structured program we utilize functions and other Shell programs that we call from our main Shell program. Essentially we want to divide our program into manageable and logical chunks. These chunks take the form of functions and Shell programs. Our goal is to avoid building what we will loosely call the "run-on" program. This is a program where all the functionality and logic are built into a single main procedure. While it is easy to get away with a "run-on" program when it is small, larger programs quickly become unmanageable. The advantages of dividing up your program are:

1. makes the program easier to understand

2. reduces redundant code (calls the function instead of repeating the code many times)

3. makes debugging much easier

4. increases maintainability

5. encourages reusing code

6. decreases testing time

Of course, all of these traits are closely tied to software quality.

When building a structured program, try to build a short main procedure (Section 2 in the skeletal Shell provided in the previous section) that provides the general flow and logic of the program. Perhaps this main program ensures that correct arguments and options have been selected and, based on those arguments, calls a number of functions or Shell programs to accomplish the task. When you are designing your program for the first time, try to think about dividing it up based on some logical functional division. For each logical division, create a separate function or program that will work to accomplish that task. Of course, these Shell programs and functions can call other functions and programs as needed. When developing Shell programs, my goal is to develop a main procedure that is no longer than one or two printed pages. All other functionality is placed in Shell functions and called Shell programs. The two-page guideline could be applied to any Shell function or program that you develop. If any program gets too long, it becomes difficult to understand and debug. Your goal should be to develop small, manageable, reusable functions.

When you are in the process of coding your program, you may find yourself coding the same thing over and over again. Any time that you find yourself copying or duplicating code, you should consider utilizing a function. Some things that often end up being functions in many of my Shell programs are:

1. Error routines— No need to produce the same code for every error; make it a function.

2. Input/output routines—Often you will read/write to/from the terminal or a file in several places. No need to create the code in all places; make it a function.

3. Any repeated process—Any procedure that you repeat more than two times should be a function.

DESIGNING REUSABLE FUNCTIONS

If you really want to become a productive Shell programmer (or any kind of programmer, really), you must work to reuse your code. This means that the functions and programs you develop should be shared with other programs and functions as much as possible. When you are writing a new function or program to accomplish some task, you should ask yourself the following questions:

1. Is there some way I could generalize this function so that it could be used in many different programs to accomplish the task at hand?

2. Is there a way to make the module independent from the current calling program so that other programs can share the code?

As an example of what we mean by generalizing, let's look back at some code we wrote in Chapter 6. In this example we had developed a program that cut particular fields from a password file record based on the user ID. Instead of building a program that cut just a particular field, we developed a program that would cut any field from the password file record based on user ID. Since cutting fields from the password file is a common process in the UNIX environment, there is a good chance that we may be able to use this procedure elsewhere in our programming efforts. So we place this in a common program or function, making it accessible to any Shell program. The original code in the Shell program looked like the following:

```
grep $userid /etc/passwd | cut -f5 -d:
```

We generalized this to the following Shell program:

```
# A general purpose password file grep and cut
if [ $# -eq 0 ]
then
  echo "No args supplied for passgrep - Arguments are userid and\
    field number to cut"
fi
grep $1 /etc/passwd | cut -f$2 -d:
```

Now any user ID and field can be specified.

This also demonstrates how we can accomplish making the function independent from the current Shell program. In this case we have elected to make the function work with arguments passed to the function instead of depending on global variables that would be shared with the calling Shell program. Sharing global variables couples the function to the calling environment. This is what we want to avoid when trying to construct general-purpose functions and programs. Avoid interacting with other Shells through the use of shared information that links the programs together. Build a barrier or wall around your function so that it uses information passed through arguments and produces specific, well-identified results.

The goal is to build up a library of reusable Shell programs that can be linked together later, in some modified way, to accomplish a different task. In order to do this well, you must keep the rules of reusability in mind.

Recursive Functions

The Shell supports recursive function calls. A recursive function is a function that calls itself. At first this can seem like a confusing concept, but actually recursive function calls are just another form of looping. You are repeatedly performing the statements in the function call by calling the function multiple times. In most cases it is possible to perform the same task using an iterative loop in place of the recursive function call. But a recursive function can solve some problems, very elegantly, that would be awkward using looping.

When designing a recursive function, a call is placed in the function to the function itself, as shown:

```
calculate ( ) {
  statement_list;
  calculate;     # Call the calculate function again
  }
```

The function, calculate, is called in a recursive manner by calling the function within the function itself. While this example shows how to make a function recursive, it also brings up a rule concerning recursive functions. You must provide an exit condition that eventually becomes true when building recursive functions. This exit condition is used to stop the recursive calling of the function. If you do not do this, the recursive calls never stop and the function ends up looping, endlessly calling the function. Eventually the recursive call will make your Shell session run out of system recourses and it will terminate. This is probably not exactly what you had in mind. How to set up recursive function calls should become a little clearer when we look at an example.

Let's take a Shell program that we developed previously and turn it into a recursive procedure. This Shell procedure adds the integers 1 through 100 and is shown next basically in its original form except that it has been formed into a function called sum_em.

```
sum_em ( ) {
while [ ${i:=1} -le 100 ]
do
  total=`expr ${total:=0} + ${i}`
  i=`expr ${i} + 1`
done
}
```

Now to modify this into a recursive function, we remove the while loop and replace it with a call to the function. Note that the function has also been generalized so that it can now accept the integer values to sum. The first argument is the starting integer, and the second argument is the ending integer. The Shell function to accomplish this task is shown:

```
sum_em ( ) {

if [ $1 -lt $2 ]      # This is the exit condition check to stop
                      # the recursion
then
  sum_em `expr $1 + 1` $2     # Call the function again with the
                             # next integer
  total=`expr $? + $1`       # Total the return from sum_em with
                             # current $1
  return $total              # Return the new total
else
  return $2                  # Return $2 if we have made all the
                             # calls
fi

}
```

At first glance, this may seem confusing. To get a better understanding of how a recursive function operates, let's turn on the debugger and take a look at the Shell as it executes. For this example we will only add the numbers 1 through 10.

```
set -vx
sum_em 1 10
+ sum_em 1 10
+ [ 1 -lt 10 ]
+ expr 1 + 1
+ sum_em 2 10
+ [ 2 -lt 10 ]
+ expr 2 + 1
+ sum_em 3 10
+ [ 3 -lt 10 ]
+ expr 3 + 1
+ sum_em 4 10
+ [ 4 -lt 10 ]
+ expr 4 + 1
+ sum_em 5 10
+ [ 5 -lt 10 ]
+ expr 5 + 1
+ sum_em 6 10
+ [ 6 -lt 10 ]
+ expr 6 + 1
+ sum_em 7 10
+ [ 7 -lt 10 ]
+ expr 7 + 1
+ sum_em 8 10
```

```
+ [ 8 -lt 10 ]
+ expr 8 + 1
+ sum_em 9 10
+ [ 9 -lt 10 ]
+ expr 9 + 1
+ sum_em 10 10
+ [ 10 -lt 10 ]
+ return 10    # This is the end of the recursive calls
+ expr 10 + 9
total=19
+ return 19
+ expr 19 + 8
total=27
+ return 27
+ expr 27 + 7
total=34
+ return 34
+ expr 34 + 6
total=40
+ return 40
+ expr 40 + 5
total=45
+ return 45
+ expr 45 + 4
total=49
+ return 49
+ expr 49 + 3
total=52
+ return 52
+ expr 52 + 2
total=54
+ return 54
+ expr 54 + 1
total=55
+ return 55
```

If you examine the output, you can see that the sum_em function is called ten times. Each time, the current invocation waits until the next invocation of the function completes. So in the first phase the function calls stack up until the exit condition is satisfied. Then the tenth invocation of the function returns a value of 10 to the ninth invocation of the function. The ninth invocation then adds the returned 10 with the value of $1 (in this case, 9) giving 19. This value is returned to the eighth invocation of the function. This continues until all invocations have been satisfied. At the end, all the integers have been added and the value for total returned is the sum we desired.

There are many uses for recursive functions. As you begin to explore recursive functions, their power will become evident. At first they may seem awkward, but after a little practice they will seem more natural and you will develop a sense for which problems can best be solved using a recursive technique.

SUMMARY

This chapter has explored use of Shell functions. A function is a series of Shell commands that are given a name. This name is then used as a handle to execute the statements declared as part of the function. To execute a function, you type its name on the command line or in your Shell program just like any other command. In order to execute a function, it must first be declared. Use the **set** command to list functions declared in your current Shell environment and **unset** to remove already existing function definitions. Shell functions can be used to enhance your login Shell environment by placing commonly used functions in your .profile so that they are defined when you log in. Unless you are using the Korn Shell, function definitions are local to your current Shell and cannot be exported to sub-shells. Variables declared and used in functions are global unless you are using the Korn Shell, which supports both global and local variables. Functions can be called with arguments. When building a Shell program, functions are very useful for structuring your program to make it easier to understand and maintain. Functions also encourage code reuse.

EXERCISE

Take any of the Shell programs in previous chapters and convert them to Shell functions.

PART THREE

SHELL PROGRAMMING
FOR MASTERY

Many men go fishing all of their lives without knowing that it is not fish they are after.

Henry David Thoreau

Chapter Nine

Rapid Prototyping and Reuse

Do it badly, do it quickly, make it better, and then say you planned it.

Tom Peters (1990)

The preceding chapters have delved into the detail of Shell programming. For a chapter, I want you to take a moment and rise up above the din and detail and view the Shell from a totally different angle. I learned virtually everything I know about creating software systems from working with Shell programming. It taught me how to be fast. The Shell taught me how to stop coding and start composing systems from reusable components. It taught me how to rise above everyday programming and start thinking functionally. If you let it, Shell will teach you how to *grow* applications four times faster than you can *build* them using conventional coding languages. Let's look at how rapid prototyping and the Shell complement each other and see the different colored glasses we need to use to see the power of these two together.

We should focus on solutions that will bear fruit quickly, within a manager's 12-month planning horizon.

Brad Cox (1990)

Rapid prototyping relies on speed, simplicity, and a shared vision to create a desired product. In rapid prototyping, prototypers create a basic working system that does not contain all of the infinite variety the customer ultimately desires, but that does work and provides the essential initial elements of the system. A baby has all of the bones, muscles, and organs it will ever need, but none are full sized

255

or fully developed. Once this basic working system is installed and turned over to the customer, a series of step-like improvements — evolutions — turn the system into the customer's desired Garden of Eden. Sounds like a utopian fantasy, doesn't it? And it's much more likely to occur this way than through software construction.

Rapid prototyping flies in the face of almost everything we believe about setting and achieving goals and objectives. Rapid prototyping demands that we embed the decision making and direction setting in the fabric of the ongoing processes of creation and evolution. Paul MacCready, inventor of the ultralight Gossamer Condor aircraft, put it this way: "If it's worth doing, it's worth doing badly. If you can make it crudely, you can make it fast and it doesn't cost much. You can test it easily . . . fix it crudely." He insists that this approach maximizes the speed of learning, and I agree; the same applies to software and especially Shell programming.

Unlike the traditional development life cycle, speed is required more than direction. Once you're rolling, you can change course at will. If you're not moving, you have no feedback to guide your first steps. For those of you who know how to ski or have ever thought of learning, you can't position or turn the skis until you are moving. The faster you move, the easier it is to turn. At too slow a speed, skis are rigid and inflexible, and it takes just plain work to direct them anywhere. Just like skiing, rapid prototyping requires that we point our skis downhill and build up some momentum before we start setting directions and goals.

BENEFITS

Compared to standard development processes, rapid prototyping offers several benefits.

1. *It achieves more effective communication* because prototypes demonstrate what is happening, rather than representing it. Designs are maps of the world. Prototypes are the territory. Prototyping simplifies demonstration, evaluation, and modification of the growing system.

2. *It reduces risk* by eliminating uncertainty. The initial system often is created with fewer people in less time. Cycle time to proof of concept is dramatically reduced.

3. *It increases the ability to deliver* desired functionality. Customers continuously refine their needs by using the prototype and offering feedback. This reduces the need for maintenance and enhancement when the system is delivered.

4. *It incorporates a learning process* into the development process. Since we know that we are operating on *incomplete knowledge* whenever we start a development process, rapid prototyping encourages us to learn as we go, backtracking and changing things until we get them right. It encourages

change rather than stifling it. Frozen requirements cannot reflect the dynamics of the organization or market.

5. *It encourages discovery and serendipity* in the development of desired functionality. If we learn as we go, there is a much greater chance of discovering opportunities along the way that will shape the course of the system and possibly the course of the company.

6. *It chops cycle time* from concept to delivered product by a factor of four or more. Since we are only creating the 20 percent of the product that provides 80 percent of the value, the infant system comes into the world with incredible capabilities. "80/20 solutions . . . have a great deal to recommend them — 80 percent of the ideal result, achieved through *20 percent of the effort* that might have been expended. Companies can gain strategic advantage . . . through 80/20 solutions, when aggressive company-wide efforts are judged to take too long and cost too much" (Ernst and Young, 1989).
   Evolution then expands and enhances these capabilities to quickly converge on the desired solution, even though we couldn't see it when we began the journey. Rapid prototyping allows information systems to be created quickly and effectively at low cost. Kraushaar and Shirland (1985) suggest that the cost of a micro-based system can be as low as $10,000 to $50,000 for a three-to-twelve-month effort. It also permits early availability of a working system to begin exploiting the opportunities in the market.

7. *It reduces defects* through continuous testing and evaluation of system components during the initial prototyping and ongoing evolutionary phases. User manuals and training can be developed *using* the working prototype to ensure accuracy.

8. *It encourages the creation of evolutionary systems* that are easy to maintain because every step of development is an evolutionary step as well.

9. *It continuously involves users in the solution*, which encourages ownership and commitment, and a level of cooperation rarely experienced. It also encourages product acceptance. The marriage of information systems (IS) and users creates a healthy environment for the system's growth and development.

> The "objective" is to nudge forward the process of *discovering* goals
> along the way to induce the largest number of people possible
> to quickly engage, to try *something*; to maximize the odds of serendipity.
>
> *Tom Peters (1990)*

Peters suggested in his article that "'having goals' and 'making plans' are two of the most important pretenses." But they are dangerous in that they prevent us from getting into the thick of things and discovering the "real goals" and needs of our customers. Our customers often don't know for sure what they want, specifically, but they know it when they see it. Our job is to help them discover what they're really after as quickly as possible.

In Davis et al. (1988), the authors observed that user needs are always changing and that software, by nature, is always late and falls short of the user's expectations. Evolutionary prototyping, however, minimizes delay and shortfall when compared with conventional, incremental, or throwaway prototype development approaches.

Attempts to establish software factories have often failed, largely due to a failure to understand the nature of the methods and tools required. In many cases, software factories need a toolsmith to create the tools and bridges to support the team. In others, managers mistakenly believe that their staff doesn't want to change, when what the staff really wants is to clearly understand the new process and tools. Managers often tend to view new methods and tools as a quick fix, but fail to train their personnel in even the basics of using the methods and tools. Most managers are looking for microwave solutions, not the kind of steadfast, consistent attention to training and evolution required to create an environment that fosters rapid evolutionary development.

RAPID PROTOTYPING

> The rapid prototyping method of development is contrary to our standard method of developing systems. There was a problem getting technical people to work that way. They had a concern that they were generating a poor quality system.
>
> *Boeing project manager (Rockart and DeLong, 1988)*

Different cultures view things differently: Americans and Europeans have a distinct past, present, and future; Hopi Indians have no words for any time except the present; and Arabs generally look no further than a week or two into the future. This puts Americans in the unique category of those able to plan for the future; but compared to most Asians, Americans are quite primitive. In America, the focus is on this quarter's profits and "What have you done for me lately?" In many Asian cultures, future time spans hundreds of years. The Chinese leased Hong Kong to the British for 99 years, and now they are about to get it back. In Japan, for another example, mortgages may span three generations — father, son, and children not yet born. Rapid prototyping is sometimes viewed as yet another American desire to reap a crop almost as soon as the seed is sown.

For those of you who are paralyzed by the thought of doing things wrong, prototyping will kill you. Indecision is usually the worst mistake you can make. By design, prototyping ferrets out the fatal flaw and drags it into the open for all to see. Then and only then can you take the kind of action required to change direction and solve the user's dilemma from a different perspective.

Rapid prototyping is the starting point of rapid evolutionary development (Figure 9.1). Rather than a minor part of the development process (as it is in the requirements specification portion of a more traditional "construction" development process), prototyping plays a vital role in both the creation and the evolution of software. Rapid prototyping, when done well, can reduce risk, enhance customer perceptions, and deliver more value in less time than any other method for software

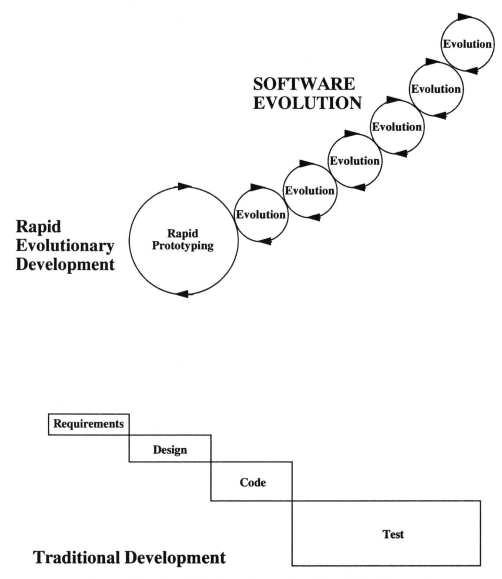

Figure 9.1   Rapid Prototyping vs. Traditional Development

creation. Your customers, of course, will expect you to deliver whatever you show them. Satisfy their expectations and you will win a great victory. If you tell them that they will have to wait a couple of years for the "real" system to be delivered, you may lose the war.

Fortunately, if you work together with the customer using the "right" tools in the "right" environment and with an eye on the vision of the future, you *can* use prototyping to create and deliver useful products quickly. Then you can grow and evolve the simple starting system into its future place in the business. If, however, you use the latest technical fad in an underpowered platform and ignore the ecology of the metasystem and the evolutionary path of the product, you are doomed to some of the worst technical and customer relations failures of your career.

> The school of data-driven prototyping . . . believes that prototypes should not be thrown away. Instead, they should evolve, extending the data architecture of the business in a process somewhat akin to learning.
>
> *Daniel Appleton (1983)*

The best way to know what you want is to experience it firsthand. Think about it: You experience cars, electronics, and numerous other products *before* you buy; why not software? Evolutionary prototypes help customers and prototypers get a hands-on feeling for the system as it develops. This ongoing, experiential feedback allows us to learn from our mistakes and make continuous corrections as we move toward the customer's desired system.

Have you ever noticed that customers don't actually want systems; they want what the system will do for them—the benefits. If you think of a system as providing a service that will assist customers in achieving their goals and objectives, you will be that much closer to being able to meet their needs in a timely fashion.

Imagine walking into a car dealer's showroom and seeing that perfect red sports car you've always wanted. The salesperson takes you for a test drive and it feels like a dream. It corners as if it's on rails and the acceleration is second to none. You know that in this car, you'll feel unstoppable, on top of the world. This car is everything you've ever wanted. You say, "I'll take one" and the salesperson says, "I'm sorry . . . this is only a prototype, but I can have one ready for you in 24 to 36 months." How would you feel? disappointed? angry? Would you take your business elsewhere?

This is the common mistake most prototyping projects make using the construction paradigm. They believe that the customer will stand still, waiting while the IS staff redevelops the "production" version of the system based on the prototype's demonstrated requirements. If you can show it to them, they'll want it and you had better be ready to deliver, or there will be hell to pay in terms of customer relations and lost credibility.

If you are going to create a prototype, it must be a deliverable prototype that can then be evolved to meet the customer's desires and expectations. It is much easier to manage the momentum of a system in operation than it is to shout "STOP!" when the prototype is completed and start building the production system.

When I put up the first UNIX system in the company where I worked, IBM was the "standard." To simplify the learning process and to create acceptance, we created over 200 look-alike IBM TSO commands in just under six weeks. Except for the screen editor, our system behaved just like TSO, only faster. This is the power of rapid prototyping with Shell to create usable applications.

One way to look at rapid prototyping would use a logical view of what happens:

```
Grow (initial prototype)        Creation
Until (replaced)                Evolution
   Grow (expanded version)
enduntil
Grow (system)
     Until (converge to a solution)
          Plan Analyze the customer's needs
                 • people, tools, environment
                 • processes
          Do Create a demonstrable prototype
          Check closeness of fit
          Act to improve
     enduntil
     Deliver the system
End (Grow)
```

First, we create and grow the initial working system. Then, until the system is replaced by a "younger" one, we continue to expand and grow the system from infancy to maturity using PDCA (plan, do, check, act). Amazing things can happen using this approach.

Rapid Evolution Metaphors

Another way to look at rapid prototyping is to liken it to human courtship and family development.

Courtship

First you have to choose the right mate. Initially, there's a lot of courting as the software developer and customer romance each other. Eventually, they decide to "get into bed" together. A prenuptial agreement is often a great idea.

Pregnancy

Prototyping is much like pregnancy. First, the customer conceives an idea. Together the software developers and the customer work together as the fertile nucleus develops into the initial version of the system. This pregnancy is accompanied by tremendous enthusiasm and growth.

Notice that mothers never ask fathers, "How many corners do you want me to cut in the construction of our child?" Systems with birth defects usually carry them for the rest of their life unless a highly skilled software surgeon makes the necessary repairs. Lots of prenatal care will prevent such problems.

And notice that fathers never ask, "How long will this take? Couldn't you deliver it in four months instead of nine?" Everyone knows it takes nine months, no matter how many people you put on the task. Children born prematurely need a lot of care, most of it expensive. Children born too late are a burden on the mother and cause endless anxiety. It's best to let the prototyping process take its natural course and deliver the baby when it's ready.

During this period, the parents must prepare a loving environment to receive the new child. Everyone has to be trained in child care, feeding, and so on.

Birth

Finally, the system is formed sufficiently to live in the world. The initial version (a small one) is "delivered" and installed for use. Like most newborns, it will wake us up in the middle of the night with all kinds of problems—it can soil itself, it can get sick, it can get hungry. Brand new systems need a lot of initial care. Parents don't say, "When is this child going to be able to take care of itself?" because they know it will take time for the child to reach a level of maturity where it can do things for itself.

The Terrible Twos

The system needs a lot of care and feeding in its first few years as it continues to grow. Like expectant parents, the software developers and the customers continue to care for its needs. The rampant enthusiasm of the pregnancy yield to a feeling of confinement. A lot of preparation and work must go into any outing with the new system. The baby system continues to grow organically and naturally—no new hands, feet, or organs are added. It is a good idea at this point to immunize the system against all of the childhood diseases.

Childhood

Look who's talking! At this point the system is fairly well mannered. It continues to grow and learn at a reasonable rate. Customers and IS both enjoy this period of working together to help the system develop.

Adolescence

The system will continue to grow, gain weight, and learn. At this stage, changes in markets or organizations can cause problems. The software may develop some wild hormonal urges that will test the mettle of the developer and customer. The software may need braces for its teeth or strong guidance to set its path.

At this point, the system may get the urge to spin off some children of its own. JUST SAY NO!

Adulthood

Maturity develops. We can no more create a mature system than we can create a mature person. As the system matures, however, it will provide increasingly more benefit to the customer and will require less support and attention from the developer.

At some point in their life, systems may put on some extra weight and need to reduce some of the flab—both data and processes. Some systems will opt for plastic surgery and various creams and balms to postpone the aging process. This is okay! No one likes ugly, old systems; we appreciate elegant, mature ones. Through good nutrition and balanced effort, the system can stay younger longer than we perhaps ever thought possible.

Old Age

Through proper exercise and diet, software can thrive. It can live a long and healthy life and retire, or it can develop all kinds of health problems and require expensive medical care. All of this depends on how it was treated during its lifetime. Rapid prototyping demands that we examine the overall ecology of any change in the system during its life.

I prefer this metaphor of courtship and childbearing to the more algorithmic model offered previously. The question on your mind now, however, might be: "How do I begin to use the model?"

RAPID PROTOTYPING PROCESS

History has shown us that large, cumbersome software methodologies will only fit a certain size of project, not all projects. These heavy methodologies also generate masses of paper and require extensive paper support systems that further impede productivity.

A flexible, evolutionary prototyping methodology lays out the fundamentals of software creation and evolution using PDCA. It can significantly improve productivity and quality. The methodology works like the expansion unit in a personal computer: The application creation or evolution team can choose the specific *methods* (expansion cards) to customize the prototyping methodology to match their application.

Using a flexible methodology, we can then integrate software tools with the methods to create an integrated *technology platform* to automate the software processes. The technology platform will then support all of the activities of software creation and evolution.

The creation process for rapid prototyping is simple (Figure 9.2).

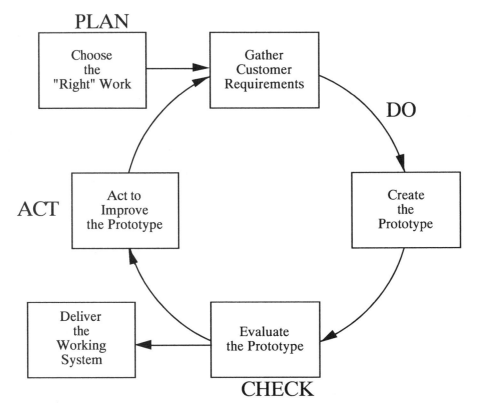

Figure 9.2   Rapid Evolutionary Development

Plan the Project

- *Choose a project that requires fast delivery and is not well understood.* This means that there must be rapid growth and evolution of the requirements and the whole product during its development. Iteration and evolution will occur whether they are planned for or not. Planned evolution before the product escapes is better than unplanned evolution after a failure in the field.

- *Gather and define customer and market requirements.* It is useful at this point to begin framing the user's expectations of the creation process. We will focus on user *needs*, not *wants or wishes*. It will require many rounds of mutual negotiation, participation, and feedback to evolve the prototype to the point that it can be used effectively. This repeated assessment of the customer's and market's requirements will ensure rapid convergence on the best possible solution.

- *Begin the analysis of the customer's process.* As we gather requirements, we need to begin sorting and chunking the customer's requests into needs, wants, and wishes. We need to begin anticipating the evolutionary path of the system as it grows. Process analysis helps IS guide the technical evolution. Will the system be a plant, rooted in one place, or a more mobile system that can move quickly to attack various markets?

Create the Prototype

- *Create a prototype or model.* The prototype plays a key role in the success of the software mission. A demonstrable behavioral model provides so much feedback that you can't help but come up with better products. Static, two-dimensional representations (i.e., design documents) of dynamic software systems that are supposed to move and grow and process information cannot help but be incomplete.

Check Closeness of Fit

- *Evaluate the prototype using customer feedback.* Given a working, demonstrable system, customers can tell you how far or how close you are to their goal. They can give you better feedback about how to make the system better.

Act to Improve

- *Act to improve the prototype.* Using customer and prototyper feedback, identify the next steps required to ecologically grow the fetal system to the next step in its evolution.

SOFTWARE EVOLUTION

Unlike a car that rolls off an assembly line or a house ready for occupancy, software systems continue to expand and change over time. The next step of rapid prototyping delivers the system into everyday use. From here on, the freewheeling accelerated growth of the prenatal system slows. The system grows and evolves in a more carefully orchestrated and focused process of software evolution (Arthur, 1988).

The software creation process can be used throughout the system's life to create major enhancements and extensions of the system's knowledge and abilities. Using the software evolution and the rapid evolutionary development (Arthur, 1992), prototypers can continuously improve and enhance the system as the environment changes around it. The system, however, is not the only thing that needs to evolve.

Evolution of the Methodology

One of the problems with most "construction" or "manufacturing" methodologies is that they rarely evolve to meet the changing needs of the business or technology. When a methodology does change, it is typically too little too late. The methodology and technology must evolve to match the needs of the customer. The PDCA process will assist you in keeping the process and technology up-to-date with the evolutionary life forms created using rapid prototyping.

INNOVATION

"The greatest pleasure in life is doing what people say you cannot do." Innovation occurs when a small team of key people combines with resources, isolation, and esprit de corps and does the seemingly undoable. This "skunkworks" approach changes the essence of how software is conceived and created. An evolutionary development team consists of top people, usually less than 25 percent of the normal team size. Prototypers share communication in many ways — sharing the same location, electronic mail, voice mail, and visual work areas all around. Prototyping projects also minimize paperwork.

Prototyping is a great way to converge on an innovative solution, but it can also be a way to go wrong in a hurry. To succeed, the team needs to focus on a small subset of the entire functionality. People have only a limited ability to reason about complex systems and their use.

The Process

Consider the Genesis model of software development — creation and evolution. God created this earthship in six days, according to Judeo-Christian beliefs. Similarly, the genesis of most prototypes is an intensive period of creation followed by a never-ending series of periodic evolutions. The initial prototyping process is a vibrant period of prototypers and customers working together to create a little, test a little, and tune, tailor, and tweek the system toward its initial incarnation. Every day during the prototyping process consists of many miniature software development life cycles — plan, do, test, and act to improve. Prototypers make user needs operational as quickly as possible to generate feedback that allows growth and evolution to occur at a phenomenal pace.

There are several types of prototyping processes:

- *Exploration* of various alternative approaches to verify feasibility
- *Experimentation* to clarify and verify requirements for development (an original model on which something is patterned — provides a demonstration prototype)
  - simulation of interfaces, functioning, etc.
  - closest to original meaning
  - also a dead horse
- *Growth and evolution* to deliver a working product (first full-scale and functional form of a new type or design)

- field and production prototype
- farthest from original meaning of the word *prototype,* but also most powerful
- *Incremental evolution* to develop expanding versions of the system

Any of these approaches may focus its efforts on data or processing. Data-driven prototyping is better for business applications. Process-driven prototyping is better for real-time applications.

Simple Prototyping Process

> The price of success: "Dedication, hard work, and an unremitting devotion to the things you want to see happen."

A strong but flexible methodology ensures the success of the project. Rapid prototyping with Shell can create small, one-shot programs or large, complex applications. The prototyping process follows the plan-do-check-act cycle of growth and evolution. A simple version of this methodology would be:

1. Gather a small, focused set of requirements.
2. Evaluate alternatives and create a working model.
3. Test for correctness with the user.
4. Act to improve the set until both IS and the user are satisfied.
5. Loop through steps 1-4 until sufficient functionality is available that the users are licking their chops in anticipation of using the system.
6. Test to ensure that the system is industrial strength.
7. Release the system to a pilot group.
8. Loop through steps 1-7 until everyone is satisfied.
9. Release the system for general use.

On-Line Systems

To develop an on-line system using Shell:

1. Focus your energy in three main areas to begin with:
   - Data models to begin creating the databases for the system as a stable, reusable platform for development of the system processing.
   - On-line screens and reports to begin developing the look and feel of the system from the user's point of view.
   - Transactions required to accomplish the system's objectives (e.g., calcula-

tions, add customer, update tax table). Model the simple transactions first and then the more complex ones.

2. Once these are somewhat stable, you can begin creating the processing required to:
   * Access and update the databases (using information hiding principles).
   * Transform the user's inputs into stored data and useful outputs.

3. Continue to grow the system to a working level that would provide at least 50 percent of the functionality required.

4. Put the system into a pilot location to work the remaining bugs out while continuing to evolve the system toward excellence. Remember: There is no failure, only feedback. Add only user *needs* to the system at this point, keeping the overall ecology of the system in mind. It has to be able to grow from this infant stage into adulthood. In other words, minimize birth defects in the system.

5. Deploy the system across its user base and begin the evolution of the system toward its desired capabilities. Use the evolutionary process to schedule important enhancements to the system and keep ecology and evolutionary ability continuously in the forefront of everyone's mind. You can continue to apply rapid prototyping to the creation of major system enhancements as well.

Ecology Issues

For an evolutionary prototype to survive in the "real" world, it will need to take into account the ecology of the entire metasystem it enters. Living systems focus energy on maintaining ecology through:

* minimizing impacts on existing systems and cultures
* providing adequate documentation and training
* ensuring quality—maintainability, flexibility, reusability, portability, reliability, efficiency
* focusing on needs versus wants or wishes
* ensuring security
* ensuring performance and response time of the delivered system
* evaluating and providing evolutionary hardware requirements
* minimizing cost
* maximizing error handling and recovery (immune system response)
* allowing backup and recovery
* providing adequate resources for the task

If a developing prototype changes too fast without regard for ecology, no one can keep abreast of the changes or manage to synchronize all of the documents and deliverables. It can become impossible to adequately test the system in such tumultuous times. It will take time for the system to become self-sustaining. Prototypers must keep their thoughts on the system's future, not only its present. Toward this end:

1. No poorly structured design should be accepted.

2. Any change that causes design deterioration must invoke a redesign of the affected system parts.

3. Code that becomes obsolete through evolution must be replaced, not patched.

Rapid prototyping gives you the time that "construction" takes away. In rapid prototyping, you always have time to make the system right *before* you release it, but you will never have time to do it over. You must keep ecology in mind.

During World War II, huge formations of bombers would gather to assault specific targets. It often took them hours to form the force that would attack a target, and many times whole groups would miss the rendezvous. In today's world, a few highly trained, heavily armed forces flying the latest in advanced technology can strike with lightning speed against targets of opportunity as they are identified.

The old construction model of software development mirrors the World War II bombing raids. Rapid prototyping teams mirror the aerial strike forces of today.

To tell you a little story, I wrote my first software metrics analyzer in UNIX Shell, and the next one in awk, and the final versions in the UNIX lexical analyzer. Each successive tool and environment took less time because I more thoroughly understood the application. I'm sure that if I had tried to learn the application and the lexical analyzer all at one time, I would have given up. As it was, though, it took me only six months to go from the Shell version to the complete suite of lexical analyzers I created for COBOL, PL/I, and C.

Software Issues

A major factor in prototyping software selection should be its speed, flexibility, and familiarity among the prototyping team. There are four key technological components that must be created for any software system:

1. the user interface — input, output, and query

2. databases, tables, files, and so forth

3. processing — algorithms, computations, and so forth

4. interfaces to other systems

Open Architectures

> [The personal computer is like] an old testament God, with lots of rules, and no mercy.
>
> *Joseph Campbell*

Several different alternatives exist for prototyping platforms: desktop computers or desktop workstations connected to one or more larger computers. Prototypers are only as efficient as the environment they use. Open hardware and software architectures allow the maximum flexibility for changes in functionality and technology. Closed architectures tend to trap prototyping teams in technological quicksand. Proprietary technology is its own tar pit.

From this perspective, an operating system such as UNIX that runs on a wide variety of platforms is a strategic weapon. UNIX offers portability and flexibility that you will be hard pressed to find elsewhere. It has several strategic advantages:

1. It frees you from dependence on a single hardware vendor.
2. It runs on a broad range of computer architectures, from PCs to supercomputers.
3. It comes with loads of reusable components.
4. It is the user interface of the future. (Workstations all run UNIX.)
5. Expert systems and parallel processing environments rely on UNIX.
6. The tools you've grown to love in MS-DOS are migrating to UNIX.

UNIX runs on more types of computers than any other operating system (Cureton, 1988). It offers windowing (X Windows among others), relational and semantic databases, extensive networking and communication, and expert systems. Sun, Digital, IBM, Apollo, and HP all have some form of UNIX workstation.

Virtually all of the vendors are working toward a true IPSE—integrated project support environment—a software cockpit where prototypers can grow and evolve software with ease. Visions of a software cockpit grew out of the dynamic changes that have rocked the software industry. Most companies have a large suite of relatively independent applications that were developed both internally and externally. It has become essential, however, to realign and integrate our information systems to meet the competitive challenges of the 1990s.

Based on the three key elements of an effective software cockpit—people (the pilots), process (how to fly a software mission), and tools (the plane)—the analogy between pilots and software professionals is so apt that the "software cockpit" can serve as the overriding vision of how people will create software in the future.

VISION

During World War II, the outcome of the war was largely decided by control of the air above the battle. In the latter stages of the war, huge constellations of bombers and fighters pounded the Axis. In today's combat environment (we call it competition), a few high-tech aircraft with advanced weaponry can perform these feats. The battleground of the 1990s will be information. To meet the challenges of the information economy, the massive software efforts of the past must give way to smaller, faster, more versatile groups of highly trained software pilots working in advanced software environments.

The analogy can be extended further to describe software projects as one of the following:

general aviation   commercial aviation   military aviation   space exploration

general aviation	end-user computing (EUC)
commercial aviation	IS software creation and evolution
military aviation	offensive and defensive product deployment
space exploration	new market development

Each of these analogies can benefit from rapid prototyping. To develop the software cockpit of the future, the hardware and software tools and methods must be chosen to reflect the type of mission a software "pilot" performs. For example, the personal computer of an end user may be completely inappropriate for a quick strike into an information technology market, and vice versa.

Yet, like aircraft pilots, software pilots will share certain common needs and abilities. For example, all three of these missions — EUC, IS, and product — require a plan for completion — a flight plan. Some of the requirements that software pilots might share are:

project management (flight planning)

flexible methodology to match the type of software mission

instrumentation — measurement of progress, direction, altitude, and so on

advanced human factors interfaces — heads-up displays, sound, video

These skills can be likened to ground school (programmer basic training) and flight school (evolutionary training). They teach a software pilot to fly — but only the basic skills needed for general aviation. To become a commercial or military software pilot, we will need additional rigor, discipline, and training to handle the specifics of each type of mission. A strong training program helps eliminate the cultural shock of change.

This evolutionary environment is a conceptual view of the software cockpit for development and evolution. It exists independently of methods, tools, and hardware platforms. It incorporates the critical success factors of people, process (how work is done), and technology (to support the process).

The Cockpit

Engineering workstations (cockpits) coupled to a dynamic repository (mission control) seemed the best route to follow. Most available vendor products, however, offer one of two things: only a small part of the cockpit or a closed architecture that would prohibit integration and choice.

Since vendors have no incentive to achieve integration and openness, you might as well do the best you can with the available packages that are both open and extensible.

Cockpit Overview

If you want an open architecture, about the only way you can get it from more than one vendor is through UNIX. Only through the multitasking and integration capabilities of UNIX can you create the desired environment. UNIX workstations offer an excellent hardware platform for the software cockpit. The Japanese reusability project (Sigma) has moved in this direction, using a UNIX-like variant.

To simplify creation and evolution, the cockpit will need a repository of data, designs, code, and other reusable components that can be shared by all the pilots. You can't create the super software cockpit of the future until, like aviation of the past, you have some sort of an initial dashboard that can then evolve to fully meet your needs. The SEI maturity framework will cause rapid shifts in methods and tools if you move rapidly toward excellence. The cockpit needs the flexibility to change and grow with the software process.

Begin building your software cockpit on UNIX workstations coupled with other host computers — UNIX, IBM, and so forth. Choose platforms and tools that offer:

1. open architecture — for flexible choice
2. extensibility — to allow growth
3. availability — to ensure reliability
4. performance — to ensure productivity
5. support of a defined process methodology

Choose your software pilot's basic instrumentation first. During a flight, for example, a pilot uses only five or six instruments to keep the aircraft aloft; choose a core of five to seven tools to aid the software pilot. Just as first-generation aircraft contained very primitive tools, so too will the initial cockpit. The seven areas of concern are:

1. project management
2. quality management
3. prototyping
4. code generation
5. documentation management
6. change and configuration management
7. release control

These seven items constitute the minimum set of tools for a successful mission. Other valuable tools include:

- a repository of data and reusable components
- screen prototyping
- report generation
- measurement and analysis
- query facilities
- document creation (text, graphics)
- fourth-generation languages
- relational database management systems
- application generators

Process

Many companies have found that in the race to automate the software process, tools can lock you into an ineffective process. These tools are ultimately abandoned because they don't help people get the job done. W. Edwards Deming (1986) suggests that any process (including software) that is not under some form of quality management wastes 25-40 percent of all effort and expenditures. Looking at the "debugging industry" that threatens all software projects — either creation or evolution — you have to address not only the technological aspects of the cockpit, but the process issues as well. Before you can automate the process, you must define and streamline the software process. Florida Power and Light, winner of the 1989 Deming Prize, found that methodology was more important than tools for improving productivity and quality in their Information Systems department. Projects are not all alike. One process or methodology cannot encompass the full range of software missions, just as no one flight plan, airplane, or pilot can perform all aviation missions. There are, however, some common activities that must be addressed; but the bulk of the methods used in any project should be modular and flexible and fit into this backbone process. This leads us to the concept of a flexible, evolutionary methodology that supports a wide variety of methods that can be selectively chosen for a given project.

> Tests cannot establish the absence of errors.
>
> *Edgar Dijkstra*

RECOMMENDATIONS

The people and organization are the keys to the success of prototyping projects. These people then select the project management, creation, and evolution methods and tools that allow them to achieve the result required. The team chooses the technology required to support the rapid evolutionary development using these methods.

Creating a team of customers and prototypers will produce the vital initial 20 percent of a system's ultimate functionality in record time.

In spite of what might on the surface appear to be a chaotic development process, prototypers follow a rigorous methodology that includes project management, quality control using inspections and testing, requirements specification, architecture and data design, detailed design, and code. High-caliber prototyping staffs recognize the value of defined processes and standards. Together, prototyping team members can apply their cumulative experience to customize a streamlined methodology to match the project's objectives.

The use of rapid prototyping will result in a more usable and responsive system to meet the customer's needs. Evolution of the system will consume as much as 50 percent of the prototyping staff for problem solving and "baby sitting" the existing system. To succeed at innovation and rapid evolutionary development, you must choose the right people, process, technology, and environment.

REUSE

> Why do schools teach almost nothing of the pattern which connects?
>
> *Gregory Bateson (1979)*

Using DNA, cells reproduce to create exact copies of themselves. Entire beings are created from a single initial cell. As the fetus grows, cells *differentiate* to form the various organs, tissues, muscles, nerves, and bones. To succeed at software reuse, we will need to follow a similar strategy.

The continuing success of rapid evolutionary development depends on the reuse of system parts and components—data especially, and then other components such as processing, documentation, and training. We must ask how one thing is related to another. What pattern connects them? One human is much like another, with two legs, two arms, a torso, and a head. Legs are much like arms, with five toes or five fingers and similar bone structures. Humans are also similar to horses and dolphins: We breathe air; we share limbs or fins, and a head with two eyes and a mouth. What are the similarities among software systems, and how can we reuse them?

By emphasizing the creation and reuse of system components from current prototyping projects, a resource pool of data, software, and design documentation can begin to grow to meet the future needs of the corporation. Using these resources, prototypers can maximize their effectiveness and efficiency during the creation of new projects. This is especially important when working with third-generation programming languages and tools.

> There is an untapped potential for productivity gains through the reuse of standard software components.
>
> *Ted G. Lewis and Paul W. Oman (1990)*

People sometimes ask, "If reusability is so great, why haven't we already done it?" Good question, and the answer is largely because reuse requires an investment. In a world of "get rich quick" schemes, reuse makes money the old-fashioned way: over the long haul. Let's look at the basic laws of reuse:

1. Part of all you code is yours to keep. (Write Shell programs that you can reuse.)
2. Start thy software repository to fattening. (The UNIX library has a vast store of tools.)
3. Make thy software multiply. (Reuse the Shell programs you've created.)
4. Increase thy ability to develop reusable software. (Learn reuse from UNIX and Shell.)

Software will form the competitive edge of companies in the next decade. IS departments must step off the slow productivity improvements of the last few decades (approximately 5 percent per year) and explore the new paradigm of software creation that will double or triple productivity in three to five years. Eric Sumner, AT&T Bell Labs' vice-president for operations planning, put it this way: "If there's a single key, it's reuse." Ted Biggerstaff said that improvements of 20 to 50 percent are reasonable *within a narrow application domain.* He also said that quality improves with reuse. "Quality comes along for free because you use the components that have been debugged and used extensively." Reuse offers prototypers a way to stop reinventing the wheel for common elements, parts, components, and subsystems and to improve quality through rigorous testing of the reusable components. The incentives to reuse software parts in the creation of new systems are:

- economic savings, especially for large, complex projects
- customer satisfaction through more reliable systems
- prototyper satisfaction through faster creation of systems
- prototyper stress reduction through focus on the creation of new components

Reuse changes the whole software process. The game becomes one of putting the puzzle together, not creating the pieces. This is a wonderful change because there's never a project that isn't under the gun.

Reuse Process

The reuse process is actually very simple; doing it rigorously is what takes time and effort. In the reuse process, you will need to:

1. identify reusable designs, parts, and components (Figure 9.3)
2. create the reusable components

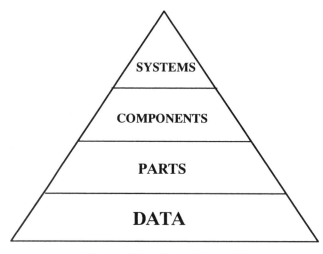

Figure 9.3   Reuse Pyramid

3. certify the quality of the reusable parts

4. catalog and store them for easy retrieval

5. manage change to these reusable items

Identifying Reusable Parts

There is a simple test that will help you determine how easily you can grasp and use reusability techniques. Before you read the next paragraph, take a handful of coins out of your pocket and describe what you see.

There are two common and two more unusual responses to what people see. People who have the easiest time reusing software will notice first *how the coins are alike and then how they are different.* For example, some people will respond that they see American coins that are all round that have faces of former presidents on them. Others will see what they add up to: 72 cents or some such thing. These people first see how things are alike and then how they are different, which allows them to see how two functions are alike so that they could be reused. Then they see how the functions are different so that they know what will need to be uniquely created.

People who will have more difficulty reusing software will first notice how the coins are *different and then how they are similar.* For example, they will say things like: "There's a penny, nickle, dime, and quarter. The penny is a copper color and they all have different obverse designs. They are all different sizes." These are all statements of difference. These people will then follow by saying how the coins are alike: "They're all cents and round." A few people will be at the poles of this discussion: The coins will all be *exactly the same or completely different.* Any of these people will have problems relating to reuse. To reuse software easily, you will need to first notice how things are alike and *then* how they are different. You learned this mental strategy early in life, and it's easy to borrow and apply the optimal strategy to reuse once you know how your strategy is similar or different.

To initiate reuse, you must begin by defining the typical issues that arise when building some *class* of systems. Then you can begin to create reusable designs, code, and data from these generalizations. There are several types of reuse:

- design, code, and data extraction and adaptation from other products
- direct reuse from component repositories and databases
- program generation
- 4GL (Fourth-Generation Language) usage

Design and code adaptation reflects that software engineering often is re-engineering, not art or invention. Adapting existing software requires clear documentation so that changes can be made safely. Adaptive reuse creates maintenance and configuration control problems. (Yet another component joins the family.) Adaptive reuse can be achieved by:

- chunking designs, code, or data to extract multiple functions or views of the data
- combining designs, code, or data into higher-level, reusable functions or databases
- generalizing an existing part or component into a reusable design, module, or database
- customizing designs, code, or data to prepare it for a specific application or environment

Chunking helps us identify the different functions or data woven together in a module or database. These can then be separated and reused. Data normalization, for example, progressively chunks data down into its component groupings.

Combining these elemental units into higher-level organs or organisms enables us to reuse the power and elegance of the smaller parts to create even more powerful reusable components.

Generalizing lets us look at two or more similar yet different functions or data structures and observe their similarities. Once we know how they are alike, we can create higher-level abstractions that allow us to reuse the basic principles. In object-oriented programming, for example, we can define a class of objects called "door" that has hinges, latches, and states of being open or closed. We can then reuse these abilities to describe car doors or house doors or even hoods and trunks.

Customizing, on the other hand, invites us to look at how the function or data is different and unique. Continuing the door example, we could define classes of doors for hoods, trunks, and car doors that specify their unique function or application.

Regardless of how we identify and create a reusable component — design, code, data, or test case — we will need some way to store and retrieve it on demand.

Reuse Repositories

Component repositories are a form of long-term "memory" that facilitate reuse. They encounter initial success and enthusiasm as people begin to add parts to the repository. Difficulties occur when these same people are called upon to reuse the components in the library. Initial components may lack the robust functionality required to ensure reuse. As a result, there will be some technical difficulties in applying reuse to achieve customer needs. This is okay because there is no failure, only feedback. These early components can be evolved into important members of the reuse repository. To encourage reuse, programmers and analysts should be challenged to argue their use or avoidance of reusable components during an inspection or walkthrough.

Reusable designs increase the possibility of code reuse and make the resulting programs more maintainable. Strict focus on reusing designs, however, can cause designers to overlook better alternatives. Use your common sense; reuse only what is reusable.

Program generators capture similarities among applications and apply knowledge at higher conceptual levels. Fourth-generation languages do the same thing. They are a powerful tool in the hands of a prototyper who has access to a reusable repository of data, information, and knowledge about the business.

Reuse opportunities vary with the class of system and its environment. Ground-breaking new systems will initially have fewer reuse opportunities than existing, known application domains. Japanese software houses, for example, reuse up to 80 percent of existing application software when creating a custom configuration for a customer. Creating space station software, on the other hand, is a less-understood application domain; reuse may be more difficult. You can measure the value of reuse by counting every incident of reuse. It costs more to set up a reuse program initially, and then it begins to repay itself over time. The Japanese Sigma project has allied over a hundred different companies to produce reusable components for the UNIX environment. Toshiba's Heavy Apparatus Engineering Lab uses real-time Fortran for 60 percent of its reusable code and is moving toward the C language for the remainder. GTE Data Services uses COBOL and assembly because of the transaction-processing nature of their business (Gruman, 1988).

Reuse can happen anywhere in the software process — from project plans to design documents, from code to data, from test cases to user training. Figure 9.3 (shown earlier) shows the reuse pyramid. The foundation of most effective business-oriented reuse strategies is data. By creating pools of shared data, prototypers can begin to leverage their work with each successive application created. These pools also provide a strategic resource for the user to evaluate the customer base, identify new markets, be more responsive to changes in market conditions, and counter competitive threats. One of the reasons that the "Information Center" concept never caught on was that the data for one of these was often spread across dozens if not hundreds of applications. This is why executive support or decision support systems, which are vital to the strategic health of the organization, have had a hard time getting started and delivering return on investment.

> [Data] is an open system . . . that learns from its experiences.
> It has adaptive mechanisms. . . . It is, in a sense, organic.
>
> *Daniel Appleton (1983)*

This philosophy of shared data pools often seems strange to those of us who were brought up with structured programming and data flows. To be successful at rapid evolutionary development, most of your data can't flow; it must remain in one place where people can use and reuse it. It can be managed and duplicated where required. It can be syphoned off, transformed, and streamed into other pools. In event-driven, real-time systems, this obviously isn't so, but in application creation it is.

Another advantage of data pools (i.e., tables or databases) lies in the ability to create, maintain, and share documentation and training in their use. Then, with this foundation to stand on, prototypers can create reusable parts to access and process the raw data into forms more suitable for human consumption. Data pools simplify the development of the processing required to meet a customer's needs — another advantage of creating the data first.

The data pools or repositories form a more object-oriented or information engineering strategy for software creation. Customers, for example, would know their own names, addresses, phone numbers, and so on. They might also know what kind of products or services they buy on a regular or irregular basis, and how much money they have to spend. This object orientation can benefit rapid evolutionary developers because it focuses on organisms, organizations, and elements of the total system and can be implemented in any language, not just object-oriented ones.

Regardless of which reuse level interests people the most, the most important key to rapid evolutionary development is data.

Reusing Data

If we look at the eons of time, evolution seems to take forever. Insects, however, evolve quickly to deal with pesticides through their rapid generational turnover, which provides massive and frequent opportunities for genetic recoding. The rapid rate of human evolution, however, depends on our ability to change and adjust our conceptual, logical, and physical worlds to our needs. Rather than change the human organism, we change the programs we put into the biocomputer we call a brain (training) and we extend the reach of our physiology through the use of machines — cars, planes, boats, rockets, or computers. Satellites in space vastly extend our ability to see changes on the planet. Our personal evolution grows each time we expand our understanding of the world. In this way, we change without having to resort to genetic mutation and natural selection. Data evolves in much the same way as human knowledge, by learning as it grows. As we add data to a database, the information or knowledge contained in that database increases just like the mind of any child.

Data-driven prototyping develops and maintains open, shared databases that can constantly be extended to accommodate new information requirements. Reusable data will need to be normalized. Over the years, several genetically advanced forms of data have appeared—normal forms. First normal form simply deals with establishing a consistent number of fields per record, all of the same size. Second and third normal forms introduce *key* fields and their relationships to other nonkey fields. Second normal form ensures that all nonkey fields relate to the entire key. Third normal form ensures that no nonkey field relates to another nonkey field. Fourth normal form ensures that a record contains no more than one independent, multivalued field. Fifth normal form simplifies things even more by creating smaller groups of data from which larger, more complex groups of information can be derived.

Using this model as the basis of creating and growing evolutionary software systems, we can begin to see that we must have ways of storing our model of the world in such a way that it can be changed easily. You can change your mind, but can you change your software? Typically not very easily, because the knowledge is hard-coded into the program or inflexible data structures. Through proper use of data, evolution becomes a process of changing the data stored in databases, not genetically re-engineering the software system. The database, like the human mind, can code, store, and retrieve data; generate decisions; and much more. Successful data design is the foundation of evolution and reusability.

There are three levels for data architecture: a conceptual or enterprise level, a logical or functional level, and a physical level.

Just having the right data and information can have a strategic impact because it will enable customers to identify new markets, evaluate trends, and increase sales through the application of "end-user" tools for database analysis.

The technical, physical, and political barriers to data can be a major roadblock in the rapid evolutionary development of any project. For prototyping to succeed, the prototyper must have access to any and all data, regardless of how far back in the woods it may be.

For data to be as reusable as possible, IS prototypers must use the same name for data elements with as few synonyms as possible. Unfortunately, during English classes in school, some teachers instilled in students that repeating the same word over and over again would be boring for the reader. Bore me! Especially in computer programs. Bore me! Make it easy for me. Simple subject, simple verb, and simple object: MOVE COLORADO TO STATE, and then simply refuse to give COLORADO and STATE more exotic names. Bore me!

Reusing Processing

There are many levels at which reuse can be achieved. Fred Brooks suggests three levels (Gruman, 1988)—algorithm, code component, and design reuse. Algorithms validate fields such as employee and customer names and numbers and crunch arithmetic calculations. Code components can update databases, communicate with users and other systems, and process specific types of application problems. For example, the common Ada missile parts—a generalized cruise-missile guidance system that uses Ada packages—has been widely reused (Gruman, 1988). At Toshiba's Heavy Apparatus Engineering Lab, reuse rate is 55 percent of delivered code. The challenge for reusable components is to create ones that can do a lot of work, but can also be flexible enough for broad application and reuse to defray the cost of creating them. Design reuse takes software up a level of abstraction such that a design can be tailored and delivered in any software or hardware domain. Compared to code or algorithm reuse, design reuse offers the flexibility to choose hardware and software platforms. Design reuse begins at the system's conception. Prototypers must constantly be on the alert for an opportunity to create or reuse portions as they chunk the system into subsystems and components. Early identification of reusable design pieces also tends to result in the creation of reusable code components.

At the lowest level, module designs and code can be *adapted* to work with new data. This implies genetic re-engineering of the element or cell to allow for evolutionary growth and development. In evolutionary terms, this is known as adaptive radiation—the rapid divergence of many new forms of life from some common ancestor. Although a valuable way to reuse software, it creates problems because:

1. It can propagate defects to a wide range of components.
2. It creates new parts that have to be maintained.

At the next level, data tables, databases, software modules, and documentation are used *as is*. This cellular approach maximizes the benefit of any given part. Nothing need be changed. The only drawbacks to this approach are:

1. Changes to the part can impact many applications and will require extensive testing.
2. The part can try to be all things to all users and may eventually fail to be of value to any.
3. It may be difficult for prototypers to evaluate which parts offer the right features for their application.

At the next higher level, a more object-oriented level, data and processing combine into reusable components that perform higher-level functions. At this level, the component acts like an organ in the body, processing specific inputs and developing specific outputs. As a prototyper moves toward higher-level reusable components, the value of each instance of reuse increases and the number of times a component can be reused decreases because it becomes more specific. The more stable the data pool, the more likely it becomes that major reusable components can be created.

At the highest level, whole applications can be reused. This is like cloning whole organisms. In Japan, software houses provide custom systems from reusable applications. Banking applications, for example, are created for one customer and then customized for each additional customer. Because the core of the processing is reusable, the custom features can be added at a low cost, maximizing customer satisfaction and profit per system. Comparing this to our biological example, there are similarities among different races and species of humans and useful specializations as well.

At this high level of reuse, reusable documents and training can assist in delivering the maximum productivity and quality with minimal cost. This is how software houses make a profit, through development and continuous reuse of existing components and applications. This is why so many companies are writing software for desktop computers; the opportunities from reuse on a grand scale reduce the cost per copy to a level that almost anyone can afford.

Fred Brooks (Gruman, 1988) said that "in UNIX, the power of the whole pipes-and-filters and unified files structures . . . lets people lash together pieces they have lying around. These kinds of reusability are immediate." Having used UNIX extensively in the 1970s and 1980s, I can agree. Programming in the UNIX Shell can teach you a lot about reusability. I liked it so much that I wrote a book about it (Arthur, 1992).

Types of Reusable Processing Modules

There are six key kinds of business-processing modules:

1. data gathering — getting input for the process
2. data storage — updating data in memory or magnetic media
3. data processing — converting the raw data into information or knowledge
4. data retrieval — selecting stored data and information
5. data presentation on various media
6. communication

Data-gathering modules include user and system interfaces. Storage modules take the gathered data and store it in appropriate databases. Processing modules transform the raw data into information and knowledge. Data retrieval modules include queries and extracts for reports. Data presentation modules include reports and screens. Communication modules connect the system with its external and internal components.

At minimum, these reusable software modules should have the qualities of being general, flexible, reliable, modular, simple, and self-documenting. Generality implies that the module is usable in many circumstances. Flexible modules evolve easily. Reliable modules rarely fail. Modular components have a single entry and exit point, and perform a single function. This singularity brings about simplicity (7±2 decisions). These modules document their abilities through clear use of the programming language, data names, and comments.

Unfortunately, most of today's programmers tend to subtly encode specific information about the operating environment—operating system, database, hardware, and interfaces—into modules. To enhance their reliability, modules should be as independent of the data as possible. Using "information hiding," the structure and origin of the data can be hidden from the module's processing. Reusable modules may also practice "mutual suspicion"; this paranoid practice ensures that the data passed from some other module is valid before it is used. Other fault-tolerant practices can be employed to trap errors when they occur and to exit gracefully.

Reusable Documentation

Looking at the coding process as the only place to reuse things often is shortsighted. If, as Capers Jones suggests, paperwork is 25 percent of the total effort in a software project, then documentation is another great place to generate a return on investment by creating everything from boilerplate to complete documents that can be reused to provide:

1. requirements for similar applications or portions (e.g., security, reporting, error handling)
2. designs—system and detailed designs
3. plans—project management, test plans, quality-assurance plans
4. methods and procedures—design and testing methods and procedures
5. user guides

Reusability Tools

The most innovative and successful software creation in the 1990s will be done by organizations that have specialized tools such as the reuse catalog and reusable, evolutionary components and computing abilities that match their business. The Japanese Sigma project has three major design principles for reusability tools (Akima and Ooi, 1989):

1. Let users create an optimal integrated environment for their needs.
2. Promote technology transfer through use.
3. Encourage development of future third-party tools that can be integrated or used to replace or mask existing reusability tools.

Some of Sigma's existing tools include documentation, networking, and project management tools. Project management tools include the plan, do, check, act (PDCA) cycle for continuous quality improvement. There are over 40 Sigma tools consisting of two million lines of C code. Other tools include integrated screen, form, file, and database design tools.

The Sigma design environment consists of 32-bit workstations with powerful networking functions, resource-sharing functions, advanced user interface, and the minimum resources needed to run the UNIX-like OS and Sigma tools.

Central Software Repository and Catalog

Reuse can begin immediately. Many small, one-celled modules and databases can be created as projects develop. These can be added to the ever-growing wealth of software in the repository. As projects grow and mature, other, larger components differentiate and grow from the smaller pieces. Ready-made tissues and organs — menuing, graphics, application libraries — can spawn from the creation process. These various components can be created to be portable across computing systems to facilitate rapid and inexpensive transition to new or additional platforms.

As the population of reusable components expands, we must be able to catalog and reuse information, ideas, and knowledge, as well as various software parts and components. An effective and efficient cataloging system is essential to successful software reuse. The reusable software repository or catalog should match the sophistication of the public libraries. Storing components is one thing; retrieving them is another. People think in ideas, concepts, and facts. The catalog should think in the same way. Most catalogs, unfortunately, are rigid; human minds are not. Prototypers should be able to tag and link components on the fly as they discover relationships. Prototypers may also want to add notes in the margin or bookmarks into the repository so that they can return to a reference after they have finished looking around. The catalog can also enable a user to navigate through the webs of reusable components demonstrating connections and interactions.

Prototypers need a rapid method for identifying available candidates for reuse (Figure 9.4). If it takes too long, they will turn to creating the parts all over again. The model suggested by Prieto-Diaz and Freeman (1987) looks first at how one component is like another and then how they are different:

```
begin
  search library
  if identical match then select and terminate    (direct reuse)
  else
    collect similar components
    for each component
      compute degree of match
    end
    rank and select the best
    modify component to fit                        (adaptive reuse)
  endif
end
```

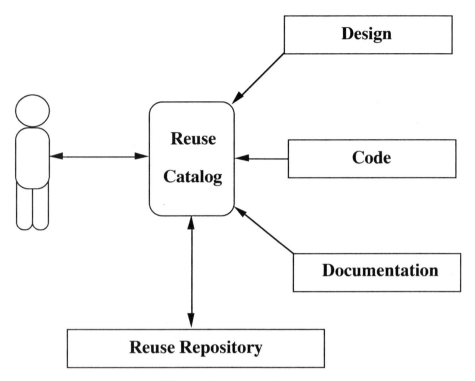

Figure 9.4   Reuse Catalog

For information, knowledge, designs, code, and data to be accepted into the repository, it will need to pass the following tests:

```
if an object is
  hardware independent and
  software independent and
  general and
  modular and
  self-documenting
then
  it is reusable
endif
If the object
  fits the business model and
  fits the architecture and
  is reusable
then
  it can go in the repository
endif
```

Problems

There are several reusability issues. How much will it cost to save money with reuse? How much will it improve productivity? How do I estimate return on investment? What are the employee incentives and barriers to reuse?

Roadblocks to reuse include the not-invented-here (NIH) syndrome, WISCY (Why isn't Sammy coding yet?), and the investment in learning and understanding reuse. Training designers and programmers to use the reuse repository costs time and money. Tracking usage of components makes configuration management costs higher. Elevating the creativity level to the design or requirements stage and rewarding early product delivery often will knock down these roadblocks.

Reusable components cost more to build, test, and document, but you can use them repeatedly in endless variations. Reuse dramatically reduces the time required to create and deliver a system. Reuse increases confidence in estimates and allows for ongoing evolution of requirements.

The technical problems of creating, cataloging, and recovering components are complex. Noboru Akima, planning director of the Japanese Sigma (reuse) project (Gruman, 1988), said that "these problems are exactly the ones that prevent the idea from realization. It [is] difficult to define the component size, interface, and functionality."

Programmer productivity, if measured in terms of just lines of code produced, tends to punish groups that reuse code extensively. Prototypers will generate less code and reuse more. One way to overcome this is to measure total functionality delivered in *function points* or to include all instances of reuse in the productivity calculation.

Some languages, COBOL specifically, do not encourage modularity, but rather encourage large, ever-expanding programs consisting of dozens to hundreds of paragraphs that, because of their custom nature, are difficult if not impossible to reuse.

Reuse is most effective at solving routine common problems. Within the confines of known application domains, reuse offers great potential. New application domains, however, require innovative solutions. Innovative designs, by their very nature, will require innovative approaches that may or may not be able to leverage the existing base of software components. At best, innovative solutions will be able to use the most basic elements of software, but possibly not the larger components.

Reuse is still struggling to establish itself in environments where the underlying technology is changing rapidly. COBOL and Fortran, for example, are stable and relatively unchanging. In parallel processing environments, however, reuse may be difficult initially. Rapid technological changes require more innovation and risk.

SUMMARY

In this chapter we've explored the benefits, critical success factors, and process of rapid prototyping. By using the metaphor of evolution, we can drop the constraints of the "construction" paradigm and discover new ways to quickly grow working systems that can surprise and delight both users and IS personnel. We've also looked briefly at the other evolutionary processes that support continued growth of the software, software processes, and technology. In the next chapter, we'll look at ways to gather customer requirements in ways that allow us to focus on the vital 20 percent of the functionality that will provide 80 percent of the benefit. We'll learn how to separate customer needs from wants and wishes. Once we know a user's needs in sufficient detail, we can begin to use rapid prototyping to create systems in record time.

The prototyper's job becomes easier as we learn to take advantage of reusable data, processing, and documentation. Reusable components may take a little longer to create, but they will serve the corporation for many years, perhaps even decades, as they grow and evolve. Vast improvements in productivity are possible when we adopt a mindset that we will reuse what is reusable and create new reusable components where none were previously available.

To maximize the benefits from rapid prototyping, reusability has to be one of the arrows in your quiver.

EXERCISE

Create a reuse catalog using Shell. As you create the catalog, create reusable Shell components that comprise at least 10 percent of the total catalog.

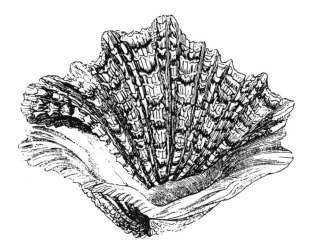

Chapter Ten

Shell for Programmers

C programmers have a wide variety of Shell tools and utilities at their disposal to aid in the development process. The beauty of the UNIX Shell toolset and utilities is that they are an integrated part of UNIX and are available on almost all UNIX platforms. When used together they form a comprehensive, flexible, and portable foundation for developing the complex software systems of the 1990s. While today's complex systems require a host of high-powered tools to yield maximum programmer proficiency, the UNIX Shell toolset still offers a great foundation for any development project.

This chapter explores the basic tools and utilities that C programmers will find useful. While the chapter will not contain exhaustive coverage on any particular tool, it will provide an overview and a description of the basic ways that the tools work and how they are used on many software development projects. C programmers (or aspiring programmers) as well as software project managers will find this chapter most interesting and informative.

C LANGUAGE PROGRAMMING

The Shell, especially the C Shell, is oriented to work with C language programming. The Shell can assist in all phases of C language development: prototyping, coding, compiling, and testing. The Shell provides the means to try out new ideas quickly and easily. C language is the vehicle to construct an efficient program once its design has been established and tested with Shell.

Chapter 7 described the five major types of programs: input, output, query, update, and interface. Each can be prototyped easily with Shell. Then begins the important task of translating the Shells into C language. One of the best ways to speed up the process of writing C language programs is to establish a directory containing skeletal programs of the five major program designs. These can easily be copied into the programmer's directory for expansion using Shell:

```
# Proto skeleton newname.c
skeletondir=/global/C/skeletons
case $# in
  0|1)
      echo "Prototype List:\n"
      ls $skeletondir
      echo "Enter skeleton type"
      read skeleton
      echo "Enter newname.c"
      read cname
      ;;
  2)
      skeleton=$1
      cname=$2
      ;;
    *)
      echo "$0 syntax: $0 skeleton newname.c
esac
while [ ! -f ${skeletondir}/$skeleton ]
do    # Prompt until they get a valid skeleton type
    echo "Skeleton $skeleton not found"
    echo "Enter skeleton type"
    read skeleton
    echo "Enter newname.c"
    read cname
done
cp $skeleton $cname    # Copy skeleton to newname.c
echo "Skeleton module $cname has been created"
```

C or Shell skeletons of the five major program designs should be created and maintained for the prototyping staff. Reusing designs and code is much more productive than reinventing the wheel. So let the Shell handle as much of the typing and logic as possible. A simple C language skeleton is shown in Appendix B.

Aside from the **proto** command which you can develop for your own use to speed up the coding process, UNIX provides a series of commands (shown in Table 10.1) to aid the programming process. These commands handle concerns such as structuring the code for readability, printing the code, and documenting what the code does.

The C language beautifier, **cb,** lets the programmer enter the code in any format and then transforms the code to one of several standard conventions. It

TABLE 10.1   C Language Coding Commands

Command	Description
cb	beautifier
cflow	flow analyzer
cxref	cross-reference listing
list	print listing
lint	syntax checker
nl	print numbered listing

straightens up the code and makes the logic more visible. The readability of the code is enhanced and so is the maintainability. **Cb** provides a consistent format for the code.

List and **nl** provide two means of printing C language listings. **List** works on object files that contain symbolic debugging symbols; **nl** provides a numbered listing of C source code. Either can be combined with **pr** to produce a clean listing of a C program:

```
# clist cnames.c
for file in $*
do
  nl $file | pr -h "Source listing for $file"
done
```

In Berkeley systems, there is a formatting program called vgrind. It emboldens keywords and sets comments in italics. Its output is in troff (-t) format. It can be invoked as follows:

```
# cprint files.c
vgrind -t $* | lpr -t
```

What if you don't have vgrind on your system? In Chapter 13 we'll look at how to write your own filters to format code any way you want.

As programmers create programs, they often include data names that aren't used, statements that can't be reached, or other problem code. **Lint,** the C program checker, finds all kinds of stylistic problems and bug-prone code. The output produced by **lint** can be selected, cut, pasted, and reported in ways that help clean up the code before compilation. **Lint** also helps spot C language portability problems when invoked with the -p option. **Lint** is an important tool in the development of portable, bug-free C language programs.

Cflow and **cxref** help document how the program works—which module calls another, which data names are referenced and where, and so on. **Cflow** works on any combination of C, yacc, lex, assembler, and object files. The output from a run of cflow is a listing of the call pattern of a set of C programs. For example, if function A calls function B, this fact will appear in the cflow listing. **Cxref** works only on C language files. The output from a run of cxref is a cross-reference listing of all variables declared in a set of C programs and how they are used by the set of functions listed.

By keeping all of the source code for a single program in a single directory, **cflow** can be executed simply as:

```
cflow *.[closy] | pr -h "Cflow listing for program `pwd`" | lp
```

Similarly, **cxref** can operate on all C language files:

```
cxref *.c | pr -h "Cross Reference for `pwd | basename`" | lp
```

The commands presented — **cb, cflow, lint,** and so on — are not the only ones that can be used during the coding process, but they are the major ones. Inventive toolsmiths will find others that can aid the coding process.

You can also call the Shell from a C language program using the system call. This is especially helpful when putting together the first draft of a system. Use Shell calls to handle things in stubs of modules that you will construct later. The Shell calls then serve as pseudocode for the routine you will ultimately construct. System calls are as simple as:

```
system(who; date);
```

Now that your program has been coded using the finest tools available, it must be compiled and tested.

COMPILING

C language programs are created in three separate steps: preprocessing, compiling, and link editing (see Figure 10.1). The commands that perform these processes are shown in Table 10.2. The Shell is the glue that links these commands together.

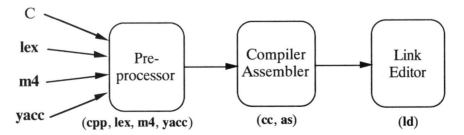

Figure 10.1   Steps in Compiling a Program

TABLE 10.2 **Preprocessing and Compiling Commands**

Command	Description
`as`	assembly language compiler
`cc`	C language compiler
`dis`	object file disassembler
`ld`	link editor
`lex`	lexical analyzer preprocessor
`make`	compile and assemble programs
`m4`	macro preprocessor
`regcmp`	regular expression compiler
`strip`	strip symbol tables
`yacc`	yet another compiler compiler

Phase 1: Preprocessing

Preprocessing occurs before compilation and provides the programmer with the ability to alter the source code in some particular way. The C preprocessor is a program that scans C source code looking for preprocessor macro commands and performing the actions specified by those commands. The preprocessor can define constants in the program, include external source files into the program, and conditionally include source code.

There are five major preprocessors for C language: the C language preprocessor (cpp), which is invoked automatically by the C compiler; lex, which generates lexical analysis programs; yacc, which generates grammar analysis and parsing programs; m4, which allows for macro substitution; and regcmp, which compiles regular expressions for use with the function regex (which examines text in much the same way as grep). Simple commands to preprocess lexical analyzer or yacc code into C language and then compile it look like this:

```
lex file.l && cc lex.yy.c -ll
yacc file.y && cc y.tab.c
```

The m4 macro processor was designed as a preprocessor for C and assembly code. It allows the definition of macros which are then expanded by m4 prior to compilation. Many of the abilities of m4 are included in the C preprocessor. Only on rare occasions will a programmer need to use the macro preprocessor. Some of the assemblers (as), however, use m4 as a preprocessor. It can be invoked whenever needed:

```
m4 file.m > file.c && cc file.c
```

The regular expression compiler, regcmp, performs most of the work done by the C function by the same name. It allows regular expressions to be compiled (an expensive process) before a C language program is compiled or tested, thereby saving execution time. It creates an output file, file.i, which can be included directly into C language code. Once compiled, regular expression analysis can be performed directly by regex:

```
regcmp regfile && cc file.c
```

where file.c contains a statement of the form:

```
# include "regfile.i"
```

In most cases the standard C preprocessor, cpp, is utilized. It is automatically called when using the standard C compiler, cc. There is no need to call the cpp preprocessor separately.

Phase 2: Compiling

Compiling is a process that translates the source program into a language that the machine can understand (machine code). Once the preprocessing stage is completed, the compiler (cc) and assembler (as) are brought into play. As previously stated, these two invoke their own preprocessors (cpp and m4). The output of these two processors is then compiled into what are commonly referred to as object modules. Object modules usually end with the .o suffix. Once a successful compilation has occurred with each C source program being translated into a corresponding object module, phase 3 begins.

Phase 3: Link Editing

The linkage editor (ld) has the task of taking the object modules, created by the compiler, and creating an executable module. An executable module can be run directly from the Shell command line by typing the name just like any other command. The linkage editor ensures that all called functions are accounted for and finalizes the relative machine addresses for all variables. Unless ld is told otherwise, the output of the linkage editor phase is stored in a file named a.out.

The three steps just described are most often accomplished automatically by using the standard UNIX C compiler command **cc.** Compiling a program is most often a single step for the programmer with the preprocessor, compiler, and linkage editor being called directly.

Simple C language programs can be compiled and tested easily:

```
cc file.s && a.out
cc file.c && a.out
```

More complex programs containing several modules must be compiled and then linked into an executable module. As pointed out previously, the linkage editor, ld, is automatically invoked by **cc** when needed:

```
cc file1.c file2.c file3.c -o ctest && ctest
```

In this example, all of the C files are compiled into their respective object files: file1.o, file2.o, file3.o, and file4.o. These are then linked together by ld, which is executed automatically by **cc.** The output of the linkage editor phase will be the executable program ctest. There are many options that can be passed to the **cc** command. Please refer to your manual pages for complete details.

One of the possible options that can be used when compiling is an option that tells the compiler to include debugger information into the object module (-g). This debugger information is stored in a table called the *symbol table.* Several of the most widely used C debuggers use this table to ascertain information about the program while it is executing. For improved efficiency, the linkage editor, or *strip*, can be used to strip the symbol tables out of an executable program. The benefit of removing the symbol tables is that the programs load more quickly and require less disk space. The drawbacks are that the program cannot easily be debugged without the symbol tables, and the executable program may not be portable between different releases of the UNIX operating system. Only final, production versions of programs should be stripped of their symbol tables.

Compiling Using Make

Because the Shell scripts to accurately preprocess, compile, and link large programs and entire systems would be overly complex, UNIX provides the **make** command to handle the complexity of preprocessing, compiling, and linking in more complex environments. A prototype makefile is available in Appendix C.

Make is a command generator that understands dependencies between files. In particular, **make** most often generates compile commands based on relationships between C source files, object files, and executables. By using the date and time stamp stored on files, **make** can determine which modules need to be recompiled.

Make knows about all of the different file types in UNIX: SCCS (s.filename.c), C language (filename.c), assembly language (filename.s), lex (filename.l), yacc (filename.y), object files (filename.o), and libraries (library.a). **Make** knows, for example, that to create an object file, it must first compile a C language or assembly language file by the same name. It also knows that it may have to get the file from SCCS (Source Code Control System is part of the UNIX change control management system — see the next section for details) if it does not exist. **Make** decides what to do based on the last modification time of each file. If the object file is newer than either the SCCS or C language file, **make** assumes that the object file is the most current and does not compile anything. If the SCCS file is newer, **make** gets the file from SCCS and compiles it to create the object module. The makefile to accomplish this task for a single source file would be as follows:

```
OBJECTS = cmdname.o            # Name of the object file
cmdname: $(OBJECTS)            # Command depends on cmdname.o
    cc $(OBJECTS) -o cmdname   # Compile & link cmdname
```

Make automatically knows to look for the SCCS (s.cmdname.c) and source files (cmdname.c). Once a makefile is created, correctly compiling a program is as simple as

```
make
```

The output from this command using the previous makefile would be:

```
get -p s.cmdname.c > cmdname.c
cc -c cmdname.c
cc cmdname.o -o cmdname
```

Since the date on s.cmdname.c was newer than either the C or object files, **make** executed **get** to retrieve the file from SCCS. Then, **make** executed the C compiler to create an object module (cmdname.o) from the source file. Finally, **make** executed the C compiler to link the object file into the executable program (cmdname).

Sometimes a C language file will include a data header file, filename.h, which may change and affect the resulting program. **Make** can know about these files and invoke the compiler when the header file changes:

```
OBJECTS = cmdname.o                   # Name of the object file
cmdname: $(OBJECTS)                    # Command depends on cmdname.o
   cc $(OBJECTS) -o cmdname           # Compile & link cmdname
cmdname.o: cmdname.c cmdname.h        # Cmdname.o depends on
                                      # cmdname.c and .h
```

Similarly, a single program may depend on many object files. **Make** can be instructed, via the makefile, to compile all of the modules and link them together:

```
OBJECTS = file1.o file2.o file3.o file4.o
cmdname: $(OBJECTS)             # Command depends on all objects
   cc $(OBJECTS) -o cmdname     # Compile & link the command
file1.o: file1.c file1.h        # Object depends on header
```

This makefile will instruct **make** to compile all of the objects including file1.c, which also depends on file1.h. All four objects are created and then linked together. Since these larger compilations take longer to accomplish, the C language programmer should put the whole process into background and continue working on other activities:

```
nohup nice make&
```

A listing of commands executed by **make** and the resulting errors will be stored in the file nohup.out for later examination.

Besides the variable, *OBJECTS,* there is another important **make** variable used to set the C compiler flags for all compiles and links — *CFLAGS.* This single variable can affect how all modules are compiled. To optimize the output of the compiler, for example, set *CFLAGS* to "-O":

```
CFLAGS = -O     # Optimize executable code
```

Similarly, to include the regular expression and lexical analyzer library (PW and l) with the resulting executable program, set *CFLAGS* as follows:

```
CFLAGS = -O -lPW -ll    # Optimize and include RE & LEX libs
```

To invoke the inclusion of test code defined in preprocessor statements, use *CFLAGS* to set the "-D" flag:

```
CFLAGS = -DTEST
```

which would cause the inclusion of code such as the following:

```
# ifdef TEST
  fprintf(stderr,"Entering Main\n");
# endif
```

Using this technique, instruments can be left in the code to test its functioning, but turned on and off with the **make** variable *CFLAGS.*

In summary, UNIX comes with a variety of preprocessors, compilers, and a linkage editor that facilitate the construction of C language programs. The Shell and **make** are both useful for executing these commands in the proper order to create executable programs. Once compiled, however, C language programs must be tested and debugged.

CREATING AND MAINTAINING LIBRARIES: AR

The UNIX archive utility, **ar,** gives programmers the ability to store compiled object modules in a common library that can be used by the link editor. Building libraries using **ar** allows for the grouping of object modules under a common name. These grouped modules can then be shared by other functions. This makes it possible to maintain a single version of source code and related object code that can be utilized freely by other modules. Large numbers of related object modules can be stored in a single library. The library, when created, is given a name that can then be used in conjunction with the C compiler, cc.

The archive utility provides ways for fully maintaining libraries. This includes creating libraries, adding modules to libraries, deleting modules from libraries, and listing the contents of libraries. The syntax of the archive command is shown as:

```
ar [-] keywords [posname] archive_file_name [object_file_list]
```

where keywords are one of those shown in Table 10.3 and the archive_file_name is the name of the archive file that is to have the actions performed. Following the archive_file_name are the names of object files that are to be added, deleted, and so forth.

Each of these keywords performs the primary function listed. In addition, there are keyword modifiers that can be used in conjunction with the keywords that modify the normal behavior. Please refer to the manual pages on ar for details.

The following command would create a new archive library, if one does not already exist, and place the named modules in the archive:

```
ar r ioarch iomod1.o iomod2.o iomod3.o
ar: creating ioarch
```

In this example, the archive file ioarch is created and the object modules iomod1, iomod2, and iomod3 are added to the archive. If the archive file already exists, then the r keyword will replace an object module in the archive if one by the same name exists, or it will add the module to the end of the archive if the module does not exist.

To list the modules in our archive, we can use the t keyword as shown below:

```
ar t ioarch
iomod1.o
iomod2.o
iomod3.o
```

The x keyword can be used to extract the listed object modules from the archive file:

```
ar x ioarch iomod1.o
```

TABLE 10.3 Ar Keyword Commands

Keyword	Description
d	Delete object files named in the object file list from the named library.
r	Replace existing object members with those named in the object list in the named library.
q	Quick add of objects named in the object list. No check is made to see if the object name already exists.
t	List the object modules found in the named archive file.
p	Print the object files listed in the object list.
m	Move the named object file to a new position in the archive file.
x	Extract named object files from the archive.

Now that we can create and maintain an archive, we need to be able to utilize created libraries with the linkage editor. This really is very straightforward: Simply list the library name just as you would any other object module that you would like to have linked into the final executable. The linkage editor is trained to search libraries looking for modules that are needed to resolve function calls. This is shown in the following command that utilizes the ioarch created previously when compiling a module.

```
cc mygame.c -o mygame ioarch
```

In this example, if the source code in mygame.c made a function call to iomod1 to perform some input/output processing, the reference would be resolved by the linkage editor simply by listing the ioarch archive since it contains the iomod1 object module. Similarly, if the source in mygame.c made references to all three modules contained in the ioarch archive, they would likewise be resolved by the linkage editor simply by listing the library name on the compile line.

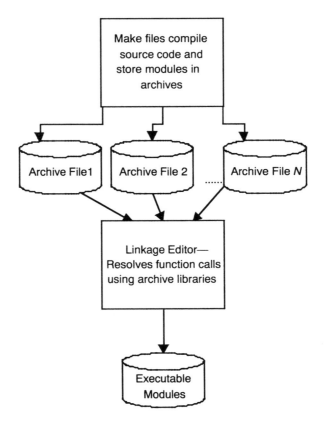

Figure 10.2   Utilities

Figure 10.2 shows how a typical C software project utilizes tools to create and maintain an up-to-date executable program module.

TESTING AND DEBUGGING

The major UNIX commands that aid testing and debugging are shown in Table 10.4. **Adb, sdb,** and **dbx** are the three major debugging facilities. **Ctrace** is a more primitive debugging tool that allows for the tracing of C programs as they execute. **Prof, time,** and **timex** are all useful for determining a program's efficiency. All of these commands are useful for testing.

    Adb, a debugger, is available with various versions of UNIX and is the most primitive of the three debuggers. It is primarily an assembly-level debugger and is not widely used. **Sdb,** the symbolic debugger, is available with virtually all systems and debugs at a source level. **Dbx,** like **sdb,** is a symbolic source-level debugger that is mainly available on Berkeley UNIX systems. **Sdb** is perhaps the more powerful and more widely used of the two symbolic debuggers, but really both **sdb** and **dbx** work in very similar ways and accomplish similar tasks. When a program aborts or requires specialized testing, these debuggers can analyze compiled C language programs, core (a file left behind when a program terminates that shows its final state) images of the program when it failed, and aid the programmer in analysis of the problem. To maximize the effectiveness of **sdb** and **dbx,** the program must be compiled with the -g option and the symbol table must not be stripped from the executable file:

```
cc -g *.c -o ctest && ctest || sdb ctest
```

Or the *CFLAGS* variable could have been changed to include the -g option and the program would be compiled and tested as follows:

```
make && ctest || sdb ctest
```

TABLE 10.4   Testing and Debugging Commands

Command	Description
adb	a debugger
ctrace	C program execution trace
dbx	Berkeley symbolic debugger
diff	file comparison utility
dump	dump object file
od	octal dump
prof	execution profiler
sdb	symbolic debugger
time	timer
timex	timer and system activity reporter

This command stream will compile all C language modules in the current directory, link them into a program called ctest, execute ctest, and, if it fails, invoke **sdb.** Since most programs are compiled without the -g option or the symbol tables, this compilation and retest are required to generate all of the information needed by **sdb** and **dbx.**

A simple use of **sdb** traces the path the program took before ending abnormally. After executing **sdb** and receiving the **sdb** prompt (*), enter a lowercase *t:*

```
sdb ctest
*t
doprnt()
sub1()
main()
```

In this example, the program ended in doprnt (a printf function) and was called from sub1. Sub1 was called from main. The C programmer can now trace potential paths of error in the subroutine sub1. To get a more specific trace, ctest would have to have been compiled with the -g option, but this example is sufficient for tracing most errors.

Sdb and **dbx** can also execute a program one line at a time allowing the programmer to watch its progress as it steps toward completion. Both of these facilities are useful when testing and debugging programs.

Ctrace is a utility that allows you to trace the execution path of a C program. It is not as powerful a symbolic debugger as **sdb** or **dbx,** but is easier to learn and to use. It is very similar to using the -x option on Shell programs and tracing the flow of the program as it executes. **Ctrace** inserts printf statements to modify your program for you. For each line in the program, printf statements are generated to show you the line that is executing along with any variable values that were used on that line. To use **ctrace** you specify a C source program as input. The modified version of the program is placed on the standard output. The output can be captured to a file and compiled by the C compiler cc. The **ctrace** command has the following syntax:

```
ctrace [options ] [filename ]
```

where filename is the C source program. To create a trace program for the **ctest** module, the following would do the trick:

```
ctrace ctest.c > ctsttrace.c      # Capture new source program to
                                  # ctsttrace.c
cc ctsttrace                      # Compile the modified program
```

After creating the new program and compiling it, we run the executable to get trace information. Each line is displayed as it executes, along with any variables and their values. As you can imagine, tracing programs in this way can get quite cumbersome. A great deal of output can be generated very rapidly. In order to help control the scope of the tracing, **ctrace** provides a few options. The -f option allows you to specify tracing in particular functions in the program. The -v option is the complement of -f, telling **ctrace** to trace all functions that are not in the list.

The three commands **prof, time,** and **timex** can help identify programs that are resource hogs. **Time** and **timex** both give rudimentary indications that a program takes too many resources, either CPU or disk. **Prof** encourages a more exacting analysis of a program's efficiency. These three commands can be executed as follows:

```
time command
timex command
cc -p *.c -o command && command && prof command
```

The last command compiles the program command with a -p option to invoke the creation (the mon.out) file readable by **prof.** The command is then executed and **prof** profiles the execution of the command using mon.out in conjunction with the program symbol table. The output of **prof** can be directed to a file, printer, or terminal as required.

Each of these commands—**time, timex,** and **prof**—allows analysis of a program's execution in ways not possible with **sdb.** Once a program has executed, however, analysis focuses on the program's output.

The remaining commands—**diff** and **od**—help analyze the results of a program test. **Diff** compares files, and **od** generates an octal dump of a file. **Diff** is useful with standard files that end with a newline character (\n). **Od,** on the other hand, prints the unprintable, showing normally unreadable octal characters as their octal value. Because many terminals require control strings that may be unprintable, **od** provides a simple means to examine the output of commands that generate terminal control strings. Other files, such as SCCS files, have embedded octal characters that cannot be detected without **od.** Both **diff** and **od** help analyze test results.

Diff, a file comparison utility, can examine two output files and display only those lines that differ. It shows which lines were added, changed, or deleted from the test output. This comparison aids a technique called regression testing—comparing the old to the new to ensure that only the desired changes occurred. Eliminating identical information from both tests helps the programmer determine the success or failure of a change:

```
oldcommand [args] > oldstdout 2>oldstderr
newcommand [args] > newstdout 2>newstderr
diff oldstdout newstdout | pr      # Compare the output from the
                                   # old and the new
diff oldstderr newstderr | pr
```

Examination of **diff**'s output should indicate that the changes were made successfully or incorrectly.

Diff has several sister commands: **bdiff, sdiff,** and **sccsdiff. Bdiff** works on larger files than **diff** can handle; **sdiff** gives a side-by-side difference listing; and **sccsdiff** compares two versions of an SCCS file. **Sccsdiff** is one of the best ways to determine the changes that occurred between two versions of a program's code, providing that the source code is stored in SCCS in the first place. SCCS is a major portion of the change control and configuration management facilities of UNIX.

CHANGE CONTROL AND CONFIGURATION MANAGEMENT

Change control and configuration management are the way that programs are built and changed in an orderly fashion. SCCS stores C language code, documents, Shells, or anything consisting of text. (The available SCCS commands are shown in Table 10.5.) When you are developing new Shells or C language programs and you complete an early working version, store the version in SCCS so that you can recover it later if required. When changing a program, get the source code out of SCCS, change it, store it back, and then build the changes to the program into the SCCS source.

SCCS can hold all versions of a program, from its infancy through adulthood, until it is scrapped. Most library systems hold only the most current version of the source; the older versions are backed up on tape somewhere. Recovering old versions is no fun. With SCCS, however, it is simple. Even programmers on single-user systems will find SCCS of immeasurable value for controlling software and documentation changes.

SCCS files can be kept in any directory, but for convenience it is best to store them in one location so that Shells for accessing them can easily be built. Normally, they are stored under a directory called "sccs," which can exist under the user's home directory or the group's file system (see Figure 10.3). Some users prefer to store documentation with the program, whereas others favor a separate directory. Once the organization of SCCS directories is decided, Shell interfaces are easily created to add or change SCCS files.

TABLE 10.5   SCCS Commands

Command	Description
`admin`	add a file to SCCS
`comb`	combine two versions of an SCCS file
`delta`	create a new version of an SCCS file
`get`	get a file from SCCS
`prs`	print a description of an SCCS file
`rmdel`	remove a delta
`sccsdiff`	compare two versions of an SCCS file
`val`	validate an SCCS file
`what`	look for *what* strings in an SCCS file

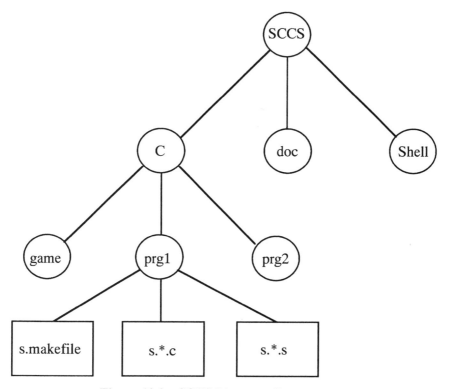

Figure 10.3   SCCS Directory Structure

The command to add files to SCCS is **admin.** It has a variety of options that often are unclear to new users. A simple Shell interface would accept the type of file, program name, and source name and add the file as follows:

```
# cadd program file
sccsdir=$HOME/sccs/C
if [ $# -eq 2 ]    # Two arguments?
then
  if [ ! -d $sccsdir/$program ]    # New program?
  then
    mkdir $sccsdir/$program         # Create a directory
  fi
  echo "Enter one line description"
  read desc
  admin -n -i$file -y"${desc}" $sccsdir/$program/s.$file
else
  echo "$0 syntax: $0 program file
fi
```

A user easily could add a program to SCCS with the following command and the code would be equally easy to retrieve:

```
cadd prg1 main.c
```

Similarly, editing an SCCS file would require the following command:

```
# cedit program file
if [ $# -eq 2 ]
then
  sccsfile=$HOME/sccs/c/$program/s.$file
  if [ -r $sccsfile ]
  then
    get -e -s $sccsfile
    echo "$file has been retrieved for editing"
  else
    echo "File $sccsfile does not exist"
  fi
else
  echo "$0 syntax: $0 program file
fi
```

A user could retrieve the source as follows:

```
cedit prg1 main.c
```

To save the changed file back into SCCS requires a similar command:

```
# csave program file
if [ $# -eq 2 ]
then
  sccsfile=$HOME/sccs/c/$program/s.$file
  if [ -r $sccsfile ]
  then
    echo "Enter one line description of change"
    read comments
    delta -y"$comments" $sccsfile
  else
    echo "File $sccsfile does not exist"
  fi
else
    echo "$0 syntax: $0 type program file
fi
```

A user can save the changed source as follows:

```
csave prg1 main.c
```

SCCS also provides numerous ways to print information about SCCS files and the changes applied. **Prs** prints the status of various releases and levels of the source code. **Get** can retrieve the source code with the release and level number preceding each line of text. A simple command to print the history of changes to a file would be:

```
# chist program file
if [ $# -eq 2 ]
then
  sccsfile=$HOME/sccs/c/$program/s.$file
  if [ -r $sccsfile ]
  then
    prs -e -d":I: :D: :P: :C:" $sccsfile | pr -h "$file"
  else
    echo "File $sccsfile does not exist"
  fi
else
  echo "$0 syntax: $0 program file
fi
```

Executing **chist** on an SCCS file would print a listing of changes (:I:), the dates the changes were created (:D:), the programmer who made the change (:P:), and the comments associated with the change (:C:). Reports of this type are useful to managers, analysts, and programmers for various activities.

Programmers, however, can get more out of a program listing containing the program code and the deltas associated with each line. A command similar to **chist** could be built to get this information:

```
get -p -m $sccsfile | pr -o8 -h "Source listing for $file"
```

The output of this command would contain the SCCS release and level number from which each line was retrieved, a tab character, and then the source code line:

```
1.1  main(argc,argv)
1.1  int argc;
1.1  char **argv;
1.1  {
1.2  char c;
2.3  char *ptr;
```

Bugs often are found in recent modifications to the program. This facility of SCCS enables the programmer to quickly locate recent code changes. Managers can also track errors back to the release and level number of the source code.

The SCCS keywords can be used to automate version and run control in C language programs. The version number of each C source file can be stored in a variable using the SCCS keyword "%A%":

```
static char *version = "%A%"; /* SCCS Version information */
```

When retrieved from SCCS, the keyword would expand to a what string that contains the source type, the source file name, and its release, level, branch, and sequence number:

```
static char *version = "@(#) clang filename.c 2.3.1.1 @(#)";
```

This information can be extracted from the executable program using **what** to check for proper version information:

```
what filename
clang filename.c 2.3.1.1
clang sub1.c 1.2
clang sub2.c 1.3.1.1
```

The version information can also be printed or written to run control files to log the execution of the command. The SCCS keywords give the programmer a strong tool for tracking and controlling change in C language programs.

Other, similar friendly interfaces to SCCS can be built around the remaining commands: **comb, rmdel, sccsdiff,** and **val.** The Shell can handle many functions that not only will improve change control and configuration management, but will also improve productivity and the quality of the resulting system. Many people question the need for all of this control — especially some of the UNIX gurus — but as system complexities increase, the need for SCCS control becomes more intense.

SUMMARY

The Shell provides many tools that aid the development and maintenance of C language programs. The Shell can be used to develop working prototypes of C language programs to test the correctness of their design. It can be used to automate much of the coding, compiling, testing, and debugging processes. Even the control of changes to C language source code, documentation, and other text files can be orchestrated by the Shell. Every development project needs a toolsmith to create these productivity tools. The examples in this chapter provide a starting point for further development and enhancement of the C programming environment.

User-friendly interfaces to all of these commands can also be constructed to present the user with menus or windows into the C language. But the Shell can still automate most of the activities required during software development and maintenance. Use its facilities to maximize productivity and quality.

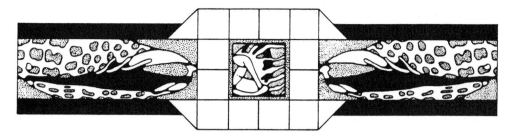

Chapter Eleven

The Shell Innovator

> The sole advantage of power is that you can do more good.
>
> *Baltasar Gracian*

Over the past 40 years we have automated virtually all of the systems that support existing business needs. Unfortunately, automation has locked us into the way we did things 10, 20, or 30 years ago, and the way we did things then were fairly inefficient and ineffective. Most of these systems are too inflexible to meet the challenges of the 1990s. Some of the concerns that face software professionals because of these dinosaurs include "manual" interfaces, redundant and inaccessible data, and the closed proprietary architectures of today's vendors. The Information Society is an economic reality, not an intellectual abstraction.

> I know of no teachers so powerful and persuasive as a little army of specialists.
> They carry no banners, they beat no drums; but where they are men learn
> that bustle and push are not the equals of quiet genius and serene mastery.
>
> *Oliver Wendell Holmes, Jr.*

The Shell power user will set the pace, direction, and inspiration for other users. As such, you will need to lead by example. If you do things in a half-baked way, so will everyone else. The Shell innovator demonstrates the power of Shell.

> Inventors and men of genius have almost always been regarded as fools
> at the beginning (and very often at the end) of their careers.
>
> *Fyodor Dostoyevsky*

UNIX and Shell offer the promised land of application portability across all types of computers. The POSIX standard put UNIX in the hands of the user, not the vendor. The long reign of hardware tyranny is coming to an end. UNIX will be the software cockpit of the 1990s and Shell will be one of the weapons in your arsenal.

This ability to develop applications that run in UNIX but need no specific hardware environment gives users freedom of choice and a way to lower overall costs. This is why UNIX is often called an open system. It also gives you connectivity to all existing applications via the communication tools, which will ultimately lead to increased vendor and hardware independence. This freedom will also:

- protect your application portfolio
- give you leverage with vendors
- increase organizational flexibility to use the same software everywhere
- simplify application maintenance
- reduce risk of technological change
- increase user control
- provide full suites of programming, text, interface, and support tools
- encourage continuity of user knowledge from MS-DOS
- enhance access to corporate data as needed

Using UNIX and Shell to integrate existing systems and develop new strategic ones is a global solution that leads to:

- lower costs
- greater results
- reduced time-to-market
- empowered employees
- increased competitive advantage

The winners of the future will need to:

1. select the right opportunities
2. apply the appropriate methodology and technology

The right opportunities for the businesses of the 1990s include integration of existing systems and the development of strategic information systems. The right methods and tools include graphical-user interfaces (GUIs), object-oriented programming (OOP), rapid application development (RAD), and open systems architectures (OSA). The absence of these foundations causes entropy, illness, and the death of information systems (IS). IS death occurs when management retreats behind policies and procedures to preserve the status quo. Those who fail at these two key activities will fumble their future. The key issues at stake in this information revolution are:

- survival
- revenue
- reputation for quality, price, and service

True simplicity is not easy.

The challenge facing all users and software developers will be to *redesign existing processes* to be more effective and efficient, and *then* to automate them. While we're doing this, however, we will have to keep the old systems growing and evolving. This is no simple challenge. The systems we have today live lonely, separate lives. In today's business climate, however, systems need to share data and information to meet the company's information needs (see Chapter 7). Rather than build a whole new system to replace several others, we can use 80 percent of the existing system or systems to perform the core processing and use UNIX and Shell to integrate the user interfaces. Using this strategy, we can integrate existing systems at 20 percent of the cost of building new ones.

SYSTEMS INTEGRATION

All "operating cost reduction" software was built in the 1960s and 1970s. These tactical systems are getting older every day, while vast hordes of programmers add new functions and patch bugs in the software. Unless someone is actively rejuvenating this software, entropy is moving it and your company closer to the software graveyard. Information managers keep waiting for some magic to appear that will redesign and rewrite these systems overnight. Alas, no such luck.

If users are the least flexible element in any system, then existing software systems must be the second most inflexible element. Fortunately, however, we can use UNIX and the Shell to rapidly create user-seductive interfaces, integrate existing systems, and breathe a few more years of life into these dinosaurs (Figure 11.1). By using the Shell to build the user interfaces, we can save money and time in comparison to developing a full GUI. This is useful for updating systems that are slated for redevelopment but may need to live on for a few more years. The data we need is available from existing screens or reports; all we need to do is extract it using Shell tools such as **grep** and **awk.** Consider the following examples:

1. Two (or more) systems maintain the same data (e.g., an employee record, the area code of your phone number, or a state code table). Use Shell as a front-end preprocessor and build a single update screen (as we demonstrated in Chapter 7), manage the data, and update the data in both systems (Figure 11.2) using Shell communications.

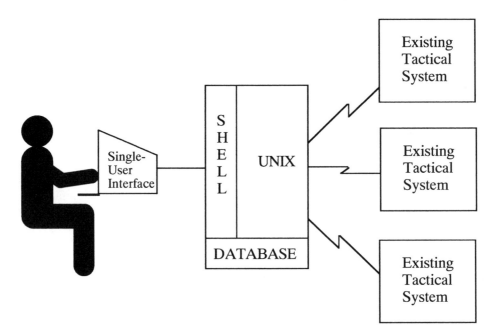

Figure 11.1   Systems Integration

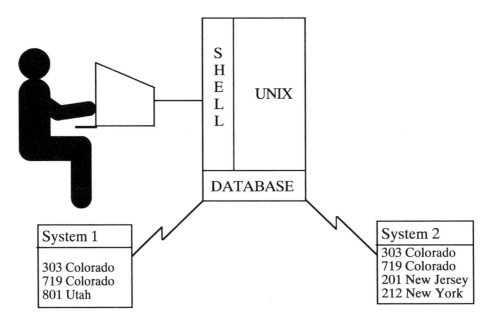

Figure 11.2   Systems Integration of Databases

2. Your company buys a smaller company with its own suite of systems and programs. Use Shell (Figure 11.3) to bridge the chasm between the two companies' systems until you can merge them.

There are, however, a few drawbacks to this technique:

1. The response time of the integrated system is equal to the response time of the slowest system.
2. Functionality is impaired when one of the systems is down.
3. The integration is highly dependent on existing screen and report design. If these change, then the integration package must change as well.

Aside from these minor drawbacks, systems integration is an excellent way to maximize the benefits of Shell. Most computer vendors specialize in certain areas — data management, real-time transaction processing, or whatever. Unfortunately, their architecture is closed. Vendors are like a railroad: you have to stay on their line and only stop in certain places, which makes it difficult to share data among disparate systems. Connecting diverse vendor systems is like trying to connect short stretches of superhighway with long, narrow dirt roads that wind through mountains, deserts, and rolling plains. Using the open architecture of UNIX and the Shell, you can build your own superhighway between these systems to help you access data, and then do what you want with it. This is the power and freedom of Shell.

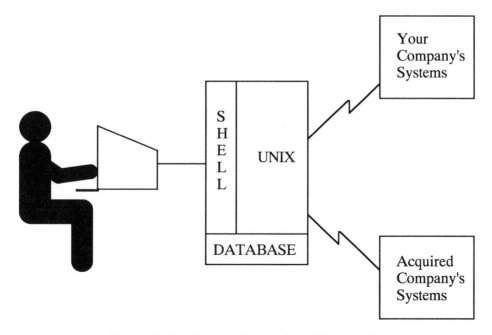

Figure 11.3   Systems Integration of Companies

STRATEGIC INFORMATION SYSTEMS

> The one that controls the software controls the war.
>
> *Katsuhide Hirai*

Estimates project that the world software market will explode from $50 billion to $1 trillion during the 1990s. The United States consumes 52 percent of the world's software and controls 70 percent of the market (Rifkin and Savage, 1989). And yet, today's businesses are suffering from an advanced case of information starvation and indigestion. Marketing types hunger for the information to forge new markets. They need real-time customer information to find and develop in new markets. Strategic information systems help you identify markets and decide where you'll be in three to five years; tactical systems maintain the status quo. Existing systems feed a flood of data into the corporate hierarchy — far more information than can be digested. Using the power of Shell and UNIX to glue these systems together and scrub their combined outputs into meaningful information will accelerate the growth and power of your company.

Existing systems are tactical in nature: They keep the business running from day to day. Although they provide value by keeping the business going, they are rarely of strategic value (Figure 11.4). The future belongs to the companies that can access their information in new ways to identify strategic opportunities. Information technology is a competitive weapon. Most information systems managers are just beginning to hear of and see the potential of strategic information systems. With the power of UNIX and the Shell, you can create strategic systems today.

An example of a strategic system might include a frequent flyer system in an airline company: If you know the 20 percent of the people who supply 80 percent of your business, would you be in a better position to target your marketing and

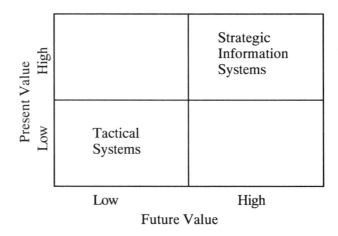

Figure 11.4   Information System Value — Tactical and Strategic Systems

sales to those people? You bet you would. If, in the case of a public service company, you knew that you could gather data from several different systems and provide service within an hour of when a customer calls in a request, would that generate more revenue? Yes, of course. Or if you knew that a call was coming in from an upscale neighborhood, wouldn't you like to know that you should try to sell more upscale services that appeal to that neighborhood? You bet. These are strategic uses of information.

> An information tool like an electronic mail system can have a tremendous effect.
>
> *Walter B. Winston (CEO, Citibank)*

In 1984, as the Bell System approached divestiture, U S WEST was formed from three existing Bell operating companies (BOCs) — Mountain Bell, Pacific Northwest Bell, and Northwestern Bell. Facsimile transmission didn't exist at the time, and we needed a way to connect the presidents of the three companies. Of course, there were three different kinds of office automation systems that simply refused to talk to one another. There were, however, UNIX systems in all three companies. In less than three days from the announcement of divestiture, the system administrators in each company had connected the three presidential offices via UNIX mail and uucp. Did this have an impact on U S WEST's ability to cope with the change? It must have. Now, of course, there are more standard networking tools for communication of this nature (e.g., INTERNET).

The growth of information databases such as Dow Jones and networks such as Usenet offer unlimited opportunity for information gathering. Unfortunately, it would take a herd of analysts to pull all of the information every day and then digest it. Using the Shell tools we've discussed so far, you could automate this process (see Figure 11.5):

1. Access these services using dial-out facilities such as **cu** or via INTERNET.

2. Use a script to interact with the database to retrieve any pertinent information.

3. Store the data in a simple UNIX database or file.

4. Scrub the stored data against the other data collected.

5. Filter the information.

6. Compose it in some usable format.

7. Mail the information electronically to interested people.

With UNIX and the Shell, you can use the open communications facilities, bring in data, manipulate it with Shell, and present the information in any desired fashion. *That* is power.

The Shell, coupled with the vast toolkit at its disposal and the simplicity of the UNIX file system, can accelerate the development and deployment of these strategic information systems. Some people have asked: "Why not buy an existing

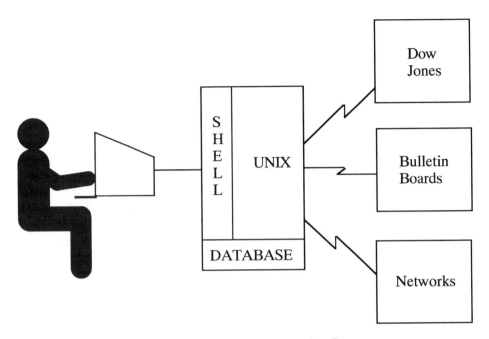

Figure 11.5   Strategic Information System

application system that provides this strategic ability?" Simple. Purchased systems only "level the playing field." If everyone else can buy it, there is no strategic advantage. Purchased systems, however, might be an extremely valuable way to deliver tactical systems—accounting, payroll, and so forth. Strategic systems are not off-the-shelf.

Why not use our existing mainframe computers? Mainframe computers are great for the centralized, tactical systems that require high transaction volumes and the like. They are terrible, however, for strategic applications. The centralized architecture of the past is inappropriate for strategic information systems, which draw their power from putting the data and processing power close to the customer. A distributed systems architecture, which is perfectly suited to UNIX and the Shell, is essential to successful implementation of strategic information systems.

Strategic systems also require quick development to maximize their benefit. To build a strategic system, therefore, will require very different tools and techniques than we have used in the past for conventional development. You just can't wait 18 months for a strategic system; you need to know *now* where you should be in 18 months. A few weeks or a couple of months at the outside often is all you have. You must choose your weapons to match the war. Strategic systems will rely on rapid prototyping and rapid development methods and tools to achieve their goals.

UNIX and Shell provide those tools.

RAPID PROTOTYPING

A complex system that works is invariably found to have evolved
from a simple system that works.

A complex system designed from scratch never works and cannot be
patched up to make it work.

Strategic information systems lend themselves to prototyping and rapid application development. Prototyping allows us to manage the expectations of our customers by involving them deeply in the project from the outset and to construct a
system quickly to meet the needs of the business.

Building the strategic and integration systems of the future will require a software attack team (SWAT) that is highly skilled in the application of the rapid
development tool suite. To succeed at rapid prototyping and rapid development,
we must shift from custom coding to composition of systems from libraries of
existing tools (Figure 11.6). The Shell provides these capabilities. Using Shell and
prototyping can dramatically reduce the time-to-market for a strategic system or
the integration of existing ones. To give you an idea of how dramatically Shell
can impact productivity, consider the following: Bruce Cox, the father of Objec-
tive-C — an object-oriented C language — gave the following comparison of productivity when using Shell, object-oriented programming, and C language:

Shell   1 line of code

Object-oriented   10 lines of code

C language   100 lines of code

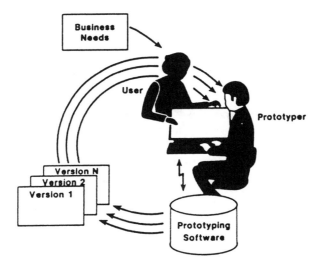

Figure 11.6   The Prototyping Life Cycle

As you can see, Shell helps you quickly evaluate various design alternatives and then convert them into more rigid languages. Since requirements and design inject over 60 percent of all system defects, it is important to weed these out before we implement the system. Shell programs play an important part in prototyping full-scale applications. Using the hundreds of tools in Shell, we don't have to start from scratch. We can compose, extend, and create whole systems, as we demonstrated in Chapter 7, which gives us:

1. the ability to build things quickly
2. the ability to rapidly identify a user's real requirements
3. portability at the system level (UNIX), not at the hardware level

Given a prototype, users can always tell you what they don't like. That saves a tremendous amount of effort that might have been wasted developing the *wrong* system. Customers don't want data or information; they want knowledge they can act upon to create value for the corporation. More importantly, customers always want more of everything. Prototyping lets us add that functionality *before* we deliver the system, not during the two years after release.

The goal of prototyping is to deliver the 20 percent of a system's functionality that provides 80 percent of the customers' needs. Rapid iteration, as shown in Figure 11.6, can rapidly converge on customers' key requirements. To deliver the full system, however, requires additional effort—typically to develop the other 80 percent of the functionality that satisfies the customers' remaining needs. Using the Shell as described in Chapter 7, we can determine most of the customers' requirements for a system. It may then require the use of a true relational database management system (RDBMS) to achieve the levels of security and response time required in the final system. With most of the clients' demands met by the Shell prototype, however, rapid implementation of the end product is much easier. And it's typically easy to integrate a relational database into Shell programs using SQL—the structured query language:

```
echo "select first, middle, last, salary from employee" | sql
Lowell Jay Arthur 35000
```

Chapter 7 described the five basic types of program designs: input, output, query, database update, and system interface. It also described the various tools available to a Shell programmer for implementing these designs. These tools can be used to develop a working version of any program design. The resulting Shell program is a prototype of the final working version that can be created in the C or C++ language, or any other for that matter.

One of the best design tools for describing new programs is the data flow diagram (see Figure 7.2). Shell is one of the best tools for implementing a working model—a prototype—of a data flow. Because of facilities such as pipes, tees, and input/output redirection, an idea can be prototyped in Shell, tested, changed as required, and then implemented in C. Many different designs can be tested, rejected, and accepted in a short time frame using Shell. The triumphant design can then be created in C language for efficiency. In many cases, however, the Shell program will be sufficient. In the instances that require C programming, the program design evolved using the Shell will be more resilient and open to change.

Data flows have long been recognized as excellent methods of describing system, as well as program, designs (Stevens, 1982). Shell helps implement those designs. In a UNIX environment, prototyping works best with a small design team that is experienced with Shell programming. The result of such a design process is a simple, economy-grade, working system.

C Shell provides an excellent pseudocode for C. The following example is a C Shell prototype of a C language main program:

```
        BOURNE                          C SHELL
for file in *                   foreach file ($argv[*])
do                                  process $file
  process $file                 end
done
```

```
                C LANGUAGE
main(argc,argv)
int argc;      /* number of args */
char **argv; /* argument array */
{
int i = 0;
  for(i=1;i<argc;i++) {
    process(argv[i]);
  } /* END FOR */
} /* END MAIN /*
```

The Shell takes the complexity of data definition out of the program and allows the designer to concentrate on *what* the program should do, not the intricacies of *how* it should be done. The Shell serves as a clear design definition as well. Shell prototypes can also be used to design and test enhancements to the program as they are required.

C Shell and Korn Shell (see Chapter 5) can also implement the use of tables and accessing the elements of those tables more effectively than the Bourne Shell:

```
           C SHELL                              C LANGUAGE
set table=(John Jerry Terry)        static char **table =
                                      { "John", "Jerry", "Terry" };
foreach person table[*]             for(i=0;i<3;i++) {
  process $person                     process(table[i]);
end                                   }
mail $table[2] < letter             sprintf(cmd,
                                      "mail %s < letter", table[2]);
                                    system(cmd);
```

The Bourne Shell, unlike the C Shell and Korn Shell, cannot directly access any item in the table. To obtain the last name, Terry, it would have to be cut out of the list or processed with **awk**:

```
lastperson=`echo $table | cut -f3 -d" "`
echo $table | awk '{ process $1; process $2; process $3 }' -
```

There are other advantages to the C Shell. The C Shell CASE construct, switch, is identical to the C language construct except that it will work with strings, whereas the C language switch works only on characters. The IF-THEN-ELSE construct is also identical to the C language syntax. This parallel design allows quicker understanding and translation of designs into code.

The CASE construct translates into C language differently depending on how it is used. If switch is used with characters or integers, the translation is identical:

C SHELL	C LANGUAGE
`switch $variable`	`switch(variable) {`
`  case 'a':`	`case 'a':`
`    whatever`	`    whatever;`
`    breaksw`	`    break;`
`  case 10:`	`case 10:`
`  case 11:`	`case 11:`
`    whatever`	`    whatever;`
`    breaksw`	`    break;`
`  default:`	`default:`
`    default action`	`    default(action);`
`    breaksw`	`    break;`
`endsw`	`} /* END SWITCH */`

When the switch works on strings, however, the C language switch cannot be used. A series of IF-ELSEIF statements must be used along with the string comparison functions:

`switch $variable`	`if(strcmp(var,"Jan")==0) {`
`  case "Jan":`	`    January();`
`    January`	`} else if(strcmp(var,"Feb")==0) {`
`    breaksw`	`    February();`
`  case "Feb":`	`} else if ...`
`    February`	
`    breaksw`	
`  default:`	`} else {`
`    default action`	`  default(action);`
`    breaksw`	`} /* END CASE */`
`endsw`	

Aside from the Shell constructs—IF-THEN-ELSE, CASE, FOR, and WHILE— just about anything else required of a C language program can be implemented in Shell. Writing to a terminal and reading a response are easy with **echo** and **read**:

C SHELL	C LANGUAGE
`echo "Enter filename"`	`printf("Enter filename");`
`read file`	`gets(file);`

More complex processes, involving pipes and several commands, often translate into submodules in C language. For example, the best way to process the following command in C language is to open /etc/passwd, match the name, and then print the required values:

```
grep lja /etc/passwd | cut -f1,5
```

Throughout the course of these examples you have seen the possibilities of using the Shell to prototype C language programs. A rudimentary working system can be constructed quickly and tested easily. Different design choices can be evaluated and accepted or rejected. Design changes can be accomplished quickly before coding begins. As much as 80 percent of the errors in developed systems can be traced to problems in the design phase. Using Shell to weed out those problems can keep a software development project on track and produce a higher-quality product. Once coding begins, the Shell takes on other duties that aid in the development and maintenance of C language programs: coding, compiling, testing, debugging, configuration management, and release control.

TOOLS FOR STRATEGIC SYSTEM DEVELOPMENT

Most software managers and their clients will agree that the biggest problem facing business today is programmer productivity: how to get new systems more quickly and how to maintain those that already exist. Toward this end they seek "magic" solutions that will improve productivity from 100 percent to 1000 percent. Is this unrealistic? Yes and no. Depending on a single tool, such as a fourth-generation language, to accomplish a 1000 percent improvement is unrealistic. Using an integrated family of products and tools to achieve these increases is not.

> In the universe, great acts are made up of small deeds.
>
> *Lao Tzu*

Many managers overlook quality improvements (from local tool construction) as the steppingstone to vast productivity improvements, but this is one of the lessons of Tom Peters' book, *A Passion for Excellence:* One thousand percent improvements are possible by small improvements in many aspects of the work. Part of the problem with software manufacturing is that much of the critical work is tedious or time consuming. Fortunately, the Shell offers a vast arsenal of tools to handle much of the effort. Toolsmithing can create the pathways of information and automate day-to-day tasks. These small improvements attain the productivity goals, not the other way around.

> For better or worse, man is the tool-using animal,
> and as such he has become the lord of creation.
>
> *William Ralph Inge*

Many software managers and clients try to solve their problems by depending on a single hardware system and a group of unrelated software products to handle their programming needs. As evidence of this, one need only look at large main-frame development groups and stand-alone personal computer users. The PCs are excellent for word processing and graphics, but are deficient for sharing information, which is essential to successful software development and maintenance. Mainframes are excellent for compiling and testing products, but are clumsy for editing, word processing, and similar human-intensive activities.

The productivity and quality solution should use an integrated network of mainframes, minis, and microcomputers for each task required of a programmer or analyst. Software for these hardware components (see Figure 11.7) should:

- provide the strongest integrated tools for each programming or analysis need—development or maintenance
- allow for exchange of text and data among the machines and people
- minimize the training required to use each tool
- maximize product quality

UNIX fits virtually all of these categories for virtually all types of software development and maintenance. If it is also the target machine for the developed software, it can be used for compilation and testing. UNIX is also used to simulate PC operating systems, thereby emulating the target machine for faster testing in more powerful machines. In fact, in today's modern UNIX environment, many of the most popular MS-DOS word-processing and graphics programs are available. This allows many users who are familar with MS-DOS to run their favorite applications on a more powerful operating system. In addition, the ability to run UNIX on virtually any hardware platform makes it an ideal choice for the modern software development project. The ability to run UNIX on INTEL-based microprocessors has opened up many exciting new avenues for streamlining software development projects. It is now much more cost-effective to have a large number of UNIX-based machines sharing information and being used as personal development machines.

Because of UNIX's communication and networking facilities, it can provide many of the development and maintenance activities for any host system. As such, programmers and analysts need only learn this one environment to develop and maintain programs for a wide array of host machines. This minimizes retrain-ing costs when moving from one host to another.

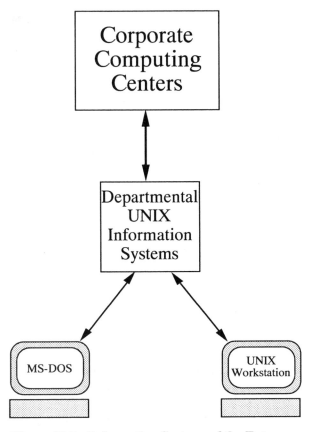

Figure 11.7   Information Systems of the Future

Technology is a jealous god. It can demand more and more from people, but not serve them. Managers often ask: "Why isn't Sammy coding yet?" In the rush to deliver products, we often forget the keys to success: people, process, and then technology (Figure 11.8). People are the most costly part of most software devel-

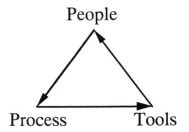

Figure 11.8   The Three Keys to Productivity

opment efforts; finding out what they do and how they do it (the process) and then automating the process will lead to powerful improvements in productivity and quality for both development and maintenance.

DEVELOPMENT AND MAINTENANCE TOOLS

To maximize productivity and quality, we must automate those development and maintenance activities that are human-intensive. These are:

1. *Documentation* — requirements, designs, plans, and all operational documentation or user guides. Word-processing facilities are essential to productivity improvements. Graphics tools to create the pictorial representations of designs, such as data flow diagrams and hierarchy charts, are important tools as well.

Admittedly, **nroff** and memorandum macros are not the most user-friendly of word-processing facilities, but micro-based packages written in C have now moved into the UNIX environment, as was mentioned previously. Graphics tools are available in UNIX environments and are important as well. Productivity improvements using these tools vary from 3 to 25 percent for people whose major work products are written documentation.

2. *Communications* — keeping users and programmers informed of changes in an ongoing maintenance or development effort improves productivity and quality. Programmers can waste up to 30 minutes per day playing telephone tag and leaving notes. Electronic mail can be sent anytime and read when time is available. Electronic mail, unlike its paper counterpart, will not get lost on someone's desk.

Mail and **uucp** are inexpensive methods of communicating in a UNIX environment. Electronic mail costs little (less than 1 percent of the machine usage), but will average 20,000 messages per month. In an environment with 100 users, that means 200 messages per user per month. Most studies have found a 3 to 5 percent improvement in productivity with the use of **mail.** In today's modern networking environment, it is easier than ever to utilize **mail.** Mail can be sent and received just about anywhere in the world with ease.

In addition to sending messages, a modern UNIX TCP/IP network allows a vast array of information to be shared between UNIX platforms that sit side by side on a desk or are separated by thousands of miles. It is now quite easy to log in to machines that are located halfway around the world and copy files back and forth as if the machines were located next to one another. In addition to moving files around, it's possible to remotely mount hard disks located over just about any distance and access them as if they were located on your machine. This type of communication ability opens up a whole new world of productivity enhancements that are centered around more effective sharing of information and resources.

3. *Editing* — entering and editing source code is another human-intensive activity that is best performed on a highly responsive hardware platform. This often

implies personal workstations or PCs since larger machines often are used to support production systems and should not be burdened with the editing task.

There are many sophisticated UNIX and PC full-screen editors that will meet this need. Editing is best performed in PCs and minicomputers; it is a waste of resources to use a host machine. Programmers spend up to 75 percent of their time editing. Any improvement in their response time and effectiveness will significantly improve productivity. No expense should be spared here. The best possible editor(s) should be available, and all programmers should be trained to be as effective as possible in utilizing this tool.

4. *Project management*—scheduling of work and resources needs to be updated as events complete. This software should reside on a shared resource and be available for update and review by all project members.

Scheduling of work and resources is available on micros and UNIX minicomputers. With its existing graphics and documentation facilities, UNIX can easily exchange information among these tools. Project management keeps projects on schedule and therefore contributes to productivity.

5. *Configuration management*—all of the source code and documents should be controlled under a common configuration management system. The object and executable programs should be controlled on the target system. Configuration management improves the quality of the delivered software and often productivity by reducing the chaos surrounding software evolution.

UNIX has possibly the best configuration management systems— Source Code Control System (SCCS) and Revision Control System (RCS)—for controlling all of the source code and documents developed or maintained for a given software project. Control of software and documentation rarely appears to improve productivity, but it can reduce delivered errors in systems by 20 to 30 percent, which drastically reduces overtime costs for corrective maintenance.

6. *Change management*—mechanizing change requests will improve communications with the client, improve the quality of information collected from maintenance, and automate much of the auditing and quality-assurance processes. When coupled with the configuration management system, change management can secure the software from unauthorized modifications, which is especially important in financial systems.

The change management tracking system under UNIX mechanizes change request initiation and tracking. It can be coupled with SCCS to prevent unauthorized changes. It ensures that changes are not lost, misplaced, or ignored. It can also feed the project management systems with information about project status. It automates the audit trail and the collection of quality-assurance data such as programs or modules with reliability or maintainability problems that are candidates for restructuring or rewrites. By identifying and correcting these wayward programs, maintenance and downtime costs can be reduced by as much as 60 percent.

7. *Application generators* — the tools available for rapid prototyping have grown tremendously in recent years. The ability to use these tools to specify system requirements undoubtedly improves the quality of delivered systems by reducing requirement defects. It also improves productivity by speeding up the requirements process and providing a working system for the developers to expand upon.

The Shell command language is an excellent tool for rapidly prototyping UNIX applications. Entire systems can be created with Shell and rewritten in C as the requirements settle down. There are other tools (e.g., C English) and databases (e.g., Oracle) that can prototype UNIX and IBM DB2 systems, respectively. These application generators improve development productivity by 50 percent or more.

8. *Toolkits* — the need for integrated tools and a Shell command language to encourage automation of mundane manual tasks should be recognized. Integration of all types of analyst and programmer tasks has been greatly improved over the past several years through the use of GUIs. A GUI can make tools from many different vendors fit together in ways never before possible. In addition, there are toolkits that specifically aid in the software development process and are very highly integrated and can aid in overall productivity. Automating repetitive tasks eliminates defects and improves productivity. Programmers and analysts who understand how to use these tools consistently outperform their counterparts.

Integrated tools and Shell command language encourage automation of mundane manual tasks. The authors' studies and those of Boehm et al. (1984) have shown that this toolkit improves productivity by 15 to 25 percent. It often takes several years to learn all of the facilities of UNIX and the Shell, so these improvements occur not once but progressively over time for several years.

9. *Database management systems* — a portable relational DBMS that spans micro, mini, and mainframe lines would allow for development and prototyping to occur in any environment and would minimize training costs. Larger information-crunching databases should remain in the host, while distributed relational databases will more readily serve the decision support needs of clients. These systems will need to work with the office automation systems and virtually all of these tools to provide business information.

A host of databases span the decision support system needs of most users. Oracle, Ingres, Informix, UNIFY, and a host of SQL-compatible relational databases span the micro- and minicomputer environments. This vertical portability of applications enhances productivity and allows selection of hardware based on user needs.

There is a vast array of hardware and software that can be brought to bear on the existing productivity and quality problems. Selecting an integrated set of tools and an environment that will meet future requirements will ensure continuous productivity and quality improvement.

SHELL TOOLS

Shell can automate activities for everyone, including the Shell toolsmith. Hundreds of tools lie waiting for discovery. How do apprentice, journeyman, and master Shell builders find these tools? Well, in some systems, the **man** command has an option to search the documentation by keyword. We could create a Shell browser that searches by keyword:

```
# Browser keyword
if [ "$1" ]
then
  while [ "$1" ]
  do
    echo $1
    man -k "$1"
    shift
  done
else
  clear
  while
    echo "Keyword: "
    read keyword
    test ! -z "$keyword"
  do
    man -k "$keyword"
  done
fi
```

What if we didn't have this extension to the **man** command? Could we create a database of commands and keywords, and the commands to search it? Of course. Using the previously developed commands **keyword** and **plural**, we could examine all of the man pages, extract their keywords, and create a database. Using the query and reporting options we covered in Chapter 7, we could compose commands to search the database based on the toolsmith's keyword choice. To do this we would first need to build the database for the browser. First we could create a list of all of the commands in /bin, /usr/bin, /usr/5bin, and so on:

```
ls /bin /usr/*bin | sort | uniq > cmdlist
```

Next, we need a command that can build database records for each command using **keyword** and **plural**:

```
# Builder
cmd=$1
CMD=`echo $cmd | tr "[a-z]" "[A-Z]"`
man $cmd | sed -e "/$CMD/d" > /tmp/$cmd      # Delete uppercase
                                             # headers
keyword -20 /tmp/$cmd | sed -e "/$cmd/d" | plural | \
head -14 | paste - - - - - - - | sed -e "s/^/$cmd\t/" >> browse.db
rm /tmp/$cmd
```

This command will build records for the database containing the 14 most common keywords in the document (after removing headers and references to the command itself, which can skew the results). Next, we need a simple command to execute this command on all of our commands:

```
# build_db cmdlist
while
  read cmd
do
  builder $cmd
done
```

Now we can run the whole thing overnight to create the database:

```
nohup nice build_db cmdlist&
```

This will give us a database like the following:

```
adb  print address value systems command names symbol
adb  source objectfile file default current subprocess
cp   copy directory file contents system subdirectories ls
grep expression regular match string character line file
...
```

Now all we need is a command to search the database for us. The **browser** we wrote before can be changed to meet our needs:

```
# Browser keyword (s)
if [ "$1" ]
then
  clear
  while [ "$1" ]
  do
    echo $1
    grep $keyword browse.db | cut -f1 | sort | uniq | pr -7
    shift
```

```
    done
else
  clear
  while
    echo "Keyword: "
    read keyword
    test ! -z "$keyword"
  do
    grep $keyword browse.db | cut -f1 | sort | uniq | pr -7
  done
fi
```

This is just one of the many tools that a toolsmith can formulate to aid in the construction of systems. This type of browser would be effective for C language programs. Just extract the comments and build a database from there. This is what I love about toolsmithing. One idea just leads to another and another. This ability drives high levels of productivity and can increase project team effectivness.

UNIMAGINABLE SYSTEMS

Judging from the negligible impact of personal computers in 1980 to their ominous presence in all walks of life by 1990, the 1990s will deliver completely unimaginable systems. Multimedia systems will stimulate the senses with graphics, text, sound, animation, and video. Computer animation houses have discovered that UNIX and Shell fit their needs. Specialized software coupled with UNIX and the Shell are winning animation awards all over the world. Animation tools are created in UNIX and C so that they can be picked from the toolbox and hooked together with pipes! The biggest advantage of UNIX and Shell for animators is that they can develop software today without knowing what machines they'll be running on tomorrow.

Technological innovation requires an open, loosely structured, risk-taking, forgiving environment. The Shell innovator will be at the core of this information revolution. The challenges are to discover creative ways to meet your company's information needs as these toolkits emerge.

SUMMARY

As a power user of Shell, your future and your company's future depend on your ability to create the information bridges and strategic information systems that will drive your company's success in the 1990s and beyond. Because of the diversity of options available for system integration and strategic information systems, this chapter discussed only possible opportunities. As you read this chapter, I hope you saw, heard, or felt the creative challenges that a power user can look forward to in the use of Shell.

EXERCISES

1. Build a rapid prototype of an airline reservation system, based on what you know about the airline industry.

2. Build a rapid prototype of a frequent flyer system, based on what you know about the airline industry.

3. Build a strategic system to capture data from both of these systems (exercises 1 and 2) to develop marketing data for the holiday and summer travel seasons.

4. Use a Macintosh running Hypercard, connected to a UNIX system, to deliver a button-driven interface to the Time Worked system described in Chapter 7.

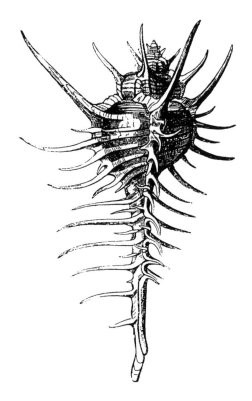

Chapter Twelve

Shell Mastery

Order and simplification are the first steps toward the mastery of a subject —
the actual enemy is the unknown.

Thomas Mann

Any hack can cobble together a few tools. Making them robust enough to withstand the brutality of daily use is another kettle of fish. A major concern of advanced Shell programming is not special tools, fancy techniques, or exotic human–machine dialogues, but a concern for quality. Shell, just like any other programming language, can be used elegantly or shoddily. Quality is the highest concern of a Shell guru. But what is quality?

It is easier to confess a defect than to claim a quality.

Max Beerbohm

Quality consists of several factors: reliability, maintainability, reusability, efficiency, portability, and usability. Each has a place in advanced Shells. *Reliability* is concerned with Shells that rarely fail and always perform the correct actions. *Maintainability* ensures that a Shell can be enhanced or repaired easily when the need arises. *Reusability* demands that Shell programs be as flexible and reusable as any other UNIX command. *Efficiency* cares about the machine resources used — the fewer the better, because new machines are expensive and the longer their purchase can be delayed the better. *Portability* is a key factor in the popularity of UNIX; Shells should remain as portable as possible. *Usability* is a key feature of Shell: Native UNIX is not that friendly, but Shell is the means to overcome that problem.

> Trouble is easily overcome before it starts.
> Deal with it before it happens.
> Set things in order before there is confusion.
>
> *Lao Tzu*

Shell wizardry is to ballet what hacking is to hockey. Shell programs are born in the fire of creative activity. These draft programs, however, must be edited and improved to maximize their usefulness. This evolution of draft Shell programs leads us to quality. It is the essence of advanced Shell programming. The Shell, in its creator's wisdom, provides many facilities that encourage quality programming. The following sections discuss their use.

RELIABILITY

The costs of reliability problems can be found easily: waste, defect investigation, rework, retest, downtime, and productivity losses. *Waste* costs involve the machine and user time lost when a command fails or works incorrectly. *Defect investigation* is the time it takes to identify the cause of a defect in a Shell program. *Rework* includes the labor to fix the command and to rerun the command. *Retest* includes the resources necessary to test a repaired command. *Downtime* includes the cost of the users' inability to do their work. *Productivity losses* include all of the costs of delaying work.

Shell facilities to handle reliability fall into two broad areas: default actions and fault handling. Default actions help eliminate waste, rework, and downtime. Fault handling reduces waste, defect investigation, rework, retest, and downtime. Both help eliminate productivity losses.

Default Actions

One of the simplest default actions occurs when a user executes a command that requires certain input parameters. If the user executes the command without any parameters, a simple Shell command will exit with an error message. An advanced Shell program, however, will prompt for the missing arguments and only exit if the user interrupts the processing. On the other hand, if the user gives many file names, the Shell will process each file. In either case, the Shell can prevent scrapping this execution of the command and the rework of reentering the command with the proper arguments.

Variable substitution offers another means of taking default actions. If a variable has no value, a default value can be substituted. If a variable has a value, a default value can still be substituted. Or, if the variable has no value, the Shell could issue an error message and exit from the Shell. Invoking these defaults instead of using undefined variable names will help make any Shell more reliable. Consider the output of the following commands:

	OUTPUT	${NAME} BECOMES
`name=/usr/bin`		
`echo ${name}`	/usr/bin	/usr/bin
`echo ${name:-"/dev/null"}`	/usr/bin	/usr/bin
`echo ${name:="/dev/null"}`	/usr/bin	/usr/bin
`echo ${name:?"Error"}`	/usr/bin	/usr/bin
`echo ${name:+"/dev/null"}`	/dev/null	/usr/bin
`name="" # set name to NULL`		
`echo ${name}`		
`echo ${name:-"/dev/null"}`	/dev/null	NULL
`echo ${name:="/dev/null"}`	/dev/null	/dev/null
`echo ${name:?"Error"}`	Error	NULL (exit program)
`echo ${name:+"/dev/null"}`		NULL

Omitting the colon (:) in any of these examples causes the Shell to check only the variables' existence. The Shell will not check for a null variable. In the previous example, the variable *name* is set, but has a null value. The results change as follows:

`name="" # set name to NULL`		
`echo ${name}`		
`echo ${name-"/dev/null"}`	NULL	NULL
`echo ${name="/dev/null"}`	NULL	NULL
`echo ${name?"Error"}`	NULL	NULL
`echo ${name+"/dev/null"}`	/dev/null	NULL

Other examples of using default actions requires a look at the Shell constructs IF-THEN-ELSE and CASE. To display the best Shell programming style, every IF should have an ELSE and every CASE should have a default action:

```
if [ -r $filename ]
then
  process $filename
else
  while [ ! -r $filename ]
  do
    echo "File $filename does not exist"
    echo "Please enter the correct filename"
    read $filename
  done
  process $filename
fi

case $TERM in
  vt100)
```

```
    tabs
    ;;
  630)
    tabs
    TERM=450
    ;;
  *)    # Default
    echo "Setting up terminal as tty37"
    TERM=37
    ;;
esac
```

In either of these two examples, a default action prevents the unexpected from occurring. The absence of a default path is one of the hardest errors to find in programs. IFs without ELSEs and a CASE without a default are often suspect when a Shell program is unreliable.

Taking intelligent default actions is one of the cornerstones of UNIX philosophy. Advanced Shell programs echo that philosophy. Errors and faults are usually avoidable in most Shell programs — an extension of UNIX reliability.

Fault Handling

Fault handling is another feature of the Shell. The two major commands that handle error detection and correction are **test** and **trap**. **Test** helps detect errors before they occur; **trap** catches interrupts and takes intelligent default actions.

As shown in previous examples, **test** can check for the presence of files, directories, or devices. It can compare the value of two variables or test the value of a single one. **Test** can prevent many errors from happening and thereby prevent waste, rework, downtime, and productivity losses.

Some Shell programs are made to run in either foreground or background. A file run in the background should not interrupt the user with spurious errors. It should mail them for later reference. **Test** can help direct error messages to the terminal or the user's mail as follows:

```
# If the terminal is associated with standard input
if [ -t 0 ]
then
  echo "Execution message"
else
  echo "Execution message" | mail $LOGNAME
fi
```

Test can also check for the presence of a variable:

```
# If $1 is non-null
if [ "$1" ]
```

```
then
  process $1
else
  echo "Enter file name"
  read filename
  process $filename
fi
```

The importance of **test** is to detect problems before they occur and then take an intelligent default action.

Trap works with system interrupts such as the break and delete keys. The most common interrupts are hangup (1), interrupt (2), quit (3), alarm clock (14), and software termination (15). All of the available interrupts were shown in Table 6.8. Another useful interrupt (0) occurs at the successful termination of a Shell command. With it, **trap** can take default actions upon completion of the command.

Trap often is used to clean up after a Shell when it ends. Temporary files are created in /tmp, /usr/tmp, or the user's directory. Whether the command ends or is interrupted, these files should be removed:

```
trap "rm -f /tmp/tmp$$ tmp$$; exit 0" 0 1 2 3 14 15
```

Trap can also identify the last file processed when a process is interrupted:

```
trap "echo $filename | mail $LOGNAME" 1 2 3 14 15
```

Trap can also ignore interrupts while the Shell does tricky stuff that is not easily fixed after the command has been interrupted and reset itself after the operation is complete:

```
trap "" 1 2 3 14 15          # Ignore common signals
cp /tmp/tmp$$ /etc/passwd     # Copy updated password file
trap 1 2 3 14 15             # Reset signal traps
```

Trap can handle increasingly complex jobs as required. These few simple examples are a beginning. Reliability is integral to UNIX; fault handling with **trap** is an important method of achieving that reliability.

MAINTAINABILITY

> Though a program be but three lines long, someday it will have to be maintained.
>
> *Geoffrey James*

Maintainability depends on quality factors called consistency, instrumentation, modularity, self-documentation, and simplicity. *Consistency* recommends doing things in the same way from Shell to Shell. *Instrumentation* gives indications of the success or failure of the Shell as it processes its input. *Modularity* is one of the keys to the success of UNIX; Shell programs should be modular. *Self-documentation* assumes that the Shell program will document itself. *Simplicity* says it all — a simple command is easily understood, modified, and maintained.

One facet of maintainability that is difficult to quantify is programming style. The examples in this book attempt to present a "good" and consistent programming style. To improve consistency, use the skeletal Shell program in Appendix A as a starting point for all Shell programs. It contains most of the information needed for good self-documentation and online help facilities. Indenting Shell control structures to show the structure of the program is another form of consistent programming style (see Figure 12.1). Programming style is also concerned

IF-THEN-ELSE

```
if [ conditions ]              if ( conditions ) then
then
  process1                         process1
else                           else
  process2                         process2
fi                             endif
```

CASE

```
case $var in                   switch ($var)
  match1)                          case match1:
     process1                          process1
     ;;                                breakswk
  match2)                          case match2:
     process2                          process2
     ;;                                breaksw
  *)                             default:
     default process                  default process
     ;;                                breaksw
esac                           endsw
```

FOR

```
for variable in list           foreach variable (list)
do
   process $variable               process $variable
done                           end
```

WHILE

```
while [ conditions ]           while ( conditions )
do
  process                          process
done                           end
```

Figure 12.1   Shell Programming Style

with simplicity. Because of the wealth of operators available with UNIX, any required program can be created in a number of different ways. Only a few of those ways will be simple and easy to maintain. Programming style is also reflected in the use of program development tools, such as SCCS, to manage change to Shell programs and thereby simplify maintenance.

As Shell users become more sophisticated, they will begin to see new opportunities for using existing commands. This means that Shell commands, no matter how well written, will need to evolve to meet those needs. Keeping Shells in SCCS will help track the evolution of a command. The reasons for changing the commands will be stored with the SCCS file, so there is no documentation to lose. A list of changes and their reasons are as close as the **prs** command. Furthermore, as one UNIX machine grows to two or three or to three dozen, the process of administering changes to the system can be simplified by extracting commands only from the SCCS libraries.

Before the commands are stored in SCCS, however, they have to be developed. Self-documentation is an important part of that development. Comments can easily be inserted into the code: they can be on a line by themselves or after an executable statement. The pound sign (#) begins all comments:

```
# If the user supplies an argument use it
if [ "$1" ]
then
  process $1
else # prompt for an argument
  echo "Enter file name"
  read filename
  process $filename
fi
```

These comments are essential to program maintainability when Shell commands become more complex. If the developer is struggling to understand how all of the commands fit together to accomplish the task, just think what the person who later maintains it must think.

Just about every Shell programmer runs across ways of doing things that are more elegant than others. Whenever possible, store these methods and use them in new Shells or use them to replace complex code in existing Shells. Simplicity should prevail over complexity. Otherwise, it eventually becomes impossible to maintain all of the existing Shells without an army of Shell gurus.

Keeping things simple is why modularity was invented. Cars are made of small, modular components. The parts are easier to design and build than complex hand-built components. The parts are also easier to replace when they fail. The same is true for Shell programs. Modularity will improve maintainability.

Modularity can be obtained in two ways: simplifying processing and creating subshells. Any Shell program over two pages in length is too complex. In some cases, the program can be simplified. The Shell may have one central process with various input and output filters. A simple, modular design would be:

```
choose input filters
choose processing parameters
choose output filters
execute input filters | major process | output filters
```

An example of this modular program can be seen in Appendix F—nroff and troff.

Creating subshells allows the main Shell to control the actions of several others to obtain the required result. Rather than having one huge Shell, each subshell can do its unique part and then pass control back to the parent Shell. Subshells are also an important feature of reusability.

Modular Shells can execute as follows:

```
edit inputfiles
update datafiles
select reportdata
print reports
```

Each subshell creates outputs that are used by future processes. The subshells can also be executed individually when required.

Subshells can also be executed directly inline with the parent Shell's code so that the subshell can access and modify any of the parent's variables:

```
BOURNE/KORN SHELL          C SHELL
# Parent Shell             # Parent Shell
variable=/usr/bin          variable=/usr/bin
. subshell                 source subshell
# Subshell
cd $variable
ls -l
variable=/bin
```

From a pure programming standpoint, this is somewhat dangerous because the subshell can change the parent's variables. Otherwise, the parent would have to export the variable for the subshell to have access to it:

```
# Parent Shell
variable=/usr/bin
export variable
subshell
```

In this example, the subshell would have access to the variable but would not be able to change it. Also, any changes made by the subshell to the current environment (such as changing directories) would not affect the parent Shell.

Making small, modular Shell programs helps improve maintainability. Small programs are easily understood. Modular programs also affect reusability.

REUSABILITY

One of the reasons that Shell is so popular is that each command is modular and reusable. Each command can easily be mated with other commands via the pipe. In the process of building commands to automate repetitive tasks for the users, functions are repeated from Shell to Shell. Creating a separate Shell for these functions improves maintainability. (There is only one copy to maintain.) All of the Shells that need the reusable function can then invoke it as a subshell.

When using Shell to prototype C language programs, reusable Shells often indicate the need for reusable C programs as well. Current technology has demonstrated that as much as 80 percent of a program's code is reusable, leaving only 20 percent to develop uniquely. This can increase programmer productivity and quality by a factor of two to five.

A simple way of affecting reusability is to create a library of generic Shell programs that can be copied and then enhanced to fit the need. These skeletons should include all of the quality features described in this chapter. (A good skeleton for Shell development is contained in Appendix A.) As described in Chapter 7, there are five basic types of programs: input, output, query, update, and interface. A reusable Shell skeleton can be built for each.

EFFICIENCY

"Techies" often worry about efficiency to the exclusion of effectiveness. To maximize efficiency, focus on people effort first and machine effort second. Once you've minimized the effort required to use and maintain a Shell program, then worry about improving the machine efficiency.

Shell runs on a wide variety of hardware, but it still concerns itself with efficiency. Spending money for additional hardware is never easy, so it makes sense to take efficiency into consideration whenever you build a Shell. Some efficiencies are handled by the system administrator; others are available to the common user.

The system administrator (superuser) can set the "sticky bit" on a program. Once the program has been loaded into memory, a copy is retained until the system is brought down. Keeping a copy of the program means that it can be swapped in when requested rather than read from disk, thereby speeding up processing. UNIX programs that are used extensively in Shell programs should be stored in memory using the sticky bit:

```
chmod 1777 shell_pgm
```

Each user can further improve efficiency by simple actions. The most obvious one is to run commands during non–prime time. Commands can be queued via the **at** command (if it is available on your system). The **at** command can offload the processor during prime time and improve response time. The following example would execute a Shell accounting report called acctrpt at 6 P.M. on Sunday:

```
at 6pm Sunday acctrpt
```

Shell efficiencies involve the number of variables, commands, and files. The number of bins searched for commands and their ordering are often prime candidates for efficiency improvement. These two criteria are established by the PATH variable:

```
PATH=:/bin:/usr/bin:/global/bin
```

The search order for this PATH is the current directory — /bin, /usr/bin, and /global/bin. If the user rarely uses the current directory and almost always uses /global/bin, then efficiency can be increased by switching the search order:

```
PATH=/global/bin:/bin:/usr/bin::
```

Other users will put all possible bins into their PATH:

```
PATH=:/bin:/usr/bin:/global/bin:$HOME/bin . . .
```

To find the requested command, the Shell must search through many directories and hundreds of files. A simple solution is to invoke the Shell itself as a subshell with the expanded PATH list:

```
# Home
PATH=$HOME/bin:${PATH} PS1="HOME> " sh $@
```

This command will change the *PATH* variable to include $HOME/bin and change the user's prompt to "HOME>" so that he or she is aware of the change. When finished using commands in $HOME/bin, the user presses Ctrl-d to exit the subshell.

Another way to improve efficiency is to change into a directory rather than use a long path name repeatedly. This eliminates the need for the Shell to search through directory after directory for each file:

```
cd $HOME/RDBMS/employee          for file in $HOME/RDBMS/employee/*
for file in *                    do
do                                 process $file
  process $file                  done
done
```

The user can also affect efficiency by reducing the number of temporary files used in a Shell. Pipes and better selection of commands can reduce the number of temporary files:

```
cut -f1,5 /etc/passwd > /tmp/tmp$$
pr -h "Password listing" /tmp/tmp$$
rm /tmp/tmp$$

cut -f1,5 /etc/passwd | pr -h "Password Listing"
```

In this example, the number of commands was reduced by one and temporary files were eliminated totally. Pipes do create temporary files of their own, but **pr** can begin executing as soon as the **cut** has passed a line to the pipe. Herein lies the advantage of the pipe.

This example also showed how programming style can reduce the number of commands required. Similarly, the commands **fgrep** and **egrep** can be more efficient than **grep** for special data-selection requirements. There are a multitude of available commands in UNIX. Often, one can be substituted for several others, thereby reducing complexity and improving efficiency.

The number and length of variable names can also influence efficiency. But the advantages of having good variable names and using them to represent only one variable instead of many outweigh the efficiency considerations.

Also, for efficiency, use *built-in* commands instead of called programs. Slowness of Shell programs occurs when the system must create a new process (**fork**), search the PATH to find a given command, and then execute it. Built-in commands are executed directly. So use **read** instead of **line**, and so on.

And, as we've demonstrated in other examples, put *reducing* filters — **grep, cut,** and **awk** — first in a pipe. This will reduce the amount of data that must be transferred by the Shell:

```
grep $1 employee.db | sort | pr
```

For users running System V, there is a facility that allows users the same capabilities of the "sticky bit." The Bourne and Korn Shells allow the use of Shell functions. Shell functions can be included in the user's .profile — or anywhere, for that matter. Once a command containing the function is executed, the Shell retains a memory copy of the function for later execution. When the user executes the command again, the function is invoked from memory instead of from disk. Response time is much faster. Shell functions are formed as follows:

```
functname()              alias functname shell_command
{
  Shell commands
}
```

For commands that are frequently executed, Shell functions will be the fastest way to obtain a response. For more examples, see the section on Shell functions in Chapter 8.

Efficiency is still a concern in UNIX systems. As UNIX users learn more about the system, their ability to use its resources expands exponentially, making it hard to obtain enough hardware to satisfy their cravings. The commands **time** and **timex** can examine resource usage of commands and be used to improve efficiency. Efficiency is one way of ensuring that there will be plenty of resources for all.

PORTABILITY

Portability is another major concern of the UNIX system. Shell programmers should also be concerned because there are three different Shells: C Shell, Bourne Shell, and Korn Shell. And there are many different versions of UNIX. The C Shell and Bourne and Korn Shells are also incompatible in many of their control constructs. These incompatibilities raise portability issues. The same utility (e.g., **pr**) may perform differently in different systems.

Every UNIX system provides new tools that are not part of standard UNIX. These are then used in Shell programs, which then lose their portability. Binary copies of UNIX sold by third parties often have nonstandard utilities that are not portable to other systems.

To maximize the chances that Shells can be ported from one machine to another, stick to the standard UNIX commands contained in /bin and /usr/bin. A Shell command using any other commands will need some work when moved from a micro to a minicomputer or mainframe environment. But standards are not the only key to portability. Portability consists of three key elements:

- design for portability
- management for portability
- standards

To achieve portability of your Shells, you must begin with the design. To achieve any quality for that matter, you begin with design. By simply focusing on a quality such as portability, you will be more likely to achieve it. Then, as you move forward with development, manage the evolution of the Shell to ensure portability. Shell checkers, such as **lint** for C, are under development and should appear soon. Finally, use standard commands (e.g., those defined by POSIX).

USABILITY

Probably the major problem with UNIX is its usability. Users complain, for example, about cryptic commands. Shell is the bridge to improve usability. The best Shells will need default actions, help facilities, and possibly online instruction.

Usable Shell commands do not give cryptic error messages and exit when the argument list is deficient. They should prompt for the proper information, as described in the reliability section of this chapter. Usable Shell commands should anticipate the user's needs and meet them wherever possible. The use of the **trap** command to handle interrupts is another means of making a Shell more usable; a Shell that cleans up after itself and restores order before exiting is more usable than one that does not.

Online Help

Online help facilities are another usability concern. The files contained in /usr/lib/help are not very beneficial, but they can be beefed up by the system administrator. User-developed Shell commands have other possibilities. Embedding help information in the Shell command is a good way to improve self-documentation and provide help facilities for locally developed commands.

Since Shells should be stored in SCCS, the **what** command provides a facility for extracting help information from Shells. The **what** command extracts lines from files containing the SCCS keyword string "%Z%", which expands to @(#). This keyword can be embedded in Shell commands:

```
# %Z% syntax: command [parameters] [files]
```

which expands as follows when the file is retrieved from SCCS:

```
@(#) syntax: command [parameters] [files]
```

What can examine the Shell file and produce the following:

```
syntax: command [parameters] [files]
```

Grep can also be used. Some users will require just a simple example of the command's syntax; others will need more extensive assistance. Two levels of help information can be provided by combining **grep** with **what**:

```
#localhelp
grep "@#@" $1                  # Print syntax line
echo "More Information?"
read answer
if [ ${answer} = "y" ]
then
  what $1                      # Print extended description
fi
```

Examples of the **grep** and **what** strings are shown in Appendix A. The local help command can be enhanced to look for the command in any of the bins specified by $PATH:

```
bins=`echo $PATH | tr ":" " "`    # Remove : delimiters
bins="$bins `pwd`"                # Add current directory
for dir in $bins                  # Check each bin
do
  if [ -r ${dir}/$1 ]             # If command exists
  then
```

```
        localhelp ${dir}/$1          # Print help information
        break                        # Leave FOR loop
    fi
done
```

This help command can be enhanced as required. Online help for Shell commands, as shown in these commands, is a necessary part of productive use of UNIX. Usability is a major factor in the acceptance of UNIX and new commands. Online tutorials, such as those available with microcomputer packages, will be essential to reduce the training costs for new users. Local commands will need to take advantage of these packages to ensure that proper training is received by all. Training is a major part of usability. Developing a Shell often is easy; creating help and training materials often takes longer, but is perhaps more important than the resulting Shell.

Documentation

> All words are pegs to hang ideas on.
>
> *Henry Ward Beecher*

A system is composed of more than just software or Shells. A system includes the hardware, software, documentation, and training to help make users effective. Effective, high-quality Shell programming requires the development of man pages and other supporting documentation. A basic outline of a man page is shown in Figure 12.2. Use it to document local commands. Manage the document's evolution using SCCS, just as you would the code.

Shell is a simple language compared to written language. Shell has but a few hundred verbs (e.g., **grep**), while written language has tens of thousands of verbs and words. Do not look down on the written word; it is the complex programming language of the mind.

SUMMARY

Expert Shell programming is concerned with the quality of the programs produced. It demands reliability, maintainability, reusability, efficiency, portability, and usability. A Shell could be complex and intricate, a brilliant piece of work, but without self-documentation and maintainability, it cannot be what I call expert.

> It is a simple task to make things complex,
> but a complex task to make things simple.

Appendix A contains a skeleton of a Shell that can be used to improve reliability, maintainability, and usability. The principles that involve advanced Shell programming are not ones of complexity, but ones of simplicity and elegance.

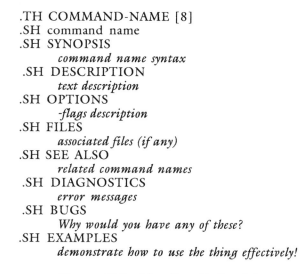

```
.TH COMMAND-NAME [8]
.SH command name
.SH SYNOPSIS
        command name syntax
.SH DESCRIPTION
        text description
.SH OPTIONS
        -flags description
.SH FILES
        associated files (if any)
.SH SEE ALSO
        related command names
.SH DIAGNOSTICS
        error messages
.SH BUGS
        Why would you have any of these?
.SH EXAMPLES
        demonstrate how to use the thing effectively!
```

Figure 12.2   Man Page Boilerplate

EXERCISES

1. What is the single major concern of an advanced Shell programmer?

2. What are the major factors that make up quality?

3. What is, in your words, programming style?

4. What Shell commands and features help provide reliability, maintainability, reusability, efficiency, portability, and usability?

5. Write a Shell program to test the various default values assigned to a variable that is:

    a. not set

    b. set but has no value (NULL)

    c. set and has a value

6. Write the **trap** command to ignore the interrupt and quit signals. Use it in a Shell command and test its performance with the break or delete key on your terminal.

Chapter 13

The Shell Filter Builder

Shell does 98 percent of what you will need for most prototyping and tool building. Sometimes, however, you will need to write a custom filter. Although it's a bit afield from Shell, lex — the lexical analyzer — can do wonderfully complex filtering, allowing you to design and build your own custom filters.

Lex is a powerful tool for looking at text — documents, C language, or data — to either transform or analyze it. Lex lets you build filters quickly and easily.

Lex lets you specify regular expressions (REs) for words, strings, or constants and then generate a C language program from the lex source specifications. You can then execute the compiled program to process the matched regular expressions. Lex acts as program generator — it takes your specifications and generates the C language statements to lexically analyze input text.

Programs written in lex can act as filters — transforming the input according to your rules (Figure 13.1) — or they can pass information about matched text strings back to a calling C language module.

You can use lex to create filters if the change depends on just the expressions found. If you need to know the grammar or *syntax* of the input (e.g., a compiler or English analyzer) to process it, then a module that understands syntax (e.g., yacc)

Figure 13.1   Lex Filters

should call lex. Lex then returns a value that the syntax analyzer can understand, called a token, that it uses to examine the syntax.

LEX SOURCE STRUCTURE

Let's look at the structure of lex source shown in Figure 13.2. First, in the *definitions* section you can specify global data used within the *rules* and *user routines*. Lex also has a number of internal tables. As the number of regular expressions grows, these tables need to grow. The lex parameters allow you to specify sizes for these tables. Don't worry about them initially; lex will let you know when you exceed one.

Then, in the *rules* section (within the %% delimiters), you can specify up to 256 rules. Each rule consists of an RE to be matched and the actions to take when a match occurs. For example, a simple lex filter might have the specifications shown in Figure 13.3. Given these rules, the resulting program takes three actions:

1. When the analyzer program finds the word "lex", it prints "LEX" on standard output.

2. When it finds a string of one or more alphabetic characters, the lex statement, ECHO, prints the matched text on standard output.

3. The program passes any unmatched characters onto standard output. This is the default action for all unmatched input.

```
%{
        /* global C language Data and Definitions
%}
```
lex parameters (%e, %p, etc.)

```
%%
```
RE { actions }
```
%%
```

C language subroutines called by *actions*
```
main()
{
.  .  .
}
yywrap()
{
.  .  .
}
```

Figure 13.2   Detailed Lex Structure

```
%%

lex        printf("%s", "LEX");  /* print uppercase LEX */

[A-Za-z]+  ECHO;                  /* match longer words like LEXical */

%%
```

Figure 13.3 The Longest Match Rule

This example also highlights one of the major *ambiguous rules:* lex always prefers the longest match. Without the second rule, the first one would match the first three characters of words such as *lex*ical; the output would be "LEXical". These ambiguous rules are essential to the simple specification of lexical programs.

The *user routines* section is a good place to put *actions* that would otherwise clutter the rules sections. Write subroutines to handle complex actions and call them from the rules section. Sometimes, you will want to perform some processing *following* the lexical analysis. At end of input, the program generated by lex automatically calls yywrap. You can code your own yywrap and include this subroutine in the user routines section to handle any postprocessing or compile and link it separately. It should return a value of one (1) for end of input or zero (0) if there's more input.

LEX FILTER PROGRAMS

Now, let's look at a couple more examples and compare them to Shell commands. The first example is a simple translator from lower- to uppercase. The command to accomplish this is:

```
tr "[a-z]" "[A-Z]"
```

When a lexical analyzer program finds text that matches an RE, it puts the

```
%{
#include <ctype.h>
char *c;  /* character pointer to matched text */
%}
%%
[a-z]+  {
            /* convert matched lowercase to uppercase */
            for(c=yytext; *c=toupper(*c) ;c++);
            printf("%s", yytext);
        }
%%
```

Figure 13.4 A Filter to Translate Lowercase to Uppercase

```
%%
[Aa]m      |
[Aa]re     |
[Bb]e      |
[Bb]een    |
[Bb]eing   |
[Ii]s      |
[Ww]as     |
[Ww]ere   {
            printf("\\fB%s\\fR", yytext);  /* BOLD to Roman */
         }
[A-Za-z]+ {
            /* match longer words that contain the above
                like care, his, aware */
            ECHO;    /* print them as is */
         }
%%
```

Figure 13.5   A Filter to Embolden Passive Verbs in nroff Text

matched text in an external character array called yytext. Using yytext, an identical translator could have been written as shown in Figure 13.4.

The lex statement, ECHO, uses yytext to reproduce matched input on standard output. ECHO is defined as printf("%s",yytext);.

Another example (Figure 13.5) specifies a simple filter to embolden passive verbs (is, was, were) in nroff text. The output could be piped into nroff to aid the writer in finding passive verbs. In this example, rather than repeating the action for each word found, the vertical bar (|) symbol works as a logical OR to connect many regular expressions with the same action.

By now, you're probably wondering how this lex source code becomes an executable program (Figure 13.6). Suppose the lex code, for this example, was in a

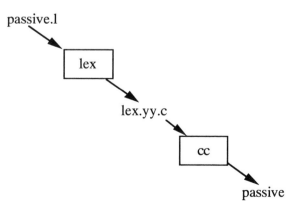

Figure 13.6   Lex Filter Creation

```
CFLAGS      = -O
OBJECTS     = main.o lex.yy.o yywrap.o
LIBS        = -ll
shellmet: $(OBJECTS)
            cc $(CFLAGS) $(OBJECTS) $(LIBS) -o shellmet
main.o:     shellext.h
lex.yy.o:   shellmet.h lex.yy.c
lex.yy.c:   shellmet.l
yywrap.o:   shellext.h
```

Figure 13.7   Shellmet Makefile

file called passive.l. (The **make** command, Figure 13.7, recognizes files with a .l suffix as lexical analyzer code.) To generate, compile, link, and execute passive.l, you would enter the following commands:

```
lex passive.l              # Generate lex.yy.c
cc lex.yy.c -ll -o passive  # Compile and link lex (-ll)
passive < textfile | nroff
```

The command **lex passive.l** creates a function called yylex() in the file lex.yy.c. The yylex function will process the input according to the specifications in passive.l. Next, you have to compile the generated C language (lex.yy.c) and link in the lex library (-ll), which contains default main and yywrap routines.

```
#include <stdio.h>

main(argc,argv)
int argc;
char **argv;
{       /* for all arguments */

    for(argc--,argv++ ; argc > 0 ; argc--,argv++)
    {   /* for all arguments */

        if( freopen(*argv, "r", stdin) ) {
            yylex();                          /* call yylex */
        } else {                              /* NULL */
          fprintf(stderr, "Unable to open %s\n", *argv);
        }    /* END IF */

    }    /* END FOR */

}
```

Figure 13.8   Listing of main Module That Calls yylex

Of course, redirecting standard input can be tiring. To specify file names on the command line, you can write your own main module that calls yylex (see Figure 13.8). This module will reopen standard input and call yylex for each file on the command line. The main module can do most of the preprocessing that any lexical analyzer requires. Any postprocessing can be handled by yywrap.

A SHELL QUALITY ANALYZER

Let's use these three parts — preprocessor, lexical analyzer, and postprocessor — to write a complexity analyzer for Shell script programs. Complexity is a function of the number of decisions and size of a program. The verbs in the Shell programming language are case, for, foreach, if, repeat, switch, until, and while. Let's write a lexical analyzer that counts the occurrences of each of these keywords and prints them if the decision count exceeds 7±2 (one of the rigorously proven limits of human understanding).

We'll use the main program shown in Figure 13.8. Figure 13.9 shows the lex source for the analyzer, shellmet.l. Figure 13.10 shows the include file for the keyword counters, and Figure 13.11 shows the yywrap module that will accumulate the decision count, compare it to a maximum value, print the results, and reinitialize the counters. Figure 13.12 shows the include file that yywrap and main use to reference the external data declared by shellmet.l.

```
%{
#include "shellmet.h"
%}
%%
case        case_cnt++;
for         for_cnt++;
foreach     foreach_cnt++;
if          if_cnt++;
repeat      repeat_cnt++;
switch      switch_cnt++;
until           until_cnt++;
while           while_cnt++;
#[^\n]*     comment_cnt++;
[\n]            line_cnt++;
[ \t]           ;
[A-Za-z0-9_.]+ { ;  /* match and delete anything else that
                        might contain the above (e.g. filenames) */
                }
[^#A-Za-z0-9_.]     { ;  /* match and delete anything else
                            (e.g. numbers, punctuation) */
                }
%%
```

Figure 13.9   The Lex Code for the Analyzer

```
/* count decisions and lines */

int case_cnt        = 0;
int comment_cnt     = 0;
int for_cnt         = 0;
int foreach_cnt     = 0;
int if_cnt          = 0;
int repeat_cnt      = 0;
int switch_cnt      = 0;
int until_cnt       = 0;
int while_cnt       = 0;
int line_cnt        = 0;

#include <stdio.h>
#include <shellext.h>
```

Figure 13.10   The include File for shellmet.1

Note that in Figure 13.9 we had to make allowances for Shell comments, any part of a line beginning with a nanogram (#) and ending before a newline (\n). We don't want to count the strings case, for, foreach, if, repeat, switch, until, and while if they occur *inside* a comment. Similarly, I had to define a regular expression, [A-Za-z0-9._]+, to rule out the possibility of these words' occurring inside another word. For example, consider a file name (e.g., *case*01 or *for*eign). It's simple to create regular expressions for the words you want to find, but not so easy to create the REs that represent larger strings that might include your keywords.

Also, since I didn't want any of the input to fall through to standard output, I had to include rules for blanks, tabs [\t], and any other input [^#A-Za-z0-9._ \t\n] that prevents them from passing onto standard output. The circumflex (^) causes the RE to match any character other than the ones within the square brackets.

I could have used a period (.), which matches any character, instead of the more complex RE with the circumflex, but I prefer to specify REs exactly to simplify future maintenance. For example, '.*' matches any number of occurrences of any character. Because of the ambiguity rule (lex always looks for the longest match), this RE could easily override other REs that have been specified.

Lex also takes the *first* and *longest* match. The first and longest rule takes *precedence*. Because of these two ambiguous rules, the longest REs should be placed at the end of the rules section. Consider the order of the following lex rules:

```
[a-z]+ identifier action;
for keyword action;
```

In this example, the first rule would always match the word *for* because the first rule has precedence; the *keyword action* would never be executed. If you have problems with a lexical analyzer, examine your lex code for ambiguity and precedence violations.

```
yywrap()
{

#define MAX_DECISIONS 10
#define MAX_LINES     100
int decision_cnt = 0;

decision_cnt = case_cnt + for_cnt + foreach_cnt + if_cnt +
    repeat_cnt + switch_cnt + until_cnt + while_cnt;

if(decision_cnt <= MAX_DECISIONS && line_cnt <= MAX_LINES) {
    printf("Quality Okay!\n");
    printf("Comment count = %3d\n", comment_cnt);
} else {
    printf("Case count = %4d\n", case_cnt);
    printf("For count = %4d\n", for_cnt);
    printf("Foreach count = %4d\n", for_cnt);
    printf("If count = %4d\n", if_cnt);
    printf("Repeat count = %4d\n", Repeat_cnt);
    printf("Switch count = %4d\n", switch_cnt);
    printf("Until count = %4d\n", until_cnt);
    printf("While count = %4d\n", while_cnt);
    printf("Total = %4d\n", decision_cnt);
    printf("\nTotal Lines = %4d\n", line_cnt);

    if(decision_cnt > MAX_DECISIONS) {
     printf("\nDecisions exceed quality standards\n");
    }
    if(line_cnt > MAX_LINES) {
     printf("\nTotal Lines exceed quality standards\n");
    }    /* END IF */
}    /* END IF */

case_cnt        = 0;   /* reinitialize the variables */
comment_cnt     = 0;
for_cnt         = 0;
foreach_cnt     = 0;
if_cnt          = 0;
repeat_cnt      = 0;
switch_cnt      = 0;
until_cnt       = 0;
while_cnt       = 0;
ine_cnt         = 0;

return(1);  /* end of input */
}
```

Figure 13.11   Listing of the yywrap Module

```
extern int case_cnt;
extern int comment_cnt;
extern int for_cnt;
extern int foreach_cnt;
extern int if_cnt;
extern int repeat_cnt;
extern int switch_cnt;
extern int until_cnt;
extern int while_cnt;
extern int line_cnt;
```

Figure 13.12   The shellext.h include File

A PRETTY FILTER

If you're looking at code hour after hour, your mind can begin to miss key constructs and keywords. To make these stand out on the printed page, we could create a lex filter that emboldens the keywords in C language, Shell, or anything else for that matter. A simple program, pretty_pr, to embolden these words would be:

```
{
#define BOLD printf("\fB%s\fR", yytext);
}
%%
if |
else |
switch |
case |
default |
until |
while |
[{ }] BOLD;
[a-z]+ ECHO;
%%
```

We could then embolden and print file.c as follows:

```
pretty_pr < file.c | nroff | lp
```

OTHER LEX ROUTINES

Let's look at some of the more infrequently used features of lex — input( ), output( ), unput( ), yyleng, yymore( ), and yyless( ).

input( )   gets a character from *stdin*

output( )   writes a character on *stdout*

unput( )   puts a character back on *stdin*

yymore( )   looks for additional matching characters

yyless( )   trims characters from yytext and puts them back on *stdin*

The input( ) and unput( ) routines provide a "look-ahead" capability. The two routines, yymore( ) and yyless( ), tell lex to look for longer matches or cut characters from the matched text. The lexical analyzer keeps the string length of yytext in an external integer variable called yyleng. We could use these functions to analyze C language comments. In C language, comments begin with the string "/*" and end with "*/". Figure 13.13 shows a lex source program to strip and print comments from C language.

The lex rule begins with "/*" and looks ahead for every character up to, but not including, the next "/". Using C language, I then check for a leading /* and a trailing * in yytext and add the trailing "/" using **input( )**. Next, if yytext begins with a /* but doesn't end with a "*", then the trailing "/" is embedded in the comment. I use yymore( ) to expand the comment. Finally, if yytext begins with other than "/*", I delete the matched text.

I should warn you that you can get into trouble if the matched text gets too long. The yytext[ ] array can be up to 200 characters in length. It isn't big enough to handle comments that span multiple sentences. To handle such problems, you'll need a syntax analyzer.

```
%%
[/][*][^/]+    {
          if( yytext[yyleng - 1] == '*') { /* end comment */

               yytext[yyleng++] = input();  /* get '/' */
               yytext[yyleng] = NULL;
               printf("%s\n", yytext);

          } else {

               yymore();  /* keep looking */

          }  /* END IF */
     }
[^/]+          /* delete everything else */ ;
[/]       ;
%%
```

Figure 13.13   A Lex Program to Strip and Print Comments from C Language

```c
#include <stdio.h>
#include "shellext.h"
#include "shelltoken.h"

main(argc,argv)          /* main for shellmet */
int argc;
char **argv;
{
int token = 0;
    for(argc--,argv++ ; argc > 0 ; argc--,argv++)
      {
        if( freopen(*argv, "r", stdin) ) { /* successful */

            while(( token = yylex() ))      /* NULL at EOF */
              {
                switch(token)
                  {
                    case CASE:
                      case_cnt++;  /* increment token counter */
                        break;
                    case COMMENT_START:
                      comment_cnt++;  /* increment token counter */
                      /* delete tokens except terminating NEWLINE */
                      while(( token = yylex()) != NEWLINE);
                          /* fall through */
                    case NEWLINE:
                      line_cnt++;  /* increment token counter */
                        break;
                    case FOR:
                      for_cnt++;  /* increment token counter */
                        break;
                    case FOREACH:
                      foreach_cnt++;  /* increment token counter */
                        break;
                    case IF:
                      if_cnt++;  /* increment token counter */
                        break;
                    case REPEAT:
                      repeat_cnt++;  /* increment token counter */
                        break;
                    case SWITCH:
                      switch_cnt++;  /* increment token counter */
                        break;
                    case UNTIL:
                      until_cnt++;  /* increment token counter */
                        break;
                    case WHILE:
                      while_cnt++;  /* increment token counter */
                        break;
                    default:
                      break;  /* ignore other tokens */
                } /* END SWITCH */
            } /* END WHILE */
        } else {
          fprintf(stderr, "Unable to open %s\n", *argv);
        } /* END IF */
    } /* END FOR */
}
```

Figure 13.14   The main Module (Syntax Analyzer Version)

USING LEX WITH A SYNTAX ANALYZER

Let's use the previous example, the Shell complexity analyzer, to explain how to analyze syntax. Figure 13.14 shows the new main program and Figure 13.15 shows the new lex program that returns tokens to the main program. Figure 13.16 shows the definition of the tokens. The yywrap routine stays the same.

```
%{
#include "shelltoken.h"
#include "shellmet.h"
%}
%%
case        return(CASE);
for         return(FOR);
foreach     return(FOREACH);
if          return(IF);
repeat      return(REPEAT);
switch      return(SWITCH);
until       return(UNTIL);
while       return(WHILE);
[#]         return(COMMENT_START);
[\n]        return(NEWLINE);
[ \t]          ;
[A-Za-z0-9_.]+ {    /* match and delete anything else that
                       might contain the above  */
            }
[^#A-Za-z0-9_.]    { ;  /* match and delete anything else
                    (e.g. numbers, punctuation) */
            }
%%
```

Figure 13.15   Lex Code (Syntax Analyzer Version)

```
/* shell tokens */

#define CASE            1
#define FOR             2
#define FOREACH         3
#define IF              4
#define REPEAT          5
#define SWITCH          6
#define UNTIL           7
#define WHILE           8
#define COMMENT_START   9
#define NEWLINE         10
```

Figure 13.16   The shelltoken.h include File

Notice how the yylex routine returns tokens to the main program, which now tallies them. Also notice that "#" is defined as COMMENT_START and that a NEWLINE is the end of a Shell comment.

In the main module, a return of COMMENT_START causes the logic to loop until it finds a NEWLINE to end the comment. Then, it falls through and increments the NEWLINE counter. As you can see, syntax analysis of language simplifies the regular expressions used in the lex code and places the burden of analysis on the calling module.

If you need to get into complicated grammars or syntax, yacc — the parser generator — generates programs from more easily understood syntax specifications. The two, in tandem, are powerful tools to analyze text and its grammar or syntax.

SUMMARY

I've covered the lexical analyzer and many of its robust features in just enough detail to make you dangerous. I recommend reading the documentation on lex to discover its other capabilities. To write your own lexical analyzer, see Kernighan and Plauger (1976). For a more thorough understanding of parsers and lexical analyzers, I recommend Aho et al. (1985).

I hope this chapter has given you some understanding of lex and how to use it to build filters and syntax analyzers. And I hope you are intrigued by the joy of lex.

EXERCISES

1. Write a lexical analyzer to embolden all of the control keywords in C language: if, else, switch, case, default, while, until, and { }.

2. Expand the Shell metrics analyzer to count all files and variables.

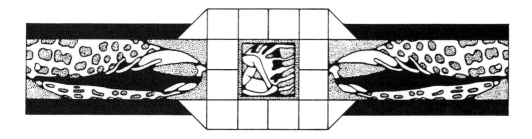

Chapter Fourteen

The UNIX System Administrator

A well-administered UNIX system is a joy to both the administrator and the system's users. A poorly administered system can be painful and is the cause of much of the bad publicity about UNIX today. The key to proper system administration is the Shell.

Successfully administered systems are popular. From one can mushroom dozens of others. From 1979 to 1984, for example, the first system I installed grew to a crop of seven that coupled with half a dozen more across U S WEST. In industry today, fields of UNIX systems — workstations, minis, and mainframes — support hordes of users worldwide. Automating the administration of your first system will greatly simplify the growth that will follow.

Shell programs can automate most of the activities of the day-to-day administration and operation. Automating activities such as adding users or backing up the file systems helps ensure that nothing is forgotten or done incorrectly. Even the best of typists (which most UNIX administrators are not) have a hard time entering the complete command to **volcopy** or **dump** (csh) a disk to a backup disk or tape without errors. Since file system backups are often done at night when even the best console operators are not totally awake, errors can occur unless the system does most of the work for them.

Other administration activities will require no human intervention at all. These can be automated with Shell and executed as required by **cron,** the clock daemon that executes commands based on the system's internal clock.

This chapter covers how the Shell can automate many of the administrator's activities and the files used for system administration. Because of its ability to handle complex processes reliably, the Shell is the key to productive, high-quality system administration.

ADMINISTRATION DUTIES

The UNIX system administrator has several key duties, most of which can be automated with Shell:

1. Add, change, and delete
   a. Users
   b. Software
   c. Hardware

2. Prevent problems through routine maintenance
   a. Back up daily activity
   b. Restore files

3. Diagnose and fix problems
   a. Monitor system usage — disk, cpu, network
   b. Maintain services — mail, uucp, network

4. Ensure system security

5. Provide user assistance

This chapter covers the routine activities of administration, not the nitty-gritty stuff of changing kernels. Why the day-to-day activities? Because the system never stays the same. Shell is a powerhouse for doing your daily grunt work. Let the Shell work for you. First, however, let's look at where the administrator's tools reside.

ADMINISTRATIVE DIRECTORIES AND FILES

A UNIX system administrator is directly involved with the directories shown in Table 14.1. Each of these directories contains files and commands that affect system administration. The major files and commands of concern to the system administrator are shown in Tables 14.2 and 14.3. The file system, /etc, contains most of the commands required for system operation.

The UNIX system administrator is also responsible for the Shell and C commands that are developed locally. The source code as well as the commands themselves should be maintained on one system and *delivered* to all other systems. Shell can help automate building and delivering locally developed software to other systems. Once the software is received, the other Shell administration systems can automatically install the software in the appropriate bin directories.

The other files that a system administrator deals with are not really files at all,

TABLE 14.1   Administrative Directories

Directory	Description
/etc	administrative and operational commands reside here, as well as passwd and group files
/usr/adm	accounting directories
/usr/docs	system documentation
/usr/games	games
/usr/lib	operational logs, cron tables, commands
/usr/lib/acct	accounting commands
/usr/lib/uucp	**uucp** commands
/usr/lp	line printer spooling system
/usr/news	local news directory
/usr/pub	public directories
/usr/rje	remote job entry system
/usr/tmp	temporary directories

but devices — terminals, disks, tapes, and line printers — that handle special functions. These are known as special files and come in two varieties: character and block special. The various UNIX files are shown in Table 14.4. Block, character, socket, and named pipe files are created with the **mknod** command.

TABLE 14.2   Administrative Files and Shell Commands

File or Command	Description
/etc	
/etc/brc	executed at startup by **init**
/etc/checklist	default file systems checked by **fsck**
/etc/group	listing of group IDs and passwords
/etc/inittab	event list for **init**
/etc/motd	message of the day
/etc/mnttbl	list of mounted file systems
/etc/passwd	login and password file
/etc/profile	custom Shell executed by **init**
/etc/rc	startup Shell executed by **init**
/etc/termcap	terminal capabilities database
/etc/wtmp	log of login processes
/usr/adm	
/usr/adm/pacct	accounting log
/usr/lib	
/usr/lib/cronlog	log of **cron** processing
/usr/lib/crontab	event list for **cron**

TABLE 14.3   Administrative Commands in /etc

Command	Description
config	configure a UNIX system
crash	crash the system
cron	execute commands in /usr/lib/crontab
dskfmt	format a disk pack
f sck	check a file system
f sdb	debug file system errors
init	initialize the system
killall	kill all process
labelit	label a disk or tape volume
mkf s	make a file system
mknod	make a special file node (e.g., named pipes)
mount	mount a file system
shutdown	gracefully shut the system down
startup	gracefully start it up
umount	unmount a file system
volcopy	volume-to-volume file system copy
wall	send a message to all users

TABLE 14.4   File Types

File Type	Description
Regular	standard UNIX file
Directory	standard UNIX directory
Character devices	
/dev/acu	auto call unit (**cu, uucp**)
/dev/console	system console
/dev/rdsk*	disk
/dev/rmt~	tape
/dev/lp	line printer
/dev/tty	terminals
/dev/vpm	virtual protocol machines (RJE)
Block devices	
/dev/dsk*	disk drive
/dev/mt~	tape drive
Named pipe	FIFO pipe created with mknod
Hard link	
Symbolic link (BSD)	
Socket (BSD)	similar to a named pipe

Shell commands write to character special files directly; block special files require special commands. Character special files act just like regular files, except that they are hardware devices. The following examples echo the system date onto the console, copy the contents of a directory to a tape, and print a file on the line printer:

```
date > /dev/console      # Print date on console
find . -cpio /dev/rmt0   # Back up a directory to tape
pr file > /dev/lp        # Print a file on a line printer
```

Special files can also be restricted with **chmod** to prevent users from writing to them. For example, terminals (/dev/tty) should be mode 700 to prevent other users from writing directly onto their terminal while they are working. Only /etc/wall overrides this protection.

Most of the block and character special files are the province of the system administrator. They facilitate disk and tape backups, console messages, terminal communications, and so on. Administrators will gain the most familiarity with their use and benefits when used in the Shell. Again, any activity an administrator performs on an hourly, daily, weekly, or monthly basis should be automated with Shell.

Aside from locally developed commands and special files, the administrative files, commands, and directories can be broken into several categories: daily administration, automated administration, system startup, and system shutdown. The following sections cover the application of Shell to these activities.

DAILY ADMINISTRATION

Day-to-day work is where Shell truly shines as an aid for productive system administration. Hardly a day goes by that the administrator is not asked to add or delete a user or group from the system, restore a file, or inform the users of changes in commands, operations, or whatever. Each of these activities represents various levels of effort required of the system administrator. Possibly the most frequent activity required is the addition of a user.

Add, Change, and Delete Users

Adding a user is not as simple as it sounds. Entries must be made in the passwd and group files. Directories and files must be created. Environment variables must be established to point the user's login toward correct line printers, RJE lines, and so on. Because remembering all of these things is difficult, we can follow Einstein's advice: Never keep anything in your mind that you can look up. Rather than miss your vacation, it makes sense to automate this activity with Shell. To add a user, the passwd file must be updated first:

```
usrno=`tail -1 /etc/passwd | cut -f3 -d:`      # Get last user no
usrno=`expr $usrno + 1`                        # Increment user no
echo "Which group will user belong to?"
read group                                     # Get group number
grpno=`grep $group /etc/group | cut -f3 -d:`
echo "User's login name?"
read logname
echo "User's name and phone?"
read usrname
echo "File system?"
read fs
echo "${logname}:..,:${usrno}:${grpno}:${usrname}:\
  /${fs}/${logname}: /bin/sh" \
  >> /etc/passwd    # Add user entry to password file
```

Next, **adduser** will have to create the user's directories and files:

```
homedir=/${fs}/${logname}
mkdir ${homedir}                # Make login directory
mkdir ${homedir}/bin            # Make other required directories
mkdir ${homedir}/doc
mkdir ${homedir}/rje
mkdir ${homedir}/src
cp /unixfs/proto/profile ${homedir}/.profile   # Add profile
chmod 755 ${homedir} ${homedir}/*              # All dirs readable
chmod 777 ${homedir}/src ${homedir}/rje        # Writeable
chmod 700 ${homedir}/.profile                  # Unchangeable
#
# Make all files and directories owned by user & group
#
chown ${logname} ${homedir} ${homedir}/* ${homedir}/.profile
chgrp ${group} ${homedir} ${homedir}/* ${homedir}/.profile
```

These few Shell commands comprise the basic needs of the **adduser** command. As the user population requires more hooks into the additional subsystems of UNIX—lp, lpr, rje, etc.—the **adduser** command should be enhanced to establish all of the environment variables required to make the user's entrance into the system as comfortable as possible. Taking care of all of these details when adding a user to a system not only helps the user, but keeps the administrator from having to answer numerous phone calls from frustrated users.

The command to add a group to the /etc/group file would be similar in format to **adduser. Addgroup** can be created easily with a few modifications to the commands shown.

The next frequent requirement is to delete a user. To delete a user, all references to the user must be removed from the system including /etc/passwd,

/etc/group, and /fs/logname. Using the same variable names as used in **adduser,** **deluser** executes as follows:

```
# deluser - remove /etc/passwd entry
sed -e "/^${logname}/d" < /etc/passwd > /etc/opasswd
cp /etc/opasswd /etc/passwd     # Replace passwd file
ed /etc/group <<!               # Remove group entry
g/${logname},/s///
g/,${logname}/s///
w
q
!
cd /${fs}/${logname}     # Change dir to user directory
if [ $? -eq 0 ]          # Successful cd?
then
  rm -rf *               # Remove all files and directories
  cd ..
  rmdir ${logname}       # Remove user directory
else
  echo "OOPS - /${fs}/${logname} not found"
fi
```

Again, as more hooks are added to a system's users, **deluser** will need to delete more references to the login name. Aside from administering logins, the system administrator must restore files and directories when a user inadvertently removes a semiprecious file. Note that this is less likely to happen in a C Shell system when the user has the noclobber variable set.

Add, Change, and Delete Software

Figure 14.1 shows a UNIX environment of the future — workstations in a local area network (LAN) tied into larger, distributed systems that include both UNIX and other operating systems via various network protocols. The challenge for power administrators will be to develop, build, install, and maintain all of the software from a central point and distribute it to remote sites. To accomplish this, you will need to create a system that:

1. builds the software from SCCS
2. sends the software via the network or uucp
3. loads the software on the remote systems during off hours
4. sends confirmation of installation to the administrator

Since this varies widely from environment to environment, you will want to develop such a delivery system for your individual configuration. Automating this

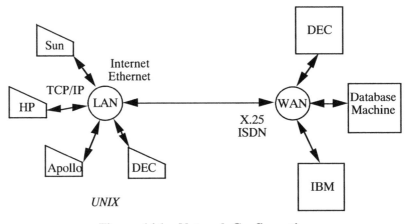

Figure 14.1 Network Configurations

process in Shell took only a couple of days and saved countless thousands of hours over the ten-year life of the seven-system configuration.

Much of daily administration work occurs in the off hours, while users and administrators rest. The tool that pilots this work is **cron.**

Cron

Cron reads /usr/lib/crontab and executes the commands found according to the time specifications. **Cron** gives the system administrator a handy way of being everywhere, doing everything, without having to be on the system.

Crontab entries have six fields. The first five fields tell **cron** when to execute the command: minute (0-59), hour (0-23), day (1-31), month (1-12), and day of the week (0-6; Sunday = 0 and Saturday = 6). To match a number of different times or days, a field may contain comma-separated numbers. To match any time or day, an asterisk (*) can be used in any of these fields. The sixth field contains the command to be executed.

A simple crontab will have entries to print the date and time on the console every 30 minutes and to sync the super block every 10:

```
0,30 * * * * date > /dev/console; echo "\n" > /dev/console
0,10,20,30,40,50 * * * * /bin/sync > /dev/null
```

To execute the calendar program every weekday morning at 5 A.M., add the following line to /usr/lib/crontab:

```
0 5 * * 1-5 /usr/bin/calendar -
```

The system administrator should use **cron** to handle as many routine tasks as possible. These include activities such as monitoring disk usage; cleaning up temporary files; validating SCCS files; keeping system logs to a reasonable size; printing accounting reports (**acctcom, sar**); administering subsystems such as lp, lpr, and rje; or any related administrative task. The system can handle all kinds of detective work in nonprime hours when the administrator is home having dinner or sleeping. Use **cron** like an army of administrators and have it send detected errors to the real administrator for resolution.

Cron is started when the system is brought up and stops when the system is shut down for backups. Both of these two activities — startup and shutdown — can be automated with Shell, to further reduce operational costs and errors.

Startup

> Trouble is easily overcome before it starts.
>
> *Lao Tzu*

Starting the system is handled by **init.** The /etc/inittab file controls the actions of **init** in each of its states — mounting disks and bringing all of the terminal devices (/dev/tty) on line.

/etc/rc checks all of the file systems for errors using **fsck**; mounts the file systems; and starts process accounting, **cron,** the RJE, lp, uucp, and anything else that should be available when users enter the system.

Since /etc/rc is a Shell, it can be modified to ensure that the system comes up cleanly, ready for users. /etc/rc can execute special Shells to handle the requirements of the system administrator, such as mailing the date and time of system startup. All of these files are under the control of the system administrator and should evolve to simplify system operation.

Shutdown

> Give as much care to the end as to the beginning, then there will be no failure.
>
> *Lao Tzu*

Shutting the system down is probably more important than how it is started. Rash actions such as halting the machine from the console before all commands are killed, file systems unmounted, accounting stopped, subsystems stopped, and so on, can generate all kinds of problems that can be avoided by using the **shutdown** command. Since **shutdown** is a Shell command, it can be modified to improve system reliability.

Once the system has been gracefully shut down and placed in single-user mode, and file systems checked, the **shutdown** command should ask the operator about disk or tape backups and execute these commands as required.

ROUTINE MAINTENANCE

A system administrator can reduce the possibility of lost files by requiring nightly backups and by automating the backup process with Shell commands to mount the proper backup disk or tape and **volcopy** the file systems. Disk and tape backup commands are fairly similar. The following command will back up the root and usr file systems:

```
# diskbackup
day=`date +%a`     # Get day of week Sun-Sat
echo "Backup volume name is bck${day}
echo "Mount backup pack labeled FILE SYSTEM = root"
echo "Hit return when ready"
read answer
mount /dev/rdsk14 /bck > /dev/null     # Mount root backup
volcopy root /dev/rdsk0 unix0 /dev/rdsk140 bck${day}
volcopy usr /dev/rdsk2 unix0 /dev/rdsk142 bck${day}
umount /dev/rdsk14 > /dev/null     # Unmount backup drive
```

The command could also use **labelit** to check the volume name of the backup pack before continuing. Disk and tape backup commands should be developed for each system to ensure the accuracy of the backup procedures. There is nothing more vicious than a user who has lost data and work. Do not let this happen to the users on your system.

Restoring files requires that the operations staff mount the correct backup disk or tape. What better way to ensure that the most current backup copy is used than to let the Shell request the backup disk from a history log? Assuming that the disk backup command creates a log of the file systems backed up and the volume names of the backup disks, a command called **file_restore** could determine which disk to use:

```
# file_restore
echo "Enter full path name: /fs/userid/dir.../filename"
read path
fs=`echo $path | cut -f2 -d"/"`
backup=`grep $fs /etc/backuplog | tail -1`     # Get latest log
backupvol=`echo ${backup} | cut -f2 -d:`     # Get volume
special=`echo ${backup} | cut -f3 -d:`       # Get special name
echo "Mount $backupvol on backup drive"
echo "Hit <return> key when ready to continue"
read answer
mount ${special} /bck          # Mount backup as bck
file=`echo $path | cut -f3- -d/`   # Cut filesys from path
cp /bck/${file} $path          # Copy backup file
umount ${special}              # Unmount backup drive
echo "${path} restored from /bck/${file}"
echo "Remove $backupvol from backup drive"
```

If the backup log contained the following information:

```
unix1:bkuptues:/dev/rdsk140
unix2:bkuptues:/dev/rdsk142
unix1:bkupwed:/dev/rdsk140
unix2:bkupwed:/dev/rdsk142
```

then the command to back up the file /unix1/lja/src/main.c would ask the system administrator to mount the disk labeled "bkupwed" on the backup drive (in this case, dsk14). The **file_restore** command would then mount the backup file system as /bck and copy the previous version of the file into the requested directory and file.

DIAGNOSING AND FIXING PROBLEMS

No computer system is impervious to errors. You will, however, find it much easier to prevent problems than to fix them when they occur. This is also less costly. Prevention involves monitoring the system's functions and taking corrective action *before* problems occur. Fix it before it breaks!

Monitoring System Usage

> Because the sage always confronts difficulties, he never experiences them.
>
> *Lao Tzu*

The first thing to manage on most systems is disk usage. The disk free (**df**) command can help pinpoint rapidly growing disk usage. If the amount of free space under a file system drops below a certain level, you will want to request free spaces from the user community or consider expanding their file system:

```
df /userfs
```

You may also find it useful to fully automate this process so that the system tracks changes in disk usage, comparing one day against the next, and notifies you of any untoward activity. You may also want to monitor remote systems using **uux**:

```
uux `df / | mail home!yourself' remote_system
```

Then you can use the disk usage (**du**) command to identify the 20 percent of the users who use 80 percent of the disk space. Pareto's rule often holds true for all system resource usage.

CPU and access times can be monitored via the accounting data. In my experience, UNIX systems experience a slow initial growth rate, then modest growth, and, toward the end, massive growth. By tracking and plotting the trend, you will have sufficient advance warning to install hardware upgrades and tune the system to meet the demands.

You will need to develop additional commands to monitor the other services on the system: **mail, uucp, lp, lpr,** and networking.

ENSURING SYSTEM SECURITY

The Shell administrator has four key jobs with respect to system security:

1. prevent unauthorized access
2. maintain system integrity
3. preserve data privacy
4. prevent interruption of service

To prevent unauthorized access, you need to make sure that all of the users and groups have passwords and that there are no duplicate user IDs:

```
awk -f: 'if ( $2 == "") { print }' /etc/passwd /etc/group
cut -f1 -d: /etc/passwd | sort | uniq -d
cut -f1 -d: /etc/group | sort | uniq -d
```

To maintain system integrity, you will need to manage the permissions on executable files and directories. Following are the three permissions that allow a user to assume someone else's identity, even the superuser's, for the duration of the command:

4000	set user ID (*setuid*)	changes to the owner of the executable program
2000	set group ID (*setgid*)	does the same for the group
1000	sticky bit	keeps a program in memory

The most dangerous of these, of course, is the first, especially when the owner is root. To find these programs, **cron** should periodically search the system as follows:

```
find / -user root -perm 4000 -exec ls -lg {} \;
find / -perm 2000 -exec ls -lg {} \;
find / -perm 777 -type f -print
```

To preserve data privacy, the administrator will need control of the **mount** and **umount** commands, and file and directory permissions. Mounting and unmounting file systems lies in the control of the superuser, who has access to /etc/mount and /etc/umount. Controlling data security is augmented by the **umask** command, which determines the default file permissions. To prevent anyone except the user and the group from accessing files created by the user, we could put the following statement in /etc/profile or .cshrc:

```
umask 027
```

As a backup procedure, we could periodically check for directories that can be read and written by anyone in the "world":

```
find / -perm 777 -type d -print
```

We could also encourage users to set their own default security and use **crypt** for really important files. All of these activities are designed to help prevent loss of data or loss of the system. To further prevent interruption of service, we could place external users in a restricted Shell (**rsh**).

Restricted Shells

Occasionally, the system administrator will need to allow a group of users access to the machine without giving them all of the power of UNIX. In these instances, he or she can create a restricted environment that lets them perform some necessary work, but prohibits them from going crazy in the system.

Creating restricted Shells is easy. First, the administrator creates a restricted login that points to /bin/rsh instead of /bin/sh. When a user logs in, he or she will be prohibited from executing the **cd** command, changing the value of PATH, redirecting output, or executing commands beginning with "/". These restrictions are enforced only after **login** has executed the commands in the user's .profile.

By creating the proper .profile and not allowing the user to change it, the system administrator can put him or her in any directory, supply any commands required with PATH, and be assured that they can do little damage.

The commands required are often linked from /bin and /usr/bin to a set of restricted bins: /rbin and /usr/rbin. A simple .profile to restrict a user's activities would be:

```
PATH=:/rbin:/usr/rbin
cd /unixfs/rdir
export PATH
```

The user could then execute the commands in the current directory, /rbin, and /usr/rbin. He or she would be restricted from moving about the system. This will only occasionally be useful, but it is an option for good system administration. Use it sparingly; the goal of administration is to help users do whatever they need to do.

PROVIDE USER ASSISTANCE

The final requirement of daily administration is to communicate all system changes to the user population. A knowledgeable user population minimizes the number of phone calls an administrator will receive. The commands that handle user communication are **mail, news,** and **wall.** The file /etc/motd (message of the day) can also be used to provide daily information when the user logs into UNIX. The following example shows various entries for /etc/motd:

```
/etc/motd
The system will be down for preventive maintenance Sunday,
July 17 from 9AM to 6PM. Please refer questions to x1234.
```

News is used for changes to the system or system commands. Users can read the daily news (**rn**) when they have time. News files are kept in the directory /usr/news. **Mail** communicates directly with specific users or groups of users. **Wall** writes to all users who are logged in when immediate communication is required (e.g., when the system is coming down for emergency maintenance).

Shell programming can aid the system administrator in all phases of daily administration. Shell commands should be developed to automate any activity that happens frequently, such as adding or deleting users, or for restoring files. Other administration tasks must occur on a set schedule. Rather than demand that these be done by the administrator, they can be executed automatically by **cron.**

Help

Nothing is more frustrating to a UNIX user than to need help and not know where to get it. Consider building a simple command, called **helpme,** that prints the administrator's work and home phone numbers. If there is more than one administrator and each specializes in certain UNIX subsystems, then include that information too:

```
# helpme
cat /global/help/oncall    # Print list of administrators
```

Periodically, check all of the system logs for signs of trouble. As certain kinds of errors rise to the surface, develop Shell commands to **grep** for errors in the logs and mail them to the system administrator nightly using **cron.** The sooner errors are detected and corrected, the sooner the administrator can kick back and spend his or her time developing new and better tools to support the user population.

SUMMARY

The UNIX system administrator has as much to gain from Shell usage as any UNIX user. Much of the work of administering a system can be handled with

Shell commands, **cron,** and the startup and shutdown procedures. Productive UNIX administration relies on extensive use of the Shell and all of its facilities. From the UNIX guru to the simplest user, Shell is the way to help a user accomplish his or her goals. May you spend your time collecting rare and beautiful Shells to satisfy your every need.

EXERCISES

1. Write the command to allow users to create news files in /usr/news.

2. Write the command to send mail to groups of users by extracting their user IDs from the /etc/group file.

3. Write the command to back up file systems to tape on your system. (Look up your device types for magnetic tape.)

4. Write the commands to restore files and file systems from tape.

5. Modify the backup command to include all of the disks and file systems on your UNIX system.

6. Write the crontab entry to print the accounting reports in /usr/adm/acct/fiscal on a line printer.

7. Write the crontab entry to validate all of the SCCS files on the system and send mail of the corrupted files to the system administrator.

Appendix A

Reusable Shell Code

```
# %M% %Y% %I%
#
# Most recent update: %G% at %U%
#
#%z% Function -
#%Z%
#
# @#@ Syntax -
#
#%Z% General Instructions
#%Z%
#%z% Parameters -
#%Z% Required -
#%Z%
#%Z%Optional -
#%Z%
# store the flags
while [ `echo $1 I cut -f1` = "-" ]
do
    parms="${parms) $1"
    shift
done
case $# in
    # if they don't give any files, prompt for them
    0)
```

```
                echo "enter filename"
                read filename
                ;;
        # if they give exactly the right number, do something
        1)
                filename=$1
                ;;
        # if they give a whole bunch, process all of them
        2)
                filename="$*"
                ;;
esac
#describe actual processing
for file in $(filename)
do
     process $file
done
```

Appendix B

C Language Prototype

```c
char mainrel[] = "%A%";

#include <stdio.h>
#include <string.h>

maintargc, argv)
int argc;
char **argv;
{
 /*****************************************************
  *                                                   *
  * main program:                                     *
  *                                                   *
  * program description:                              *
  *                                                   *
  * subroutines called or required:                   *
  *                                                   *
  * reference: (job definition, etc)                  *
  *                                                   *
  *                        %A%                         *
  *                                                   *
  *****************************************************/
char *cmdname;
cmdname=argv[O]; /* save pointer to the commandname */
argc--; argv++;
```

```
/*
          check for control flags
*/
while (argc>1 && *argv[1]=='-') {
    switch(argv[0][1]) {
        case 'f': /* flags */
                  /* insert -f processing */
            break;
        default:
            fprintf(stderr, "%s: invalid parameter %s\n",
                cmdname, *argv);
            return(1);
            break;
        } /* END SWITCH */

    argc--; /* decrement the argument counter */
    argv++; /* increment the argument pointer */
} /* END WHILE */
while(argc>0){
    /*
        if the file exists reopen it as standard input
    */

    if (freopen(*argv, "r", stdin) == NULL) {
        fprintf(stderr,"%s: can't open %s\n", pgm, *argv);
        return(1);
    } /* END IF */

} /* END WHILE */
} /* END PROGRAM */
```

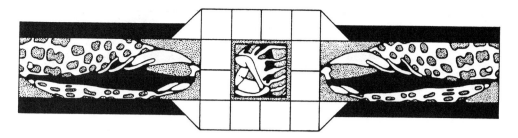

Appendix C

Makefile Prototype

```
OBJECTS = main.o sub.o lex.yy.o y.tab.o
LIB = -ll -lm
CFLAGS = -O
BIN=/usr/local/bin

command: $(OBJECTS)
    cc $(CFLAGS) $(OBJECTS) $(LIB) -o command

main.o: command.h main.c

sub.o: command.h sub.c

lex.yy.o: command.h lex.yy.c
lex.yy.c: cobmet.l
    lex cobmet.l

y.tab.o: command.h
    y.tab.c

y.tab.c: command.y
    yacc command.y

clean:
    rm *.o

install:
    cp command $(BIN)
```

Appendix D

Shell Syntax

BASIC COMMAND SYNTAX

command   *options arguments*

ITEM	EXAMPLE	DESCRIPTION
command	**grep**	name of executable command
options	-a	single letter representing an option
	-f filename	single-letter option requiring an argument
arguments	$*	pathname or other argument
	-	*stdin*

LOOPING AND DECISION SYNTAX

FOR

```
for variable in wordlist
do
  commandlist
done
```

ITEM	EXAMPLE	DESCRIPTION
variable	file	For each loop through the *commandlist, variable* is set to the next word in *wordlist.*
wordlist	$*	List of words, files, directories to be used as fodder for the *commandlist.*
commandlist		Any sequence of Shell commands.

WHILE

```
while comparison
do
  commandlist
done
```

ITEM	EXAMPLE	DESCRIPTION
comparison	($1 == "a")	Test the expression and if there is a zero (good) exit status, execute *commandlist*.
commandlist		Any sequence of Shell commands.

BREAK

break *n*   Escape from level *n* for or while loop.

CONTINUE

continue *n*   Resume next level *n* for or while loop.

EXIT

exit *n*   Exit Shell with *n* return code.

CASE

```
case variable in
  RE) commandlist ;;
  . . .
esac
```

ITEM	EXAMPLE	DESCRIPTION
variable	choice	Compare variable to the RE (regular expression); if it matches *commandlist, variable* is set to the next word in *wordlist*.
RE	1 | 2 | [7-9])	REs (In this example, if $choice is 1, 2, 7, 8, or 9, then execute *commandlist*.)
commandlist		Any sequence of Shell commands.

IF

```
if comparison then
  commandlist
elif comparison then1
  commandlist
else
  commandlist
fi
```

ITEM	EXAMPLE	DESCRIPTION
comparison	`($1 == "a")`	Test the expression and if there is a zero (good) exit status, execute *commandlist*.
commandlist		Any sequence of Shell commands.

( )

   (*commandlist*)   Execute *commandlist* in a subshell.

{ }

   {*commandlist*;}   Execute *commandlist*.

;

   `grep "a*" file; cat file2`   Command separator.

COMMENTS

   #   Everything that follows is a comment.

VARIABLES

${*variable*}	`${file}`	variable name
$*variable*	`$file`	

INPUT/OUTPUT REDIRECTION

< *input*	Open *input* as *stdin*.
> *output*	Open *output* as *stdout*.
>> *append*	Append *stdout* to *append* file or device.
<<*delimiter*	Read following *inputlist* as *stdin* up to *delimiter*.
inputlist	
delimiter	
<&*digit*	Link file descriptor *digit* to *stdin*.
>&*digit*	Link file descriptor *digit* to *stdout*.
<&-	Close *stdin*.
>&-	Close *stdout*.

Appendix E

Reference:
Shell Built-in Commands

This appendix lists the Shell built-in commands along with a brief description of what each command does. In addition, an example of how to use the command is provided. The notation used is fairly standard. Anything enclosed in [ ] is optional and anything followed by ... means that the argument can repeat.

: Null Operation

Syntax

```
: [arg ... ]
```

Usage

This is the null command and performs no action. It always returns a zero return code. The argument list is optional. If it is included, any arguments are evaluated by the Shell. If it is not included, it simply returns the value of true and can be substituted for the value true.

Example

```
while :
```

will perform the same as a while true statement.

. **Execute Shell Commands Contained in a File**

Syntax

```
. filename
ksh: . filename [args .. ]
```

Usage

The . command causes any Shell commands found in the file to be executed. The file name can be either an absolute path or a relative path. If it is a relative path, the environment variable *PATH* is used to search for the file name. The . command does not execute the commands contained in the file as a subshell, and thus variables set or changed while the commands in the file are being executed are a permanent change to the current environment. This is very useful when you write a Shell program and wish to have it alter your current environment in some way.

The Korn Shell enhancement allows arguments to be passed to the Shell named in *filename*. These arguments are passed in the standard way as positional parameters—$1, $2, $3, etc.

Example

The following command

```
. .profile
```

will cause your .profile to be executed and any changes made will have a permanent effect on your current login session. This is a convenient way to have changes that were made to your .profile active in your current environment without the need to log in again.

---

alias   Create a New Name for a Shell Command

Syntax (Korn Shell Only)

```
alias [name=[value] ... ]
```

Usage

Use the **alias** command as a convenient way to provide different or shorter names for commands or as a method of providing commonly used options to commands.

Example

If you are an MS-DOS user, you may be familiar with the command **dir** used to list the contents of a directory in DOS. To make a **dir** command in the Shell, we can use the **alias** command. The following command does the trick:

```
alias dir='ls -ld'
```

Now if you enter the command:

```
dir
```

then the **ls** command is executed with the -ld options.

---

bg   Place Job in the Background for Execution

Syntax (Korn Shell Only)

```
bg [job ...]
```

Usage

The **bg** command is part of the Korn Shell job control extension. It permits jobs to be executed in the background. If no job is provided, then the current job is placed in the background. In order for a job to be moved to the background, the job must be stopped. To stop a job that is currently executing in the foreground, the suspend key sequence is issued. This is usually the Ctrl-z key combination. Job names can take on various forms and are described in detail in the **jobs** built-in command later in this appendix.

Example

```
jobs      # List the jobs that are executing
[1] + Stopped    struct
bg %1     # Place the program struct to run in the background
```

---

break   Escape from a Loop Command

Syntax

```
break [n]
```

Usage

The **break** command is used to exit the enclosing loop or case command. The loop command can be any of the Shell looping commands — for, while, until, or select. The command will also exit from a CASE statement. The next command executed after a break is the command that follows the enclosing loop(s). The optional argument *n* is an integer value that represents the number of levels to break in the case where loop commands are nested. This is a convenient method to exit a deeply nested looping structure when some type of error has occurred.

Example

In the following example, the while loop is set to continue forever. But within the while loop a conditional IF statement causes a **break** command to execute, which exits the loop.

```
while true     # Do the loop until some user id's are entered
do
  echo
  echo "You have not provided any user id's. You must provide a \
      user id(s)"
  echo "you wish to have userfix clear. "
  echo "Enter the user id's separated by a space (e.g., tburns \
      freddy guest)"
  echo
  echo "Enter valid user id's ==> \c"
  read USERS
  if [ "$USERS" != "" ]     # Any user id's entered?
                            # If so break the loop
  then
    break
  fi
done
```

---

cd   Change the Working Directory

Syntax

```
cd [pathname]
cd old new
ksh: cd -
```

Usage

The **cd** (change directory) command is used to change the working directory to some new directory name specified in the path name. If no path name is specified, then the default path becomes the path specified in the environmental variable *$HOME*, which usually specifies your home directory. If an absolute path name is provided, then that directory is made the current working directory. An absolute path name starts with the /, ./, ../ characters. If a relative path name is provided, then the environment variable *$CDPATH* is used to search for the path name. When a change of directory takes place, the environment variable *$PWD* is set to the current working directory.

In the second form, the **cd** command replaces the string "old" with the string "new" in the current directory name.

The Korn Shell extension provides a mechanism for returning to the most recently visited directory path. Using a "-" in the place of the path name will return you to your previous working directory.

Example

```
cd                        # Return to $HOME directory
cd programs               # Change to directory programs - If not
                          # a subdirectory of current directory
                          # Then search CDPATH path for a direc-
                          # tory named programs
cd ~/programs             # If using Korn Shell then switch to
                          # $HOME/programs
cd -                      # If using Korn Shell return to the
                          # previous directory
cd /user/john/mailstuff   # Go directly to a fully qualified path
```

---

continue   Skip to the Next Iteration of a Loop

Syntax

```
continue [n]
```

Usage

The **continue** command is used to skip to the top of the next iteration of a looping statement. Any commands that follow the continue statement but are part of the enclosing loop command are skipped, and execution continues at the top of the loop. If an integer value is provided after the continue, that number of enclosing loop levels are skipped.

Example

This example reads standard input (a redirected file name, for example) and performs some processing on the input lines. Note that if it is the first line, then processing is skipped.

```
FIRST=1
while read INPUT
  do
    if [ $FIRST = 1 ]
      then
        FIRST=0
      continue
  fi
  CON_NUM=`echo $INPUT | cut -c9-14`
  echo $CON_NUM
  grep "$CON_NUM" /user/list >/dev/null
  if [ $? = 0 ]
    then
      echo "$INPUT" >> inlist_con
    else
      echo "$INPUT" >> new_con
  fi
done
```

---

echo   Write Arguments to the Standard Output

Syntax

```
echo [arg ..]
```

Usage

The **echo** command is used to write strings and Shell variables to the standard output (usually your terminal). This is very useful for producing messages to the screen when writing Shell programs and for examining the value of Shell variables stored in your environment.

Example

A very common use for the **echo** command is to see the value of a Shell variable in your current environment. If we wanted to see the value of our home directory path, we could enter the following command at the prompt:

```
echo $HOME
/usr/tburns
```

You can see that the Shell responds by returning the value of the variable *$HOME* to the terminal. Any text that is not a variable is reproduced on the screen directly. So, for example, we could enhance the preceding example by typing the following:

```
echo My home directory is $HOME
My home directory is /usr/tburns
```

In this example each word is considered an argument to the **echo** command and is echoed to the terminal. The arguments may be enclosed in quotes, which allows for the interpretation of the special formatting escape sequences such as \b, \c, \f,\n,\r, \v, \\, and \n where *n* is octal code for some ASCII character.

For example, the previous example could be enhanced so that the terminal skips to the next newline (nice for skipping lines in output) by embedding \n in the command

```
echo "My home directory is $HOME \n"
My home directory is /usr/tburns
```

---

eval   Evaluate Arguments as Input to the Shell and Execute

Syntax

```
eval [command_line]
```

Usage

The **eval** command evaluates the command line to complete any Shell substitutions necessary and then executes the command line. This is most often needed when a single pass of Shell substitution does not complete all needed expansions. Often this arises when a Shell command is constructed in a Shell variable (a very flexible and powerful technique in Shell programming). When this constructed command contains variables that must be expanded, the **eval** command does the trick. The following example should make this clear.

Example

```
OUTPUT="macfact > macfactout"
eval cat $OUTPUT
```

In this example the information in the file macfact is placed in the file macfactout, as was intended. If, however, we remove the **eval** from the cat line, then cat will get confused looking at each argument in OUTPUT as a file. When looking for a file named ">", an error will be produced, as:

```
cat: cannot open >
```

exec   Run Specified Command without a New Process

Syntax

```
exec [command_line]
```

Usage

The **exec** command is used to run the specified command without starting another subshell process. This is efficient since no new UNIX process is created and the existing environment is replaced. This aids in the removal of subshells that no longer need to be maintained by the system. These subshells are created each time a command that is not built in is executed from the Shell.

Example

Let's say that we have some users on our system that do nothing but execute an application program called PIGGY. To accomplish this, we run PIGGY directly from the user's .profile as the last command. But in order for PIGGY to run correctly, some environment variables must be set and exported. Once we have done this, we no longer need the current Shell. Instead of just running PIGGY directly at the end of the .profile, which would create a new subshell process, we instead **exec** PIGGY, replacing the current log on Shell with PIGGY. This allows each user to have only a single process instead of two, which saves system resources.

```
$ cat .profile
HOUSE1=straw
HOUSE2=sticks
HOUSE3=brick
WOLF=bad
export HOUSE1 HOUSE2 HOUSE3 WOLF
PIGGY
```

The preceding .profile would create two processes—one for the .profile Shell and one for the PIGGY program. But the following would create only a single-user process at login through the use of the **exec** command:

```
$ cat .profile
HOUSE1=straw
HOUSE2=sticks
HOUSE3=brick
WOLF=bad
export HOUSE1 HOUSE2 HOUSE3 WOLF
$ cat .profile
```

```
HOUSE1=straw
HOUSE2=sticks
HOUSE3=brick
WOLF=bad
export HOUSE1 HOUSE2 HOUSE3 WOLF
PIGGY
exec PIGGY
```

---

exit   Exit from Current Shell and Return Exit Status

Syntax

```
exit [n]
```

Usage

The **exit** command is used to exit the currently running Shell. If the **exit** command contains an integer value *n*, then *n* is returned as the exit value from that Shell. If no value is provided for *n*, then the exit value of the last command is returned. It should be noted that if you perform an **exit** command and the only Shell running is your login Shell, then you are returned to the login prompt, effectively logging you off the system. If a Shell program does not have an **exit** command, then the end-of-file has the same effect as exiting without a value supplied for *n*.

Example

Our goal in this example is to write a Shell script that will tell users to log off the system. We could write a Shell script that checks to see if anyone is logged onto the system. If this is the case, then the Shell returns an exit value that indicates this condition and our parent Shell can then issue an appropriate message to all users on the system. It might look something like:

```
$ cat parent
if [ `anyone` = 1]
then
  broadcast "LOG OFF NOW EARTH SCUM OR DIE! UNIX GOD";
  exit 1
else
  exit 0
fi
$cat anyone
if [`who | wc -l` > 1]
```

```
then
  exit 1
else
  exit 0
fi
```

---

export   Add Variables to the Global Environment

Syntax

```
export [variable_name]
```

Usage

This command is used to make Shell variables available to all subshells. Exporting a variable is a method of making a variable defined in the current Shell global so that all subshells will have access to the variable. In reality, the variable is copied to the subshell environment. If a variable is not exported, then it is local to the current Shell. It should be noted that it is not possible for a subshell to alter the value of a variable in a parent Shell even when it is exported; the exported variable is copied and upon returning to the parent Shell that copy is destroyed, thus returning to the original value in the parent Shell.

Example

Let's say that we have a few Shell programs — set1, set2, set3.

```
$ cat set1
SHAPE=round
COLOR =red
# Make shape global
export SHAPE
```

Now if we execute set1 and check the value of SHAPE and COLOR, here is what we get:

```
$set1
$echo $SHAPE
round
$echo $COLOR
$
```

As you can see, only SHAPE was made available to our login Shell since it was the variable that was exported. Once the Shell set1 finished running, its environment was removed and thus all local variables were destroyed.

Now let's look at a variation.

```
$cat set2
SHAPE=round
COLOR =red
# Make shape color global
export SHAPE COLOR
echo "Before set3 SHAPE = $SHAPE, COLOR= $COLOR"
set3
echo "After return from set3 SHAPE = $SHAPE, COLOR= $COLOR"
```

You can see that set2 calls set3. Let's see what set3 does:

```
$cat set3
echo $SHAPE $COLOR
SHAPE=square
COLOR=blue
export SHAPE COLOR
echo "After export in set3 SHAPE = $SHAPE, COLOR=$COLOR"
```

Now when we run set2, we get the following output:

```
$set2
Before set3 SHAPE=round,COLOR=red
After export in set3 SHAPE=square,COLOR=blue
After return from set3 SHAPE=round, COLOR=red
```

This demonstrates the fact that exported variables are passed to subshells as copies (passed by value) and that a subshell cannot change a value in a parent Shell even when using the **export** command. If, however, another Shell had been called from set3 (perhaps set4), it would have had the values of square and blue placed in its environment.

---

fc   Reexecute a Command on the History Stack

Syntax (Korn Shell Only)

```
fc [ -e editor ] [ -nlr] [ first_line] [last_line ]
fc -e - [old=new] [line ]
```

Usage

The **fc** command allows previously executed commands, stored in the command history file, to be edited and reexecuted via an editor. Editing and listing commands are accomplished by the first form of the command just shown. Each command is stored in the history file and has an associated line number that is used to access the command directly via the **fc** command. Use the -l option to list the last 16 commands entered into the file along with their associated line numbers. It is also possible to access the commands in the history file by specifying a relative line number or a command name that is used to search the stack. Use the -e option to specify an editor to edit and reexecute a particular command. A default editor can be specified by using the Shell environment variable *FCEDIT*. The meaning of the options for the first form of the command are:

-n   no number in listing

-l   list the contents of command file; don't edit and execute

-r   reverse the listing order

To reexecute commands directly, without editing, use the second form of the command, fc -e -, which tells **fc** that you do not want to use an editor but instead want to directly reexecute the command. The Korn Shell alias *r* provides direct reexecution of the last command entered.

Example

```
fc -l            # List the last 16 lines in the history file
fc 6426          # Edit line number 6426 using editor specified
                 # in FCEDIT and reexecute
fc -e emacs -4   # Edit and execute the command in position -4
                 # (4th previous command)
fc -e - 6426     # Re-execute command at line number 6426 directly
```

---

fg   Move a Job to the Foreground

Syntax (Korn Shell Only)

```
fg [job_name]
```

Usage

The **fg** command is part of the Korn Shell job control extension. This command is used to move a job that is stopped or is executing in the background to the foreground. Job names can take on various forms and are described in detail in the **jobs** built-in command later in this appendix. The stopped or background job becomes the foreground job and will continue to execute in the foreground unless it is stopped again using a Ctrl-z. If no job name is given, then the last stopped job is used to bring to the foreground.

Example

```
fg %2        # Bring the job numbered 2 into the foreground
fg 23456     # Bring the process id(pid) number 23456 into the
             # foreground
fg           # Current job into the foreground
```

---

getopts   Parse the Argument List Passed to a Shell Program

Syntax (Korn Shell Only)

```
getopts options_str opt_variable [args .. ]
```

Usage

Used to parse argument lists passed to a Shell in a standard manner. This is the Korn Shell version of the **getopt** command. This new version should be used in place of the UNIX **getopt** command wherever possible. This new Korn Shell version is more powerful and also functions as a built-in command instead of a UNIX call.

Example

```
USAGE="showopts [-q] quit mode [-v] verbose mode(default) [-h] \
   help -f filename"
   while getopts :qvf: h WHICH_OPTION
     do
       case $WHICH_OPTION in
         q) echo "You selected the option $WHICH_OPTION indicating\
            Shell is in quit mode"
         echo "No messages will be displayed during Shell execution"
            Q_MODE=1;;
         v) echo "You selected the option $WHICH_OPTION indicating \
            Shell is in verbose mode"
            echo "All informational and error messages will be \
               displayed"
            V_MODE=1;;
         f) echo " You selected to work with file named $OPTARG";;
         h) echo "You selected the help option. The format of this \
            command is $USAGE"
         exit(-1);;
         ?) echo "$USAGE"
            exit(-1);;
     esac
done
```

```
if ([ Q_MODE -eq 1] && [V_MODE -eq 1])
then
  echo "Quit mode and verbose mode are exclusive of each other; \
    pick one or the other"
  exit(-1)
fi
```

Now if we enter the following command, let's see what happens:

```
showopts -q -f FRED
You selected the option q indicating Shell is in quit mode
No messages will be displayed during Shell execution
You selected to work with file named FRED
```

---

hash   Control Command Hashing

Syntax

```
hash [ -r] name..
```

Usage

The **hash** command is used to control the internal hash table used by the Shell to increase performance. Each time that you enter a command it is stored in the hash table to improve efficiency. The Shell uses the hash table to locate commands you have already used. By doing so it saves on searches of the PATH you have defined. These PATH searches can be very costly since they require disk access. You can control what is in the table by adding entries to it or removing entries from it. To add a command to the hash table, give the command:

```
hash command_name
```

To remove a command from the hash table use the command:

```
hash -r command_name
```

To view a list of what is in the hash table, enter the **hash** command alone with no other options.

It should be noted that the Korn Shell does not utilize the hash table. Command tracking is implemented using tracked aliases. The **hash** command is actually aliased to the **alias** command itself in conjunction with the -t option. You can see this by typing `alias` to see a list of all aliased commands for your session. For more information on tracked aliases, please see the **alias** command earlier in this appendix.

Example

Let's say that we have a Shell command that resets our modem so that it will be in auto-answer mode. This Shell is called, surprisingly enough, reset. We will be using reset often so we want to hash the command. If we enter the **hash** command with no arguments, we see something like:

```
hash
hits    cost    command
1       2       /usr/bin/pg
3       1       /bin/ls
1*      7       ./junk
```

This shows all the commands that have been placed into the hash table so far along with the number of times the hash table has been used to locate the command (hits) and a relative cost of looking up and executing the command. Now let's say we want to add **reset**.

```
hash reset
hash
hits    cost    command
0*      7       ./reset
1       2       /usr/bin/pg
3       1       /bin/ls
1*      7       ./junk
```

You can see that the **reset** command has been added to the hash table. Now the command will be found in the hash table each time it is executed. To remove it from the hash table, enter:

```
hash -r reset
```

---

jobs   List Stopped and Background Jobs

Syntax (Korn Shell Only)

```
jobs [ -lp ]
```

Usage

The **jobs** command is used to display the stopped and background jobs that are currently active for your session. The list produced is used to manage the jobs using the other Korn Shell job management commands (**bg, fg, kill**). By using this list you can tell the Shell which job to work with when using the other commands. The two options control how the display is sent to your screen. The -l option tells the **jobs** command to list UNIX process ID numbers. These are numbers used by UNIX to keep track of your running programs and are in addition to the other job information that is provided. The -p option just prints the process ID of all jobs and no other information. This is much like the UNIX **ps** command. In addition, the **jobs** command indicates the state of the job. It will list whether the job is running, stopped, or done. The job name in Korn Shell job processing can take on several various forms, as outlined in the table that follows.

Korn Shell Job Identifiers

JOB IDENTIFIER	WHAT IT REPRESENTS
number	the UNIX process ID
% number	job control number printed by jobs command
%+	current job
%-	previous job

Example

```
jobs
[1]+ Stopped      emacs tester.c
[2]- Stopped      zap
[3]  Running      counter
[4]  Done         magic
```

kill   Send a Signal to a Job

Syntax (Korn Shell Only)

```
kill [ -signal] job
kill -l
```

Usage

The **kill** command is used to send a specified signal to a job. The signal can be either the name of any of the signals used in UNIX or the corresponding number that is related to the signal. The available signals and their related numbers are shown as:

Table of UNIX Signals

Signal Name	Signal Number	Signal Description
SIGHUP	01	hangup (user disconnects in some way)
SIGINT	02	interrupt (user hits DEL key on keyboard)
SIGQUIT	03	quit (user hits Ctrl - \ on most keyboards)
SIGILL	04	illegal instruction (not reset when caught)
SIGTRAP	05	trace trap (not reset when caught)
SIGABRT	06	ABORT instruction
SIGEMT	07	EMT instruction
SIGFPE	09	kill (cannot be caught or ignored)
SIGBUS	10	bus error
SIGSEGV	11	segmentation violation
SIGSYS	12	bad argument to system call
SIGPIPE	13	write on a pipe with no one to read it
SIGALRM	14	alarm clock
SIGTERM	15	software termination signal
SIGURG	16	urgent condition present on socket
SIGSTOP	17	stop (cannot be caught or ignored)
SIGTSTP	18	stop signal generated from keyboard
SIGCONT	19	continue after stop
SIGTSTP	20	child status has changed
SIGTTIN	21	background read attempted from control terminal
SIGIO	23	I/O is possible on a descriptor
SIGXCPU	24	CPU time limit exceeded
SIGXFSZ	25	file size limit exceeded
SIGVTALRM	26	virtual time alarm
SIGPROF	27	profiling timer alarm
SIGUSR1	28	user-defined signal 1
SIGUSR2	29	user-defined signal 2
SIGPWR	30	power fail
SIGPOLL	31	selectable event pending

This list is a typical list of signals or system interrupts. While it would be possible to send a job or process any of these signals, it is typical to send signals 1, 2, 3, 9, and 15. Many of the other signals are used by the system to communicate with executing processes. The way that any particular program or Shell responds to a received signal varies. Some processes may ignore a signal; others may try to perform some action and exit gracefully. For this reason, the sending of signals should be done very cautiously since a program may not respond in a desired manner. The only signal that cannot be ignored by a program is KILL(-9). This is a sure kill and will not allow the executing process to exit gracefully. *It should be used with caution and only when no other signals kill the process in a graceful manner.* Some programs do not like being killed with KILL(-9) and doing so can cause problems. The other common signals — TERM(-15), HUP(-1), INT(-2), and QUIT(-3) — are much friendlier ways to kill a process and most Shells, including any you write, should handle them in some graceful manner.

If no signal is specified, then the TERM signal is sent to the job. The job name can be any of the job names described in the **jobs** built-in command.

With the second form of the command, using the -l option, a list of all available signals is presented.

Example

Let's say we stopped our emacs edit session using the ^Z command. We would see the following:

```
[1] + Stopped     emacs
jobs -l
[1] + 6362  Stopped     emacs
kill %1
jobs -l
[1] + 6362  Terminated     emacs
```

So you can see that the emacs edit job was sent the default TERM signal and that emacs terminated after receiving the signal. It would also have been possible to perform the same kill by providing the following command:

```
kill -15 6362
```

This says to send a -15(TERM) signal to the process ID 6362. Or if the job was very stubborn and seemed to be ignoring all signals, we could send the **kill** command as the last resort.

```
kill -KILL +%
jobs -l
[1] + 6484  Killed     emacs
```

---

let   Evaluate an Arithmetic Statement

Syntax (Korn Shell Only)

```
let expr..
```

Usage

The **let** command forces evaluation of an arithmetic expression when using the Korn Shell. The **expr** can be any valid numeric expression(s) as defined by the

Korn Shell. If the expression has any special Shell characters, it must be enclosed in quotes. The Shell command ((..)) is equivalent to **let "expr"**.

An advantage of using the **let** command is that since it is a Shell built-in, it executes much faster than the **expr** command. It also has the advantage that, when using Korn Shell, it recognizes whether the assignment is being done to an integer variable or a string variable. If it is an integer variable, the **let** command performs integer arithmetic; otherwise it converts the variables to strings as needed. The **let** command always regards the expression passed as a numeric expression, unlike the **expr** command. This is convenient since it removes the need to place a $ in front of variables. The **let** command recognizes only numbers, variables, and arithmetic operators.

The expression does not need to be an assignment statement. The **let** command returns an exit value that indicates whether the last expression evaluated to a non-zero number or a 1. This allows the **let** command to be used in conjunction with an IF statement and makes a more natural arithmetic statement than what is usually created with the test statement.

Example

```
n=1
let "n = n+1"
```

The preceding statement adds 1 to the number *n*. Note that the *n* on the right-hand side of the assignment did not require a $n.

```
a=5
x=5
n=1
let "n = n +1" "q = (a+5 + (x *100))"
print $n $q
2 510
```

Note the use of parentheses in the preceding statement, which contains two numeric expressions.

```
i=9
if (( i < 10))
then
  print Yes it is
fi
```

In the preceding statement, the **let** command is used in the form ((..)) and is used to test an arithmetic expression. Notice that that is much easier to write and understand than the test command shown next:

```
if [ "$i" -lt 10 ]
then
  ...
fi
```

---

newgrp   Switch to a New UNIX Group

Syntax

```
newgrp [-] [group_name]
```

Usage

The **newgrp** command is used to switch to a new UNIX group in order to alter a user's access to UNIX files. The user's login ID must be listed as a part of that group (/etc/group). If no group name is provided, then the user is switched to the default group as defined in the /etc/passwd file entry for that user.

When a user issues the Korn Shell built-in command **"newgrp"**, it is like executing the UNIX command:

```
exec newgrp group_name
```

The user's current Shell is replaced with a new Shell that has the real and effective group identifier set to the group listed in *group_name*. If the group is not found, then the Shell is still replaced and the group remains the same. Please note that any variables that are not exported will be lost as when you **exec** any command.

If the first argument to newgrp is a -, the environment is altered to look just as if the user had logged in under that group ID. This includes the resetting of environment variables and the reexecution of .profile.

The user is prompted for a password if the group has a password and the user does not, or if the group has a password and the user is not in the group indicated in *group_name*. To be a group member, the user must be listed in /etc/group.

Example

```
id
uid=413(tburns) gid=400(progmrs)
newgrp general
id
uid=413(tburns) gid=600(general)
```

The preceding command sequence shows that tburns was a member of group progmrs before the **newgrp** command was issued to switch to the group general.

---

print   Print Arguments on Standard Output

Syntax (Korn Shell Only)

```
print [ -Rnprsu[n ] ] [ arg ... ]
```

Usage

The **print** command is the Korn Shell output command that is used in place of the
Bourne Shell **echo** command. The **print** command can perform just as the **echo**
command does, simply by using no command options, or it can support extended
functionality through the use of the command options. The **print** command provides more flexibility in formatting and direction of Shell output, as outlined next.

OPTION	DESCRIPTION
-R	Places the **print** command, which specifies that all escape sequences are to be ignored. The escape sequences \t (tab), \n (newline), and \c (escaped special char) are ignored as special and are printed. All command-line options that follow the -R , except for the -n option, are ignored.
-n	Do not place a newline character at the end of the output.
-p	Write output to process spawned with |& instead of standard output.
-r	Raw mode just as -R but no other command-line options are recognized.
-s	Write the output to the history file.
-u	Write the output to the file descriptor specified with number (one digit only). Default is 1.

Example

```
print HELLO CRUEL WORLD
HELLO CRUEL WORLD

STRING1="I am not who I appear to be\n \tJust as expected!

print -r $STRING1
I am not who I appear to be\n \tJust as expected!

print $STRING1
I am not who I appear to be
  Just as expected!

STRING2="THE MAN IN THE MOON"
STRING3="\027 EATS GREEN CHEESE! "
print $STRING2; print $STRING3
THE MAN IN THE MOON
EATS GREEN CHEESE!
print -n $STRING2; print $STRING3
THE MAN IN THE MOON EATS GREEN CHEESE!
```

---

pwd Display the Current Working Directory

Syntax

pwd

Usage

The **pwd** command shows the current directory in which you are working. The path name printed is the full path name.

Example

pwd
/usr/tburns

KSH

When using the Korn Shell, the **pwd** command is often used in the primary prompt string (PS1) to show your current working directory as part of your prompt. This way you are always aware of your current working directory. Very convenient!

```
PS1='${PWD}: '
export PS1
```

Now when you change directories your prompt will contain whatever your working directory is. For example:

```
/usr/tburns: pwd
/usr/tburns
/usr/tburns: cd src
./src
/usr/tburns/src: cd rules
/usr/tburns/csrc/rules
/usr/tburns/csrc/rules: cd
/usr/tburns:
```

---

read Read an Input Line from a File and Parse

Syntax

```
read [name ... ]
ksh: read [ -prsu[n] ] [name ? prompt] [name ...]
```

Usage

The **read** command is used to obtain input from a file. In the case of the Bourne Shell, the file read is the standard input. In the case of the Korn Shell, the file can be, in addition to standard input, a pipe created with |& or a file descriptor. The line read from the file, whatever that file happens to be, is parsed using the IFS environment variable as a delimiter. Using this delimiter, the first field is sent to the first name, the second field to the second name, and so on. Leftover fields are sent to the last name. In this case, a name represents a Shell variable. If all goes well, then the **read** command returns a 0. If the end-of-file is reached, then a nonzero return code is issued.

KSH

As was just mentioned, the file read can be other than standard input when the Korn Shell is being used. The following options control the file being accessed:

-p   Read from the input pipe of a process spawned using |&. If an end-of-file is read, then the spawned process is cleaned up so that another can be spawned.
-u [n]   Read from the file associated with file descriptor n. If n is not supplied, then 0 is used.

As well as being able to control what file is being read, the Korn Shell also provides some options for being able to control how the input line is read and where to place the input if no name is provided.

-r   Raw mode — this implies that a \ at the end of the line does not signify a line continuation.
-s   Save the line read as a command on the history stack.

If no name variable is provided, then the Korn Shell uses the default variable named REPLY (very handy). If the first variable name is followed by a ? then the text to the right of the ? is used as a prompt when entering the data interactively.

Example

```
echo $IFS
read JUNK?"What would you like master? "
What would you like master? FOOD PLEASE
echo $JUNK
FOOD PLEASE
```

In this example, the full string is assigned to the variable *JUNK*, even with the IFS variable set to a space because there is only a single variable. Let's try it a different way:

```
IFS=" "
read JUNK?"What would you like master? " STUFF
What would you like master? FOOD PLEASE
print $JUNK
FOOD
print $STUFF
PLEASE
```

As you can see, the line is parsed into the two variables, *JUNK* and *STUFF*.
A file can also be read by redirecting standard input to the Shell:

```
shellpgm < filename
```

And shellpgm can then contain a while loop that is used to read the input fields:

```
while read field1 field2 field3
do
  process input line
done
```

---

readonly   Prevent Variables from Being Changed

Syntax

```
readonly [ variable_name ... ]
```

Usage

The **readonly** command is used to specify variables that should not be allowed to change. Once a *variable_name* has been specified in a read-only statement, the variable is unalterable. Any attempts to change the variable will cause an error message to be generated. With the Bourne Shell, once a variable has been declared as read-only, it is not possible to make the variable modifiable again. Note that variable names are used without the $; we are assigning an attribute to the variable itself and not the value the variable contains.

The Korn Shell provides a few nice enhancements to the read-only typing of variables. First, it is possible to assign a value to a variable when you declare it as read-only; this cannot be done when using the Bourne Shell. Second, it is possible to change the variable back to being modifiable again. This can be done by using the **typeset** command, available with the Korn Shell.

Example

First, let's set a variable and declare it as read-only. Then we can try to change the value. The resulting messages are shown:

```
readonly TEST_MACHINE="explorer"
TEST_MACHINE="stargazer"
ksh: TEST_MACHINE: is read only
unset TEST_MACHINE
ksh: TEST_MACHINE: is read only
```

Now let's try to make the variable modifiable again using the **typeset** command. The +r option tells the Korn Shell to turn off read-only mode on the named variable. (Please see the **typeset** command later in this appendix for details.)

```
typeset +r TEST_MACHINE
TEST_MACHINE="stargazer"
print $TEST_MACHINE
stargazer
```

Now let's switch to the Bourne Shell and try the same thing. The error message shows that we are not able to assign a value to a variable when we declare it.

```
sh
readonly TEST=1
TEST=1: is not an identifier
```

In order to accomplish this assignment in Bourne Shell, we must assign and then declare it as read-only.

---

return   Return from a Shell Function and Assign a Return Code

Syntax

```
return [n]
```

Usage

The **return** command is used with Shell functions. It will return from a function to the point where that function was called. The Shell continues execution from that point. The optional value, *n*, is returned as the value of that function. If you do not specify *n*, then the return value of the function is the value of the last command. If return is not used in a function, then it behaves the same as the **exit** command.

Example

Let's define a function that returns a value 1 if the *TEST_MACHINE* variable is "stargazer" and 0 otherwise. Then we can check the return value from the function by using the $? variable.

```
echo $TEST_MACHINE
stargazer
mach_test() { if [ "$TEST_MACHINE" = "stargazer" ]
    then
      return 1;
    else
      return 0;
    fi
  }
mach_test
echo $?
1
```

The mach_test function could be called from another within a Shell script and the return would cause execution to begin at the statement following the call to mach_test.

---

set   Change the Shell Invocation Options and Arguments

Syntax

```
set [ -+aefhkntuvx [ arg ... ] ]
ksh: set [-+aCefhkmnopstuvx] [+o option]...[+A name] [arg...]
```

Usage

The **set** command is used to turn on and off the various Shell control options and to change the values of any arguments passed to the Shell when it was invoked. This is very useful when you wish to alter the behavior of the Shell dynamically. To make an option active you use the -; to make the option inactive you use the +. The current list of active options can be viewed by looking at the value of the variable $-. A list of the various options and the functionality they control within the Shell is listed in the following table. Please note that all these Shell options can be set upon invocation of the Shell. The args are passed to the Shell as positional parameters $1, $2, and so forth.

Bourne Shell Options

-a	Mark variables that are modified or created for export.
-e	Exit immediately if a command exits with a nonzero exit status.
-f	Disable filename generation.
-h	Locate and remember function commands as functions when they are defined. (Function commands are normally located when the function is executed.)
-k	All keyword arguments are placed in the environment for a command, not just those that precede the command name.
-n	Read commands but do not execute them.
-t	Exit after reading and executing one command.
-u	Treat unset variables as an error when substituting.
-v	Print Shell input lines as they are read.
-x	Print commands and their arguments as they are executed.
--	Do not change any of the flags.

Korn Shell Options

-A	Assign values sequentially from the list arg. If +A is used, the variable name is not unset first.
-a	All subsequent variables that are defined are automatically exported.
-C	Turn off directory caching. Pwd will use the actual path instead of following links.
-e	If a command has a nonzero exit status, execute the ERR trap if set and exit. This mode is disabled while reading profiles.
-f	Disable filename generation.
-h	Each command becomes a tracked alias when first encountered.
-k	All variable assignment arguments are placed in the environment.
-n	Read commands and check them for syntax errors but do not execute them. Ignored for interactive Shells.
-o	The following argument can be one of the option names outlined in the table following this one.
-p	Use the /etc/suid_profile instead of .profile whenever the ENV profile was to be executed. This occurs only if the group ID or user ID of the process is not the same as the effective ID.
-s	Sort the positional parameters and gid.
-t	Exit after reading and executing one command.
-u	Treat unset parameters as an error when substituting.
-v	Print Shell input lines as they are read.
-x	Print commands and their arguments as they are executed.
-	Turn off -x and -v flags and stop examining arguments for flags.
—	Set $1 to a value beginning with -. If no arguments follow this flag, then the positional parameters are unset.

Option (-o) Arguments for Korn Shell Set Command

-O ARGUMENT	DESCRIPTION
allexport	Same as -a.
bgnice	Run all background commands at reduced priority. This is just like using the **nice** command for background jobs. No need to use **nice** if this is set.
cache	Same as -C.
errexit	Same as -e.
emacs	Use the emacs editor commands for command-line editing.
gmacs	Use the gmacs editor commands for command-line editing.
ignoreeof	The Shell will not exit on end-of-file. It will ignore the eof key sequence (^d) and will not exit the Shell when this occurs. You must use the **exit** command to exit the Shell.
keyword	Same as -k.
markdirs	Place a / after all file names generated.
monitor	Same as -m.
noclobber	Prevent existing files from being overwritten when the > or >> redirection is used on a Shell command.
noexec	Same as -n.
noglob	Same as -f.
nolog	No function definitions in history file.
nounset	Same as -u.
privileged	Same as -p.
verbose	Same as -v.
trackall	Same as -h.
vi	Use vi commands as the command-line editor.
viraw	No buffering of characters — processed as they are typed.
xtrace	Same as -x.

Example

```
set -a          # Tell the Shell to export all variables
set -o ignoreeof  # Don't log me off when I hit ^d -Thank you
```

---

shift   Shift Passed Arguments to the Left

Syntax

```
shift [n]
```

Usage

The **shift** command is used to shift arguments to the left and is usually used to gain access to arguments that are > $9. (Really, this is only necessary with Bourne

Shell since Korn Shell allows > 9 arguments.) In general, the (n+1) argument becomes the $1 argument, ($n$+2) becomes $2, and so on. The default for n is 1. The arguments that are shifted over are no longer accessible and the value of $# is adjusted accordingly.

Example

The following while loop will process all the arguments passed to a Shell program by shifting until no arguments remain.

```
while [ "$1" ]
do
  process $1
  shift
done
```

---

test   Evaluate a Conditional Expression to True or False

Syntax

```
test [ cond_expr]
[ cond_expr ]
ksh: [[ .. ]]
```

Usage

The **test** command, in any of its forms, is used to evaluate the cond_expr and return a value of true (0) or false (any other number). The result of the test can therefore be used in conjunction with an **if** or **while** command to test a particular condition and take some action based on its outcome.

Example

The following code checks to be sure that the previously executed command had a successful return code and, if not, takes some error action:

```
if ( test $? -eq 0 )
then
  echo "There is an error in the program"
    exit (1)
fi
```

The same test condition could be written in the following abbreviated format:

```
if [ $? = 0 ]
  then
    echo "There is an error in the program"
      exit (1)
fi
```

---

times   Determine Time Used by a Command

Syntax

```
times
```

Usage

The **times** command is used to display the user and system time consumed by the Shell and by any commands run from the Shell. The output is shown in minutes and seconds. The output from the **times** command is a little less than user-friendly, but in its raw form it looks something like:

```
0m0.68s 0m2.05s
0m8.83s 0m7.66s
```

This output can be interpreted as the following:

	USER TIME	SYSTEM TIME
Time consumed by Shell	0m0.68s	0m2.05s
Time consumed by commands		
run from Shell	0m8.83s	0m7.66s

Example

```
times
0m0.68s 0m2.05s
0m8.83s 0m7.66s
```

---

trap   Set Action for System Interrupts

Syntax

```
trap [ command ] [signal]
```

Usage

The **trap** command is used to take some action when the Shell receives a signal from the system. This action can be some further commands to be executed or can be no action at all. Taking no action is like ignoring the signal. In the case of the Bourne Shell, the signal must be a numeric integer. It should be noted that the command is scanned once when the trap is set (this of course implies that variables will be substituted when the command is scanned — you may need to protect variables by quoting them) and once when the command is executed after receiving the signal. The **trap** commands are executed in signal number order. (Please see the **kill** command earlier in this appendix for a list of all signals and their related names and numbers.)

Please note that it is not possible to trap a signal 11 (memory fault) or a signal 9 (sure kill). If a Shell ignores a signal, then all subshells also ignore that signal. If, however, a Shell takes some action based on a signal, then all subshells take the default action on that signal. In other words, trap actions are not inherited by subshells.

If no command is given (as opposed to the null string), then the trap is reset to the default action for that signal. The default action for all signals is to terminate the Shell. The only exception to this is that interactive Shells automatically ignore interrupts and terminate signals.

A command associated with signal 0 is executed when the Shell exits. Typing trap with no arguments prints a list of all currently active traps.

Example

The following **trap** command placed at the start of a Shell procedure would remove the file /tmp/caldate and then exit the Shell upon receiving any of the signals listed.

```
trap "rm -fr /tmp/caldate; exit" 1 2 3 4 5 10 12 15
```

This next example would ignore the signals listed:

```
trap "" 1 2 3
```

---

type   Determine Type of Command

Syntax

```
type command_name
```

Usage

This command is used to determine if the argument given, *command_name*, is a known command and if so, what type of command it is. If the command is known to the system (can be found in your $PATH or is a built-in command or a defined function), then a path name is provided, where it applies, as well as a description of the command. In the case of a function, the definition of the function is provided. When using the Korn Shell, the **type** command is set up as an alias for the **whence -v** command. The types of commands identified are:

- a normal command with the full path of the command
- a Shell built-in command
- a command that is currently in the hash table due to recent use
- a function identified as such, followed by the function's definition

If the command is not found, then an error message indicating that it is not found is produced on the standard output. (For details on additional functioning in the Korn Shell, please see the **whence** command later in this appendix.)

Example

```
type cast
cast not found
type cat
cat is /bin/cat
type cd
cd is a Shell builtin
```

---

typeset   Set the Type for a Shell Variable

Syntax (Korn Shell Only)

```
typeset [ -FLRZefilprtux[n] ] [name[=value]..]
```

Usage

The **typeset** command is a Korn Shell command that allows Shell variables to be of special types. These types allow special processing to occur for a variable that has the type assigned. For example, a variable that has been assigned an integer type can participate in Korn Shell integer arithmetic directly without using the **expr** command. Note that when used inside a function, a new copy of the parameter and its type is created, and this definition lasts only for the life of the function invocation. After leaving the function, the variable is returned to its original form.

Using a + instead of a - on the option will turn that option off. This is sometimes useful when trying to control variable assignment.

Following are a list and description of each option available with the **typeset** command:

Typeset Options

OPTION	DESCRIPTION
-F	Provide a UNIX to host-name file mapping on non-UNIX names.
-Ln	Left-justify the variable and remove all leading blanks from the variable. If a value for n is specified, then that becomes the width for the variable. If no value is provided, then the width of the field is determined by the first assignment. If a value is assigned to the variable and does not entirely fill the width, then the variable is padded on the right with blanks. If the assignment is too long for the width of the variable, then truncation will occur on the right.
-Rn	Right-justify the variable and fill with blanks on the left. As with the -L option, the length of the variable is determined by the value of n or by the length of the first assignment. Filling and truncation occur on the left on all subsequent assignments to the variable name.
-Zn	The -Z flag is a zero-fill indicator. It can be used in conjunction with either the -R or the -L flag. If used alone, the variable is right-justified and zero filled to the left if the first nonblank character contained in the variable is a digit. As with -L and -R, the value of n determines the width of the variable; truncation and padding will occur.
-e	Tag the variable as having an error. This currently is not used in any way by the Korn Shell, but it can be set or unset by the user.
-f	The -f option is used to indicate that the variables listed in the **typeset** command are actually function names. This allows functions to have properties assigned and can only be used with the -t, -u , and -x options.
-i [n]	The variable is assigned an integer type and can participate in Korn Shell arithmetic statements directly. The base used for the arithmetic operations can be set by setting a value for n. Default is determined by the first assignment. Simply exclude a value for n for normal base 10 arithmetic.
-l	Convert all uppercase characters to lowercase characters when assignment occurs.
-p	The output of the command is written to a two-way pipe.
-r	The variable named is set to read-only and cannot be changed except by using the **typeset** command again either to assign a value to the variable (name=value) or to turn off the read-only indication (+r).
-t	Places a tag on the named parameter. These tags are not used by the Korn Shell. If used in conjunction with the -f(-ft) option, the -t sets the xtrace option for the named function.
-u	Convert all lowercase characters to uppercase characters when assignment takes place. If used with the -f(-fu) option, the named function becomes undefined.
-x	The names provided are marked as automatic export to the Shell environment. This is for both variables and functions. To use with function names, the -f variable must be applied.

Example

```
typeset -i counter
                    # Set the variable counter to be of integer type
typeset -L5 part_number
    # Left justify the part number and make it have a length of 5
```

---

ulimit   Set Process Limits

Syntax

```
ulimit [-acdfmst ] [ n ]
```

Usage

The **ulimit** command is used to impose limits on any process that runs under the current Shell. In general, this means limiting the size of some system resource. The size is always given by the value of *n*. The meaning of each value is outlined in the following table:

OPTION	DESCRIPTION
-a	Display the values of all the currently active limits.
-c	Limit the size of a core dump output file for the process to *n* blocks.
-d	Limit the size of the data area for a running process to *n* kilobytes.
-f	Limit the size of an output file created by a process to *n* blocks.
-m	Limit the size of memory used to be *n* kilobytes.
-t	Limit the time of execution for the process to *n* seconds.
-s	Limit the size of the stack area to *n* kilobytes.

If the option is given without a value for *n*, then the current value of that option is printed.

Example

```
ulimit -f        # What is the limit on my output file size ?
4069
ulimit -f 5000   # Increase that limit
ulimit -t        # How much time do I have?
unlimited
```

---

umask   Set or Display File Creation Mask

Syntax

```
umask [nnn]
```

Usage

The **umask** command is used to set the file creation mask. Any time that a file or directory is created, the permissions are controlled by the umask value. The **umask** command is used to set the umask value. The setting of a umask value often is done in a user's .profile. The values for the umask can range from 000 to 777, just like a value for setting a file permission. But the behavior of the umask is different from setting the permissions on a file directly using **chmod**. Instead of setting the value of any new file or directory to the value specified in the umask, the umask value is subtracted from the default file and directory permissions. For a file, the default is usually 777 and for a directory the value is 666. Therefore, a umask value of 000 when creating a file will yield a file permission of 777 (read, write, and execute for everyone). This is arrived at by subtracting the umask value from the default (777 − 000 = 777). Likewise, a value of 022 for the umask would yield a file permission mask of 755 (read, write, and execute for owner; read and execute for everyone else). This was arrived at by taking 022 (subtract read permissions from group and other) away from the default 777.

If no value is given for *nnn* in the **umask** command, then the value of the umask is displayed. Using umask provides a means for creating files and directories with consistent and security-minded permissions.

Example

```
umask
002
umask 033    # Set file creation mask so people other than the
             # owner can only read the file
```

---

unalias   Remove an Existing Alias

Syntax (Korn Shell Only)

```
unalias alias_name ...
```

Usage

When using the Korn Shell, the list of alias names provided in *alias_name* are removed from the alias list and are no longer available in the Shell. (See the **alias** command earlier in this appendix for details on how to define an alias in the Korn Shell.)

Example

```
alias finger='ucb finger'    # Create an alias for the finger
                             # command
unalias finger    # Remove my alias for the finger command
```

unset   Remove a Shell Variable from the Environment

Syntax

```
unset name ...
ksh: unset var_name
unset -f function_name
```

Usage

The **unset** command is used to remove variable and function definitions from the current Shell environment. The variable name and its associated values are no longer accessible after an **unset** command has been executed. With the Bourne Shell, both variables and functions are removed in the same way — the **unset** command followed by the function or variable name(s). With the Korn Shell, since variables and functions are distinguished from each other, the -f option must be used to remove functions. Also note that with the Korn Shell, a variable that has been set to read-only, using the **typeset** command, cannot be unset. In this case, use the **typeset** command to change the variable to be readable and then unset it.

Example

```
unset note_count        # Unset the variable note_count
unset -f count_em_up    # Unset the function definition count_em_up
```

wait   Wait for a Job to Finish

Syntax

```
wait [n]
```

Usage

The **wait** command causes the parent Shell procedure to wait for its executing children processes to finish. If a specific process ID (pid) is specified as a value for *n*, then the Shell will wait for that particular process to finish. If no value is specified for *n*, the parent Shell waits for all child processes to finish execution. While waiting, no other Shell statements are executed by the parent Shell. The return value is the value of the final completed child process.

Example

```
wait 14479   # Wait for process 14479 to complete before continuing
wait         # Wait for all background processes to finish
```

whence   Describe a Shell Command

Syntax (Korn Shell Only)

```
whence [ -v ] command_name
```

Usage

The **whence** command is the Korn Shell version of the **type** command in Bourne Shell. The -v option places the **whence** command in verbose mode, causing the Korn Shell to provide greater detail about the command. The output is different from the Bourne Shell **type** command when the -v option is omitted. In this case, the output is brief and can be used as input to other commands. The **whence** command provides feedback on all types of Shell commands, just as the Bourne Shell **type** command does. This is shown in the following table:

COMMAND TYPE	WHENCE RESPONSE	WHENCE -V RESPONSE
regular UNIX command	full path name of command	additional information about whether the command is a tracked alias
Shell built-in command	just the command name	additional verbiage indicating that the command is built-in
function	just the function name	additional verbiage indicating the name is a function
alias	the value of the alias	additional verbiage indicating the command is an alias
not a command	no response	verbiage indicating command was not found

Example

```
whence whence       # Describe the whence command
whence
whence -v whence    # Tell me more
whence is a built-in command
whence whog         # Describe the whog command
whog
whence -v whog
whog is a function
whence finger
ucb finger
whence -v finger
```

```
finger is an alias for ucb finger
```
whence -v uncle
```
uncle not found
```
whence cat
```
/bin/cat
```
whence -v cat
```
cat is a tracked alias for /bin/cat
```

Appendix F

Nroff and Troff

Documentation is one of the major features of UNIX. Major word-processing and desktop publishing packages such as WordPerfect, Interleaf, and Framemaker are now available on UNIX machines. Since these software tools are not part of UNIX, we'll focus on the documentation facilities that come with UNIX and how the Shell can aid their use.

> In any bureaucracy, paperwork increases as you spend
> more and more time reporting on the less and less you are doing.

In 1975, long before word processing and desktop publishing were performed by personal computers, there lived two commands, **nroff** and **troff**, that could do virtually everything that modern packages could do. **Nroff** formats documentation for the existing ocean of dot-matrix and letter-quality printers; **troff** formats documents for PostScript laser printers and phototypesetters. Using **nroff** and **troff** can be made much easier by the use of Shell. The major documentation commands are shown in Table F.1. Because of the number of commands and terminals that work with these two commands, it is often confusing to get all of the commands put together to generate the correct output. Shell helps eliminate those problems.

Otherwise, formatting documents with **nroff** would be as simple as

```
nroff document_file
```

Usually, however, it takes many parameters and a few input and output filters to format a document correctly. The most frequently used parameters invoke a macro package.

TABLE F.1   Documentation Commands

Command	Description
`checkeq`	check a document's usage of equation macros
`checkmm`	check a document's usage of mm macros
`col`	process reverse line feeds
`cw`	prepare constant-width text for troff
`deroff`	remove nroff/troff macros
`diffmk`	mark differences in two versions of a document
`eqn`	equation preprocessor for troff
`gath`	gather files
`greek`	prepare output for special terminals
`lp`	spool output to printers (System V)
`lpr`	spool output to printers (Berkeley)
`man`	format UNIX manual pages
`mm`	format documents using memorandum macros
`mmt`	typeset documents, viewgraphs, and slides
`neqn`	equation preprocessor for nroff
`nroff`	format documents for ASCII terminal
`ptx`	generate permuted index
`spell`	check spelling of documents
`tbl`	table preprocessor
`troff`	format documents for a phototypesetter

MACRO PACKAGES

There are a number of macro packages designed to handle most documentation problems. These packages are contained in /usr/lib/tmac and /usr/lib/macros. The most common ones are the memorandum macros (**mm** or csh:**ms**) and manual page macros (**man**). The available macro packages are shown in Table F.2. Typically, a separate Shell command is necessary to invoke each different macro package:

```
nroff -mm document    csh: nroff -ms document
nroff -man manpage
```

To speed up loading of the macros and to improve efficiency, use the compacted macros — a "compiled" version of the macros:

```
nroff -cm document        nroff -cs document
nroff -can manpage
```

Documentation problems that couldn't be solved easily with these macro packages required special preprocessors to prepare the input files for **nroff.** Commands were developed to handle tables and equations.

TABLE F.2   Documentation Macro Libraries

Macros	Description
`man`	manual page macros
`mm`	memorandum macros
`mosd`	operations systems deliverable documentation macros
`mptx`	permuted index macros
`ms`	manuscript macros (Berkeley)
`mv`	viewgraph and slide macros
`cm`	compiled memorandum macros

INPUT FILTERS

The commands that preprocess **nroff** files are **eqn, tbl,** and **gath. Eqn** processes equations for mathematical output. **Tbl** creates the nroff macros needed to format tables. And **gath,** which normally works with the remote job entry (RJE) facility, can be used to set keywords, include files, or execute commands and use their output as input to **nroff** or **troff.** Each of these commands expands the capability of **nroff** for text formatting.

Eqn

Eqn preprocesses mathematical equations for **troff.** Its twin, **neqn,** processes equations for **nroff.** They are useful for serious scientists, but hold little value for the average user.

They are invoked as input filters to **nroff** or **troff:**

```
eqn files | troff
neqn files | nroff
```

For the average documentation user, **tbl** and **gath** hold more interest.

Tbl

Tbl takes files of the form shown in Figure F.1 and turns them into usable input for **nroff.** The resulting output from the following command is also shown in the figure.

```
tbl document | nroff
```

To build a command to accurately format all documents regardless of content takes planning. On any system, **tbl** is a hog. It is more efficient to check the file for tables than it is to use **tbl** on all documents. We could use **grep** to check the file:

```
.TS
center tab(:)
l c c c
l n n n.
Sales:January:February:March
_
Southwest:100:1 10:120
Northwest:230: 150: 170
.TE
```

Sales	_January_	_February_	_March_
Southwest	100	110	120
Northwest	230	150	170

Figure F.1   Documentation Example Using tbl Macros

```
# get the names of any files that have tables
if [ -z `grep -l "^.TS" $* | line` ]
then
  nroff -cm $*          # no tables in the file
else
  tbl $* | nroff -cm    # process tables and format file
fi
```

The **grep** takes less time than running **tbl** on every file. It also keeps the user from forgetting to invoke the table preprocessor when required. Both of these advantages make the cost of searching each file for tables an inexpensive proposition.

Gath

Gath gathers information together just like the **send** command, but it doesn't send the information over the RJE. Instead, it puts the output on *stdout*. **Gath** can preprocess text to prompt for keywords, include files, and execute commands.

Keywords are useful when the document doesn't change, but certain key phrases do:

```
~=:FIRST
~=:LAST
~=:ADDRESS
~=:CITYSTZIP
.nf
FIRST LAST
ADDRESS
CITYSTZIP
```

```
.sp
Dear FIRST,
.sp
.fi
. . . letter
```

gath letter | nroff -cm

```
FIRST=Jay
LAST=Arthur
ADDRESS=123 Anystreet
CITYSTZIP=Anytown, AZ 12345
```

Gath will prompt for each keyword, as previously shown, and then substitute them for all occurrences. The keywords can also be supplied on the command line:

**FIRST=Jay LAST=Arthur ADDRESS="123 Anystreet" \
CITYSTZIP="Anytown, AZ 12345" gath letter | nroff -cm**

Gath can also include files in the text:

```
text...
~filename
text...
```

Gath will include *filename* at that point in the text. But **gath** can also execute commands. In the following example, **gath** retrieves a file from SCCS and runs it through **tbl** before inserting the text in the file:

```
text
~!get -p s.tablefile | tbl
text
```

Gath can even include the output from specific commands such as **ls**:

```
text
~!cd;ls -l
text
```

These are trivial examples, but they illustrate the potential for preprocessing **nroff** and **troff** input to allow for more robust documentation. The presence of **gath** commands can also be detected with **grep**:

grep -n "^~" $*

In cases where both **gath** and **tbl** are required as input filters, execute **gath** before **tbl** to ensure that all tables are included with the text before invoking **tbl.**

```
gath $* | tbl | nroff -cm
```

Once the input has been processed correctly, **nroff** or **troff** must be brought into play to format the resulting text in a way that is suitable for the output device.

TERMINAL PREVIEWING OF DOCUMENTS

Because UNIX uses mainly asynchronous communications (except for rare implementations of synchronous support), there are innumerable types of terminals that can be used with UNIX. Video display terminals vary from so-called dumb terminals to workstations. Hardcopy output devices range from dot-matrix and letter-quality printers up through laser printers. These are all available to UNIX and connected as shown in Figure F.2.

Because of the variety of output devices, **nroff** and **troff** use numerous parameters to control their output (see Table F.3). **Nroff** and **troff** also extract a heavy toll from the system when they format a document. In most active UNIX systems,

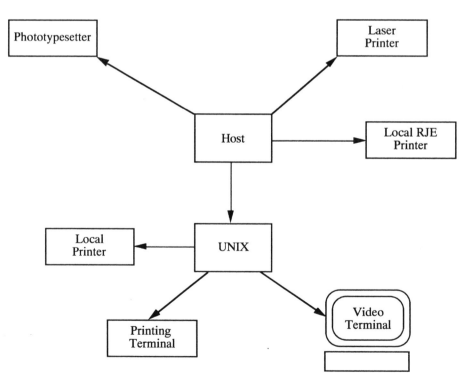

Figure F.2   Printing Options

TABLE F.3   Nroff and Troff Formatting Options

Option	Descriptions
Nroff and Troff	
-i	read standard input
-n*n*	number first page as *n*
-o	print requested pages
-q	use input.output mode of .rd request
-rA*n*	set register A to *n*
-s*n*	stop every *n* pages
-z	print messages generated by .tm requests
-c*m*	include compacted macro library *m*
-k*m*	compact the macros and store in the current directory
-m*m*	include macro library *m*
Nroff Only	
-e	invoke proportional spacing
-h	use tabs to speed output
-l*name*	format output for terminal type *name*
-u*n*	set emboldening factor to *n*

nroff and the screen editors will consume most of the system's resources. All too often, when a user enters an **nroff** command, he or she will forget to enter all of the parameters needed. So they try again and again to get everything "right" for their terminal. In the process, they eat up huge chunks of system resources.

To circumvent this resource drain, it is usually wise to develop Shell commands to handle **nroff** or **troff** output to the various terminal types. The following sections will describe using **nroff** with each terminal type.

Video Display Terminals (VDTs)

VDTs come in two screen widths—80 and 132 characters. To have **nroff** format the output correctly for comfortable viewing, the width and offset options must be set as follows:

```
nroff -rO0 -rW79 document
nroff -rO0 -rW131 document
```

Why are the line widths one less than the maximum length? At the end of each line printed by **nroff** are a carriage return (CR) and a line feed (LF). Most VDTs have what is called a wraparound feature—when a long line is not truncated at the edge of the screen, a line feed is automatically generated and the remainder of the line prints on the next line on the screen. If a line is 80 characters long, a CR would generate a wraparound LF and the LF following would leave a blank line on the screen. Line widths of 79 and 131 seem to work best. Since what people see on the screen should not differ from what ultimately prints on a printer, these width options should be used for all printer output as well.

Emboldening — making text appear darker — is possible with **nroff** and **troff.** **Nroff** emboldens text by overstriking each character as many as four times. There are several ways to embolden text:

```
nroff        mm              nroff
.bd          .B text         \fBtext\fR
text
```

The result of using **nroff** on the following emboldened text is a series of characters and backspaces:

```
\fBuser\fR
u<u<u<us<s<s<se<e<e<er<r<r<r
```

Since most VDTs switch into enhanced print via a control character sequence, all of these backspaces and extra characters are unnecessary and require longer transmission times. Unless the administrators have developed an output filter to handle these special situations, suppress them by using the -u option to eliminate emboldening:

```
nroff -cm -u -rW79 -r00 document
```

This helps speed up the transmission of the formatted document. Most other adjustments to the output are handled with output filters.

Printers

The type of printer can be specified with the -T parameter when printing directly on a given printer (i.e., when not using **lp** or **lpr**):

```
nroff -cm -T630 -rW79 -r08 document
```

This command specifies that the output is a Diablo printer (-T630) and states that the output is to be offset eight spaces to the right (-rO8).

Local line printers can receive output by I/O redirection of the **nroff** output into a device name or a spooler:

```
nroff -cm -rW79 -r08 document > /dev/lp
sh: nroff -cm -rW79 -r08 document | lp
csh: nroff -cm -rW79 -r08 document | lpr
nroff -cm -rW79 -r08 document | opr
```

OUTPUT FILTERS

The most common output filters for **nroff** are **col, pr, sed,** and **uniq.** All four are useful with VDTs. **Col** is also useful with some printers.

Col removes reverse line motions that are used to handle underlining, super-scripts, and subscripts. VDTs and a few line printers cannot handle reverse line motions, so **col** is used to convert reverse line motions into single-line combinations of backspaces and characters. **Col** removes super- and subscripts from **nroff**'s output. The output of any **nroff** command for a VDT should be run through **col:**

```
nroff -cm -rO8 -rW79 document | col
```

The output of **nroff** can be further optimized for screens by use of filters. The most obvious one is **uniq,** which suppresses duplicate lines. Duplicates are most often blank lines at the end of a page. At 1200 baud, a short last page can zip off the screen before the user can read it. To eliminate all but one occurrence of each blank line, use **uniq:**

```
nroff -cm document | col | sed -e "s/\b.//" | uniq
```

Another way to handle the problem is to present only 24 lines at a time and then allow the user to request more information with **pr, pg,** or **more:**

```
nroff -cm document | col | sed -e "s/\b.//" | pr -124 -t -p
nroff -cm document | col | sed -e "s/\b.//" | pg
nroff -cm document | col | sed -e "s/\b.//" | more
```

Pr, pg, or **more** will sound the terminal bell and the user can hit return to view each new section of a formatted document.

PUTTING IT ALL TOGETHER

Customizing document output for a particular terminal can be handled with a variety of input and output filters. The command line for each terminal type looks like this:

```
input filters | nroff [macros] [parameters] | output filters
```

Putting all of these filters together requires changes to /etc/profile and the creation of a new command that we call **output.** First, /etc/profile should ask for the terminal type and assign it to the variable *TERM*:

```
echo "Enter Terminal Type: "
read TERM
case $TERM in
    vt100|5420|tv970)
        tabs
        ;;
    lp|620|630|laser)
        ;;
    ti|700|745)
        tabs
        ;;
    *)
        echo "Setting up default terminal"
        ;;
esac
```

Users will be prompted for this information when they log in. The output command can then use $TERM to make intelligent default choices for **nroff.** It should check for tables, equations, and commands for **gath.** Next, it should invoke output filters for the terminal type:

```
# Output file(s)
if [ $# -gt 1 ]     # Check parameter count
then
# Save the parameters entered by the user
    while [ `echo $1 | cut -c1` -eq "-" ]     # Flags
    do
      parameters="${parameters} $1"     # Save flag
      shift                             # Delete flag
    done
# Check the files and save their names
    while [ "$1" ]               # While more arguments
    do
      if [ -r $1 ]               # Readable file?
      then
        files="${files} $1"     # Save file name
      else
        echo "file $1 not found"
      fi
      shift                     # Delete argument
    done
# Determine the input filters
    tblcnt=`grep -c "^.TS" $* | cut -f2 -d: | sort -nr | line`
    gathcnt=`grep -c "^~" $* | cut -f2 -d: | sort -nr | line`
    if [ $tblcnt -gt 0 ]
    then
      inputcnt=`expr ${inputcnt:=0} + 1`
```

```
    fi
    if [ $gathcnt -gt 0 ]
    then
       inputcnt=`expr ${inputcnt:=0} + 2`
    fi
    case $inputcnt in
    0)
       inputfilter="cat $files | "
       ;;
    1)
       inputfilter="tbl $files | "
       ;;
    2)
       inputfilter="gath $files | ""
       ;;
    3)
       inputfilter="gath $files | tbl | ""
       ;;
    *)
       echo "Error in output: filters $inputfilter"
    esac
    case $TERM in
    vt100|5420|tv970)
       parameters="$parameters -u -rO0 -rW79 "
       outputfilter=" | col | sed -e "s/\b.//g" | uniq"
       ;;
    lp|620|630)
       parameters="-rO8 -rW79 $parameters "
       outputfilter=""
       ;;
    ti|700|745)
       parameters="-rO0 -rW79 $parameters "
       outputfilter=" | col "
       ;;
    esac
    eval "${inputfilter} nroff ${macros:="-cm"} ${parameters} \
       {outputfilter}"
else
    echo "No files specified"
fi
```

The actual makeup of the **output** command will vary with the type of terminals in use. But the advantages of typing the following simple command to print files should be obvious:

```
output document
```

Once formatted, documents can be spooled for output to any number of devices or line printers.

SPOOLING DOCUMENTS

A line printer (**lp** or csh: **lpr**) spooler was added to UNIX Version 4 and later versions. **Lp** allows the system administrator to define the types of printers on the system. Each user can spool files to a printer without actually logging on, and the printout can be picked up later at the user's convenience. **Lp** can even send the user mail when the file finishes printing.

To use **lp,** the printers have to be defined and labeled by the system administrator. Then, documents can easily be spooled by creating a command to make a few decisions for the user. The spooler must decide whether to print an existing file or to execute a command and print its output. Using **lp** (sh) or **lpr** (csh), documents can be formatted with the **output** or **pr** command, and printed by the line printer:

```
output file | lp        output file | lpr
pr -o8 file | lp        pr file | lpr -i8
                        troff -t troff_file | lpr -t
```

In the first example, the **output** command will format the document file and spool the resulting file. In the second example, **pr** will format the text file and then print it, indented by eight spaces. The last (csh) example formats the document using **troff**; **lpr** then converts the **troff** (-t) input into PostScript for the receiving printer. Formatting requests that are more complex than those provided by **output** and **pr** will require the use of other miscellaneous filters.

To check on the status of print jobs, just enter the command **lpstat** (csh: **lpq**). This command checks the queues and lets you know if your job has finished printing.

MISCELLANEOUS DOCUMENTATION FILTERS

Figures F.3 and F.4 show the various filters available for handling documents with **nroff** and **troff.**

Troff uses the same input filters as **nroff** with one exception: **cw,** the constant width preprocessor. **Cw** uses some additional macros to handle special output requirements. Each of these filters is handy for special circumstances, but most users will rarely need them.

MISCELLANEOUS COMMANDS

There are a number of commands that work with **nroff** text: **man, mm, mmt,** and **deroff. Man** formats manual pages using a unique set of macros. It executes **nroff** with a variety of options to format the output. **Mm** invokes **nroff** using the

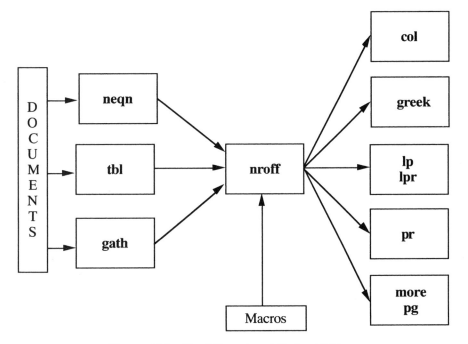

Figure F.3   Nroff Input and Output Filters

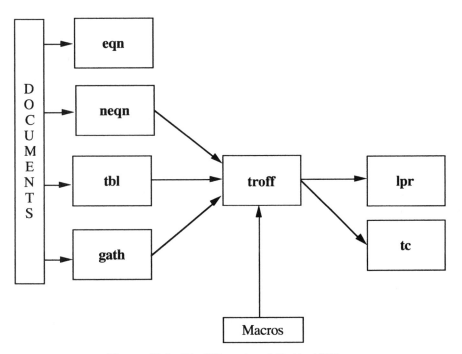

Figure F.4   Troff Input and Output Filters

memorandum macros (System V). It can do much of what the previously developed Shell commands, such as **output,** can do, but it lacks the robustness available with the Shell. **Mmt** typesets slides and viewgraphs (System V). **Deroff** removes all **nroff** and **troff** macros from a file, which occasionally can be useful.

In Berkeley systems, the formatting commands are **ms** and **me. Ms** handles standard text processing. **Me** provides multicolumn capabilities for formal papers to academia or for publication.

Document Analysis

Spell is one of the most useful document processing tools. It finds most of the spelling errors in a document. **Spell** produces its list of errors one word per line. If there are extensive errors, the list will scroll off the screen quickly. A solution is to print the output of **spell** horizontally:

```
spell document | pr -4
```

The Writer's Workbench facility also provides some excellent tools for examining and improving documents. Commands such as **style** and **prose** can be beneficial to writers. Shell commands can be created to run all of these commands against a document and print or store the results. These Shells should be created as needed.

Let's use Shell to build an analyzer of our own. One of the things I find most useful is to know what the keywords are in a document—those that are repeated most frequently. These words often capture the true content of a document. How could we do this using Shell? First, using **deroff**, we would want to remove all of the **nroff** or **troff** formatting commands:

```
deroff $1
```

Then, we would want to transform the file in the following ways:

- Convert uppercase to lowercase (so that **Troff** and **troff** would be counted as the same word).
- Convert blanks and tabs to newlines (to create one word per line).
- Convert all punctuation into newlines (so that "sentence." and "sentence" will be counted as the same word).

We can accomplish all of this using **tr:**

```
deroff $1 | \
tr [A-Z \t#',.;:()] \
   [a-z\012\012\012\012\012\012\012\012\012\012]
```

Next, we can select just the words (using **grep**), **sort** the word list in descending numeric order, and then count words using **uniq:**

```
deroff $1 | \
tr [A-Z \t#',.;:()] \
   [a-z\012\012\012\012\012\012\012\012\012\012] | \
grep [a-z] | sort -nr | uniq -c
```

If we executed this command, we'd get a listing of keywords that includes the following:

```
127 the
86 a
32 an
31 shell
27 programming
```

Words such as *the* and *a* are the most common words in the English language. We might want to use **sed** to eliminate these words. This will help illuminate the true keywords. Similarly, the numbers are only useful to get the file in order. We can use **cut** to eliminate them:

```
deroff $1 | \
tr [A-Z \t#',.;:()] \
   [a-z\012\012\012\012\012\012\012\012\012\012] | \
grep [a-z] | sort -nr | uniq -c | \
cut -c6- | sed -f conjunctions
```

The file, conjunctions, would contain entries for all filler words—*a, an, and,* and *the*. It would tell **sed** to delete them as follows:

```
/^a$/d
/^and$/d
/^but$/d
/^the$/d
. . .
```

With all of the filler words out of the way, we might want to capture just the first ten keywords. We could use **head** to do this for us:

```
deroff $1 | \
tr [A-Z \t#',.;:()] \
   [a-z\012\012\012\012\012\012\012\012\012\012] | \
grep [a-z] | sort -nr | uniq -c | \
cut -c6- | sed -f conjunctions | \
head
```

Using this command on this chapter, we might get the following results:

```
document
documents
nroff
documentation
troff
shell
printer
terminal
```

From these results you'll notice that **keyword** cannot differentiate between the singular and plural words (*document* and *documents*). To overcome this, we could write another Shell program, **plural,** to extract words that end in *s*:

```
# plural
cat $* > /tmp/tmp$$
sed -e "s/s$//" /tmp/tmp$$ | sort | uniq -d > /tmp/tmp1$$
# Find plurals
if [ -s /tmp/tmp1$$ ]     # Plurals were found!
then     # Create sed file to delete them
  sed -e "s/^/\//" -e "s/$/s\/d/" /tmp/tmp1$$ > /tmp/tmp2$$
else
  cat /tmp/tmp$$
fi
rm -f /tmp/tmp*$$
```

These commands, **keyword** and **plural,** can dramatically aid the development of an index for a book, or a reference index for an information archive. First you figure out what is most important and then you combine them into a beginning table of contents:

```
for file in chapter*
do
  keyword $file >> /tmp/tmp$$
  sort /tmp/tmp$$ > index
  rm /tmp/tmp$$
done
```

This is just a simple example of the ways that documents can be examined and evaluated using Shell. I hope it has opened your eyes to the possibilities inherent in the flexibility of the Shell.

Shell provides some excellent tools for handling documents and preparing them for output on the wide variety of devices available to UNIX. Connecting all of these tools can improve efficiency and reliability: Users type one simple command and it determines how to format each document. Commands can easily be created for each set of **nroff** or **troff** macros.

Documentation is one of the strengths of UNIX. Full-screen word processors have largely displaced **nroff** and **troff,** but there are still hundreds of thousands of **nroff** users who need simple interfaces to its facilities. Use the Shell to fill those needs.

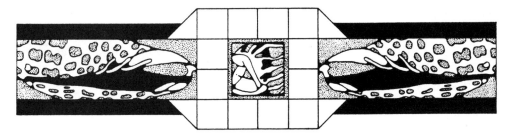

Appendix G

Sed Reference

Sed, which stands for stream editor, is a noninteractive editor that is used in Shell programs to filter information in a file, often in a pipeline. **Sed** is modeled after the **ed** command, and they share a common command set. **Ed** is the old UNIX line editor, which has been replaced by more modern editors like vi and emacs and is rarely used these days. But its sibling, **sed**, is still a useful tool in Shell programming and deserves proper coverage.

Sed works much like any other editor with one exception. It takes commands like any other editor, and acts on the file being processed based on those commands, but with the exception that the original file is not changed. The modified data is placed on the standard output as a new file. For this reason, **sed** is often considered a filter. This exception differentiates it from most editors, which take action upon the original file and permanently alter it in the process.

The syntax of the **sed** command can be summarized as follows:

```
sed -n 'edit_command' [input_files...]
sed [-n] [-e edit_command] ... -f [edit_script_file] \
  [input_files... ]
```

with the options defined as follows:

-n   Suppress printing of result lines.

-e   Use the *edit_commands* as the edit script.

-f   Use the edit commands stored in *edit_script_file* as the edit script.

Note that in the first form, no -e is needed because only a single edit command is provided. If more than a single edit command is provided, then the -e option (or better, the -f option) is needed to specify each command. It is best to enclose all **sed** commands in single quotes because many **sed** command characters overlap with Shell special characters and metacharacters.

The **sed** command operates by reading a line from the input files and applying the list of edit commands to the line in the order that they are written. The edited line is then copied to the standard output automatically. Since all output is directed to the standard output, the results often are redirected to a file using >. Don't, of course, redirect the output to the file name that you are using for input. If your intention is to replace the original file, use a temporary file for the output of **sed** and copy it over the original when the edit session is complete.

SED COMMANDS

Now that we understand how **sed** works in general, we need to look more closely at how to form **sed** commands. A series of **sed** commands is often referred to as a script. These commands instruct **sed** to perform some editing action. A script has a single edit command per line, each of which has the following syntax:

```
[line_range] [edit_command] [command_arguments]
```

where *line_range* specifies a range of lines (in the form line_num1, line_num2) relative to the start of the file, which are to have the edit command applied. If a single line number occurs, then the command applies only to that line number. The line range can also be replaced by a regular expression pattern (enclosed in /reg_exp1/,/reg_exp2/) that is used to match the line. If the line contains the pattern, then the edit command is applied. If the line does not match the pattern, then it is placed on the standard output in its original form (as long as no other edit commands apply). If a pair of regular expressions are provided, then they define a range of lines from the first line that matches reg_exp1 to the next line that matches reg_exp2. It is even possible to mix line numbers and regular expressions to define a range of lines. Note that **sed** supports regular expressions. If no line number or match pattern is provided, then by default the command is applied to all lines.

SPECIFYING MULTIPLE EDIT COMMANDS IN SED

There are times when you may want to perform several edit commands on each line of input. In order to do this, you must specify multiple edit commands in one of the two following ways:

- On the **sed** command line using the -e option before each edit command. For example, the syntax would be `sed -e 'sed_command1' -e 'sed_command2' ... filenames`.
- In a file listing each command on a separate line. Specify this file to **sed** using the -f option. The syntax in this case would be `sed -f sedscript_file filenames.`

If your script requires several commands or if you will need to run the script several times, it is easiest to use the file (-f) option. This makes modifying the **sed** script simple and reusable. Each method is demonstrated in the examples that follow in subsequent sections.

SED COMMAND LIST

The following table contains the most common **sed** commands. A brief discussion of most of the commands follows, complete with examples.

Sed Commands

COMMAND	DESCRIPTION
a *append_data*	Append the *append_data* to the end of each selected line. The append data is taken to be all data starting with \\ to the last row that does not contain a \\.
b label	Branch to the command with : label.
c *change_data*	Change selected lines to *change_data* in the same manner that was discussed in a \\.
d	Delete the selected lines and go to the next. No output is produced for this line.
g	Replace the current line with the contents of the hold buffer.
h	Copy the current line to the hold buffer.
i *insert_data*	Insert the *insert_data* before the selected lines.
l	List the selected line.
p	Print the line (used with the -n option to print only selected lines). Note that **p** normally is not needed.
q	Quit the edit session.
r *file_name*	Read the *file_name* and place its contents in output.

s/*reg_exp1*/*new*/*func*	Substitute the pattern specified in the regular expression *reg_exp1* with the *new*. If *func* is specified, then it has the following values and meaning:
	    func = g means do a global replace on all occurrences
	    func = p means to print the occurrence
	    func = w means to write the occurrence to a file
	    func = *n* (where *n* is an integer between 1 and 512) means replace the *n*th occurrence of the regular expression

t label	Jump to label if substitution is made to the current line. If no target is provided, then jump to the end of the script.
w *file_name*	Write the current line to file *file_name*.
x	Exchange contents of current line and hold buffer.
y/*str1*/*str2*	Replace all occurrences of character found in string str1 with characters found in string str2. Note that the length of str1 and str2 must be the same.
=	Print current input line number on standard output.
!*sed_cmd*	Perform the command **sed_command** only if the current line does not match the pattern or line range.
: label	A label definition for **b** and **t** commands.
{ }	Command grouper — consider all commands between { } to be a group.

SELECTING USING SED

Sed can be used to select certain lines from a file in a variety of ways. In order to do this, we utilize the -n option which suppresses output of each line and instead outputs only selected lines using the **p** command. The following example will output lines 20 through 30 of the input file into the file new_file:

```
sed -n '20,30p' > new_file
```

Of course, you can use the -n option in conjunction with **p** to select lines using a regular expression, as shown in the following example:

```
sed -n '/^..X/p' file1
```

which will print all lines in the file that have an *X* as the third character on the line. You might note that this allows **sed** to act just as **grep** does, printing matched lines on the standard output. Any regular expression pattern can be used, which makes this method of selecting lines very powerful.

SUBSTITUTING USING SED

The easiest way to understand **sed** is to look at some examples. This section shows some examples of using the substitution command in a **sed** script. Following are some examples with a brief description.

```
sed 's/korn/Korn/g' chapter5
```

The preceding statement will replace all occurrences (based on the g option) of the string korn with the string Korn for all lines in chapter5. Note that without the g option, the substitution will occur on the first occurrence in the line only. Each line is output to the standard output.

```
sed '1,10s/korn/KORN/g' chapter1 chapter2 chapter 3 chapter 4 \
    chapter5
```

The preceding **sed** command will replace all occurrences of korn with KORN in the first ten lines of each of the files chapter1 through chapter5.

```
sed '/^FILEINFO/s/filename = Z.*\.dat/filename = NONE/'
```

The **sed** command just shown uses a regular expression pattern to select lines. Any lines that start with the string FILEINFO will have the substitution command executed. The substitution command replaces the first string that matches the string "filename = Z *something* .dat" with the string "filename = NONE". For example, the string "filename = ZEBRA.dat" would be replaced with the string "filename = NONE".

```
sed `s/ */ /g'
```

This **sed** command will replace all occurrences of two or more spaces by a single space on all lines in the file. Likewise, the substitution command can be used to remove matching characters from a file. For example:

```
sed -e `/price/s/^...//' -e `/budget/s/^...//'
```

would remove the first three characters of any line that contained the word *price* or *budget*.

DELETING LINES USING SED

To delete lines using **sed**, the **d** command is used in conjunction with a line range. Each line that matches the line range, which of course may be a regular expression, is deleted. It is not printed on the standard output and the next line is read. Following are a few examples of using the delete command:

```
sed `1,5d'                 # Delete lines 1 through 5
sed `/^$/d'                # Remove all blank lines from the file
sed `/^BEGIN/,/^END/d'     # Delete the lines between the line
                           # that starts with BEGIN
                           # and the next line that starts with END
sed `/[A-Za-z]/d'          # Delete all lines that contain any
                           # alphabetic characters
```

APPENDING OR INSERTING LINES USING SED

In order to append lines after a particular line, we can use the **a** command. If we wish to insert lines before a particular line, the **i** command does the job. They both work in the same way. The data to be appended or inserted is placed on the next line following the \ character. All lines that follow the \ are considered part of the append or insert. If multiple lines are to be part of the append or insert, then each line except the final line must end with a backslash character. Lines that are to have data inserted before or appended to are selected in the normal way using a line range. If no range is specified, then the data is inserted or appended to all lines as expected. Note that since the appended lines need to appear on the line following the \, it is easiest to use a file to store the commands in conjunction with the **sed** -f option.

```
cat sedcommand                 # Show the command file
a\
***
sed -f sedcommand namefile     # Add a new line *** after each
                               # line in namefile
Ted
***
Jay
***
Sam
***
Will
***
```

WRITING LINES TO A FILE USING SED

In addition to writing lines to the standard output, it is also possible to write selected lines or substituted lines to a particular file using the **w** command. Numerous files can be used. Note that in order to write lines that have been substituted, we use the w option at the end of the substitute command, as shown in the following examples:

```
sed -e '/UNITED STATES/w usa.data' \
   -e '/UNITED STATES/!w other.data'
```

This **sed** command essentially splits the file based on a pattern matching condition. All lines that contain the string "UNITED STATES" are written to the file usa.data; all the other lines are written to a file called other.data. Of course, any line_range specification could be made. All of the lines in the file are also placed on the standard output as would be expected.

```
sed 's/UNITED STATES/USA/gw usa.data'
```

This **sed** command would read a file and substitute any occurrence of UNITED STATES with USA and write the substituted line in the file usa.data as well as on the standard output.

Appendix H

Awk Reference

Awk is a general-purpose pattern scanning and processing language that can handle a wide variety of filtering, transforming, and reporting tasks. While it can perform many of the tasks that are done by other UNIX tools, such as **grep** and **sed,** it can also do other more complex tasks. Many of its constructs are taken from the C language; other parts of the language seem much like **sed.** It is a fairly robust language complete with variables, arrays, looping commands, and much more. **Awk** has no specified task, as many other UNIX tools do, but instead provides a flexible way for you to build a tool that solves the problem at hand without the complexities of a language such as C.

This appendix introduces a large portion of the **awk** programming language— enough to make it a useful tool—but does not attempt an exhaustive survey of **awk. Awk** comes in two flavors on some UNIX implementations—the original **awk** and a new and improved **awk** for the future, called **nawk**. Eventually **nawk** will replace **awk** on UNIX implementations where both exist. **Nawk** provides new features and functions. This reference covers **awk**, but it does not cover some of the newer features found in **nawk**. If you have **nawk** on your system, you may want to explore its extra features if you are writing larger and more complex **awk** programs. For more information about **awk** and **nawk**, see your manual pages.

AWK SYNTAX

The **awk** command has the following syntax:

```
awk [-Ffield_sep] 'program' filenames ...
```

or

```
awk [-Ffield_sep] -f program_file filenames ...
```

where *program* is the actual awk program code and *filenames* is the name of the input files to be processed by the program. In the second form of the command, the program can be read from a program file, which is recommended for more complex awk programs because it allows for reusability and makes modification of your awk program simple and straightforward. This syntax is much like **sed** syntax, with the major difference being what is contained in the program portion. In **sed** these were edit commands; in **awk** they are programming commands. Commands are discussed in detail in the next sections. The -F option is used to specify a field separator character. **Awk** uses this field, if present, as a means to determine how to divide lines into fields. If it is not present, a space character is assumed. The meaning of this will become clear as we discuss how **awk** works.

AWK MECHANICS

The **awk** command operates by reading a line from the input files and applying the list of program commands to the line in the order that they are written. Each program command has the syntax:

    [*pattern*] [*{action}* ...]

where *pattern* is a matching pattern and *action* is some **awk** command(s) that gets executed when the pattern matches the current line. Each input file is processed in order a line at a time. Note that any action performed does not alter the original file. The matching pattern and the action are both optional. If a pattern is not used, then every line of input is considered a match and the corresponding action is taken. If no action is specified, then the line is simply placed on the standard output. While this action is very similar to **sed**, note that lines are not automatically placed on the standard output after an awk action is performed. **Awk** provides a command called **print** to allow output of specified information on the standard output.

AWK FIELDS

As **awk** reads input lines from the file list, the line is automatically divided into fields for more refined processing capabilities. Fields are defined based on the field separator character (specified with the -F option), which defaults to a space. Each field is assigned a field identifier with the names $1, $2, $3 . . . $n. Do not confuse the $ with the Shell representation for variables. In **awk**, variables are not preceded by a $—only field names are. Now that the line has been divided into fields, each field can be used and manipulated independently using **awk** commands. For an example of field assignment, consider the following file:

```
cat phone_list
Burns,Ted:Denver: 303-747-8976
Hart,George:Seattle: 206-756-8907
Newberry,Sandy:Tippany: 435-356-9345
Groggy,Sam:Los Angeles: 394-987-6390
```

If our field separator was specified as a colon (-F:), there would be three fields created for each line as it was read — $1 would contain the name, $2 would contain a location, and $3 would contain the phone number. In addition, each time a line is separated into fields, a built-in variable called *NF* is set to the number of fields on the line being processed. Another default field action in **awk** is the assignment of the entire line to the field identifier $0. Referencing $0 in an action statement references the entire current input line.

We can now access the fields of each line independently, as shown in this simple **awk** example, which would print just the name and phone number from the file shown previously:

```
awk -F: '{ print $1 , $3 }' phone_list
Burns,Ted 303-747-8976
Hart,George 206-756-8907
Newberry,Sandy 435-356-9345
Groggy,Sam 394-987-6390
```

SELECTING LINES FOR PROCESSING — AWK PATTERNS

Line selection in **awk** is an extension of the regular expression capabilities found in **sed**. In addition to being able to match particular lines or ranges of lines using regular expressions, **awk** provides the ability to compare information found in the fields of the line in a wide variety of ways. Finally, **awk** provides two special patterns — BEGIN and END — which are used for further control. In summary, there are three types of pattern matching capabilities in **awk:**

- regular expression patterns
- relational expression patterns
- BEGIN and END patterns

The power of these pattern matching types is enhanced by the ability to specify compound patterns using the Boolean operations (&&, ||, !) and range patterns. These can be summarized as:

```
pattern_expression && pattern_expression      (compound and)
pattern_expression || pattern_expression      (compound or)
pattern_expression, pattern_expression        (range expression)
!patterns                                     (not expression)
```

where pattern_expression is either a regular expression or a relational expression.

Regular Expression Patterns

Regular expression patterns are specified as in **sed** and **ed** by enclosing them between forward slashes:

```
/regular_expression/
```

For example, the following **awk** command would select lines that contain the string USA from the file geo_data. Note that in this simple form **awk** reproduces the line on standard output and acts like the UNIX egrep filter since no action pattern was specified.

```
awk '/USA/' geo_data
```

Of course, all regular expressions are legal, as in the following example that prints all lines that start with the word *TOTAL*:

```
awk '/^TOTAL/' geo_data
```

Relational Expression Patterns

In addition to matching any regular expression pattern found anywhere on a line, **awk** also allows matching to portions of the line using fields, variables, and relational operators. The following example checks to see if field 1 is equal to the string Chapter1.

```
awk '$1 == "Chapter 1"'
```

If this is true, then the line is printed. The relational operators are summarized in the following table, which shows examples of using the various relational operators in a relational expression pattern:

Awk Relational Operators

OPERATOR	DESCRIPTION	EXAMPLE
= =	equality operator	`$1 = = "Fred"`
		`$4 != NF`
<	less than	`$1 < $3`
<=	less than or equal to	`$2 <= $1 + NR`
>	greater than	`$10 > 100`
>=	greater than or equal to	`mycount >= $5 + 1`
!=	not equal to	`$7 != length($1)`
~	contains regular expressions	`$4 ~ /LOC/`
		`$9 ~ /[A-Z]/`
!~	does not contain regular expression	`$9 !~/..[a-z]/`

As you can see from the examples, the relational expressions are robust and can include more than just field names and the relational operators. They can contain variables, **awk** built-in commands (such as the length command), constants, and regular expressions, as well as awk expressions (i.e., $5 + 1). These expressions work just like regular expression patterns; if the relational pattern expression is true, then the line matches and the related awk action is performed. Clearly these enhanced abilities provide a great deal of power for selecting rows to be processed in **awk.** When taken in conjunction with the regular expression pattern matching, **awk** provides a very flexible and powerful toolset.

Next is an example of using relational patterns to select rows in **awk.** The example prints rows only where the line is not blank and the first field has a value greater than 100:

```
awk '($0 !~ /^$/) && ($1 > 100) { print $0 }' dept_stats
```

The relational expression $0 !~/^$/ ensures that the line is not blank; the ($1 > 100) ensures that field 1 is greater than 100.

BEGIN and END Patterns

The BEGIN and END patterns are two special patterns in **awk** that allow actions to be taken before any lines are processed (BEGIN) and after all the lines have been processed (END). BEGIN must be the first pattern in the list of patterns and END must be the last. This is shown as:

```
BEGIN { action }
pattern { action )
...
END {action }
```

The **BEGIN** command is often used to set initial values for variables that are going to be used in your program, to print headings at the top of a report, or to set the internal field separator (same as -F on the command line). Any type of setup action can be performed in the BEGIN action. The following example sets the field separator, stored in the **awk** variable *FS*, to a colon (:) and prints an informational message about the file name being processed using the **awk** built-in variable *FILENAME*.

```
awk 'BEGIN { FS=":"; print "File name", FILENAME}' file1 file2
```

Likewise, **END** performs tasks that are often done after all processing is complete. This might include final calculations, totals that were accumulated while processing, or any other chore that must occur after all lines have been processed. The following example prints the number of records processed. This is stored in the **awk** variable *NR*. The example shown here is a simple way to count the number of lines in a file much like the **wc** command in UNIX Shell.

```
awk 'END { print NR}' geo_data
```

PERFORMING TASKS IN AWK – CREATING ACTIONS

Recall that an **awk** command has the form:

[*pattern*] [{*action*} ...]

Now that we have seen how to specify line matching patterns, we need to take a closer look at the action portion of the **awk** command. An awk action consists of one or more statements. Statements cause some form of action to occur on the current input line. This could be a very simple action, such as printing the line as we saw in some examples in the previous section, or very complex. Each statement is separated by a semicolon, a newline, or a right brace. A statement can be any of the following:

FLOW CONTROL STATEMENTS	DESCRIPTION

`if ( conditional )`
`  { statement_list1 }`
`[ else {statement_list2} ]`
	If conditional is true, then perform the actions specified in the statement list1; otherwise, perform the actions specified in statement_list2 if specified.

`while ( conditional )` `{statement_list}`	While conditional expression is true, perform statement_list.

`for ( int_expr ; condi-`
`tional_expr; ctrl_expr )`
`{ statement_list }`
	Perform the initial expression, init_expr, then execute statement_list while conditional_expr is true. After each execution of statement_list, perform control expression ctrl_expr.

`break`	Break from the containing loop and continue with the next statement.
`continue`	Go to the next iteration of the containing loop without executing the remaining statements in the loop.
`next`	Skip remaining patterns on this input line.
`exit`	Skip the rest of the input and go to the END pattern if one exists. Then exit the awk program.

PRINT CONTROL STATEMENTS	DESCRIPTION
`print [ expression_list ]` `[ >filename ]`	Print the expression list on standard output unless redirected to filename. Printed variables must be separated by a comma to ensure that the output field separator is used.

`printf format`
`[ , expression_list ]`
`[ >filename ]`
	Like the C programming language printf statement. Allows printed output to be formatted. Printed on standard output unless otherwise redirected to filename.

ASSIGNMENT STATEMENT	DESCRIPTION
`variable = awk_expression`	Assign variable the value of the awk_expression.

Awk statements contain expressions that assume string or numeric values and are comprised of **awk** variables combined with the operators, **awk** built-in functions, and built-in variables, as well as string and numeric constants.

AWK VARIABLES

Awk allows for the definition of variables. This provides a great deal of power and flexibility in the awk language. Variable names are formed with letters, numbers, and the underscore character. An alphabetic character must be the first character in the variable name. The variables can be of either string or numeric type. The type is implied from its usage as is done in the UNIX Shell. If you use the assignment operator to assign a string to a variable, then the type of that variable is an implied string type. If you assign a number, then the variable is assumed numeric. Note that there is no $ preceding **awk** variables. You can use variables, as in any other programming language, to hold information that you will need for processing later. This might be previous values of fields or a sum of fields over a range of lines.

As an example, consider the following awk program that reads a file and eliminates duplicate adjacent lines from the file. This is like the UNIX Shell **uniq** command. This is done by storing the value of the line in a variable named *prev*, which is then compared to the next line.

```
cat awk_prog
BEGIN {prev=""}
{ if ($0 != prev) {print $0}}
{prev=$0}
```

To run the program we use the following command

```
awk -f awk_prog geo_data
```

The output lines will be all the unique lines in the file geo_data.

Built-In Variables in Awk

Awk provides a number of built-in variables that store a wide range of information while your program is executing. We have already been introduced to a several of these variables. The variable *FS* holds the field separator character that is used by **awk** to divide the input line into fields. The *NR* variable holds the number of lines that have been processed by the current awk program. These are just two of the variables available in **awk.** These variables can be accessed and changed by your **awk** program as needed. Following is a list of all of the **awk** built-in variables and the value that they contain.

Built-in Awk Variables

VARIABLE NAME	DESCRIPTION
FS	Field separator character for input lines. This value defaults to tab and space if not set.
NR	Number of input lines processed by program.
NF	Number of fields in the current input line.
FILENAME	Name of the current input file.
OFMT	Default format for output numbers.
OFS	Output field separator. When fields are output by **awk** this value is used to separate them. The default is a space.
ORS	Output record separator. Value used to separate records when output by **awk.** This value defaults to a newline character.
RS	Input line separator. The value used to identify new lines on the input file. The default value for this is a newline character.

Field Names as Variables

Fields are assigned to numeric field numbers $1 . . . n. The $ is used in **awk** to define field names, which are a special form of variables. Field variables can be used just like any other type of variable in **awk.** They can be assigned values, used in expressions, and created. Using fields as variables is a very powerful feature of **awk.** This allows fields to be added or removed from input lines or simply rearranged. If a new field is created, its default position, when the line is output, is at the end of the line.

The following example shows how a new field can be added to a line. In addition, fields $2 and $3 have their position rearranged. The file contains the following fields: the account number, the number of phones at the company location, a company name, the type of phones used, and the number of employees. The field separator is a colon (:). We want to add two new fields. First, we wish to add a salesperson to each account. This is based on the first letter of the account number. Second, we want to add an indicator field that shows whether the account may be in need of new phones. If the number of phones is less than the number of employees, then we set the indicator to "Y". Finally, the company name and the number of phones fields have the position swapped. Our file looks like this before we start:

```
cat account_list
C13789:38:BIGNAME PRODUCTIONS:STANDARD:29
C67890:110:BIGSHOT OIL:SLICK:150
E45890:76:NEAR ECSTACY:STANDARD:37
E23789:200:WAYOUT WILLIE BURGERS:PORTABLE:139
E34278:10:CLYDE BASS GUITARS:STANDARD:15
G22410:4:SECOND HAND BAGELS:PORTABLE:23
G44890:310:SPACE WALKS INC:RED:110
```

The awk program to accomplish the tasks just outlined is shown next. Comment lines are placed in awk programs by using the # character to indicate the start of the comment.

```
cat awkprog
# Assign the input and output field separators
BEGIN {{FS=":"}; {OFS=":"}}
# Next three action statements assign the sales person
{ if ($1 ~/^C/) {$6="ALFRED"}}
{ if ($1 ~/^E/) {$6="MAGGIE"}}
{ if ($1 ~/^G/) {$6="DAWN"}}
{ if ($1 !~/^[C,E,G]/) {$6="UNKNOWN"}}
# Now let's determine if our potential sales indicator should be
# set
{ if ($2 < $5) {$7="Y"} else {$7="N"}}
# Output the fields in the desired order, commas cause fields to
# separate by OFS
{print $1,$3,$2,$4,$5,$6,$7}
```

After running the awk program, the file has been transformed to:

```
awk -f awkprog account_list
C13789:BIGNAME PRODUCTIONS:38:STANDARD:29:ALFRED:N
C67890:BIGSHOT OIL:110:SLICK:150:ALFRED:Y
E45890:NEAR ECSTACY:76:STANDARD:37:MAGGIE:N
E23789:WAYOUT WILLIE BURGERS:200:PORTABLE:139:MAGGIE:N
E34278:CLYDE BASS GUITARS:10:STANDARD:15:MAGGIE:Y
G22410:SECOND HAND BAGELS:4:PORTABLE:23:DAWN:Y
G44890:SPACE WALKS INC:310:RED:110:DAWN:N
```

Array Variables in Awk

Awk provides one-dimensional arrays to improve the language's flexibility and processing power. Arrays do not need to be declared in any special way. To utilize arrays in **awk**, you simply assign a value to an array element. The values contained in array elements can be either numeric or string data. Elements are referenced by using the syntax:

```
array_name[index]
```

where *index* may be either numeric or string. There is no set size for an array in **awk.** The size of an array is limited only by the amount of memory on your machine. It continues to grow as new elements are assigned.

Array elements can be accessed directly by using the index to the array element or sequentially by using a modified version of the for loop. The syntax is

```
for (var_name in array_name) statement_list
```

where *var_name* is a valid **awk** variable name and *array_name* is the name used when assigning values to the array elements. All statements contained in *statement_list* are executed in order. Each array index (not the element) is assigned to *var_name* until the end of the array is reached.

The following example shows a simple array populated for use as a verification check. For each line read, the fourth field is checked to be sure that it contains a value stored in the verification array. A running total of the number of each type of phone found is also kept and printed at the end.

```
cat awkprog
# Assign the input field separator and array variables
BEGIN {{FS=":"}
     phone["STANDARD"]
     phone["SLICK"]
     phone["PORTABLE"] }
# Check each input and assure that the phone type is found in the
# array phone
# If the type is not valid then print an error message
# If the line matches a valid type then count the number of
# occurrences
{ found = 0 }
{ for (type in phone) { if ($4 == type) {print $0; found=1; \
  phone[type]++}}}
{ if (found != 1) {print "Line",NR,"has an invalid phone type", \
  $4} }
# Print the occurrences of each phone type
END{ for (type in phone) print "Type", type, "had", phone[type],\
  "occurrences"}
```

Running this against the account file from the previous example yields the following:

```
awk -f awkprog2 account_list
C13789:38:BIGNAME PRODUCTIONS:STANDARD:29
C67890:110:BIGSHOT OIL:SLICK:150
E45890:76:NEAR ECSTACY:STANDARD:37
E23789:200:WAYOUT WILLIE BURGERS:PORTABLE:139
E34278:10:CLYDE BASS GUITARS:STANDARD:15
G22410:4:SECOND HAND BAGELS:PORTABLE:23
Line 7 has an invalid phone type RED
Type PORTABLE had 2 occurrences
Type SLICK had 1 occurrences
Type STANDARD had 3 occurrences
```

Awk Operators

The relational operators were presented previously; the remaining operators are shown in the following table. Note that many of the operators are taken directly from the C language.

Awk Operators

OPERATOR	DESCRIPTION
+	binary arithmetic addition
-	binary arithmetic subtraction
*	binary arithmetic multiplication
/	integer division
%	remainder operator — provides the remainder after division
++	unary increment; var++ is the same as (var + 1)
--	unary decrement; var--is the same as (var -1)
+= ,*= , /= , %=	assignment operator; each of these is equal to var = var op expression, where operator is +, *, /, %
No operator	string concatenation

Several examples of the **awk** operators have appeared in previous examples. These operators should be familiar to anyone who knows the C programming language. The only operator that is not somewhat standard and deserves attention is the string concatenation operator (which really is no operator). This is useful for creating or appending to strings. The following example would concatenate the string "DATE:" with the field $3 and assign the results to the variable dateprint:

```
dateprint = "DATE:"$3
```

AWK CONSTANTS

Awk constants are straightforward. Numeric constants are simply specified as numbers where needed, just as one would expect. The following example sets the variable *s* equal to 100:

```
awk 'BEGIN {s = 100}'
```

String constants are specified by enclosing the constant in double quotes. The following sets string1 to a constant value:

```
awk 'BEGIN {string1 = "BEAUTIFUL VALLEY"}
```

AWK BUILT-IN COMMANDS

In addition to variables and operators, **awk** provides a number of built-in functions that can be used in awk expressions. These functions perform some specific task and return. The built-in functions are listed in the following table along with a description of what each function does.

Awk Built-in Functions

FUNCTION	DESCRIPTION
cos(awk_expr)	Returns the cosine of awk_expr.
exp(awk_expr)	Returns the value exponential of awk_expr as in e raised to the awk_expr power ($e^{awk\text{-}expr}$).
index(str1, str2)	Returns the starting position of str2 in str1. If str2 is not present in str1, then 0 is returned.
length(str)	Returns the length of string str.
sin(awk_expr)	Returns the sine of awk_expr.
sprintf(frmt, awk_expr)	Returns the value of awk_expr formatted as defined by frmt.
substr(str, start, length)	Returns a substring of the string str starting at position start for length characters.

The following example shows the use of the **awk** built-in command length. Here we verify that a field contains only alphabetic characters and that the length of the field is 6.

```
awk '{if (($3 ~/[A-Z]*/) && (length($3) == 6)) print $0}'
```

Bibliography

Aho, A. V., R. Sethi, and J. D. Ullman. *Compilers, Principles, Techniques, and Tools.* Reading: Addison-Wesley, 1985.

Aho, A. V., B. W. Kernighan, P. J. Weinberger. *The AWK Programming Language.* Reading: Addison-Wesley, 1988.

Akima, Noboru, and Fusatake Ooi. "Industrializing Software Development: A Japanese Approach," *IEEE Software* (March 1989).

Appleton, Daniel S. "Data-Driven Prototyping," *Datamation* (Nov. 1983).

Arthur, Lowell Jay. *Measuring Programmer Productivity and Software Quality.* New York: Wiley, 1985.

_____. *Rapid Evolutionary Development.* New York: Wiley, 1992.

_____. *Software Evolution – The Software Maintenance Challenge.* New York: Wiley, 1988.

AT&T. *The Bell System Technical Journal,* **57**(6), part 2 (1978).

Bateson, Gregory. *Mind and Nature.* New York: Bantam, 1979.

Bateson, Gregory and Mary Catherine. *Angels Fear.* New York: Bantam, 1987.

Belady, L. A. and M. M. Lehman. "A Model of Large Program Development," *IBM Sys. J.,* no. 3 (1976), pp. 225-252.

Bell, C. Gordon. "The Fewer Engineers per Project, the Better," *IEEE Spectrum* (Feb. 1989).

Boar, Bernard. *Application Prototyping.* New York: Wiley, 1984.

Boehm, Barry. "Industrial Software Metrics Top 10 List," *IEEE Software* (Sept. 1987).

Boehm, B. W., et al. "A Software Development Environment for Improving Productivity," *IEEE Computer* (June 1984), pp. 30-34.

Brooks, Frederick. *The Mythical Man Month.* Reading: Addison-Wesley, 1975.

_____. "No Silver Bullet," *IEEE Software* (1988).

Clason, George S. *The Richest Man in Babylon.* New York: Signet, 1988.

Cobb, Richard H., and Harlan D. Mills. "Engineering Software under Statistical Quality Control," *IEEE Software* (Nov. 1990).

Covey, Steven R. *The Seven Habits of Highly Effective People.* New York: Simon and Schuster, 1989.

Cox, Brad. "Planning the Software Industrial Revolution," *IEEE Software* (Nov. 1990).

Cureton, Bill. "The Future of Unix in the CASE Renaissance," *IEEE Software* (March 1988).

Cusumano, Michael A. "The Software Factory: A Historical Interpretation," *IEEE Software* (March 1989).

Davis, Alan M., et al. "A Strategy for Comparing Alternative Software Development Life Cycle Models," *IEEE Trans. Soft. Eng.,* **14**(10) (Oct. 1988).

DeMarco, Tom. "Making a Difference in the Schools," *IEEE Software* (Nov. 1990).

_____. "Software Development: State of the Art vs. State of the Practice," ACM Sigsoft, 1989.

Deming, W. Edwards. "Out of the Crisis," MIT, 1986.

Drucker, Peter E. *Innovation and Entrepreneurship.* New York: Harper & Row, 1986.

Ernst & Young. "The Landmark MIT Study: Management in the 1990s." Cleveland: Ernst & Young, 1989.

Fagan, Michael E. "Advances in Software Inspections," *IEEE Trans. on Soft. Eng.,* SE **12**(7) (July 1986), pp. 744-751.

Gaffney. "Estimating the Number of Faults in Code," *IEEE Trans. on Soft. Eng.,* SE **10**(4) (July 1984).

Grady, Robert, and Deborah Caswell. *Software Metrics: Establishing a Company-Wide Metrics Program.* Englewood Cliffs: Prentice-Hall.

Gross, Neil. "Now Software Isn't Safe from Japan," *Business Week* (Feb. 11, 1991), p. 84.

Gruman, Galen, ed. "Early Reuse Practice Lives Up to Its Promise," *IEEE Software* (Nov. 1988).

Guaspari, John. *I Know It When I See It.* AMA, 1985.

Heider, John. *The Tao of Leadership.* New York: Bantam, 1985.

Hekmatpour, Sharam. "Experience with Evolutionary Prototyping in a Large Software Project," *ACM Sigsoft Eng. Notes,* **12**(1) (Jan. 1987).

Hix, Deborah. "Generations of User-Interface Management Systems," *IEEE Software* (Sept. 1990).

Humphrey, Watts S., "Characterizing the Software Process: A Maturity Framework," *IEEE Software* (March 1988).

_____. *Managing the Software Process.* Reading: Addison-Wesley, 1989.

Humphrey, Watts S., and D. H. Kitson. "Preliminary Report on Conducting SEI-Assisted Assessments of Software Engineering Capability," Tech. Report, SEI-87-TR-16, Software Eng. Inst., Pittsburgh, PA (July 1987).

Kernighan, B. W., and P. J. Plauger. *Software Tools.* Reading: Addison-Wesley, 1976.

Kraushaar, James, and L. Shirland. "Prototyping Information Systems on Microcomputers: A Design Philosophy for Engineering Management," *Engineering Management International,* **3** (1985), pp. 73-84.

Kuhn, T. *The Structure of Scientific Revolutions.* Chicago: Univ. of Chicago Press, 1962.

Laborde, Genie Z. *Influencing with Integrity.* Palo Alto: Syntony, 1984.

_____. *90 Days to Communication Excellence.* Palo Alto: Syntony, 1985.

Lakoff, George, and Mark Johnson. *Metaphors We Live By.* Chicago: Univ. of Chicago Press, 1980.

Lewis, Ted G., and Paul W. Oman. "The Challenge of Software Development," *IEEE Software* (Nov. 1990).

Lind, Randy K., and K. Vairavan. "An Experimental Investigation of Software Metrics and Their Relationship to Software Development Effort," *IEEE Trans. on Soft. Eng.,* **15**(5) (May 1989).

Luqi, "Software Evolution through Rapid Prototyping," *IEEE Computer* (May 1989).

McCabe, T. J. "A Complexity Measure," *IEEE Trans. Soft. Eng.,* **2**(4) (Dec. 1976), pp. 308-320.

McEachron, Norman B., and H. S. Javitz. "Quality in Research and Development, *SRI International,* Report no. 750 (1987).

McWilliams, John-Roger and Peter. *Life 101.* Los Angeles: Prelude Press, 1990.

Miller, George A. "The Magical Number Seven, Plus or Minus Two: Some Limits on Our Capacity for Processing Information," *The Psychological Review,* **63**(2) (March 1956).

Miller, James Grier. *Living Systems.* Princeton: McGraw-Hill, 1978.

Mills, Harlan D., Michael Dyer, and Richard C Linger. "Cleanroom Software Engineering," *IEEE Software* (Sept. 1987).

Misra, Santosh K., and Paul J. Jalics. "Third-Generation versus Fourth-Generation Software Development," *IEEE Software* (1988).

Moad, Jeff. "The Software Revolution," *DATAMATION* (Feb. 15, 1990), pp. 22-30.

Parnas, David L., Paul C. Clements, and David M. Weiss. "The Modular Structure of Complex Systems," *IEEE Trans. on Soft. Eng.,* SE **11**(3) (March 1985), pp. 259-266.

Peters, Tom. "Do It Badly, Do It Quickly, Make It Better, and Then Say You Planned It," *Rocky Mountain News* (Dec. 4, 1990), p. B14.

_____. "A Passion for Excellence." New York: Random House, 1987.

Potosnak, Kathleen. "Modular Implementation Benefits Developers, Users," *IEEE Software* (May 1989).

Prieto-Diaz, Ruben, and P. Freeman. "Classifying Software for Reuse," *IEEE Software* (Jan. 1987).

Rifkin, G., and J. A. Savage. "Is U.S. Ready for Japan's Software Push?" *ComputerWorld* (May 8, 1989), pp. 1, 114-116.

Rockart, John F., and David W. DeLong. *Executive Support Systems.* Dow Jones-Irwin, 1988.

Ross, Niall. "Using Metrics in Quality Management," *IEEE Software* (July 1990).

Royce, W. W., "Managing the Development of Large Software Systems: Concepts and Techniques," *Proceedings* (WESCON) (Aug. 1970).

Shaw, Mary. "Prospects for an Engineering Discipline of Software," *IEEE Software* (Nov. 1990).

Shmucker, K. J. "MacApp: An Application Framework," *Byte* (Aug. 1986).

Stevens, W. P. "How Data Flow Can Improve Application Development Productivity," *IBM Syst. J.,* **21**(2) (1982).

Thadhani, A. J. "Factors Affecting Programmer Productivity during Application Development," *IBM Syst. J.,* **23**(1) (1984), pp. 19-35.

Thomas, Lewis. *The Lives of a Cell.* New York: Bantam, 1975.

Withrow, Carol. "Error Density and Size in Ada Software," *IEEE Software* (Jan. 1990).

Zultner, Richard. "The Deming Approach to Software Quality Engineering," *Quality Progress* (Nov. 1988).

Index